The Study of Leisure

An introduction

The Study of

L E I S U R E

An introduction

JARMILA HORNA

OXFORD UNIVERSITY PRESS

Toronto • New York • London

Dedicated to the memory
of my father, Josef

Oxford University Press
70 Wynford Drive, Don Mills, Ontario M3C 1J9

Oxford New York
Athens Auckland Bangkok Bombay
Calcutta Cape Town Dar es Salaam Delhi
Florence Hong Kong Istanbul Karachi
Kuala Lumpur Madras Madrid Melbourne
Mexico City Nairobi Paris Singapore
Taipei Tokyo Toronto

and associated companies in
Berlin Ibadan

Oxford is a trade mark of Oxford University Press

Canadian Cataloguing in Publication Data

Horna, Jarmila L.A., 1932–
    The study of leisure: an introduction

Includes bibliographical references and index.
ISBN 0-19-540921-3

1. Leisure.   I. Title

GV174.H67 1994   306.4'812   C94-931903-1

J.L.A. Horna, Figure 5.2 is from 'Family and Leisure', in *Family and Marriage: Cross-Cultural Perspectives*, edited by G.K. Ishwaran (Toronto: Thompson Educational, 1992):302.

N.J. Osgoode and C.Z. Howe. The table 'Roles and Changes over the Adult Life Course: The Traditional Pattern' from 'Psychological Aspects of Leisure: A Life Cycle Developmental Perspective', *Loisir et Société/Society and Leisure* 7 (1):175–96.

Contents

Preface

The growth of all aspects of leisure is widely recognized in our society. Leisure has become much more than what little is left over after the day's or week's work, to be spent on renewing workers' energy for more labour. Both scholarly publications and popular opinion claim that leisure, at least in the industrialized countries, will likely become one of the crucial components in our lives, eventually resulting in a future 'society of leisure'.

We all know about leisure or a perennial lack of it. After all, people do things at their leisure, mothers complain about never having any leisure, workaholics don't ever seem to care about leisure, while others work hard only because they want leisure after their work. Some individuals watch television in their leisure time, but others avoid television in order to spend their spare time in leisure courses, and many parents give up their spare time to drive their children to their leisure activities.

Beyond everybody's personal experience with it, what is the definition of leisure? Do we mean the time after work and, if so, would it include or exclude regular meals? Maybe preparing them is not your idea of leisure, but the pleasure of eating in the company of friends is. Does it matter what you do and when, or do you need to feel free to decide whether to participate or not in order to turn any activity anywhere at any time into your leisure? Some individuals may insist that their leisure is associated with what little free time is left after all the day's work and chores are done, while others would argue that any pleasurable discretionary activity, even work or household duties, can be viewed as real leisure. For some linguistic groups, talking about their leisure is even more complicated because their language does not distinguish between leisure and free time. For instance, English *leisure* or French *loisir* are *Freizeit* in German, *tiempo libre* in Italian and Spanish, *vrijetijd* in Dutch, *svobodnoje vremja* in Russian, *volný čas* in Czech—all of these words literally meaning *free time*.

If leisure is interpreted as a counterpart to work, do the unemployed or retired live a life of complete and perennial leisure because they no longer make their daily trip to the workplace? And what about those hobbyists whose eyes gleam with just a mention of their most preferred leisure activity—gardening, of course! Scores of others, meanwhile endure the drudgery of annual planting, seeding, weeding, watering their yards and gardens and wish these 'leisure' rituals of suburban living would end. This is the same activity, but what a difference in its interpretation!

In this book I argue in favour of a definition of leisure as an enjoyable experience in which people choose to participate with relative freedom in terms of discretionary time and particular activities, within the context and limitations of culture, socio-economic factors, and gender. Leisure experience can be objective and/or subjective, long-lasting or brief, planned or spontaneous, an end in itself or therapeutic/compensatory, sociable or solitary.

This book provides a concise, encyclopaedic review of theory and research topics and developments in the study of leisure. The parallel foci throughout the book are leisure and leisure studies from theoretical and empirical as well as historical and international perspectives. The illustrative material originates primarily from contemporary (both anglophone and francophone) Canadian data, some of them collected in the province of Alberta and the city of Calgary, thanks to the support given to me from the Social Sciences and Humanities Research Council of Canada.

Part 1 gives a historical overview of leisure across the world in Chapter 1, and an account of the development of leisure in Canada in Chapter 2. Part 2 is concerned with definitions, disciplinary perspectives, theories, and paradigms found in leisure studies. Chapter 3 presents an overview of numerous earlier and current definitions of leisure and classifications of these definitions, then proposes a complex definition stemming from those previous definitions by various authors. Chapters 4 and 5 focus on theoretical discussion of leisure from the psychological, social-psychological, and sociological perspectives. Chapter 6 examines theoretical conceptualization of the development of leisure over the three stages of life: the preparation period that includes childhood and adolescence, the establishment period with particular emphasis on the parental phase, and the stage of life culminating in the 'third age'. Chapter 7 presents two issues: the institutionalization of leisure studies, in academia in particular, and the types and methodologies of leisure research.

Part 3 focuses on the applied side of leisure studies as it provides empirical evidence and examples to support the discussion in Part 2. Chapter 8 examines the inequitable and asymmetrical distribution and allocation of leisure time among various population groups, and between core and peripheral leisure activities. Chapters 9 and 10 are devoted to popular culture and élite culture, sports, and other forms of leisure, including activities that are morally controversial and marginal. Chapter 11 complements at the empirical level the developmental-theoretical and feminist perspectives on the life cycle presented earlier. Finally, Chapter 12 examines the constraints and barriers to leisure participation, leisure enjoyment, and freedom of leisure choices.

Extensive references to leisure and leisure studies publications supplement these twelve chapters and provide a good starting point for serious students of leisure.

The leisure domain is broad and interwoven with other life domains, so consequently its field of study has become complex as well. Collecting, selecting, and finally presenting this information on leisure and leisure studies has been challenging and taken more time than initially anticipated. It is encouraging to find that in addition to the earlier publications and surveys, the tide of material published recently has swollen so greatly that just monitoring and cataloguing it can become a full-time occupation. The sources selected for our discussion offer considerable amounts of conceptualizations and theoretical approaches to leisure as well as emphasis on methodological rigour that are noteworthy indeed.

PART 1

The evolution of leisure

■||| This section gives a brief historical overview of leisure. Contemporary life patterns — occupations we hold, the technology we use, the clothes we wear, the homes we inhabit, and the knowledge we possess — obviously differ from those of our ancestors. What about leisure? How much leisure did they have, and what were their philosophies, pursuits, and policies with regard to leisure? When and how did it all start? Has leisure as we know it today always existed, or does it appear somewhere next to the steam engine and electricity whose beginnings are associated with the Industrial Revolution? To search for answers to these intriguing questions, we need to turn to those historians and sociologists who have examined the history of leisure and its development. We need to ask anthropologists about leisure in contemporary and past simple societies. We should consult those sociologists, social psychologists, and philosophers who compare leisure and its underpinnings in contemporary societies under different political and economic regimes and cultures around the world.

Many works have already been written just on leisure and its styles in the past or in different cultures and indeed a long treatise might again be composed about these issues. Our present discussion will only highlight selected major patterns and crucial similarities or differences. The works that provided the base for this summary primarily include those of Sebastian de Grazia, Foster Rhea Dulles, Geoffrey C. Godbey, Thomas L. Goodale, Hilmi Ibrahim, John R. Kelly, Richard Kraus, Thorstein Veblen, and several others. Their own studies are based on recorded historical materials as well as on rich oral history, and many are rooted in comparative anthropological studies.

1

Leisure across the world and over the centuries

IIII   Life patterns in simple societies

Most historians of leisure assume that leisure in its present form is a relatively new phenomenon that came about in the Industrial Revolution. This does not mean that members of non-industrial societies have never had or do not have any leisure. Rather, their leisure experience or their time off from work and other obligations appear to be distributed differently from ours. It is not possible to draw a clear distinction between work and leisure; work and non-work are inextricably intertwined (Thomas 1960). Thus one of the main characteristics of life in simple social systems is the lack of clear boundaries between activities such as production of goods, family life, child-rearing, music and dance, affective expression of relationships, and maintaining social order (Kelly 1982). In such simple societies, life seems relatively seamless and undifferentiated. As Margaret Mead (1928) observed in Samoa, a day in such a simple society passes as a tidal ebb and flow, a rhythmic flow of life in which elements of the necessity we call work and the freedom we call leisure are integrated rather than segmented. There in 'time, place, mode of behaviour, companions, and even mood, the clear divisions between work and play, home and workplace, duty and choice almost disappear' (Kelly 1982:39). In simple societies of this type, the schedule and rhythm of the seasons, of planting and harvest, determine the time frame of the culture, while life's major uncertainties stem from the climate, weather, and harvest rather than the economy. In fact, the slack periods of agricultural production allowed for far more holiday periods compared to what is allowed by the regimentation of the production line or the nine-to-five office.

According to Ibrahim (1991) and Turner (1982), rituals in which the early human community participated ushered in those activities that are now considered recreation or amusement. These authors assert that the rituals were a part of people's obligation, not choice; however, they were and still are the hallmark of the 'works of the gods' as well as sacred human work. As such, these activities were originally means to an end, not an end in themselves (to promote rain and fertility, to cure the ill, to avert disasters, etc.). Moreover, in a subsistence-level economy, any surplus food was used for ceremonial purposes and prestige, not for trade.

Furthermore, as Kelly (1982) suggests, preindustrial leisure is more limited by isolation than by lack of space. It tends to be either integrated into the work and survival patterns of life or is related to special events, for example, holy days during which people gather for religious or secular celebrations. The gathering itself might provide the opportunity for games, spectacles, and various forms of social interaction that would not be regularly available because of the dispersed population.

It appears that for our early ancestors, their life, including leisure, was like interlocking pieces of a giant jigsaw puzzle—their experiences consisted of interrelated and overlapping activities. Let us look now at a few historical periods to see when and how the old patterns changed into our contemporary life domains and leisure patterns. We will examine what the historians tell us about the historical periods that still influence our present life. Our Eurocentric, Judaeo-Christian orientation in studying history is responsible for somewhat slanted views of leisure throughout millennia. Most historical accounts of leisure deal only with Europe and White inhabitants of North America. However, other continents and countries have histories that are perhaps even richer than those we know in detail. We will turn at the end of this section to a brief overview of what is known about leisure in other parts of the world.

▥ Leisure in ancient societies

Most readers will recall their history classes about the Western heritage derived from the Egyptian, Greek, Roman, and Judaeo-Christian traditions. We have learned in our history classes that as the division of labour gradually took hold in previously undifferentiated societies, the ruling class, along with soldiers, craftsmen, peasants, and slaves, appeared as a consequence. For the first time in history, the upper-class strata gained increased power and wealth as well as leisure that did not overlap with work or other activities. It is assumed (Kraus 1984) that the landed aristocracy of the first civilizations that developed in the Middle East during the five millennia before the Christian era represented the first leisure class in history.

According to our limited knowledge, the leisure class of ancient Egypt, which consisted of the nobility and high officials, led a colourful and pleasant life. Ibrahim (1978) described their formal banquets where men and women ate together, while wrestlers, dancing girls, or storytellers entertained them. The commoners soon started to imitate the nobility, and a number of festivals with music, dancing, and drinking took place in the larger rooms of the village houses and on open land around the village. The early Egyptians engaged in many sports for education and recreation, while music, drama, and dance formed part of religious worship as well as social entertainment. Ancient records document, for example, wrestling, gymnastics, weightlifting, and ball games. Many historians believe that such games as chess, checkers, backgammon, and other table games also originated during this period. In general, athletics were performed chiefly by the lower classes and the soldiers; the upper classes were more sedentary and enjoyed being entertained. Groups of female performers were affiliated with temples, and royalty had troupes of entertainers who performed on sacred or social occasions. In the later Egyptian dynasties, many slaves constituted a special class of professional entertainers. The diversions of peasants and field labourers, however, were few and inexpensive. After the Roman conquest, Egypt was much influenced by the Roman way of life. During this period, clubs and drinking societies became common, and both private and public festivals on imperial and religious holidays were frequent. Most large towns had theatres and regular mass athletic contests.

As in Egypt, ancient Israelis used music and dancing for rituals as well as for social activities and celebrations. The early Hebrews distinguished between sacred and pagan dances. The Old Testament contains numerous references to dancing, and it seems that this activity complemented most festive occasions. Kraus (1984:58) suggests that the idea that recreation is related to morality was already established during this period.

The Greek idea of leisure may sound familiar as leisure literature and policies have often referred to it since the turn of the twentieth century. Today, proverbial couch potatoes are admonished to follow a noble Greek ideal of leisure instead of watching television. The proponents of the Greek ideal typically advocate the ancient Athenians' belief in the unity of mind and body, in the interrelationship of all human qualities and skills, in the total cultivation of the body and the emotions, in a sound intellectual and physical life — all of this encouraged through, for example, gymnastics and music. Consequently, Athenians considered play activity to be essential to the good physical and social health of all citizens, particularly children. Plato is credited with the idea that all children should be instructed in the performing arts and tested with frequent contests. Regarded as an obligation to the state, gymnastics and sports were performed by all citizens. Even when they were essential for maintaining national security, exercises were regarded not as a grim discipline but as a creative and enjoyable experience.

The concept that a society might be strengthened or weakened through leisure and its uses was expanded by the Greeks and Romans, who believed it was the state's responsibility to provide entertainment for the masses and such leisure facilities as small parks and gardens, open-air theatres and gymnasiums, baths, exercise grounds, and stadiums (Kraus 1984). It should not be forgotten, however, that in the city-states of ancient Greece, particularly in Athens from about 500 to 400 BC, the philosophical and cultural developments affected the people unequally. The ideal pursuits of a well-rounded person were generally restricted to the noblemen who had full rights of citizenship, including voting and participation in affairs of state. Craftsmen, farmers, and tradespeople, although they were citizens too, had limited rights and less prestige, while slaves and foreigners had neither prestige nor citizens' rights. The amenities of life were generally restricted to the most wealthy and powerful citizens, who represented the Athenian ideal known to us today: the well-balanced man, who was a combination of soldier, athlete, artist, statesman, and philosopher. This ideal was furthered through education and various religious festivals, which occupied about seventy days of the year and included music, poetry, theatre, gymnastics, and athletic competition. Sports appear to have been part of daily life and to have occurred chiefly when there were mass gatherings of people. When boys reached the age of seven, they were enrolled in schools in which gymnastics and music were stressed.

The original Greek approach to leisure and play, however, experienced a gradual transition in the religious and cultural functions of the Olympic games and other festivals. The change resulted in athletic specialization and commercialism. Sports, drama, singing, and dance came to be performed primarily by highly skilled specialists.

The accounts of life in the ancient Roman republic during its early development document that like the Greeks, the Roman citizens too participated in sports and gymnastics to keep the body strong and the spirit courageous. A member of the privileged class, the Roman man was always ready to defend his society and fight in its wars (Kraus 1984). Numerous games held in connection with worship of various Roman gods later developed into annual festivals. Such games were carefully supervised by the priesthood and supported by public funds, frequently at great cost. Young Roman children engaged in many sports and games; young boys in particular were taught various sports and exercises. Roman towns generally had public baths, open-air theatres, amphitheatres, stadiums, colonnades for sports in bad weather, and sometimes parks and gardens.

In spite of many similarities with the Greek practices, the Romans had a different philosophical concept of leisure. The Latin words for 'leisure' and 'business', *otium* and *negotium*, suggest that the Romans regarded leisure as positive and work as negative. Kando, however, points out that the Roman society represented the first manifestation of the expansionist work society that culminates 2,000 years later in the industrial West. Empire building and bureaucratic organization are Rome's legacy to the world. They developed out of hard and frugal work. Leisure to Romans meant primarily rest from work (Kando 1980). The evidence can be interpreted to indicate that the Romans tended to support play for utilitarian rather than aesthetic or spiritual reasons. In general, they valued sports chiefly because of its practical benefits. Although they had many performing companies, the Romans themselves did not actively participate in theatre or dance. As leisure increased and the necessity for military service and other forms of physical toil declined for

Roman citizens, they began to do fewer and fewer things for themselves. Their normal practice was to be entertained or to follow a daily routine of exercise, bathing, and eating. The Roman baths became popular social and athletic clubs, but were not exclusive to the nobility, as gradually public baths were established throughout Rome. Athletes now performed as members of a specialized profession with unions, coaches, and training schools. Gradually the traditional sports of running, throwing, and jumping shifted into an emphasis on human combat, and then displays of cruelty in which gladiators fought to the death for the entertainment of mass audiences.

When the simple democracy of the early republic shifted to an urban life with sharply divided classes, a huge urban population of plebs lived in semi-idleness, while most of the work was done by *coloni* (lower-class tenants of the land) and slaves. The Roman emperors and senate found it necessary to pacify, amuse, and entertain the restless plebs by providing doles of grain and public games—thus the expression 'bread and circuses'. It may come as a surprise to many of us who believe that today's shorter work week and long weekends are of a fairly recent origin. In fact, as historians tell us, there were 159 public holidays during the year, ninety-three of which were devoted to games at public expense, as early as the reign of the Emperor Claudius in the first century AD. By AD 354, there were 200 public holidays each year, including 175 days of games. Even on working days, labour began at daybreak and ended shortly after noon for most of the year.

Our brief overview of the early forms of leisure has two main themes: (1) leisure in simple, preindustrial societies was not sharply segmented from other life spheres, and work and leisure were mostly integrated in time, place, behaviour, and companions; (2) with the rise of differentiated societies, different social strata gained uneven access to leisure time and pursuits, while the ideal of a well-balanced person applied unequally to men and women, as well as to individuals belonging to different groups.

▌▌▌ From the Middle Ages to nineteenth-century Europe

After the collapse of the Roman Empire, which was attacked by successive waves of northern European tribes, Europe was in disarray for several centuries, overrun with warring tribes and shifting alliances. Gradually the Catholic Church emerged to provide a form of civil order within Europe. Having suffered under the brutal persecutions of the Romans, the early Christians condemned all that their oppressors had stood for, especially their hedonistic way of life. The early church fathers believed in a fanatical asceticism, the dignity of labour, and self-deprivation in order to save one's soul. Not surprisingly, all forms of pleasure were seen as evil and leisure became viewed as sinful idleness.

Despite the church authorities' disapproval, many forms of play continued during the Middle Ages. In Veblen's (1899) opinion, early communities did not have a leisure class per se; it gradually emerged during the later stages of the barbarian culture and was associated with the beginning of private ownership, particularly in feudal Europe. During the Middle Ages, noblemen in particular had a great amount of leisure, which they spent in various pastimes, including games, gambling, music, dance, sports, and jousting. At the outset, tournaments had violent and dangerous martial combat between large numbers of knights, but gradually tournaments became more stylized and eventually represented a form of war game. Hunting skills were not only considered virtues of medieval noblemen, but were used to keep hunters from the sin of idleness and to prepare them for war. Peasants, meanwhile, usually worked as long as twelve hours a day and craftsmen and other city workers laboured daily from fourteen to eighteen hours. Only during the winter months were the work hours shorter and holidays plentiful. The Catholic Church had replaced the original pagan or Greek and Roman festivals with Christian holidays and made Sunday the day of rest. There were village feasts and sports, practical jokes, various games, dancing, and forms of popular religious drama and pageantry. Many modern sports were developed at this time and other types of entertainment became popular, for example bear-baiting, bull-baiting, and other cruel shows. In the summer, English parish festivals called wakes weeks celebrated the founding of the parish church.

The European Renaissance—which historians place at about 1350 in Italy, about 1450 in France, and about 1500 in England—introduced profound social and cultural changes that affected leisure as well. In Italy and France in particular, the nobility became patrons of artists, who were no longer dominated by the Catholic Church. People pursued new forms of entertainment and amusement, while the courts enjoyed lavish entertainments and spectacles. Some games were designated for certain social classes. For example, football was seen chiefly as a lower-class sport, while Henry VIII tried to restrict tennis to noblemen and property owners. As the Renaissance continued, opera-houses, theatres, and ballet companies were founded under royal sanction and subsidy, and music, dance, theatre, and opera again became professionalized. The feasts covered both work and play since the two were interconnected, and the contrast between them was not as significant as today (Dumazedier 1974).

In the countryside, work followed the natural cycle of the seasons, intense during the good season and slower during the winter. Its rhythms were natural, interrupted only by breaks, songs, games, and ceremonies. In the relatively warm climate of southern France, the village square and town formed the foci of male leisure, while in the colder and damper regions of England, the alehouse performed a similar function (Cross 1990). Small groups, mostly men, gathered, especially on damp and cold days, for cards, conversation, and drink. Women had limited access to these public and carefree opportunities for leisure; their social pastimes revolved around the church, market, well, or mill, and the get-togethers they had when they worked. Especially during the winter months, women knitted or crocheted while talking, sharing information, and even singing. It is assumed that poverty may have dictated these collective pleasures. Cross (1990) cites evidence of French *veillés* that were similar to the sewing bees of American pioneer women. Apparently, the intimacy of the dining-room or the drawing room was unknown in the seventeenth century, even for royalty. Popular leisure activities were often chaotic and crude, even violent and critical of the status quo, but the powerful often patronized them nevertheless. Often an aristocrat, even one trained in the good manners of the gentleman, would wrestle with his peasants or join them in a dance or song. There is some evidence that at least until the seventeenth century, popular leisure was enjoyed jointly by both the rich and the poor.

The preindustrial European enjoyed lengthy breaks from the drudgery of manual work (Cross 1990). During the early eighteenth century in particular, Sundays and holidays were often occasions for feasts and were the opposite, even negation, of everyday life:

> Feasting was inseparable from ceremonies and generally closer to religious ritual than to leisure. Thus, although there were more than one hundred and fifty-five workless days per year, I do not feel that the concept of leisure is applicable to ·their analysis. To take France as an example, Vauban (1707) distinguished feast days, often imposed by the Church against the peasants' and artisans' will, in order to ensure the performance of religious obligations, and non-work days. In La Fontaine's fables the poor man complains that his parish priest is 'forever adding some new saint to his sermon'. In early 18th century France there were 84 such saints days, to which should be added some 80 days a year when work was impossible (due to sickness, frost etc.). Peasants and artisans, who made up approximately 95% of the French labour force, were idle, according to Vauban, for 164 days per year, mostly because of religious observances or lack of work (Dumazedier 1974:14).

Historian Philippe Ariès (1962) argues that before the eighteenth century, both the young and the old played the same games and shared in the same leisure pursuits. From about four years of age, children joined in the dancing and card-games of alehouses. They were allowed to gamble. Rough outdoor sports like bull-baiting and seemingly childish activities like swings, teetertotters, or parlour games were enjoyed by both children and adults.

Numerous festivals were central to leisure throughout the year, carnivals being the most popular among them. People even counted the passage of time by reference to festivals. These popular events usually included three elements: food, sex, and violence, and eased pent-up frustrations (Cross 1990). Festive leisure allowed for expressions of anger among the common people and at the same time pacified them with relatively harmless forms of symbolic aggression. Gradually, parks and gardens came into existence, first developed and used exclusively by the nobility and later opened to the public as well. They provided entertainment, amusements, and relaxation, complete with eating places and tea gardens. In England, the lower classes, especially in the country, continued to engage in sports, dancing, singing, and spectator events. In large cities in France, many places of commercial entertainment and taverns sprang up to such an extent that there was a concern about excessive leisure among the lower classes and its effects upon industry. People attended public festivals and theatre productions, and enjoyed walking in the city or made frequent excursions to the country where they danced in outdoor pavilions.

Together with the revival of ancient arts, the Athenian philosophy of education and leisure was revived during the Renaissance. For example, in the early sixteenth century, French writer François Rabelais advocated the need for physical exercises and games, as well as for singing, dancing, sculpturing, painting, and nature study. The philosopher Montaigne later emphasized the concept of a unity of mind, body, and spirit, opposing the medieval idea of a separation of the mind and body.

The liberalized forms of and admonitions about leisure came to an end with the Protestant Reformation. The religious Reformation brought about progressive economic, social, and political changes, but the new sects turned out to be more ascetic and austere than the Catholic Church. As the Protestants took complete control over the social and cultural life of the community, they were also determined to curtail public amusements, sports, the arts, and 'frivolous' leisure. The Renaissance's pleasures and merriment were replaced by a serious dedication to work and the imposition of the old codes against play and idleness. The English Protestants in particular required dedicated religious observations on the Sabbath and condemned or seriously limited sports and other forms of entertainment during the sixteenth and eighteenth centuries.

Despite the efforts of Puritans to reform popular leisure, these pastimes remained largely unchanged into the late eighteenth century (Cross 1990). Most typical, perhaps, were rough team and blood sports with contests often resembling slightly civilized forms of combat and tests of physical skill and endurance. Many games involved cruelty to animals, such as cock-throwing, ratting, bull-baiting, badger-baiting, bear-baiting, and cock-fighting. They cut across class lines and were even practised by pupils and their schoolmasters in the courtyard. Foot races, hammer-throwing, leaping, and similar contests, particularly in rural areas, provided diversions from everyday work, required ordinary tools, and stressed physical endurance. A great attraction of such games was gambling on the winners rather than the aesthetic of the sport itself.

Beginning in the nineteenth century in France, there were increasing concerns for the masses and their education. Leisure was connected with a type of Utopian thinking and promoted later through education for the masses, particularly workers, by 'providing them with technical qualifications as well as individual growth and morality for the benefit of the entire nation' (Olszewska and Pronovost 1982:305). This philosophy was again revived during the Popular Front in the late 1930s, with its emphasis on making 'high' culture available to the masses and the drive towards 'cultural leisure'.

This overview demonstrates that leisure was not denied to the people of Europe in spite of several attempts on the part of the Catholic and Protestant churches. When efforts to suppress leisure turned out to be futile, the clergy tried to combine religion with festivals and other leisure pursuits. The masses, on the other hand, used leisure to relax, vent their frustration, and maintain social contacts.

▥ Leisure in the New World and the United States

The Puritan settlers of New England transported their strict interpretation of the Bible and concerns against idleness, gambling, drama, dancing, and certain forms of music from their homeland to the New World. They maintained that any distraction from prayer, worship, and other sober enterprises was evil. The Lord's Day was to be regulated and kept free of frivolity, pleasure-seeking, and dissipation, while sports were accepted as discipline and training rather than enjoyment. Detached from these influences, the upper classes in southern colonies enjoyed wealth and leisure and indulged in lavish entertainment, feasts and parties, music, hunting, fishing, games, sports, and gambling.

By the early part of the eighteenth century, the Puritan influence began to decline. The erosion of Puritan restrictions made recreation acceptable, even justified, especially if it could be associated with work or turned into a necessity, as in hunting. Cross (1990) suggests that colonists sated their thirst for blood sports in frequent hunting, although the Puritan influence largely eradicated the traditional blood sports. Other similar pursuits, such as wrestling, cudgelling, backsword, singlestick, and boxing remained as common in America as in England. Nevertheless, leisure opportunities available to the poor throughout the country were constrained by a scarcity of time and resources, as well as a lack of autonomy. The large illiterate population in particular was cut off from many kinds of activities that were taken for granted by the élite.

In eighteenth-century America, taverns and other places of entertainment were soon widely established throughout the region, with wagering, card-playing, and drinking involved in most adult male leisure activities. Alcohol contributed to the relaxation of social constraints and by most accounts, drunkenness was common, although most people in preindustrial times drank in moderation. Gambling is frequently mentioned, particularly in connection with colonization and the western migration in America.

As in medieval Europe, 'the history of leisure in America runs the gamut from circuses to courting, from crowds to solitary wilderness treks, from sober meetings to wild and violent debauches' (Kelly 1982:69). The proximity of neighbours, socializing at the school and church, and visiting broadened leis-

ure opportunities for townspeople. Community events were a regular and expected part of the weekly round. The circus and exhibitions illustrating scenes
and events of the American Wild West frontier were the oldest forms of occasional popular entertainment in America (Wilmeth 1989). These American
outdoor amusements evolved from European traditions of the medieval fair
and carnival and the seventeenth-century pleasure garden. People in the country, however, were forced to find most of their leisure within the family and in
such survival-related pursuits as fishing and hunting.

The high male-to-female ratio further influenced leisure patterns, especially
on the frontier in mining boom towns and in open-range cattle country, where
the ratio was often as high as 100 men to one woman. In such a man's world,
many of the means of entertainment did not require any companions but
other men, and the commercial entertainment of the town tended to be mostly
for men (Kelly 1982). A good deal of leisure was related to work and made
games of many work tasks. For example, around the ranch, breaking horses
was not only hard and dangerous work but a contest between males too.

In the early American industrial city where the social timetable was no
longer based on the seasons of the year, the long work week and oppressive
conditions at the workplace dominated and shaped the non-work life of most
people. At first, in winter in particular, there were no parks, playing fields, or
other recreation areas that were accessible to everyone. Many workers used
their weekly break to escape and forget their misery. Cross (1990) notes that
drinking, frequently part of the traditional peasant's leisure, became part of
the industrial and urban world as well. However, the consumption of alcohol
was not necessarily only a form of escapism. Cross suggests that the pub may
be regarded as the one true institution for working men (although seldom for
women), and was the only place available to them for socializing. Women,
however, had very few places to go and were mostly confined to their tene-
ments and front steps.

Urban dwellers with families had to develop their own leisure opportunities
and forms (Kelly 1982). Making games of some chores, teasing and social
interaction, playing musical instruments at home, dancing, attending wed-
dings, funerals, and revivals all represented leisure events or opportunities for
leisure pursuits. Based on her study of New Hampshire textile families, Tamara
Hareven (1982) points out that early industrialization was associated with
the beginning of Sunday evening family get-togethers and reunions. Unlike
working-class dwellings, middle-class homes were designed to reflect a clear
separation between the formal and private, male and female, adult and child
(Cross 1990). Even the respectable working class devoted a large amount of
scarce living space to dining-room and parlour. The era of Victorian
familialism, with its emphasis on family recreation, entered the leisure scene.
The familial trend and emphasis on family recreation was evident also in
Christmas and the American Thanksgiving, which became traditional occasions for family reunion. Women were socialized to assume the role of organ-

izers of family recreation. Public walkways in parks were designed for family strolls. Furthermore, thanks to high-speed printing, cheaper paper, and the general increase in literacy, English and American publishers flooded the market with family-oriented periodicals.

Sports, for youth in particular, were developed by private organizations such as the YMCA (Cross 1990). By 1870, the American 'Y' had lost much of its initial emphasis on moral refinement and became a sports and physical fitness centre for the urban middle class. In a similar vein, the scouting movement was started in America in 1910 by Ernest Thompson Seton, who followed the initiative of the English general and hero of the Boer War, Robert Baden-Powell. The twelve- to eighteen-year-olds, mostly boys from the middle class, were organized in troops that filled a need for recreation and provided an alternative to street play. With the exception of a few efforts to organize girls' clubs or to introduce physical fitness into girls' education, the reformers were relatively indifferent to organizing leisure for girls. When Agnes Baden-Powell organized a separate organization of Girl Guides, the girls were supposed to learn domestic skills and inculcate attitudes of harmony and happiness, while the boys were trained to be loyal and competitive. Nevertheless, the movement with its summer camps introduced millions to hiking, camping, and other outdoor activities.

The American playground movement that aimed at providing alternatives to cheap amusements (such as gambling and drinking) was less authoritarian, if perhaps equally paternalistic (Cross 1990). According to its philosophy, cities were to build neighbourhood playgrounds, as opposed to downtown 'promenade parks', and organize programs; games and play areas were to be age-graded and gender-differentiated, and offer safe, regulated fun.

In the early twentieth century, several turning points and transitions refocused the leisure domain in the United States. The nationwide Conference on Outdoor Recreation, called by President Coolidge in 1924, helped to focus attention on the importance of public outdoor recreation facilities (Neumeyer and Neumeyer 1958). Rapid change and advancement in increased leisure and forms of recreation during the 1920s meant that 'the concept of recreation was expanded and the importance of leisure-time activities was increasingly recognized' (Neumeyer and Neumeyer 1958:87). Such novel circumstances prompted Lindeman to suggest that leisure was no longer only for the élite classes of society but available to all social classes. In his opinion, this has led to the situation in which the 'leisure of American people constitutes a central and crucial problem of social policy' (cited by Kraus 1984:114).

A contemporary writer, Arthur Newton Pack, wrote an account of those profound changes:

> Skillfully and very gradually the American was taught that leisure and play were not sinful if they could be classed under the head of recreation. As such they could be admitted to the category of acceptable and respectable occupa-

tions, since scientists, luckily, had found that neither brains nor bodies can work all the time and still retain full vigor and efficiency. The corollary was plain—one must play more in order to work better . . . not because these things made us any happier but because they made us work better. This health and efficiency slogan became the crowning manifestation of boom times after the World War. In 1926 it even attained Presidential recognition . . . . Thus was signalized the acceptance of leisure not as an end in itself but as a valuable handmaiden of prosperity (1934:16).

By the end of the 1920s, the American federal government became involved in providing facilities for outdoor recreation, and states began to expand their parks systems. There was increasing awareness that varied recreation opportunities were needed for all ages and social classes. Later, the Great Depression stimulated the concern of the American people about the lack of leisure and recreation opportunities. However, Americans blended private and commercial leisure provisions with those of government (Sessoms et al. 1975). Initially, the private recreation associations, primarily youth-oriented and supported by private contributions, were the backbone of organized recreation sources. Government restricted its role to acquiring and developing parks and other open spaces. The leisure business addressed itself to the growing demand for spectator sports and mass entertainment, such as movies and radio. Unlike countries disrupted by the Nazi occupation and the war, American recreation programs were curtailed only during the Second World War because of manpower shortages and travel restrictions. Concurrently, recreation and parks departments instituted special new programs to assist the war effort and to organize programs for members of the armed forces (Kraus 1984).

After the Second World War, there was a marked increase in all forms of leisure participation throughout the United States as well as the trend to 'democratize leisure'. Charles Brightbill made a humanist plea to 'let recreation help us live a really democratic life and use it to attain sound emotional and physical health and make our daily lives more zestful' (1961:38). Trends and organized recreation in the 1950s and 1960s included the national concern with physical fitness, programs for the disabled, outdoor recreation and parks development, increased federal assistance for recreation, involvement in the arts, growth of commercial recreation, unification of recreation and parks movement, concern with the poor and minority groups, and new challenges created by the youth rebellion of the 1960s and other special-interest groups such as women, the elderly, and homosexuals (Kraus 1984). A major expansion of the American federal outdoor recreation role was enacted through a series of legislative acts.

Not all of that rapid development, however, has been viewed as an unmitigated success. For example, just as two decades later Neulinger (1981) would identify a syndrome he called leisure lack, Brightbill noted that for many people, 'there can be no more vital implication than the importance of education for leisure. If we do not learn how to use the new leisure in wholesome, uplifting, decent, and creative ways, we shall not live at all' (1961:189).

Thus we can recognize at least two transformations in American attitudes towards free time during the twentieth century (Hunnicutt 1980). Initially, free time was seen by the majority of Americans as practical and as a means of promoting efficiency, production, health, safety, and social welfare, although at first, leisure was negatively perceived as a waste of time and a hindrance to production. Contrary to those attitudes, however, many reformers defined leisure in a positive fashion, made it a national issue, and understood it as a central concern of the economy and the American culture. Hunnicutt posits that during the Depression, when free time took the form of unemployment, it ceased to be a viable economic and political option. Increased leisure has not had a political constituency since the Depression. Likewise, Sessoms et al. (1975) point to three distinct periods of development of organized leisure and recreation and their related concerns: youth work, diversionary activities, and conservation. They were, in turn, reflected in three types of programs: diversionary, management-oriented, or instruments of personality development and social change.

To summarize our description of American developments of leisure, the spontaneous and mostly disorganized leisure that the Puritans found difficult to curtail later became subject to commercialization and 'amelioration' by numerous private and public organizations, business, and the government. Later sections of this book will examine specific forms of leisure pursued by individuals and families at home and elsewhere.

▮▮ Leisure in other parts of the world

As mentioned earlier, most studies of leisure and its history are Eurocentric and Judaeo-Christian in orientation. Those few historians who view the history of leisure from a world perspective have noted the popularity of various sports and entertainment in ancient China, India, and Japan. For example, the wealthy in these Eastern societies surrounded themselves with a host of retainers who became tutors, storytellers, chanters of poetry, musicians, painters, or others who gave exhibitions of cock-fighting. They had gardens, theatre, singing, dancing, and various sports, but the poor in the countryside most likely led monotonous and frugal lives. Hilmi Ibrahim (1991) posits that the nobility of the early nation-states — Egypt, Mesopotamia, China, and India — must have had different pursuits and arranged different training for their offspring than did parents among the common people.

According to Ibrahim's detailed discussion, the tradition and maintenance of acceptable and unacceptable forms of leisure are very strong factors in Eastern societies. India, China, Japan, and the Islamic society in particular, show little change between their ancient and medieval leisure activities. In ancient and medieval India, the invaders from the North developed a cult that included lengthy consecration and rejuvenation ceremonies in which gambling played a small but significant part. For example, their board game played with dice on sixty-four squares was subsequently copied by the Persians, who modified it and taught it to the Arabs, who then brought it to Europe as chess. Entertainment for the upper classes was provided by performers who included acrobats, fortune-tellers, flute players, and dancers. Early dramatic performances, mostly of religious legends, took place in the palaces of the rich, or in temple courts during the festivals. The wealthy had gardens or parks with ponds, lakes, and fountains where they spent much of their leisure time. Wealthy men used amorous adventures and erotica as their chief recreation. The rural population enjoyed religious festivals during which the temples and rulers gave public entertainment.

Ancient and medieval China developed over the centuries under the Confucian codification, which became the basis of an educational program similar to that of the ancient Greeks (Ibrahim 1991). The goal was to develop the harmonious and symmetrical aspects of body and mind, and to prepare a broadly cultivated person in both the literary and martial arts. The six subjects were rituals, music, archery, charioteering, writing, and mathematics. Chinese gentry lived in a large household with many servants, while masses of peasants tilled land that was mostly owned or controlled by the gentry. The wealthy kept a retinue of chess players, painters, writers, and setters of riddles, or they hired singing girls, musicians, acrobats, and conjurers for entertainment at parties. During the Han dynasty, military victories were celebrated by dances accompanied by music and songs, forming a kind of ballet. With the Mongol conquest, the Chinese embarked on new forms of amusement. Plays became long dramas, evolved from court entertainment into the chief recreation of the common people, and rituals changed into amusement. The pleasure grounds included instruction centres for music and drama. In thirteenth-century Chinese towns, the population watched ceremonies, then made merry in the streets and spent day and night drinking and wandering about seeking amusements like boxing matches, acrobats, singers, drama, and shadow plays.

As in China, the ancient and medieval Japanese nobles, monks, priests, and warriors were supported in increasing luxury by the farming population (Ibrahim 1991). Some of the musical instruments of China were adopted in Japan and used for court entertainment. Archery, horseback riding, and hunting with falcons were very popular among the wealthy, and even women were allowed to ride. Their less active pastimes were gambling games and a version of checkers. Among the original pursuits was the tea ceremony, which was started by the warrior aristocracy, mostly for meeting friends in a formal social gathering and the Japanese garden. Judo and ju-jitsu became uniquely Japanese sports. The Japanese also developed resorts for merchants and samurai, and bath houses where women provided singing, dancing, and other pleasures. The social gatherings of the well-to-do introduced and developed Japanese poetry and lyric drama accompanied by music. Kabuki, a popular drama, together with songs, dance, and farces, apparently satisfied everyone's tastes. At home, the nobles were entertained by musicians, acrobats, jugglers, and dancers.

Another work by Ibrahim (1982b) explains that in the Arabic language, there is no comparable term for the Western world's definition and conception of leisure. However, there are Islamic words that mean play, free time, recreation, sports, art, music, drama, and literature. Thus we have to be more specific in our terminology rather than using the general term 'leisure' when examining leisure in Arab countries. Leisure in the Arab world was influenced by the first group of caliphs who ruled from Mecca and were quite ascetic (Ibrahim 1991). It was not until the second dynasty, during which the capital was moved to Damascus, that a pre-Islamic practice was revived. Muhammad had frowned on many of the leisure activities of polytheist Mecca, particularly music and poetry. With the coming of Islam in AD 630, literary gatherings ended, but poetry recitations as a pastime returned to Damascus around AD 750. Ibrahim posits that the Islamic attitude towards leisure and recreation has been formulated differently from that of Judaism and Christianity, regardless of their time period. The leisure that flourished among lords and their entourages (from whom a leisure class emerged) was eventually shared by the rest of the population. The caliphs and their courtiers were engaged in hunting, horse racing, and playing dice; hunting as a sport developed in Arabia. Later, the wealthy created lush gardens with pavilions, pools, and fountains for relaxing, entertaining friends, and playing chess. Women were completely segregated from men and relegated to receiving visitors, playing games, music, dancing, and storytelling at home. For an upper-class Ottoman woman, a weekly visit to the public bath was her only diversion away from home and was considered a group outing. The leisure life of the masses was different in many respects from that of the wealthy. During festivals, people were amused by reciters of glory, rope dancers, street entertainers, and other performers.

There was considerable richness and diversity of leisure forms and preferences in the Islamic and Eastern societies. We have seen some similarities between those societies and ours, especially with regard to class and gender inequalities. In addition, we have become aware of considerable differences in leisure interests and their underlying factors in those societies and ours. The main purpose for presenting this cross-cultural overview is to examine leisure activities in other parts of the world, as well as to point out a few crucial specifics, some of which are being imported to Canada by the new wave of immigrants who are arriving in increasing numbers.

▮▮▮ Summary

The overview of leisure around the world and throughout history bears witness to the multitude of leisure patterns. Although contemporary forms of leisure have evolved recently, simple and preindustrial societies have long had rich and varied forms of leisure. The crucial characteristic of life in simple social systems was the lack of clear boundaries between productive activities, conjugal and parental roles and relationships, or games, music, and dance. Work and leisure were integrated in place, time, behaviour, and companions. In simple societies, the schedule and rhythm of the seasons—of planting and harvest, climate and weather—ruled people's lives. Frequent slack work periods created additional leisure time.

With the rise of class-differentiated societies, overall social inequality contributed to inequality in leisure among separate social strata, as well as between men and women. Each of the ancient societies followed its own philosophy and style of leisure. The original Greek ideal advocated the unity and total cultivation of mind and body, but eventually allowed athletic and artistic specialization, professionalism, and commercialism. The Romans adopted many ideas from the Greeks; however, they tended to support play and leisure primarily for utilitarian purposes. Roman citizens in particular preferred to be entertained by professional entertainers instead of engaging in their own active pursuits.

The Middle Ages in Europe brought profound changes in attitudes and access to leisure for both the nobility and common folk. The Catholic Church attempted to curtail leisure, but many forms of play continued during the Middle Ages despite church authorities' disapproval. The noblemen in particular spent a great amount of leisure time in games and gambling, music and dance, sports and stylized forms of war games. Gradually the Catholic Church replaced the original pagan or Greek and Roman festivals with Christian holidays, and made Sunday the day of rest. Slack periods of work and frequent holidays imposed by secular or religious authorities helped to break the monotony of work and provide additional leisure time.

The Renaissance introduced professional arts, ceremonies, and entertainment, as well as sports. For many European countries, this revival ended with the Protestant Reformation. Control over social and cultural life in Protestant countries resulted in another period of limitations imposed on public amusements, sports, the arts, and 'frivolous leisure'. Such efforts, however, turned out to be mostly futile as the masses continued their leisure pursuits nevertheless.

With the colonization of America, Puritans exported their ascetic philosophy of life and leisure, but eventually lost the struggle for control over people's leisure activities, especially in cities. Industrialization was accompanied by increasing emphasis on familial leisure, reformist movements to 'ameliorate' leisure, and the development of playgrounds, sports, and outdoor activities, especially for boys and young men. In the twentieth century, American leisure attitudes followed two paths: at first, free time was regarded by the majority of Americans as practical, promoting efficiency, production, health, safety, and social welfare, but leisure was still perceived negatively as a waste of time and a hindrance to production. Later, more positive views of leisure contributed to its growth and acceptance, but were simultaneously influenced by commercialization and commodification, particularly by the mass media, of leisure pursuits and sports.

The richness and diversity of leisure forms and preferences in Western societies have parallels in Islamic and Eastern societies. Many similarities between those societies and the West pertain to class and gender inequalities in particular. In addition, the respective social, cultural, ideological, or economic factors that formulate these different worlds contribute to considerable differences in leisure domain as well. At this juncture, however, we are not commenting on the conflicts and struggles or their underlying elements that were part of the historical development of leisure. An analytical commentary that addresses common themes in the controversies and struggles during different periods and parts of the world (namely the class and gender inequalities in leisure availability, behaviour, practices, and preferences) would be very similar to that presented in the next chapter in connection with the history of leisure in Canada. The inequalities will be seen as part of broader social relationships and inequalities among the dominant and subordinate social groups, perpetuated by the process of socio-historical reproduction and the transformation of those relations, as well as mediated through the system of hegemony and cultural imperatives.

CHAPTER **2**

The history of leisure, sports, and culture in Canada

▥ The development of leisure and sports

The history of leisure in Canada, as published to date, has chronicled almost exclusively the developments and activities of Canada's White settlers and their descendants. Leisure pursuits of the original inhabitants, the native peoples, have been largely neglected by leisure historians. Even though the anthropological studies of the lifestyles of Canada's aboriginal inhabitants are rich, they have yet to be systematically included in leisure studies. We learn from some of them, for example Blanchard and Cheska (1985) and Glassford (1976), that the life of the Inuit population in the Arctic was very simple yet playful. They enjoyed singing, storytelling, and games in their free time, and men liked wrestling as entertainment or to celebrate a successful hunt.

Because of this paucity of information about aboriginal Canadians, we focus on the leisure of the immigrant settlers. The first Canadian settlements in present-day Nova Scotia date back to the beginning of the seventeenth century and to the 1660s for some 3,000 original male settlers in New France. The founding of the Hudson's Bay Company in 1670 brought an influx of English traders and employees, who were largely recruited from the urban unemployed. The settlement of Alberta took place primarily during the 1896–1914 period. By the time of Confederation, the population was about 3.3 million; most of the early settlers—pioneers in fur trading, forestry, mining, and ranching—were single and male. Women joined the settlement of New France in the seventeenth and eighteenth centuries, arrived in the Maritimes and Upper Canada from 1780 to 1860 and throughout the prairie homesteading era between 1870 and 1914.

The historians tell us that the majority of the pioneers who came to Canada were not members of the wealthy leisure classes but peasants, craftsmen, or fishermen who were used to a hard way of life in their own countries. These pioneers faced the difficult task of building homes and establishing communities. They adapted new versions of their traditional churches, schools, local government, and social manners and customs to the new environment. In their free time, they entertained themselves by playing games or watching others play, as well as singing and telling stories. In their homes, the pioneers practised folk artistry to make practical things and to decorate their spartan surroundings. In particular, pioneering meant isolation, deprivation, and hardship. No wonder that persistence, optimism, thrift, resourcefulness, and the acceptance of unremitting hard work became character traits valued by succeeding generations.

Later, unlike most European countries, Canada was faced with three-way development. First of all, there was industrial, urbanizing development in the established areas of the East; secondly, there was extensive rural expansion into the uninhabited empty prairie regions and the lush West Coast; and thirdly, spot settlements (which were often transitory) on mineral source locations in the north and northwest became a distinctive Canadian phenomenon (Cox 1985).

The climate, terrain, and native inhabitants were major influences on the lifestyle of European settlers in Canada who pursued a range of sports, games, and play activities. Although some activities could not be reproduced in the new land, most of their traditional games were successfully adapted (Howell and Howell 1985). Thus, it is assumed that English troops stationed in Kingston from 1783 to 1855 played ice hockey—that is, their familiar field hockey—but on skates. Such pioneer attributes as courage, physical prowess, and adventure were converted into competition and athletic endeavours. Winter activities were largely confined to sports, although winter leisure in numerous prairie communities revolved around a literary society that organized recitations, songs, debates, and story readings that ended with a lunch or fraternal club activities, drama clubs, and performances by touring groups (Wetherell 1990).

According to Lappage (1985), people living in British Columbia (which is geographically isolated from the rest of the country, has a mild climate, and is influenced by a strong British tradition and the proximity of its urban centres to the United States) preferred a wide variety of sports. These sports interests included bowling, polo, skiing, gymnastics, baseball, golf, lawn bowling, sailing, yachting, rowing, hockey, rugby, cricket, soccer, track and field, badminton, and tennis.

Residents of the three prairie provinces, Alberta, Saskatchewan, and Manitoba, who also had frequent interaction with the United States in a wide variety of sports and international leagues, were inclined to interact more with Americans than with people in Ontario and Quebec. In addition to American influence, the climate, known for its long, cold winters and short, warm summers, was an important factor in the development of sports in the prairies. In particular, the natural ice conditions made hockey and curling the two most popular winter sports in both urban and rural areas. The severe winter weather also introduced an early trend towards indoor winter sports. As was the case in British Columbia, the prairies' competition in sports with eastern Canada was usually restricted to national championship events. For the most part, the prairie provinces interacted with the adjacent regions of the United States, and occasionally competed interprovincially, sometimes including British Columbia in their leagues.

Unlike the western provinces, Ontario, as the industrial and commercial heart of Canada, also became the centre of Canadian sports. Not surprisingly, sport-governing bodies were dominated by eastern representatives. For decades, Ontario had several advantages over other provinces, such as more numerous and better facilities, and, with the abundance of industry in the urban area, extensive commercial sponsorship of sports as well. Also the climate of southern Ontario was conducive to a long playing season for outdoor summer sports. The fact that the majority of the national championships were staged in southern Ontario or southwestern Quebec was advantageous to Ontario athletes, for they had shorter distances to travel, unlike competitors from the extremities of Canada, whose long travels undoubtedly inhibited their performances (Lappage 1985).

Still another pattern developed in Quebec. Its two distinct ethnic groups, with the Anglophone population as the minority, contributed to the development of sports in somewhat different ways. In rural areas, where a French-Canadian tradition prevailed, the trend towards Americanization of sports—that is, the introduction of sports and rules not indigenous to Quebec—was less pronounced than in urban centres where the sports of French and English Canadians seemed to be equally susceptible to American influence. There were a few activities like curling and cricket that were played almost exclusively by the English-speaking population. Generally, both groups competed in similar sports, although they were often polarized into teams with English Canadians on the one side and French Canadians on the other. As Lappage (1985) documents, the sports interests of French Canadians were basically similar to those in the rest of Canada, but the two combative sports, boxing and wrestling, seemed to draw much more interest than they did in other parts of the country. Winter carnivals, in which sports played a major role, were also commonplace in most French communities in Quebec. As in the West, the climate of Quebec was conducive to the development of winter sports, making hockey by far the most popular, with numerous leagues spread throughout the province. Skiing was not just an urban phenomenon; farmers discarded their slower snowshoes in favour of swifter skis. For commercial sports, which was predominantly favoured by the masses, the preferences differed more along class than ethnic lines (Metcalfe 1983). With the strong francophone rural roots, harness racing, weightlifting, and wrestling became favoured by the general population.

The Maritime provinces, bound together by similar climate and geography, similar economic problems, and a common British heritage, tended to follow similar sports patterns as well (Lappage 1985). Since outdoor winter sports were somewhat restricted by the climate, the Maritimers preferred indoor activities. Because of the depressing economic conditions, however, most of the activities tended to be those that required a minimum of expenditure.

One inhibiting factor that prevented an even greater early participation in sports, was the Lord's Day Act of 1845, which made it illegal to play 'skittles, ball, football, racquets, or any noise game on Sunday'. For example, young boys were fined for playing ball games on the Sabbath as late as 1896. Only by the mid-1880s were Saturday afternoons accepted as a time for sports (Cox 1985). Gerald Redmond (1979) argues that the traditional ascetic attitude of the Church towards sports was gradually transformed, as most religious institutions quickly became patrons of sports and found moral benefit in its practice. At the same time, sports were embraced in similar fashion by educational institutions and included into the curricula of schools and colleges in Canada.

Since the laws severely restricted physical recreation on Sundays, most sports competitions in urban centres took place on weekdays only. This typically excluded participation by the working class. When early closing became more widespread from the 1850s onward, working men were able to participate more (Lindsay 1969). Yet for many, Sunday remained the only really free day from work, and therefore Sunday sports became an issue, and violations of Sunday sports ordinances became more frequent. The Lord's Day Alliance, formed in 1899 to protect the Sabbath as a day of rest and worship, campaigned against Sunday sports, but eventually failed to stop it. If any one factor was responsible for the failure of the Alliance to restrict Sunday sports, it was the triumph of the nineteenth-century 'Muscular Christianity' movement—a concept that originated in the 1850s and emphasized manliness, determination, and fair play.

Like other facets of life in the early years, sports were based locally, followed variable rules, involved primitive equipment, and had haphazard, if any, organization. Together with the development of roads, railways, and waterways, localism soon extended into regionalism and technological developments changed not only the face of the land but the nature of the sports as well. The most significant effects were the standardization of rules and the formation of clubs and leagues at local and then regional levels. Overall, particularly in small-town Canada, hockey represented a focal point for community life (Dryden and MacGregor 1989). In addition to hockey, curling, and related activities—playing, watching, travelling to and from arenas in neighbouring communities, as well as the postgame socializing—represented some of the most distinctively Canadian cultural forms (Hall et al. 1991). Regional participation subsequently led to national and then international competitions.

The urbanization process in Canada started relatively early and increased rapidly with the industrial era in the 1870s. From about 1880, urban reformers and civic supporters attempted to develop public parks and playgrounds, although for different reasons (Markham 1991). The urban reformers were concerned about the physical, mental, and moral health of city residents and were interested in the provision of parks and playgrounds. To civic supporters, parks and, to a lesser extent, playgrounds could be attractions for new residents who would bring investments and prosperity to the city. In either case, such developments contributed to richer leisure and recreation opportunities. The concentration of power in a few major central Canadian cities, notably Montreal and Toronto, however, created tensions between the core and the periphery. The nature of Canadian settlement and the spatial structure of the Canadian economy have ensured the persistence of a complex regional character.

The multifaceted process of urbanization also replaced the traditional rural approach to recreation. Many sports were codified and played according to quite stringent regulations and within a specified duration of time. The club system came to typify organized sports (Redmond 1979). The Montreal Curling Club, the first recorded sports club in Canada, was founded in 1807. Metcalfe's (1983) study of the emergence of organized sports documents that sports organizations started primarily among the francophone population of Montreal. This organized sport was practised mostly among the French middle class, who generally rejected British forms of sports in favour of American ones, like baseball. Other teams and leagues mushroomed especially in the 1880s and 1890s, and a newly formed association attempted to organize them across the country. The first national organization, the Canadian Baseball Association, was founded in 1864, and other associations soon followed (Hall et al. 1991; Metcalfe 1987; Morrow et al. 1989).

It needs to be emphasized that not only men were involved in sports during the nineteenth century. Many well-to-do women in Canada began to break away from their traditional roles as admiring spectators of male sports or as non-competitive participants in more genteel activities. In the second half of the nineteenth century, women became involved in sports such as baseball, basketball, bicycling, curling, field hockey, golf, ice hockey, and walking, either through joining men's sports clubs or forming their own. Archival materials cited by Redmond (1979) document that women's sports clubs were founded before the end of the century. For example, the Montreal Ladies Club started in 1858 (archery), a women's baseball club was formed in Nanaimo, BC, in 1890; lawn tennis tournaments for women were organized in Ottawa (1881) and Montreal (1881), women played basketball in Toronto and Whitby, Ont. (1895), and the first women's curling club was established in Montreal in 1984.

Throughout the twentieth century, sports have been important in many Canadian women's leisure activities. Lenskyj (1991) recognizes two periods of special interest: the 1920–30s and the 1970–80s. She suggests that each of these periods may be loosely called a 'Golden Age' because of the marked increases in participation and public recognition. During the 1920–30 period, some women in sports leadership sought to increase participation opportunities for all girls and women, not just for the most talented. They considered team sports played by girls' rules as more suited to the large numbers of girls and women of average ability who wanted a recreational activity. Following their American counterparts, some Canadian female sports leaders relied heavily on conservative medical arguments about the dangers of competitive sports for women's reproductive capacity. Other proponents of female-only sports made reference to propriety and decorum.

More recently, many women have used human rights legislation to gain access to the same sporting options as men (Lenskyj 1991). At the same time, however, growing numbers of women have begun to question the uncritical acceptance of male-defined sports, particularly their values and goals, and to develop alternative models of autonomous, women-centred sports models that owe much to contemporary women's movements.

The growth of American influence in most aspects of Canadian life was clearly seen especially after the First World War. The United States exerted an increasing influence in the Canadian economy and, correspondingly, in Canadian sports. Both commercial and professional sports in the form of big business were initiated in the United States and spread into Canada at an accelerated rate during the 1920s (Lappage 1985). Furthermore, with the exception of interregional contests in the form of playoffs for national championships, each region of Canada looked to adjacent areas in the United States for competition, sometimes to the detriment of regional sports interaction within the country.

Since their beginnings in the new land, sports in Canadian life have assumed various forms. Hall and her colleagues (1991) argue that sports likely provide a common interest for more Canadians and brings them together more than any other aspect of culture—be it national competitions and events such as the Stanley Cup and Grey Cup or activities like curling, community hockey, and water sports. Canadians also participate in low-impact activities like walking and picnicking, or non-physical pursuits like watching television, reading newspapers and magazines, or listening to the radio.

▮▮ Culture and the arts

The development of the arts, particularly the performing arts, appears to be more influenced than sports by Canada's unique climate and history. The harsh living conditions of the early settlers were not conducive to the support and growth of the arts. The original settlers transplanted their songs, dances, and religious chants to Canada, and successive waves of immigrants reinforced Old World traditions, including amateur performances. For example, reminiscences of the farmers who settled Alberta in the 1920s are rich with stories of amateur theatre and music making (Horna 1979). Although some performances were given in the actors' mother tongue, they were enjoyed by people from other ethnic groups. Curiously, although the settlers readily adopted and adapted boats, skills, and activities of Canada's original inhabitants, there is no evidence that the immigrants were ever interested in aboriginal music or artistic expression.

A lack of wealthy patrons of the arts slowed the introduction, development, and performance of artistic endeavours. Thus, professional ballet was not introduced to Canada until the middle of the twentieth century. The Royal Winnipeg Ballet, the oldest surviving company in Canada and the second oldest in North America, had its origins as a ballet club organized by two immigrant English ballet teachers. It became Canada's first truly professional company in 1949. Another British dancer and choreographer, Celia Franca, founded the National Ballet of Canada in 1951; despite its title, the company never received an official national mandate. Seven years later, Les Grands Ballets Canadiens was founded in Montreal.

Canadian theatrical activity developed along linguistic lines. The promising start of the French theatre in Quebec was brought to an end by the province's isolation and the condemnation of 'comedies, balls, dance, masquerades, and other dangerous spectacles' by Monseigneur de Saint-Vallier in 1700 (Hare 1983). Professional theatre in English has been offered in Quebec since the end of the eighteenth century. In the last half of the nineteenth century, sporadic tours of professional French actors helped to develop larger audiences. At the turn of the twentieth century, several French repertory companies were formed, but most of them disappeared during the First World War when theatre and vaudeville performances gained popularity.

As theatrical performances had been imported from France for a century or more, anglophone theatres had no established professional base on which to build when the imports declined in the first half of the twentieth century. When increasing national consciousness demanded theatrical expression, it was largely amateurs who were available to provide it. The transition from a predominantly amateur to a predominantly professional theatre began with the founding of the Stratford Festival in 1953. In spite of its growth, professional theatre companies remain concentrated in only a few areas of Canada. For example, the National Arts Centre Corporation, the Stratford Shakespearean Festival Foundation of Canada, and the Shaw Festival Theatre accounted for approximately 68 per cent of the total paid attendances at theatres and art centres in Ontario (Statistics Canada 1980:17).

Historically, music in Canada paralleled the basic European style periods, usually lagging behind by a few decades. There were very few permanent orchestras before the early years of the twentieth century, and those that developed often lasted only a few seasons. After the First World War, the era of active music making waned under the impact of the new technologies of recorded and radio-transmitted sound. In 1936 when the Canadian Broadcasting Corporation was founded, it broadcast symphonic and chamber music, thus making it available to vast audiences across the country. A rapid increase in establishing orchestras and attending concerts occurred in the 1940s and continued in a spectacular fashion until the economic austerity of the 1970s and 1980s.

Similar to other performing arts, opera was slow to take root in Canada. During the second half of the nineteenth century, the majority of performances were given by travelling foreign, primarily American, companies. After the First World War, over thirty opera associations, including amateurs and students, were formed, though most of them were short-lived. Opera has been primarily promoted and disseminated through the CBC, the Banff Centre of Fine Arts, various local voluntary opera associations, and festivals. As mentioned earlier, the Canadian Broadcasting Corporation became one of the most crucial cultural institutions for the performing arts. Created as an independent Crown corporation in 1936, the CBC is required by statute to provide comprehensive national radio and television services. Over the years, Canadians without direct access to cultural amenities came to depend on the CBC for opera, classical music, and drama broadcasts. CBC television expanded those services and included ballet performances as well.

Unlike the slow beginnings of the performing arts, the museum movement swept across Canada and became a hallmark of the late nineteenth century. Large canvasses called panoramas, of English or American origin, arrived in Montreal and other cities throughout most of the nineteenth century (Montpetit 1983). In the first half of the twentieth century, many small community museums were founded in eastern Canada. As immigrant settlers moved to the West, pride in their varied ethnic origins gave birth to many collections that eventually became community or regional museums. Canada's centenary in 1967 and several provincial and metropolitan birthdays in the 1960s encouraged museum development. By 1984, Canadians could visit some of the approximately 1,700 museums, art galleries, and related institutions, although they remained unequally distributed throughout the country.

To summarize, high culture and the arts in Canada were influenced, especially during their early years of development, by the climate, the past experiences in the settlers' countries of origin, and the harsh living conditions. The scarcity of professional performing arts companies and events led to the development of amateur performances and was eventually alleviated by the CBC's radio and television cultural broadcasts.

▥ Everyday leisure and popular culture

In addition to attending 'highbrow' cultural events, many people participate in seasonal festivals that are held across the country, mostly during the summer. Smaller local and regional fairs, midway attractions, and rodeos or major events like the Calgary Stampede and Edmonton's Klondike Days, together with other occasional events, seem to be plentiful and well attended. Several cities also organize indoor and outdoor winter festivals as well; some of them were the legacy of the Canada Winter Games held in various cities in the past or the 1988 Winter Olympics in Calgary. The latest additions are multicultural festivals and ethnic events.

The everyday pastimes and leisure pursuits of Canadians are historically very similar to those of Americans. Crafts and handiwork that might be considered hobbies today most likely met dual needs by providing practical products as well as opportunities for aesthetic-creative leisure. Some chores were combined with leisure, and logging, barn-raising, or quilting bees were occasions for making necessary work easier as well as for socializing and games. Men in particular frequented taverns and inns, where drinking and gambling, with occasional blood sports, were part of men's pleasures (Gruneau 1983; Hall et al. 1991). Local inns offered places for meetings, dances, and travelling circuses or theatre performances. In some cities such as Montreal, the opening of a zoological and botanical garden modelled on the English 'pleasure garden' reflected the attraction of the times for the 'picturesque' and the exotic and offered a place for rest and recreation (Montpetit 1983). For example, the Guilbault Garden in Montreal has been the site for various attractions since its opening in 1831.

Under the strong influence of the Catholic Church in Quebec in particular, men and women were admonished to be on guard against 'bad leisure' such as night clubs and alcohol, obscene reading, houses of prostitution, and gambling (Bellefleur 1983). They were encouraged to participate in active leisure —sports, hobbies, do-it-yourself pursuits, and gardening; enriching leisure— reading, music, travel, cultural activities; or Christian leisure—attending mass, prayer, meditation and contemplation, and doing charitable activities. Women and girls were warned against frivolous leisure and entertainment or materialistic, frivolous, indecent behaviour and immodest clothes. Young women in particular were warned against sports that might impair their ability to have children.

In the twentieth century, as more people owned cars and gained greater mobility on both sides of the border, there were numerous new leisure opportunities, such as drive-in movies, drive-in restaurants, holiday travel, or driving for pleasure. In addition, popular daily leisure interests for most Canadians are based on consumption of the mass media—print as well as radio and television. Later we will examine in detail the frequency and amount of time different social groups spend on following mass media. We will briefly outline the development and history of mass media consumption in Canada.

With little surplus money or time, reading was at first infrequent among Canadian pioneers. Quebeckers depended upon France for books and periodicals, English Canada on Britain (Vipond 1989). Gradually, as the United States influenced Canada more and more over the course of the nineteenth century, English Canadians increasingly looked southward for their cultural products, especially more popular material like romance novels and poems. By the 1880s, many middle-class English Canadians read the 'better' American periodicals like *Harper's* and *Scribner's*, and the less prosperous read the cheap 'sentimental' American magazines. With the expanded transportation system, newspapers and magazines became more widely distributed and cheaper than before.

Most of the daily papers were evening editions, more convenient for people who worked outside the home and only had time to read during their leisure hours after work. Vipond (1989) points out that the principal emphasis was on facts and information, much of it trivial. The strong secondary emphasis was on entertainment, both sensational and human-interest news, and an increasing number of features were designed to appeal to different groups of readers. Many of these features—which included serialized novels, science columns, sports news, women's pages, and comics—were purchased from American syndicates. Similarly, special interest and 'sentimental' magazines, whether Canadian or American, were designed to appeal to a wide variety of readers. The Canadian middle class in particular became avid readers of these new products.

The twentieth century also introduced another popular form of leisure—the movie theatre. By the time the First World War began, all of Canada's major cities and most of the smaller ones had several movie theatres (Vipond 1989). Movie attendances increased dramatically during the Depression when the weekly visit to the movie theatre became a popular escapist luxury. However, almost all of the films were American.

Listening to the radio rapidly evolved from a novel experience to a frequent leisure pursuit. By 1931, one-third of Canadians had radios, and by 1950 almost all of them did (Vipond 1989). As with the print media and the movies, American popular culture exerted its strong influence in radio as well. From the beginning, many Canadians listened to the best and most powerful American stations. Furthermore, the CBC offered a wide range of serious and light entertainment, such as 'The Happy Gang', 'CBC Stage', and 'Hockey Night in Canada', which attracted large audiences in most Canadian households. With the arrival of television in Canada in 1952, only those living in the most remote areas were beyond the range of a Canadian TV station by 1960. In less than a decade, television became the primary entertainment and in-home leisure activity of Canadians.

In sum, everyday leisure and popular culture for most Canadians included occasional festivals, sports, or performing art events. However, in the twentieth century in particular, reading mass-circulation newspapers and magazines, listening to the radio, and watching television became a part of daily leisure. In addition, Canadians liked movie theatres, but eventually succumbed mostly to television. Of course, daily leisure always involved socializing with family and friends, parental games with the children, or simply 'doing nothing'. These other types of daily leisure have not been addressed in this section, but will be examined in detail in later chapters. What the present historical, descriptive examination cannot adequately convey are the underlying pro-

cesses and controversies over the control of leisure and sports. We shall turn
to the issues of hegemony and struggle in the following section.

▉III An analytical commentary on leisure developments

The historical overview covered the introduction and pursuit of various types
of leisure activities. It also indicated some of the differences and inequalities
between men and women, and among various social groups. Moreover, it has
pointed out that leisure has been subject to often successful attempts by the
élite and various interest groups to control, exploit, and commercialize its
forms. Some forms of control over leisure were quite direct and blatant, such
as forbidding less-privileged groups (for example, women and the lower classes)
to participate in some activities. In other instances, attendance at certain events
and selected places was prohibited or access was limited. We have seen reformists of many stripes attempting to decide what is 'good' for other people,
or the wealthy controlling other people's activities and limiting access to 'their'
activities. Likewise, we have seen how civic supporters attempted to formulate and modify leisure according to a city's image and business interests.

In addition to overt control, there are numerous subtle ways of controlling
leisure. Also, there have been instances in which sports and arts were manipulated to build national or group pride, for example, in international sporting or artistic competitions. In 1983, Sports Canada introduced its 'Best Ever
1988' program, which was designed to assist national sports organizations in
preparing the 'best ever' Canadian Olympic teams (Canada Fitness and Amateur Sport 1986). The federal sports policy documents released by Canada
Fitness and Amateur Sport (1979) indicate not only concerns about 'fitness
in the third age', women, the disabled, and 'hard-to-reach youth', but also
vigorously emphasize the goal of increasing Canada's prominence on the world
stage. Similarly, the provincial government of Quebec no longer considered
recreation only for personal development but assigned it a role in the cultural
development of the 'Québecois nation' (Harvey and Proulx 1988). The Parti
Québecois, concerned with the distinctiveness of Quebec and opposed to federal intervention in sports and recreation, promoted high-performance sports
and athletes after its 1976 election.

We have already touched upon various reformist movements and struggle
for control over leisure. The process of transformation from traditional to modern sports was not always easy. Conflicts flared up and struggles were fought
over sporting practices, the legitimacy of blood sports, 'respectable' forms of
sports, and the organization of sports associations. Theorists like Gruneau
(1988) interpret such historical transformation as a history of cultural struggle. The designation of specific pursuits as more appropriate and worthy—
typically the leisure of the wealthier and more educated classes of society, and
the corresponding devaluation of working-class skills or activities—represent
'the power to define' (Hall et al. 1991). This power is in the hands of the

privileged groups, who are able to establish their cultural practices as the most valued and legitimate.

The approach to the history of leisure and sports as part of the history of struggles among differing social classes and groups over their rights, access to power, privilege, and élite lifestyles addresses only one (albeit crucial) aspect of these processes. It needs to be pointed out that subordinate groups not only demanded access to the privileged strata's leisure but fought for the right to maintain their own non-élite life and leisure styles, which the dominant élites wanted to eradicate or change. The lower classes often engaged in their separate pursuits by choice; they devised activities that mocked the dominant classes and contributed to the building of popular solidarity, such as carnival frivolities, rough sports, or drinking and gambling. Gruneau (1983) calls them 'profane rituals'. They have never really disappeared, only assumed new forms in later societies. For example, British cultural studies theorists have documented the existence of a rich working-class world apart from the élites, expressed through its unique language, rituals, and institutions as sporting events and pubs (Hoggart 1958; Thompson 1963; Williams 1958, 1961) in the second half of the twentieth century.

Like class inequality in leisure, gender inequality, perpetuation of patriarchy, and the imposition of the norms of 'proper' leisure for women made possible by reinforcing the gender division of labour, the division of sports into male and female sports, and the marginalization of females as cheerleaders and spectators (Kidd 1987). The experience has also shown that some female athletes in competitive sports may be exploited by their male coaches and fans and subjected to sexual harassment. It is ironic that concerns voiced by the seemingly conservative proponents of female-only sports regarding propriety and decorum may have proved to be justified (Lenskyj 1991). Furthermore, given the contemporary emphasis on male professional sports (especially hockey and football), the manipulation of images and effects on the television audience, and the concentration on the individual athlete, women's sports and interests remain undervalued (Cantelon and Gruneau 1988; Hall et al. 1991).

In the twentieth century in particular, various women's groups challenged male hegemony in recreation and sports (Lenskyj 1991). They used different, sometimes even conflicting ways to do so: a popular liberal approach insisted that girls and women should have access to equivalent (also known as 'separate but equal') sporting opportunities as boys and men, while another approach, which was developed in the 1970s and 1980s, called for sex-integrated sports and teams. The radical or women-centred approach raised fundamental questions about the nature of male-defined sports, especially the élitism and win-at-all-costs mentality. The feminist assumption of the women-centred model posits that women as a group tend to value social experience above competition. This can explain why most women prefer the social aspects of sports and physical activity more than defeating opponents.

As we have seen in the historical overview, another phenomenon in leisure throughout the world and over time is spectatorship. People of all social
ranks liked to be entertained and amused by amateur and professional entertainers, athletes, or friends and neighbours at play. They flocked to fairs, theatres, or playing fields. What has became one of the distinct characteristics of
contemporary leisure is its 'entertainmentization'—the emphasis on display—
especially in sports (Frey and Eitzen 1991). It changed the nature of sports
because of the media's influence and the desire of both media entrepreneurs
and sports representatives to enhance the appeal of sports products to maintain profit margins. It is not unusual to see the media glorify violence, create
heros, or demand the shift of athletic schedules to accommodate their programming and the exorbitant amounts paid to sports organizations for broadcasting rights. Such commercialization of sports brought the decline of amateurism and the rise of professionalism. Élite amateur sports, whether the
Olympic games or collegiate sports, transformed itself into corporate sports.
Furthermore, as mass media theorists point out, the media's pre-eminent role
in sports brings about not the real but 'mediated' representation of sports. The
consumers of mass media, television in particular, receive a representation of
sports as it is depicted and editorialized by the media providers (Coakley 1990).

In sum, the controversies and struggles over leisure pursuits associated
with historical periods have had several common themes, namely class and
gender inequality in leisure availability, behaviour, practices, and preferences.
This inequality has been part of broader social relationships and inequalities
among the dominant and subordinate social groups, and perpetuated by the
process of socio-historical reproduction and transformation of those relations
as well as mediated through the system of hegemony and cultural imperatives. Although presented here in connection with the history of leisure in
Canada, the above conclusion is equally applicable to leisure in most countries around the world, including that in the United States.

▉▋▋ Summary

The history of Canadian leisure and sports falls into four phases (Hall et al.
1991): leisure and sports in early Canada (1600–1850); Victorian struggles
and transitions (1850–1920); the development of and resistance to the
commodification of leisure and sports (1920–60); and increased involvement
of the state (1960s onwards). Like the Eurocentric and Judaeo-Christian slant
in the world history of leisure, historical studies of leisure in Canada have
been preoccupied with leisure of the White settlers and their descendants.
Only a few leisure historians have studied native peoples' leisure pursuits.

Our brief historical overview of the development of leisure in Canada allows us to see how the climate and vastness of Canada, as well as the diversity
of its settlers, contributed to the uneven development and variation in preferences for different activities. Canada's immigrants have adapted their tradi-

tional forms of leisure and thus altered the nature of the country and influenced the leisure of its inhabitants. Sports, outdoor pursuits, and the arts in Canada were influenced, especially during their earlier phases of existence, by the climate, immigrants' past experiences, and the hard life of the settlers. In addition, there was a scarcity of professional performing arts companies and events. Only the introduction of the CBC radio and television broadcasts made cultural events more accessible for most people.

The chapter has also pointed out the dual influence on leisure in Canada of traditions from settlers' homelands and from the United States. Furthermore, the dividing lines within Canada run along francophone and anglophone distinctions, as well as class and gender divisions.

This historical look at leisure trends and developments should help us to understand better the contemporary patterns and controversies, including specific rates and frequencies of participation that will be examined elsewhere in the book.

PART 2

Definitions, disciplinary perspectives, theories, and paradigms

▮▮▮ Leisure scholars have strived towards conceptual clarity and paradigmatic delineations over several decades. In the course of the increasingly more systematic building of theoretical interpretations and explanations of leisure, the development has been and remains influenced primarily by three factors: the 'real world' with its changing social trends in general and changes in recreation and leisure in particular; developments in related social sciences; and self-generated change within leisure studies (Burton and Jackson 1990).

It has been widely documented that the 'real world's' social, economic, technological, political, attitudinal, and environmental conditions, trends, and changes have important implications for the form and structure of leisure. Correspondingly, these factors have also left their mark on the direction of leisure studies. Furthermore, broad social and technological changes appear not only to influence leisure but are, in turn, influenced by changes in patterns of leisure. For instance, the proliferation of television has had an impact on the patterns of home recreation and, in turn, the demands of home recreation have profoundly affected television programming. Similarly, easy access to automobiles and recreation vehicles has influenced people's vacations, while new vacation patterns affected the automotive production. Other examples of such reciprocal influences include relationships between unemployment and leisure (Glyptis 1989), or between youth and the spread of video games (Braun and Giroux 1989).

Leisure scholars also respond to the developments in particular social sciences concepts and methodologies. Such responsiveness reflects the fact that the interpretation, understanding, and theoretical approaches to leisure are rooted in psychological, social-psychological, and sociological perspectives. Leisure scholars, however, do not passively follow the progress in other sciences; they seek to actively contribute to leisure studies. The reflections on the ever-changing subject of leisure and its changing relationship to other phenomena necessarily create new or refined definitions, concepts, and paradigms in the field of leisure studies (Burton and Jackson 1990). This process takes place especially when leisure researchers want to overcome shortcomings in existing concepts or methods, or when they are faced with difficulties in adapting their research results for practical applications. Jackson's (1988) work on constraints and barriers to leisure, or the social carrying capacity research (Stankey and McCool 1989)—that is, research on how much use an area can receive before controls and limitations on use need to be introduced—are examples of such responses to conceptual and methodological concerns.

It is not surprising that in this environment of contextual and academic changes, 'the present condition of leisure theory approximates to a state of multiparadigmatic rivalry in which a number of mutually incompatible theoretical perspectives hold the terrain' (Rojek 1985:5). Furthermore, as Parry and Parry (1977) noted about Western leisure studies, tensions arise between those who see leisure from a liberal democratic perspective, principally in terms of freedom, and those in the Marxist tradition who see it in terms of social control, repression, or 'unfreedom', i.e., alienation and consumerism. Parry (1983) stresses that one of the positive tendencies of Marxism in alliance with the new feminism and the rapid rise in large-scale unemployment is a refocused attention on unpaid labour, particularly that of women, on dependency even under the welfare state, on unemployed youth, the middle-aged, and those in premature retirement.

The aim of the following discussion is to familiarize the reader with the roots of leisure studies, and with the specific contributions of different social sciences to the analysis and explanation of leisure. In line with our emphasis on the multidimensional, both the subjective and objective context and character of leisure, we will focus on the psychological and social-psychological interpretations of leisure. In particular, we will examine values, attitudes, and motivations as they pertain to leisure, their formation, change, and variations over the life course and across generations. Then we will turn to the sociological perspectives on leisure and their application to leisure within selected life domains. Furthermore, since the feminist theoretical analysis spans psychology and sociology, we will devote a separate section to the feminist orientation in leisure studies.

CHAPTER **3**

Definitions and conceptualizations of leisure

$\mathbf{A}$re the amounts and forms of men's and women's leisure identical or do they differ by gender? If they are different, whose leisure will be studied? Are leisure motivations, experiences, availability, or barriers identical or different for single people in comparison with married couples? Are there differences among the young and old, labourers and professionals, mothers/homemakers and mothers who are employed outside the home? Don't we all watch television, but most likely prefer different programs? Don't we all socialize with family members or friends, but may feel differently about it?

Most earlier studies and books had a tendency to interpret leisure as the residual time, be it at the end of the day, work week, or year (Brightbill 1960; Dumazedier 1960; Giddens 1964; Gross 1961; Soule 1957; Szalai et al. 1972). For example, Brightbill suggested that leisure is the time beyond what is required for existence and subsistence—it is discretionary time. However, he made an important distinction between 'freedom from' and 'freedom to'. Instead of using the definition simply as the absence of impediments, which would mean only 'freedom from', leisure is the discretionary time to be used according to one's own judgement or choice.

Other leisure scholars and recreation practitioners assumed that leisure can be best examined as a list of specific activities that people do in their spare time. Such lists of leisure activities aimed at being as all-inclusive as possible. These inventories often required further grouping based on various criteria; for example, the location, time, or special equipment would place pursuits into one of several leisure types or pairs of activities: outdoor or indoor, self-propelled or mechanized, contemplative or manipulative, solitary or social, serious or inconsequent.

Numerous analyses of specific leisure activities, however, documented that the same activity can mean different things to different persons, or to the same person in different situations. Have you ever experienced the freedom and exhilaration of a mountain hike, been completely absorbed in a beautiful piece of music, or enjoyed the pleasure and camaraderie of your friends' company at some point—only to feel the pain of pushing your aching body up the hill, the disappointment of being unable to master that particular piece of music, or the boredom with your companions at some other point? Which experience would you consider a leisure experience and when did it take place? Would others share your feelings and your state of mind about that particular event?

Arguing against the narrow view of leisure as only the time after work, John Neulinger stated that leisure is 'not not-work' (1981). He maintained that leisure is a state of mind that reflects one's perception of freedom or constraint and intrinsic or extrinsic motivations. According to Neulinger (1981), 'Leisure, then, has one and only one essential criterion, and that is the condition of perceived freedom . . . . *To leisure* implies being engaged in an activity as a free agent and of one's own choice.' Sebastian de Grazia, in his influential work *Of Time, Work, and Leisure*, posited that 'work is the antonym of free time. But not of leisure. Leisure and free time live in two different worlds. We have got in the habit of thinking them the same . . . . Leisure refers to a state of being, a condition of man, which few desire and fewer achieve' (1964:5).

Similarly, Goodale and Godbey (1988) argue that from the definition of leisure as free time, we learn little about what free time is. Rather, it tells us what it is not—free time is not devoted to work or other obligations. The implications often are that leisure is the absence of impediments, or that free time has to be earned. In contrast, leisure can be the time that people can use as they choose, so the focus would shift from 'freedom from' to 'freedom to'. The choice and its implementation become central elements in the notion of freedom.

In contrast to the leftover time approach, Geoffrey Godbey formulated the following definition a few years earlier (1985:9): 'Leisure is living in relative freedom from the external compulsive forces of one's culture and physical environment so as to be able to act from internally compelling love in ways which are personally pleasing, intuitively worthwhile, and provide a basis for faith.' In his approach, there is no reference to time nor to leisure as one's state of mind. Goodale and Godbey argue that by noting that leisure is living, the time and state of mind notions can be avoided. Since individuals are not and should not be free to do anything, the notion of relative freedom recognizes that freedom is necessarily and appropriately limited. Freedom from external compulsive forces of one's culture and environment means that we need snow for skiing and water for swimming, and that we need food, clothing, and shelter. How much we need depends on our environment, but beyond what is minimally adequate, it is our culture that compels us to acquire and consume as much as we do.

From the holistic perspective of leisure comes the definition by Csikszentmihalyi (1975). According to this author, leisure is a state of playfulness or 'flow' that is achieved whenever a person is in optimal interaction with the environment. Flow is possible during the simultaneous presence of four conditions: (1) the individual is free from obligation; (2) the activity pursued is a voluntary choice; (3) the participation is pleasurable; and (4) the activity pursued is culturally recognized as leisure. Also, Tinsley and Tinsley (1982) argue that the leisure state, which means a continuum of experience, resides in the individual, not in the activity. It may occur in all aspects of life, including work and other functions. Thus leisure involves (1) absorption or concentration on the ongoing experience; (2) lessening of focus on the self; (3) feelings of freedom or lack of constraint; (4) enriched perception of objects and events; (5) increased intensity of emotions; (6) increased sensitivity to feelings; and (7) decreased awareness of the passage of time.

Another leisure scholar, Max Kaplan, incorporated the factor of a pleasant expectation of a specific involvement and the pleasurable recollection of it into his elaborate, multivariable definition of leisure. Kaplan's earlier discussion of leisure (1960:22) listed seven essential elements that comprise leisure:

- an antithesis to work as an economic function
- a pleasant expectation and recollection
- a minimum of involuntary social-role obligations
- a psychological perception of freedom
- a close relation to values of the culture
- the inclusion of an entire range from inconsequence and insignificance to weightiness and importance
- often, but not necessarily, an activity characterized by the element of play

The lack of agreement about leisure definitions prompted French sociologist Joffre Dumazedier to write about the 'quarrel over definitions'. In one of his influential works, *Sociology of Leisure* (1974), Dumazedier prefers to view leisure as the time or activities that are free from institutional obligations and that are mainly oriented towards self-fulfilment. For him, leisure is activity— apart from the obligations of work, family, and society—to which individuals turn at will for relaxation, diversion, or broadening spontaneous social participation and exercising their creative capacity. However, leisure time is above all the product of economic and social evolution.

Recently, the commonly accepted definitions of leisure go beyond a unidimensional approach of viewing leisure in terms of one criterion only, be it freedom, a state of mind, designated activities, or residual time. According to one of its main proponents, a multidimensional definition of leisure incorporates all three broad elements mentioned earlier: time, activity, and experience. Thus, leisure is the quality of activity defined by relative freedom and intrinsic satisfaction (Kelly 1982:23).

The broader approach can be helpful in understanding leisure and is applicable in research as well as in leisure services and management, especially

Figure 3.1 A multidimensional definition of leisure

Leisure is:

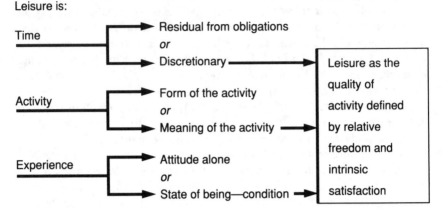

Source: J.R. Kelly, *Leisure* (Englewood Cliffs, NJ: Prentice-Hall, 1982): 23.

because leisure is seldom a yes or no phenomenon. Many situations create an ambivalent perception of a given activity that may make it difficult to determine whether it is or is not leisure. A mother playing with her child or an athlete on the playing field would most likely name at least two reasons for their engagement—pleasure as well as obligation. They may conclude that their activity is not pure leisure but is similar to it, perhaps semi-leisure or semi-work.

The proportion of leisure and non-leisure characteristics in an experience can vary along a continuum, from an unconditional leisure for its own sake to almost no leisure. Neulinger (1981:30) presents such a continuum (Figure 3.2) in which the intrinsic and extrinsic motivations and perceived freedom represent the crucial defining criteria.

Other factors for defining what is or is not leisure stem from the multitude of roles people play in their lives, or from other reasons for participation in leisure—be it for no specific purpose as in leisure for its own sake, for a specific purpose as in compensation for work, or because it is expected of a person in his or her position.

The above definitions of leisure fail to recognize specifically a unique leisure experience of some groups, women in particular (Bella 1989; Deem 1986; Henderson et al. 1989; O'Neill 1991; Shaw 1985). Leisure as non-work time has been shown as an inappropriate concept for women (Anderson 1975; Coles 1980; Deem 1982). Time left over after work or time free from obligations is rare; most women have little real freedom and choice, particularly those for whom work and leisure are interchangeable, and for whom free or unoccupied time is virtually non-existent (O'Neill 1991; Wearing and Wearing 1988). To view leisure as experience can make leisure oppressive for women (Coles 1980). Feminist scholars charge that just as society has been

Figure 3.2 Neulinger's paradigm of leisure: A subjective definition

Freedom					
Perceived freedom			Perceived constraint		
Motivation			Motivation		
Intrinsic	Intrinsic & extrinsic	Extrinsic	Intrinsic	Intrinsic & extrinsic	Extrinsic
Pure leisure	Leisure-work	Leisure-job	Pure work	Work-job	Pure job
Leisure			Non-leisure		

◀ - - - - - - - - - - - - - - - - - - State of mind - - - - - - - - - - - - - - - - - - ▶

Source: J. Neulinger, *To Leisure: An Introduction* (Boston: Allyn and Bacon, 1981): 30.

largely patriarchal, leisure has been mostly an androcentric concept, grounded in androcentrism and masculine subjectivity (Bella 1989; Henderson et al. 1989). Women's thoughts, interests, and experiences have generally been excluded from leisure literature. Deem (1986) posits that the fragmented and irregular notion of time continues for many women because their unpaid work, housework in particular, has only indirect modes of control and no clearly demarcated end or beginning. Consequently, men's and women's notions of what constitutes a working day may be very different.

Some leisure theorists have become critical of the perspectives that are rooted in individual factors and their variations in leisure. For example, Pronovost and D'Amours (1990) argue that some works have so insisted on the individual and personal traits of leisure, and have so used the notion of liberty and free access, that in the end the study of leisure is no longer possible. According to Provonost and D'Amours, the phenomenon of leisure disappears, so to speak, into a 'state' if not a global ethos. It becomes confounded with all the fields of human activity and identified with the search for pleasure and freedom. In their opinion, such approaches are countered by some scholars through the application of, for example, the role of social structures, institutions and organizations, social strata, or the observable differences in leisure habits according to different life stages, and a deluge of figures.

Many readers, particularly novices to leisure studies, might find the number and variety of leisure definitions or conceptualizations rather overwhelming, perhaps even confusing. However, we still have to acknowledge that there is more than one workable, operational definition of leisure.

▮▮ Categories of leisure definitions

To make the mass of proposed conceptualizations of leisure more manageable, several leisure theorists attempted to classify leisure definitions according to the main focus of each definition or conceptual approach. An early endeavour in creating such a classification comes from the American doyen of leisure studies, Max Kaplan. His categories of leisure conceptualizations or definitions are organized in the following outline (1975:18–26): leisure as *end*: the humanistic model in the tradition of Aristotle, de Grazia, Pieper, and the Chinese Confucian conception (the man who is wisely idle is the most cultured man); leisure as *means*: the therapeutic-change model that refers to the uses of leisure for such purposes as social status, therapy, or social control whereby leisure becomes a medicine, a symbol, or a tool; leisure as *time*: the quantitative model used by those who seek to measure, experiment, or in other ways deal with the term for 'objective' purposes, and applied in time-budget studies; the *institutional* conception of leisure that seeks to distinguish it from religious, marital, educational, or political behaviour and value patterns; the *epistemological* conception of leisure that relates activities and meanings to the assumptive, analytic, and aesthetic views of the world; and the *sociological* conception that sees leisure as a construct with such elements as an antithesis to the work of the participant, a perception of the activity as voluntary and free, a pleasant expectation and recollection—a full range of possibilities from withdrawal in sleep or drink to highly creative tasks. Elements of leisure are to be found in work, family, and education; conversely, elements from those constructs are often to be found in leisure. From this view, nothing is definable as leisure per se, and almost anything is definable as leisure.

Dumazedier (1974) examined leisure definitions from the point of view of activities or life domains and their inclusion or exclusion in a specific definition. He distinguished between (a) remunerated work, (b) family obligations, (c) socio-spiritual and socio-political obligations, and (d) activities external to these institutional obligations and oriented mainly towards self-fulfilment. Depending on whether they hold leisure to include one or more of these domains, the four types of definitions differ among themselves in the following manner. Under the first type of definition, leisure is not a definite category of social behaviour, it is a *style of behaviour* that may occur in any activity and any activity may become leisure. The second type of definition explicitly or implicitly situates leisure in relation to work only, and equates leisure with *non-work*. The third type excludes household and family obligations from the definition of leisure, but covers *socio-spiritual and socio-political obligations*. Fourthly, there is the type of definitions of leisure as the time whose content is oriented towards *self-fulfilment* as an ultimate end.

Later, Dumazedier (1990) addressed this issue of definitional classifications from yet another viewpoint when he outlined three directions in leisure studies: (1) *objectivistic* orientation that inspired many studies on the origin, distribution, and interrelationships of leisure activities and social structures in global societies; similarities and differences among social classes and groups within the same culture; tourist movements; and labour migration; (2) a focus on *social subjects*—private, commercial, associative, or public—as well as interaction among the social subjects and social situations that are found, for example, in Bourdieu and praxeology or in Mannheim's *Freedom, Power and Democratic Planning*; and (3) *phenomenological* sociology, for example, the works of Garfinkel, Schutz, and Maffesoli.

James F. Murphy's categorization of the prevalent leisure concepts is depicted in his diagram (1974:11), which incorporates the *discretionary-time* concept of leisure; leisure as a *social instrument*; leisure as a *non-work* activity associated with the characteristics of social class, race, and occupation; the *classical* view of leisure as a condition of the soul or a state of being; an anti-utilitarian view of leisure as an *end in itself*, a joy, harmony, and pleasure; and, finally, the *holistic* concept of leisure, which recognizes that everything has leisure potential and incorporates a full range of self-determined activities and experiences.

In his later summary, Murphy (1987) first divides views of leisure into the objective and subjective categories. The objective category, most frequently used by sociologists, includes several definitions or conceptualizations. The definitions of leisure as discretionary or residual time view leisure as freely chosen activities that people engage in during the time that remains after working, eating, sleeping, and fulfilling other biological necessities of life. This perspective emphasizes the freedom of the individual to select activities for personal satisfaction at his or her discretion. The view of leisure as activity suggests that leisure apart from work and other obligations, fulfils certain behavioural requirements. Leisure in this context is a diversion and an elaborate rationalization that provides individuals respite from work. It is exclusive devotion to the pursuit of personally liberating and growth-enhancing experiences. When leisure is interpreted as a symbol of social class, as it was first articulated by Thorstein Veblen in 1899, it is viewed in relation to the wealthy or élite social class, who used it to maintain position or standing in society. Especially in Veblen's times, this was achieved through the conspicuous consumption of leisure goods; the possession and visible use of leisure became the hallmark of the upper class. The interpretation of leisure as a social instrument sees leisure as a means of meeting the needs of the poor, elderly, and disabled, along with various other disenfranchised groups, through the efforts of human-service agencies. Originally an outgrowth of the early recreation and leisure movement, this idea became an essential cornerstone for the expansion of services in the 1960s. Focusing on leisure as a function of a social group addresses the provision of the most common individual leisure experiences through participation in social groups, with the family representing the most basic social unit for leisure activity.

Apart from the above objective views of leisure, there is the subjective, introspective orientation that focuses upon perceived freedom and intrinsic motivation as the basis for leisure experience. In this subjective category, the classical view of leisure, and more recently, the holistic concept figure quite prominently. According to the holistic definitions of leisure, leisure can be experienced in a wide variety of activities—work, play, education, and religion. In Murphy's opinion (1987), the works of Mihaly Csikszentmihalyi and of Tinsley and Tinsley represent the prominent interpretations of the holistic perspective of leisure.

The classification by Richard Kraus (1984:41–7) is analogous to some of the earlier ones. Kraus finds at least four traditionally held meanings of leisure and proposes the following categorization: '(1) the classical view of leisure, as exemplified in the writings of de Grazia and Pieper; (2) the view of leisure as a function of social class; (3) the concept of leisure as activity carried on in free time; (4) the concept of leisure as free time.' To this, he adds the fifth and more recent concept of leisure as a state of existence or way of being.

Unlike these more complex kinds of classification, the simplest among them is represented by Neulinger's twofold categorization (1981:21–2), which consists of the subjective and the objective approaches to leisure. The former is represented by the views of de Grazia and Pieper that portray leisure as a state of mind; the latter comprises the views that include the quantitative, residual, or discretionary time concepts.

The most recent classification originates in Quebec. Its authors, Gilles Pronovost and Max D'Amours (1990), group the best-known approaches as:

1 residual (those that stress the availability of time or define leisure as available time, notably beyond the bounds of work and family obligations)
2 those that are based on the study of activities and more or less identify leisure with free-time activities, notably sports and cultural activities
3 those that stem from the notion of culture, under two orientations:
    a) those inspired implicitly or explicitly by the notion of mass culture and that lead to either making a severe criticism of modern leisure, or proposing a sort of élitist concept of leisure (à la de Grazia)
    b) those inspired either by notions of culture in the anthropological or sociological sense of the term, or by notions of cultural development and changing values, making leisure one of the major fields of study of cultural changes in contemporary societies
4 those that stress the relationship between leisure and other phenomena, work and the family in particular, and focus on their reciprocal influence

In sum, there is a general agreement among leisure scholars that in spite of their considerable diversity, even incompatibility, leisure definitions and conceptualizations fall under a few groups. Based on their main focus, we find the objective and subjective groupings, as well as the notions of discretionary time and freedom of choice, activity, experience, and individual perceptions, at the core of these definitional groups.

When examining different authors' specific conclusions about people's leisure patterns and assessing their applicability, we will always bear in mind the particular definition utilized in the original work. Having the advantage of familiarity with those different propositions, we can now build on that base and start the work by formulating our own definition of leisure. As presented earlier, I suggest the following definition of leisure: leisure is an enjoyable experience in which people choose to participate with relative freedom in terms of discretionary time and particular activities, within the context and limitations of culture, socio-economic factors, and gender. Leisure experience can be objective and/or subjective, long-lasting or brief, planned or spontaneous, an end in itself or therapeutic/compensatory, sociable or solitary.

CHAPTER 4

Psychological and social-psychological perspectives on leisure

The individual approach to leisure can be viewed from a psychological perspective. According to one of the most prominent psychologists of leisure, John Neulinger (1981, 1987), this approach is restricted to investigating the state of mind that has traditionally been associated with the leisure experience. Leisure psychologists identify (a) the conditions that bring about the state of mind associated with the experience of leisure, (b) the nature of this state of mind, and (c) the implications of this state of mind.

The social psychology of leisure has been defined as 'that branch of scientific leisure studies which examines how the feelings, cognitions, and behaviours of one individual are influenced by the feelings, cognitions, and behaviours of others during a period of time subjectively designated as unobligated, free, or leisure' (Iso-Ahola 1980a:18). The two key points in a social-psychological analysis are individual and social influences that lead to the examination of how an individual's attitudes, motives, emotions, and behaviour are influenced by other individuals, social groups, and social structures. The social-psychological analysis of leisure is based upon the assumption that cognitive mechanisms (thought processes) mediate all human responses to a varying degree (Iso-Ahola 1987).

The factors closely associated with the leisure experience include freedom of choice, enjoyment, intrinsic motivation, relaxation, and the lack of evaluation. Since no direct causal link between leisure attitudes and leisure behaviour can be established, contextual and intervening factors of and specific barriers to participation need to be examined as well. Thus, it is essential to explore also the context of leisure experience and motivation.

The psychological and social-psychological approaches have been discussed in leisure literature for quite some time; however, a systematic psychological and social-psychological research of leisure did not start until the 1970s. Even then, much of it was scattered throughout the vast body of psychological and leisure literature (Iso-Ahola 1987). Applications of social psychology to various aspects of leisure behaviour, as well as implications for leisure counselling and therapeutic recreation, appeared primarily in the 1980s.

Roger Ingham (1986, 1987) draws attention to the diverse approaches adopted within the psychology of leisure. On the one hand, he sees the experiential approaches of Csikszentmihalyi and Neulinger in particular, who emphasize the subjective qualities of the leisure experience, regard leisure as a state of mind, and concentrate on identifying the conditions necessary for this state of mind. On the other hand, Ingham finds explorations of a wider range of phenomena that incorporate the reported motivations, satisfactions, and attributions relating to aspects of leisure behaviour. Other psychological studies of the leisure experience can be found, for instance, in a monothematic issue of *Loisir et Société/Society and Leisure* published in 1984.

Iso-Ahola (1987) contrasts his position regarding the factors external to an individual with the behaviourist approach. In his view, the narrow behaviouristic perspective examines behaviour only in terms of stimuli and responses, and assumes that human beings are robots without cognitions. Cognitive social psychology takes on an interactionist perspective, according to which leisure behaviour is explained in terms of the interaction between an individual and his or her social environment. Moreover, as Csikszentmihalyi noted in 1976, there is growing evidence of a paradigmatic shift in the study of human behaviour towards the view that external rewards are motivating only when they conform to a person's intentions and desires. In contrast to the purely stimulus-reduction view, the new interpretation suggests that leisure consists of an open stimulus/arousal-seeking model of human behaviour. According to this point of view, an individual strives to maximize control over increasingly complex challenges in the environment by developing his or her skills.

A related social-action model that views the nature of reality from a subjective/experiential perspective is elaborated by James F. Murphy (1987). The social-action model recognizes that an individual's own behaviour and goal setting will condition his or her attempts at fulfilment through leisure experiences. According to this definition, leisure is an integral part of life as a whole, and individuals determine their own goals and attempt to realize them according to their own way of life.

Iso-Ahola's theory of substitutability of leisure behaviour (1986), rooted in the theoretical and empirical literature of the social psychology of leisure, can be presented as a particular example of the recent orientation in studying leisure. In this theory, Iso-Ahola suggests that the substitutability concept is of theoretical significance because it lends itself to analyses of the antecedents of leisure behaviour and thereby contributes to the knowledge of the whys of leisure behaviour.

One of the difficulties with applying the psychological conceptualization to leisure stems from the inconsistencies between attitudes and behaviour. Because of the lack of direct causal link between leisure attitudes and leisure behaviour, Iso-Ahola (1980a) argues that in order to predict participation in a specific leisure activity, the prediction should be made from expressed intentions to engage in it rather than from an attitude towards that leisure activity. If the purpose of a project is to understand leisure behaviour, factors that affect such intentions should be studied as well. Among the empirical studies of the characteristics of leisure experience, most frequently cited are Maslow's peak experience, Csikszentmihalyi's flow experience, Mannell's findings on time duration estimates (perceptions of the loss of time), situational awareness (decreased awareness of the incidental features of physical and social surroundings), and mood change (positive effect) as variables of relevance (Neulinger 1987).

As we will elaborate in more detail later, leisure appears to be chiefly motivated by intrinsic factors; however, many activities have both intrinsic and extrinsic rewards. In addition, environmental forces help to determine to a considerable extent how intrinsic motivation influences human behaviour. Thus, although leisure goals and rewards are viewed as either intrinsic or extrinsic, much leisure behaviour seems to be externally motivated nevertheless (Iso-Ahola 1980a). However, there is also some evidence that individuals differ substantially in the frequency of experiencing intrinsic motivation. Most scholars posit that the differences are not due to demographic, social class, or occupational factors, and they argue that optimal experiences cannot be increased beyond a certain point by providing better and better leisure activities.

Neulinger's hierarchical model of leisure identifies motivation as a secondary condition for leisure that further determines the quality of the leisure experience. In this view, the proportion of intrinsic and/or extrinsic motivation for the activity affects the nature of the leisure experience. One of the implications of recognizing the nature of leisure is that it is no longer defined in contrast to work, but is seen as an overriding experience that determines the quality of both work and non-work time. According to Neulinger, recognizing leisure as an essential, perhaps *the* essential dimension of human existence, is revolutionary. Neulinger's own research instrument and technique (1981) address the effects of leisure and non-leisure experiences and allow an estimate of both the quantity and quality of a day's leisure experiences.

In sum, leisure psychologists examine the conditions and the nature of the state of mind associated with the experience of leisure and explore its implications. Social psychologists analyse individual and social influences that affect an individual's attitudes, motives, emotions, and behaviour towards leisure. More recently, several diverse approaches have been adopted within the psychology and social psychology of leisure.

We now turn to the selected issues addressed by psychologists and social psychologists, particularly the values, attitudes, motivations, and need satisfaction over a lifetime. Our main focus, of course, will be on the specific application of these concepts within the examination of leisure.

▥ Values, attitudes, and beliefs

Most authors agree that leisure participation is an expression of personal values and attitudes. However, they also recognize that attitudes do not exist by themselves within the individual as separate, independent, or isolated units but are part of an interdependent system that constitutes much of what is called personality. Other related concepts include beliefs, cognitions, expectations, intentions, and perceptions of various experiences. In spite of this overall agreement, many theorists disagree about the exact definition of such personality terms as mental dispositions, values, attitudes, beliefs, motivations, and satisfaction as they pertain to leisure. Many of these terms are overlapping or are used interchangeably in the literature.

A value is usually conceived as a broader concept than attitude, one that does not refer to any specific object (Neulinger 1974, 1981). Some authors define values as the cluster of beliefs an individual holds regarding things that are important in life. Values determine in part how an individual uses his or her resources, for example, how much time and money is invested in leisure as opposed to work and family roles. The values one holds help provide the motivation for many life choices and behaviours, including one's choice of leisure activities (Osgood and Howe 1984).

As for attitudes, most psychologists agree with Allport (1968) that attitude connotes a neuropsychic state of readiness for mental and physical activity. It is also generally agreed that this readiness expresses itself in three areas: cognitive, affective, and behavioural (Harrison 1976; Triandis 1967), although different theorists place varying emphasis on each. According to Fishbein and Ajzen's (1975:15) conceptualization, 'Attitude is a general predisposition that does not predispose the person to perform any specific behaviour. Rather, it leads to a set of intentions that indicates a certain amount of affect toward the object in question.'

Leisure attitudes are usually viewed as a person's dispositions towards leisure (Neulinger 1984). A person's attitude towards leisure is how he or she thinks, feels, and acts with regard to leisure. Leisure attitudes determine that proportion of variance in leisure behaviour that reflect the personal, subjective, and unique (Neulinger 1974). Iso-Ahola argues that leisure attitude can be defined as the expressed amount of affect towards a given leisure-related object. The object of an attitude can be leisure itself or some of its components like a leisure behaviour, a leisure activity, a person or a group participating in leisure activities, a leisure program or policy, and a place where leisure participation takes place. Thus, a leisure attitude can be both general and specific, depending on how the object is defined (Iso-Ahola 1980a).

Neulinger and Breit (1971) identified five relatively stable and independent attitude dimensions in the leisure domain: affinity for leisure, society's role in leisure planning, self-definition through leisure or work, amount of perceived leisure, and the amount of work or vacation desired. Such average attitudes do not necessarily exist in any one person, and very often what an individual would like to do in accordance with his or her attitudes is not what this person ends up doing. These authors suggest that in order to ascertain whether a leisure experience is likely to emerge, those dimensions that are viewed as the necessary conditions for that experience need to be investigated. In terms of Neulinger's paradigm of leisure, they are perceived freedom and intrinsic motivation. Thus, it is crucial to distinguish between identifying the characteristics of a phenomenon and investigating the conditions that bring it about.

Attitudes towards leisure are also linked with personality types. This position has been documented more recently by several authors (Gosselin 1985; Guthrie 1986; Ouellet 1985) who apply Holland's theory (1973) of vocational choices to leisure. Holland's theory supports the view that different personality types (realistic, investigative, artistic, social, enterprising, and conventional) would correspond to different vocational choices depending on their interests and values, and that work values reflect the personality that develops during adolescence. These authors confirm that leisure, like work, permits the expression of personality and depends on the choice and interests of the individual.

Kleiber (1979) suggests that attitudes towards leisure may be affected by one's perception of the ability to control life's consequences and by the perceived locus of control. Similarly, attitudes among married people appear to be influenced according to the stage of their marital and parental careers, more so for women than men (Horna 1987c; Horna and Lupri 1987; Orthner 1975; Rapoport and Rapoport 1978; Shaw 1984). Thus, obligatory activities tend to be defined more negatively by people with children than by childless individuals, and by housewives as opposed to women who work outside the home. Even informal, unstructured leisure situations that occur throughout the day seem to be associated with the situational factors conducive to their occurrence. Samdahl (1992) suggests that this common leisure occasion may be important because it offers relative freedom from negative judgements, allowing an individual to relax from the necessity of behaving according to others' expectations. Similarly, Unger (1984) provides evidence that the subjective labelling of a situation as leisure was tied to characteristics of the social context. According to this view, situations were particularly likely to be labelled leisure if they offered companionship or entailed activities that encouraged social interaction.

Apart from differences among individuals or groups of individuals who differ in their definitions of and attitudes towards specific leisure activities, the same individual can display internal differences as well. Shaw (1984) has shown how the day of the week, the time of the day, the location of the activity, and the presence of other people affect people's perceptions. Similarly, Mannell's s-a-e (Self-As-Entertainment) construct (1984) suggests that there may be individual differences that influence whether the amount of discretionary time available is perceived as too little or too much. The complex pattern discovered by Mannell, however, indicates no gender or age differences. The s-a-e scores increase with education; they are not significantly associated with actual income, but they are related to perceived financial comfort. Activities that require active participation and some basic skills (e.g., music, crafts, and gardening) have weak but positive correlations with s-a-e scores. Furthermore, the amount of time per week spent watching television is negatively related to the level of s-a-e, and attitudes towards television soap operas are also moderately negatively associated. Of particular interest is Mannell's finding that the self-entertaining capacity appears to be associated with an avoidance and distaste for activities that may be suggested as alternatives for people when they do not know what to do with their discretionary time.

Beliefs constitute a person's informational base and are the fundamental building blocks that determine personal attitudes, intentions, and behaviour. The two major sources of belief formation are situational/social influences and past experiences. Beliefs differ in terms of how they are formed and how long they endure. Beliefs about social institutions (such concepts as democracy, capitalism, school) tend to be relatively stable, while beliefs about consequences of behaviour and persons are quite unstable (Fishbein and Ajzen 1975).

These notions imply that beliefs about leisure activities vary, and that personal experiences play an important part in belief formation. An individual's preferences in leisure are influenced not only by his/her attitude but also by past experiences (Russell 1985). The experience is affected by the individual's attitude and opportunities in recreation, with a reciprocal or simultaneous relationship between attitude and opportunities. Situational and social influences and past experiences, in turn, give rise to beliefs, attitudes, and future intentions. If the person has a reason to believe that participation in a leisure activity will lead to intrinsic rewards, then he or she would have a positive attitude towards that activity.

▮▮▮ Need satisfaction

As discussed earlier, the experience of leisure is not directly associated with particular activities, nor with what is traditionally thought of as free time. Many people perceive leisure as a common daily experience, others as a peak experience, or as a rare and special occurrence. Most leisure theorists tend to agree that leisure activities can function as potential satisfiers of human needs. Psychologists usually distinguish between two types of general needs: primary or innate needs that include hunger, thirst, and sleep, and secondary needs that include love, achievement, companionship, artistic expression, and autonomy.

Conceptually as well as empirically, needs fulfilment is often presented as interchangeable with or similar to functions, meaning, rewards, and goals of leisure activities. Perhaps the most familiar conceptualization of human needs comes from Maslow's (1976) hierarchy of human needs: (1) physiological needs (hunger, thirst, sleep, sex); (2) safety and security, protection of the physical self and lifestyle; (3) affection, sense of belonging, and love; (4) self-esteem, esteem by others, prestige; and (5) self-actualization.

Another need conceptualization is proposed by McClelland (1961) who argues that people are motivated by one of three needs: achievement, power, or affiliation. Several theorists also apply Dubin's model (1956) of central life interests. Dubin investigated whether workers considered work and the workplace or a non-work locale as their central life interest. He found that only 24 per cent of his respondents could be defined as job-oriented in their life interests. The majority sought meaningful human relationships, feelings of worth, and enjoyment in non-work situations. Similar findings were obtained in studies by Dumazedier (1967) in France, by Blishen and Atkinson (1980), Horna (1985a) and Meissner (1975) in Canada, and Parker (1983) in England. How frequently leisure is regarded as a central life interest depends upon how broadly leisure is defined.

The choice of a particular activity to satisfy specific needs is the result of a whole system of social relationships involving other areas of an individual's life as well. Research has provided evidence that the perceived 'best' activities are those that involve both friendly interaction *and* an activity, thereby implying that satisfying the need for social interaction is rated an important motive for leisure participation if it is expected to provide feelings of interpersonal competence (Iso-Ahola. 1980a). Typically, leisure activities are not always chosen for their own sake. They appear to be selected from a range that will support systems of social relationships rooted in other spheres of life; married people or parents in particular put their families at the centre of their life interests and consider leisure as one of the crucial means of their family life (Horna 1986, 1989a; Kelly 1983; Rapoport and Rapoport 1978). The familiarity hypothesis and the personal community theory (Bammel and Burrus-Bammel 1982) put leisure in the context of personal history and emphasize an individual's personality needs, in particular the need for a comfortable routine and familiar things while avoiding uncertainty.

It has been argued (Tinsley 1978) that studies of psychological benefits of leisure activities must take into account both the primary and secondary needs of the individual. The conclusions based on Tinsley's research and on the work of several other scholars point out that (1) participation in leisure activities provides a source of satisfaction for a wide range of psychological needs; (2) leisure activities differ in the needs they satisfy; and (3) investigation of the need-satisfying properties of leisure activities contributes to further insight into leisure activities and leisure behaviour.

Additional distinction is made between improvised and stable leisure needs. Most improvised leisure needs are not new but are based on existing needs and may be directed towards activities that take place in novel physical and social settings. Successful recreation programs not only consider people's stable needs, but also provide opportunities for improvised leisure needs (Iso-Ahola 1980a). There may also be a change from 'before' to 'after' needs (e.g., going to a concert to enjoy music and the company of friends afterwards). The a priori reason may also change, for example, one day a person plays primarily for physical exercise, the next day for social interaction.

One specific point of view in this connection relates to the school of thought that interprets the mass media from the perspective of the uses and gratifications paradigm. Its adherents posit that individuals selectively use the mass media in order to satisfy their human needs (Lull 1982). Similarly, McQuail (1983) applies the uses and gratifications perspective and suggests a fourfold typology of these uses and gratifications: (1) information, (2) personal identity, (3) integration and social interaction, and (4) entertainment. The uses and gratifications perspective has been criticized already in the 1970s (Elliot 1974) from both the radical and the humanistic perspectives (reviewed by Rosengren 1983). This perspective and the gratification component of the paradigm in particular contributes to a better understanding of motivations and functions associated with the mass media use (McQuail 1983; Rubin 1981).

▮ Motivations

The psychological literature has not yet clarified the conceptual and empirical confusion with differentiating meaning from motivation. What one writer defines as a motivation for participation in leisure another labels a meaning derived from participation (Osgood and Howe 1984). Regardless of these differences, psychologists agree that a motive is an internal factor that arouses and directs human behaviour (Iso-Ahola 1989). People do not simply engage in various pursuits, they strive for some objectives and escape from others. Most human actions are directed, and actions resulting from an inner motive bring about desired goals. According to Iso-Ahola, internal and external stimuli give rise to human motivation. Most contemporary psychologists agree that a search for some optimum level of arousal or general stimulation underlies most psychological motives. Empirical findings strongly suggest that people seek neither an absence nor an excess of stimulation, but rather an optimal level.

Since intrinsic and extrinsic motivations or rewards are subjectively defined, it is critical to know how a person perceives his or her motivations. Leisure appears to be chiefly motivated by intrinsic factors; however, many activities can bring about both intrinsic and extrinsic rewards. In addition, environmental forces help to determine to a considerable extent how intrinsic motivation influences human behaviour. Thus, although leisure goals and rewards are viewed as either intrinsic or extrinsic, much leisure behaviour seems to be externally motivated nevertheless (Iso-Ahola 1980a).

An investigation of the consequences of intrinsic motivation has led to identifying the differences in types of leisure behaviours of persons with high or low intrinsic motivation. Individuals with low intrinsic motivation may resort to avoidance behaviours like entertainment activities, while those with high intrinsic motivation may become involved in more interactive activities (Kobasa 1979). Furthermore, individuals differ substantially in frequencies of experiencing intrinsic motivation. The differences are not due to demographic, social class, or occupational factors, and optimal experiences cannot be increased beyond a certain point by providing better and better leisure activities (Graef, Csikszentmihalyi, and McManama Gianinno 1983). Whenever possible, people prefer and opt for self-determined and autonomous behaviours. The two basic reasons for this general tendency towards intrinsically motivated behaviours mean that (1) they facilitate people's attempts to pursue and achieve optimum levels of sensory stimulation and arousal and, therefore, also their efforts to maintain motivational normalcy; and (2) they produce inherent pleasure and satisfaction (Iso-Ahola 1989).

As people seek to satisfy their needs, enjoyment, freedom of choice, relaxation, motivation, and the lack of evaluation are most closely associated with the experience of leisure (Shaw 1984). The freedom to choose an activity, with no external compulsion or obligation to engage in the activity for others or for their own good, one that is for one's own immediate enjoyment, leads to the interpretation of activities as relaxing and less likely challenging of one's skills or psychologically involving. Other theorists (Deci 1980; Maddi and Kobasa 1981; Weissinger and Iso-Ahola 1984) posit that intrinsically motivated behaviours may result in physical as well as psychological benefits. Maddi and Kobasa further suggest that a person's intrinsic motivation is useful in mediating the negative effects of stress and contributes directly to physical health. Considerable empirical evidence obtained from the Alberta Public Opinion Survey on Recreation (1981, 1984, 1988) brings similar conclusions as practically all Alberta respondents reported that 'recreation makes me feel good', and 77 per cent chose physical health as their reason for being involved in leisure pursuits.

Freedom in leisure, perceived subjectively, consists of four major elements: perceived competence, perceived control, intrinsic motivation, and a behavioural manifestation of these—playfulness (Witt and Ellis 1984). Also the ability to fill one's free time with activity (mental, physical, or social) that is perceived by the individual as personally satisfying and appropriate is important in this connection (Mannell 1984). Persons high in this trait find a match between discretionary time and their capacity to use or fill it, and do not experience time as hanging heavily on their hands, nor do they feel that their free time is wasted. On the other hand, individuals low in this trait perceive that they have too much free time, and that there is frequently nothing to do;

consequently, their leisure needs may be inadequately satisfied. Freely chosen activities are not only more likely to be labelled leisure, they also appear to be accompanied by higher levels of flow (Mannell, Zuzanek, and Larson 1988). Furthermore, activities perceived as intrinsically motivated are accompanied by feelings of greater relaxation/lower tension, but the type of motivation has no significant impact on affect.

In contrast to casual leisure, which ultimately tends to cause 'spiritual dyspepsia', Stebbins's (1982) in-depth studies examine the systematic pursuit of an amateur, hobbyist, or volunteer activity that is so involving and interesting for the participant that he or she finds a career in it. Stebbins envisages people who will increasingly search for leisure activities that express their abilities, fulfil their potential, identify themselves as unique human beings, and satisfy these needs through some of the three types of serious leisure, i.e., amateurism, hobbies, and career volunteering.

In spite of the apparent inclination towards intrinsically motivated behaviours, people cannot always opt for self-determined activities and, at times, their initial intrinsic motivation is significantly modified by certain factors. One such modifying factor is the use of extrinsic rewards. There is considerable empirical evidence in the literature to indicate that, in general, rewards undermine intrinsic motivation (Deci and Ryan 1985; Iso-Ahola 1989). In general, rewards for doing an activity of intrinsic interest subsequently cause a loss of interest and willingness to participate in that activity. People regard such rewards and feedback as controlling, and therefore perceive them as restricting their self-determination. There are, however, gender differences in these perceptions, in that females are more likely than males to perceive any feedback as controlling.

Other factors that undermine intrinsic motivation include the imposition of a deadline for the completion of an interesting activity (Amabile, Dejong, and Lepper 1976; Iso-Ahola 1989; Reader and Dollinger 1982; Shaw 1984), and the presence of an evaluator (Lepper and Greene 1975; Shaw 1985; Harackiewicz, Manderlink, and Sansone 1984), even if the subsequent evaluation turns out to be positive. However, a reward in the form of positive feedback that confirms or increases one's sense of competence does not undermine intrinsic motivation and can even enhance it (Iso-Ahola 1989; Koestner, Zuckerman, and Koestner 1987).

In a similar vein, other research efforts attempt to identify the role of motivation as a factor related to physical or sports activities, and to pinpoint motivational factors that influence adults to participate in physical activity (Kenyon 1968; Ruskin and Shamir 1984). The findings reveal that the three dimensions that relate most strongly to the extent and level of activity involve relaxation and release of tension, tension and excitement, and physical fitness and health. Likewise, the 1985 Canada Fitness Survey finds that about 90 per cent of Canadians participate in fitness and physical activities to feel better or for fun and excitement. These findings indicate that people do things that they think will yield gratifying or beneficial results, yet only 6 per cent say that more information on benefits would encourage their involvement (Canada Fitness and Amateur Sport 1983).

▮▮▮ Attitude formation and change

Psychologists widely recognize childhood as the primary formative period of the personality. Traditional conceptions of socialization view the family, specifically the parents, to be the principal agents of socialization in childhood (Erickson 1950; Heilbrun 1965). Children learn their parents' values, beliefs, and attitudes through direct teaching and indirect observation as part of the information and guidance that children either actively seek out or passively accept. In addition to the parents, a number of social agents, namely siblings, peers, and schoolteachers, represent major influences in the socialization process. The implicit assumption has been that childhood socialization is so intense, prolonged, and psychodynamically important that the attitudes and values formed during childhood persist well into adulthood (Adorno et al. 1950; Campbell 1969; Chodorow 1978).

Of course, socialization occurs within the boundaries established by social and cultural forces (Iso-Ahola 1980a); they also affect the range of leisure activities and the experiences available to an individual. The agents of socialization operate within such boundaries. Based on their experiences, expectations, values, and preferences, these agents of socialization shape the leisure experiences and involvement of their subjects. What becomes intrinsically motivated is determined through the socialization process; within this process, a person learns competencies and finds out about leisure activities that are compatible with his/her perceived capacities. Furthermore, the subject's accumulated repertoire of leisure experiences becomes a major factor in the development of his or her evaluation of anticipated outcomes and subsequent definition of leisure experiences. It follows that there is no better time than childhood for establishing basic leisure attitude patterns.

Findings from several surveys indeed demonstrate that the family is the primary context for leisure learning and participation (Barnett and Chick 1986; Horna 1988b; Kelly 1978b, 1982, 1987; Roberts 1981; Yoesting and Burkhead 1973; Yoesting and Christensen 1978). Research on the intergenerational transmission of attitudes documents that parents' attitudes, especially mothers' attitudes, are significant positive predictors of children's attitudes in adulthood (Acock and Bengston 1978; Bengston 1975; Dalton 1980; Glass, Bengtson, and Dunham 1986; Jennings and Niemi 1982; Smith 1983). Further reinforcement of these arguments comes from other studies, such as Greendorfer and Lewko's (1978) analysis of the role of family members in sports socialization of children. Their findings, however, suggest that when each family member's influence on children's sports participation is examined in detail, only the father's influence proves to be significant. Like Greendorfer and Lewko's study, Horna's stream model (1987c) also underscores the importance of the family in leisure learning. The latter model of leisure preferences and behaviour, which will be discussed again in connection with particular patterns of conjugal and familial leisure, is based on the life histories of married and cohabiting couples. The model suggests that most pursuits outside the core activities typically come from one stream of activities (Horna 1987c) falling under the physical or cultural category. It shows that specific preferences and forms of leisure activities within these streams are launched by the family early in one's life and individuals tend to stay with them throughout life. They might occasionally experiment with other specific activities, but will seldom, if ever, cross over into another stream. Another Canadian study, this time based on a survey of the nature of exposure to the performing arts (Bradley and Ward 1979), shows that participation by most adult audiences in the performing arts too has been influenced by early exposure to that art form.

The traditional approach to socialization has been challenged by several scholars in recent years. Family scholars in particular point to the diversity of influences on children and the complexity of family relationships. They also insist that it is important to recognize relational change beyond primary socialization, and that the family may also act as an agent of change, not an impediment to change. The narrow approaches to socialization have been labelled childhood-determination models by Kelly (1982) because they emphasize the early learning and assume that later years are characterized by the refinement and extension of earlier choices, preferences, and skills rather than by the development of new ones.

Other scholars criticize those narrow interpretations of socialization for failing to address two important issues. First, from a macrostructural point of view, parent-child attitude similarity may be viewed more as the result of social forces that generate the inheritance of social status than as a product of individual psychosocial influence. One of the central issues in the interpretation of findings is whether such similarity can be attributed to successful parental socialization, or whether it has more to do with successful intergenerational transmission of class, race, religious affiliation, marital status, and other prominent social statuses that structure life experience and mould social attitudes (Acock 1984). Thus, what parents transmit may be more social statuses than attitudes and values. In addition to the family as the major socializing agent, the educational system can be the potential promoter of attitudes and their change. Since both the family and the educational system are located within the broader social system, one of the strongest factors in the development of leisure attitudes is represented by the person's cultural and subcultural background. Many differences in peoples' attitudes in various societies are accounted for primarily by societal factors.

The second conceptual challenge stems from the possibility that similarity in attitudes between parents and children could be due equally to the influence of children's attitudes on those of their parents, especially as children age. Proponents of the interactionist perspective (Bell and Harper 1977; Bengston and Troll 1978; Hagestad 1984; Lerner and Spanier 1978) argue that children increasingly influence their parents. Thus, in view of such reciprocal effects, attempts to model intergenerational influence as a one-way process flowing from parents to children may be fundamentally erroneous. Moreover, variability in the impact of parent-child relations across social ideologies is uneven. For example, religious and political ideologies emerge as areas of strong family influence, while gender ideology seems to be less affected by internal family dynamics. However, contrary to McPherson (1976), who proposed that socialization in sports was similar to socialization in general— peer groups as the most influential for males and parents as the most influential for females—Hoff and Ellis (1992) suggest that peers are the most influential source for both males and females. These findings notwithstanding, other theorists posit that family contacts provide the initial and perhaps most lasting examples of modelled behaviour (Bandura 1986).

McGuire, Dottavio, and O'Leary (1987) argue that the childhood-determination model is insufficient for explaining the development of leisure participation patterns among older adults. Their research results provide evidence that some individuals reflect their childhood activities in adulthood, while other adults continue to alter their leisure patterns throughout life by adding new activities and replacing old ones. Similarly, Scott and Willits (1989) find that leisure patterns continue throughout life, although unevenly with regard to specific activities and gender. The overall conclusion from these findings indicates that leisure socialization is a lifelong dynamic process.

Not surprisingly, researchers question whether or not socialization to satisfying leisure behaviour enhances a person's orientation towards intrinsic motivation or satisfaction. Another question has to do with what kinds of socialization patterns are most useful—exposure to a wide variety of leisure experiences, or exposure to a few experiences with deeper involvement (Weissinger and Iso-Ahola 1984). Although there are no conclusive answers to these questions yet, the preliminary evidence suggests that leisure socialization in youth is influential in later leisure career changes (Horna 1987c). Similarly, Brooks and Elliot (1971) show that intrinsic leisure behaviour in childhood is related to psychological well-being twenty years later.

Among the most influential factors related to the formation of both leisure attitudes and behaviour are the situational interrelationships between paid work and family work, as well as the structure and the division of labour within the family (Deem 1987; Dynes 1977; Horna 1987d; Horna and Lupri 1987; Kelly 1982; Meissner 1975; Shaw 1984, 1989; Young and Willmott 1975). Women's leisure attitudes in particular are influenced by their situation and will likely remain so as long as women continue to be disadvantaged in terms of leisure, whether or not they are formally employed in the labour market. Attitudes to or perceptions of specific leisure activities (e.g., active sports, reading, and social events) are not always considered leisure among women. Such activities as cooking, home chores, shopping, child care, and travel are more frequently defined as leisure by men than by women, while gardening and social events receive higher leisure ratings from women than from men. Overall, men are more likely than women to rate obligatory activities as leisure, probably because men in general feel less obligation and more freedom of choice with respect to these activities than women do (Horna and Lupri 1987; Shaw 1984). Within such situation- or activity-specific contexts, no single pattern of attitude formation can be expected.

An additional factor that may affect leisure attitude formation and experiences is the level of stress in the lives of individuals, women in particular. For example, leisure variables and their relationships with other factors show substantial differences between high-stress wives and low-stress wives, but little difference among the husbands (Holman and Jacquard 1988). The nature of work exerts its influence as well. While women are more influenced by their employment status, the influence on men comes primarily from their occupational level. Unlike for most workers with compartmentalized work and non-work lives, a lack of free time or leisure does not seem to pose a problem on the farm. According to oral histories gathered from farm women (Henderson and Rannells 1988), these women found meaning and leisure through an integration of work, family, and community experiences.

In sum, childhood socialization is the primary formative element of the personality and thus of leisure attitudes; however, leisure attitudes do not remain unchanged throughout the life cycle. Leisure attitude, behaviour, and choices are linked with personality types, while situational/social factors and past experiences also exert influence. Gender and age, the stage of the life cycle, relationships between labour force participation and family work, and the structure and division of labour within the family affect individuals' leisure. Furthermore, these factors are linked with a person's ability and opportunity to substitute one activity for another. It must be concluded that there cannot be just one generic approach to attitude formation and change; the multitude of individual, subjective, and contextual factors must be taken into consideration as well.

▥▮ Means of attitude formation and change

The many factors involved in attitude formation and/or change are centred in three elements: the communicator (the person who attempts to bring about an attitude change); the communication (the particular message or form that the communicator uses); and the audience (the characteristics of the persons whose attitudes are being manipulated). How can people's attitudes towards leisure in general and towards a given recreation program in particular be changed? Iso-Ahola (1980a) extends Fishbein and Ajzen's argument that attitude change involves changing a person's beliefs, whether they are beliefs about the object or beliefs about its attributes. For example, instead of attacking the belief that the swimming-pool is crowded, it would be better to try to convince people that a crowd is not so bad at the pool after all.

It has been shown that actively trying out an activity is a more effective method of attitude change than passive exposure to information about it. Horna's (1987c) empirical evidence suggests that couples' continued participation in some new pursuits often started through active participation initiated by their friends. Researchers have recommended to practitioners that if they want to sell their programs, they should organize participants according to the similarity of their leisure needs, then attempt to affect their salient beliefs (needs). For example, for people looking for social interaction, the program's ability to provide it should be emphasized (Iso-Ahola 1980a). In addition, it is more difficult to change the attitudes of those who are highly committed to their attitudinal position than it is to change the attitudes of those who are not. There is an inverted-U-shaped relationship between self-esteem and attitudinal change: persons with moderate self-esteem are more receptive and are thus open to attitude change, whereas persons with either very low or high self-esteem are the least impressionable.

Another step towards attitude change consists of persuasive communication. Two-way communication is more effective under most conditions than a one-way message (as in advertising) (Iso-Ahola 1980a). Under many conditions, information that arouses fear tends to be more persuasive; for example, by demonstrating that a lack of stimulating recreational experiences is detrimental to mental and physical well-being. Conversely, the beneficial impact of physical exercise on social interaction could be shown to be indisputable.

The application of various strategies, however, does not always guarantee attitude change; it simply increases its probability. The effectiveness of different persuasion techniques in motivating people to be physically active may depend on a particular procedure. For example, simply calling people and asking them why they did not attend a recreation event, then encouraging them to participate is an ineffective strategy because it does not result in a greater or long-term turnout (Wankel and Thompson 1977). Explicitly stating a conclusion (e.g., 'It's good for your health') is detrimental under many conditions because it makes the intent of persuasion too obvious and apparently reduces the communicator's credibility (Freedman et al. 1974; Iso-Ahola 1980a). When people are encouraged to reach the conclusion by themselves, communication is likely to be persuasive. Persuasive communication is based upon an implicit assumption that changing attitudes towards an object will lead to changes in overt behaviour or behavioural patterns; Wankel and Thompson (1977) were able to increase their subjects' recreation participation because they succeeded in changing subjects' attitudes towards physical exercise or they managed to reinforce subjects' already-learned predisposition towards physical activity.

Most children and adults come in contact with one or more of the media on a daily basis, albeit at a variable rate depending on demographic and socio-economic characteristics (Godbey and Parker 1976; Horna 1985, 1987c; Kando 1975; Kelly 1978b, 1983; Parker 1983; Robinson 1981; Shaw 1984; Szalai 1972; Wilensky 1964). The news about various politicians, performers, and public personalities have become an integral part of the daily exposure for most people living in contemporary industrial societies. This information flux both invades people's leisure time and portrays celebrities' leisure behaviour and preferences. Taking into account this continuous flow of information, researchers often focus on the role of the mass media and document how the media influences and serves as an agent of socialization and attitude formation and change. Serious concerns of whether or not the media manipulates messages to consumers and distort reality are frequently raised in the literature.

However, it remains unclear whether or not (or to what degree) the media consumers form or modify their personal identity in response to the role models and values for lifestyles and leisure that are featured by the media. Some researchers suggest that celebrities likely represent the intermediary level of opinion leaders (Burt 1987; DeFleur and Ball-Rokeach 1989; Katz and Lazarsfeld 1955; Lowery and DeFleur 1983; Merton 1949). The public's interpretation of the message takes place within 'a set of presuppositions, concerns, problems, and associations held by a particular social group in a particular historical and institutional context' (Griswold 1987:1112; Rosengren 1983).

ⅢⅢ Summary

In this chapter, we have discussed the major approaches to leisure employed by psychologists and social psychologists. In particular, we have looked at the ways these theorists and empirical researchers examine the conditions and the nature of the state of mind associated with the experience of leisure as well as how they interpret individual and social influences that affect an individual's attitudes, motives, emotions, and behaviour towards leisure. Psychologists and social psychologists have shown that freedom of choice, enjoyment, intrinsic motivation, relaxation, and the lack of evaluation are closely associated with the leisure experience. The majority of them argue that leisure participation is an expression of personal values and attitudes, although attitudes do not exist by themselves within the individual but are part of the personality. Nevertheless, no direct causal link between leisure attitudes and leisure behaviour has so far been established.

In spite of the general agreement about the main themes, several diverse approaches have been adopted within the psychology and social psychology of leisure. We have seen the approaches that emphasize the subjective qualities of the leisure experience, regard leisure as a state of mind, and concentrate on identifying the conditions necessary for this state of mind. At the same time, reported leisure motivations, satisfactions, and attributions are being studied. Numerous researchers continue to attempt to identify the role of motivation and to pinpoint motivational factors that influence adults to participate in leisure, even though the psychological literature has not yet clarified the conceptual and empirical confusion with regard to what constitutes meaning as differentiated from motivation.

Since psychologists recognize childhood as the primary formative period of the personality, childhood socialization is also considered the primary formative influence of leisure attitudes. These attitudes, however, are not viewed as unchanged throughout the life cycle. They are linked not only with personality types but with gender and age, stage of the life cycle, relationships between labour force participation and family work, and the structure and the division of labour within the family in particular. Of special interest are the mass media's influence and the continuous flow of information. Furthermore, psychologists and social psychologists link these factors with a person's ability and opportunity to substitute one activity for another.

One influential approach to leisure and socialization for leisure has not been included in this chapter—the feminist perspective. Since we devote an entire section of the next chapter exclusively to feminist theories and conceptualizations, feminism has been omitted here for practical reasons only. In fact, feminists have made important and challenging contributions to the study of leisure. The leading Canadian feminist, Dorothy E. Smith, postulates that an important part of the socialization process includes taking on the standpoint of others (1987). This results in the central problem of women's relative powerlessness in society—they internalize a basically patriarchal view of themselves and the world and adopt it as their own, thus learning to undervalue themselves and their own contributions. Their powerlessness is perpetuated through the generations.

Overall, we have seen that most of the psychologists and social psychologists who study leisure behaviour, values, attitudes, motivations, and changes over the life cycle maintain that only the multitude of individual, subjective, and contextual factors can explain leisure behaviour.

CHAPTER 5

Sociological perspectives on leisure

▌▌▌ The evolution of the sociology of leisure

The founding fathers of sociology studied leisure indirectly (Wilson 1987). Notably, contemporary sociologists find references to leisure in Karl Marx's analysis of the labour process under capitalism and in his concept of alienated labour. According to Wilson's assessment, Émile Durkheim's study of the emerging complex forms of the division of labour in modern societies alerts us to parallel trends in the division of leisure forms, while Durkheim's analysis of the modern cult of the individual predicted more individuated and privatized leisure habits. Max Weber's writings on rationalization help us anticipate the bureaucratization of leisure and sports, along with the modern obsession with records and rules. His writings on lifestyles parallel some of the comments made about the leisure class by Thorstein Veblen, who viewed leisure behaviour as an instrument of social display and distinction. For Georg Simmel, play and games were part of a world of sociability in which the social game has a double meaning: society is a game that we must play to be fully involved members, but games are a microcosm of society where people learn and play society with each other. George H. Mead's focus on the socializing function of children's play contributed to the appreciation of the symbolic dimensions of festivals and carnivals.

Sociology in the first half of this century, particularly industrial or plant sociology that aimed at making work more efficient, treated leisure largely as an adjunct to work. Those who looked at leisure beyond the factory gates were usually engaged in community studies and used social/anthropological methods (Lundberg et al. 1934; Rowntree 1951). During the economic boom of the 1960s, sociologists began to speculate about the role of leisure in the coming postindustrial society. It was predicted that societies would become increasingly 'leisure-centred' (Dumazedier 1967) and oriented towards consumption for pleasure rather than work for gain and security. Georges Friedmann emphasized the democratizing and equalizing effects of leisure:

Young workers, coming out of their factories at Paris, Frankfurt, or Milan, are likely to see the same cinema and television programs, hear on the radio the same variety shows, songs, and jazz records, and look at the same magazines as the sons (or daughters) of their foreman, engineer, or overseer, and middle-class adolescents in general. Workers are to be found more and more often during their holidays with pay, frequenting the same organized holiday clubs, sunbathing on the same beaches as the middle classes (1960:517).

However, others, for example, Smigel (1963), disagreed with such optimistic predictions and maintained that previous work problems would just be replaced by leisure problems.

It becomes apparent that the international community of leisure scholars was an arena for debates and discussion (Roberts 1990). In Roberts's assessment, there was never one coherent body of orthodox leisure theory, though by the end of the 1970s, a consensus was emerging around a number of propositions about the character of leisure. One point of agreement was that industrial societies had produced a historically specific form of leisure. The definitions of this leisure—whether a time free from obligations, a kind of activity, or the quality of experience—however, continued to be debated. An earlier agreement among the scholars that leisure could and should be distinguished from other spheres of life subsequently became a point of dispute as well, especially because the nature of leisure in modern societies seems to blend elements of leisure with other life domains. Many heated debates addressed the work-leisure relationship and eventually led to a general agreement in the form of a pluralistic perspective that argues that leisure opportunities, interests, constraints, and behaviour are the outcomes of multiple influences, and as these influences could operate in numerous combinations, they result in a variety of leisure styles (Roberts 1990).

Another point of agreement concerned the anticipated long-term growth of leisure that will result from reduced work time and higher incomes. The debates in this connection focused on the pace of leisure's growth and on the kind of future society that the growth of leisure would bring about. Sociologists agreed that leisure behaviour was influenced by individuals' other social roles, including those associated with age, gender, and employment. They began to analyse those aspects that were common to all societies regardless of their levels of economic development or the types of their economies, whether ruled by planners or market forces.

■Ⅲ Sociological perspectives on leisure

Most students of general sociology are familiar with a number of schools of sociological thought, their theoretical frameworks and paradigms, primarily the structuralist-functionalist, conflict, interpretive or symbolic interactionist, developmental, and feminist perspectives. All these have been applied in sociological approaches of leisure. Structuralism, for example, examines such variables as socio-economic status and educational and demographic characteristics in their relation to leisure choices, preferences, or barriers. Many studies have examined the consensual or conflict relationships among different social institutions and spheres of life, in particular the interrelationships among the work, family, and leisure domains. Also, various contemporary conceptualizations of cultural and social reproduction have their theoretical roots in structuralism. Functionalism focuses on the social functions of leisure, for example, the role of leisure in marital and familial cohesion, and, conversely, the impact of marital relationships on leisure forms. Studies done from the structural-functional perspective may, for example, focus on socialization of youth through leisure and sports, sports as a vehicle for assimilation, the relationship of sports to other institutions, and the integrating function of sports for participants, observers, and social organizations.

In contrast to structural and functional theories, conflict theory holds that power is crucial to any given society, and conflict is a natural state in societies. Society is made up of diverse groups that fight for power and dominance. Applied to the leisure domain, this perspective argues that leisure and sports reflect and reinforce the hegemony of societal arrangements, thereby perpetuating class and power differentials (Gruneau 1983; Hargreaves 1986). Conflict theorists also focus on social inequality, sexism, racism, and oppression, as well as organized conflict and deviance, especially in sports. The concept of cultural hegemony refers to domination (Gruneau 1988), a system of cultural domination that reinforces the power of dominant classes.

Microperspectives and interpretive approaches such as symbolic interactionism focus more on individuals and their behaviour. Symbolic interactionists analyse how individuals subjectively define and interpret their environments and other people around them, and how these subjective definitions and interpretations affect their interaction with others. Symbolic interactionism applied to leisure may involve investigations of the meaning of leisure, barriers to leisure participation, or the substitutability of leisure pursuits.

Yet another framework, the developmental theory, emphasizes the evolution and changes throughout an individual's or group's life cycle. This framework is frequently applied to an analysis of lifelong changes of leisure in general or during the family life cycle in particular. Our next chapter will examine this framework and its application to leisure in considerable detail.

The following discussion of sociological perspectives documents that practically all of the above theoretical approaches have been scrutinized and criticized by numerous authors. Chris Rojek (1985, 1987) prefers the term 'social formalism' instead of functionalism, which is, in his opinion, a conservative view of society. Rojek makes three points against functionalism and other traditional theoretical positions: firstly, the interpretation of leisure relations and leisure experience is excessively rigid as it focuses only on socially approved forms of leisure—watching television, visiting the pub, family leisure. What little attention is given to the deviant side of leisure—taking drugs, stealing, football hooliganism, pornographic activity, etc.—is implicitly moralistic. Rojek further posits that the formalist association of leisure with freedom neglects to recognize that leisure opportunities and leisure activities are socially constructed and structured by relations of gender, class, culture, and ethnicity. Moreover, the extent to which values play a part in leisure relations is neglected. Rojek is also critical of the formalist equation of choice, flexibility, and self-determination, which fails to adequately recognize the variety and diversity of what people seek in their leisure, what they want to achieve, and what they want to avoid. Yet another stream of criticism of the mainstream or male-stream sociological perspectives originates with the feminists. They will be presented in a later section of this chapter.

Dissatisfaction with the limitations of any single framework has led over the years to several attempts at formulating multidimensional and multiparadigmatic perspectives that aim to overcome some of the drawbacks by combining specific concepts from several theoretical and methodological sources. Holistic perspectives on leisure, family and leisure, and the place of leisure in the overall quality of life are discussed elsewhere in the book.

Two other schools of thought that have had a profound impact on the field of sociology in general and sociology of leisure in particular are the feminist theories and critical sociology or critical theory. Critical theory originally referred exclusively to the theory developed by the Frankfurt School in Germany in the 1930s. The original Frankfurt School theorists attempted to explain why the socialist revolution prophesied by Marx did not occur as expected (Agger 1991). They argued that Marx underestimated the extent to which workers' (and others') false consciousness (misperceptions) could be exploited to keep the social and economic system running smoothly. According to the Frankfurt School theorists, capitalism in the twentieth century developed effective coping mechanisms and forestalled socialist revolutions.

In the last decades, critical theory has come to be regarded as an independent form of theorizing that has expanded to incorporate a wide range of topics. Critical theory brings new theoretical analyses of the role of the state and culture in advanced capitalism; these analyses also include critical assessments of mass culture. In particular, the argument that capitalism increases false consciousness, suggesting that the existing social system is both inevitable and rational, helps to interpret contemporary leisure trends. For example, the common values inculcating obedience and discipline contradict people's objective interest in liberation. What Marcuse (1955) calls *surplus repression* imposes discipline from the inside. People are taught to fulfil their needs through *repressive desublimination*, exchanging substantive sociopolitical and economic liberties for the 'freedoms' of abundant consumer choices (Marcuse 1964). Space limitations do not allow us to discuss critical sociology or critical theory in more detail. Readers who would like to learn more may wish to study the works by the contemporary leading critical theorists Jürgen Habermas, Anthony Giddens, and the late Alvin Gouldner.

In sum, the competing and complementary sociological theories in general approach society, including its leisure domain, from differing viewpoints. We need at least some basic familiarity with them in order to interpret their specific application to various types of leisure trends, forms, and behaviour.

▥ Comprehensive and holistic theoretical frameworks of leisure

Several leisure theorists suggested more or less comprehensive or holistic theoretical approaches to leisure in the 1970s. Max Kaplan's (1975) system included sixty illustrative propositions that incorporated objective aspects of the individual situation; external, internal, and mediating factors; manifest and latent functions; symbolic, expository, and epistemological meanings, as well as clusters of relationships consisting of person and family, group and subculture, community and region, and nation and world. All of them were positioned within four cultural systems (the energy, social, value, and symbolic systems), and the social/historical orders that Kaplan named the Conquest order, the Kilowatt order, the Cogno order, and the Cultivated order. Similarly, James F. Murphy discussed a holistic framework for understanding leisure in 1974.

More recently, the prolific theorist and researcher in the sociology of leisure, John R. Kelly, presented a complex attempt at a coherent, dialectically interrelated theoretical framework. In his work *Freedom to Be* (1987), Kelly elaborates his sociological model of interpreting leisure as a 'state of becoming' that is defined more by orientations than by time, place, form, or outcome. Kelly's analytical framework, a spiral of leisure theory, 'takes the shape of double dialectic' (1987:14). The first dialectic is hermeneutic, the second dialectic is the negation of every 'metaphor' (domain assumption or presupposition), either from its own contradictions or from external antithesis. The spiral begins with leisure as immediate experience, negated by its transitory character; the second 'loop' represents leisure as decision, negated by contextual limits and 'bad faith'; the third represents leisure as human development, negated by distortion and loss; the fourth interprets leisure from the point of view of social identity negated by inauthenticity; the fifth views leisure as social interaction negated by manipulation; the sixth relates leisure to institutional role playing, negated by normative structures; the seventh presents leisure as political freedom negated by social alienation and control; and the top of the spiral presents leisure as creativity negated by conformity and a celebration negated by false consciousness.

Corresponding theoretical perspectives in Kelly's model include the following approaches: leisure as immediate experience, existential theory, developmental theory, social identity theory, interaction theory, institutional theory, political theory, humanist theory, and a synthesis in dialectical theory. Kelly's analysis moves towards *social existentialism* because it includes both the risk of decision and the reality of social forces.

Kelly further emphasizes that any human action always has two dimensions or components. Human action is both existential and social; it involves action with meaning and takes place in a social environment of learned symbols and social contexts so that the existential and social dimensions of action are related rather than separate. Thus, leisure too is existential as action that produces meaning, it is action that both has and creates meaning. Kelly further asserts that, along with the immediate experience, there is often a dimension of becoming in the sense that it is action in which the actor becomes something more, in which the action creates novelty.

At the same time, Kelly maintains, leisure is social in both its context and orientations; it is learned behaviour, since leisure forms, interpretations, and aims are learned in a particular society. Furthermore, the resources for leisure, including time and skill-acquisition, are products of the social system's symbols, institutional role sets, socialization processes, and layers of formal and informal organizations. For Kelly, leisure includes activity that is solitary as well as social, disengaging as well as demanding of high investment, and autonomous as well as conditioned by previous activity intensity. Being entertained may be as much a part of the balance as creative action. However, the overall 'shape' of leisure is more than momentary in meaning. It is part of a whole in which social and high investment activities tend to be valued most by those who have not surrendered their existential freedom (1987:233). One orientation of this 'creation' is towards the self, the other orientation is social. In leisure we may not only create a somewhat different self, but we may create community. Kelly finds a possible paradox in such leisure, as it appears most consequential in its results when it is least focused on results. This does not mean to him that leisure carries no form or discipline. On the contrary, the freedom of leisure is freedom *for* real action, not freedom *from* form. Therefore, leisure *is* creation, not always realized but always a possibility.

The holistic leisure paradigms expanded the analysis of leisure beyond the former narrow approaches. The pluralist scenario, however, was to come under attack as well. The criticisms aimed not so much against any particular sides as towards certain underlying, taken-for-granted assumptions (Roberts 1990). We will apply some of these theoretical propositions in later sections of this book when we turn to the examination of selected empirical findings about leisure patterns, styles, and specific social groups.

▥ More challenges and propositions

Similar to the trends in sociology in general, one of the new trends in the sociology of leisure that emerged in the last few decades stems from the renewed interest in classical social theory and the more or less forgotten earlier approaches in the field of leisure studies, including the community studies by Lundberg or Robert Lynd and Helen Merrell Lynd, and the stimulating works of Huizinga and Veblen.

The faith in the adequacy of theories that proclaim the continued modernization and industrialization of an already affluent society that will develop in the direction of a leisure society has drastically declined; this decline has also affected the dominant position of neo-positivistic epistemology, operationalistic research methods, and structural-functionalism (Giddens 1984; Mommaas and van der Poel 1987). Theorists turned their attention to marginalized currents in social theory, to the challenge of seemingly unquestionable dichotomies like actor-structure, individual-society, and freedom-constraint, or to the relationships between work and leisure, family and leisure, and the reproductive or productive (i.e., creative, autonomous, and/or self-expressive) character of leisure. Thus, some posit that orthodox enquiries into leisure have artificially separated their subject from the broader socio-economic context and argue that hitherto standard ideas about leisure have little relevance beyond the lives of adult, ethnic majority, male employees (who are in fact a minority group).

Many theorists are influenced by the writings of Marx and neo-Marxists like Antonio Gramsci, Herbert Marcuse, Louis Althusser, and Henri Lefebvre (Wilson 1987), or they further expand the original Frankfurt School's critical theory. The new orientations in the sociology of leisure advance two principal arguments: first, that leisure ideas and practices are part of a larger apparatus of ideological reproduction that serves to maintain capitalist social relations, and, second, that an important part of the modern capitalist order's political economy is the culture industries that manufacture and distribute 'pleasure' for a profit within broad regulatory guidelines laid down by the state (Maltby 1983).

Recently formulated perspectives in general social theory are sometimes expressed within the sociology of sports or sociology of culture. Two new approaches—cultural studies and figurational sociology—originated in England where they exert greater influence than in the US or Canada. The specific contribution of cultural studies has been to link up the lived experience of human actors, and cultural meanings, texts, representations (culture as interpretation) with broader political and economic structures of modern industrial societies (Hollands 1984). Different traditions of cultural studies have grown out of efforts to understand the processes that have shaped modern and postwar society and culture, including the rise of mass communication, the increasing commodification of cultural life, and the worldwide dissemination of mass culture (Grossberg, Nelson, and Treicher 1991).

British cultural studies began with Williams's *Culture and Society* (1958) and *The Long Revolution* (1961) in which he theorized the relations between culture and society. The turning-point for cultural studies was the founding of the Centre for Contemporary Cultural Studies at Birmingham in 1964.

Various scholars produced important studies of politics of popular culture (Bennett and Woolacott 1987; Chambers 1986; Fiske 1989; Hebdige 1988; Winship 1987), as well as works on education, leisure, welfare policy, and history, including Clarke and Critcher's (1985) widely cited book. Readers should beware of the common misconception that cultural studies only addresses popular culture or particular cultural practices.

Figurational sociology refers to the theoretical and empirical approach that is associated with the writings of Norbert Elias and his followers, particularly his collaborator Eric Dunning. Figurational sociology is distinctive in the way it studies leisure and in the functions it attributes to leisure behaviour in modern industrial societies (Rojek 1985). Methodologically, people who engage in specific forms of leisure are studied as part of particular types of figurations. The concept of figuration, which means a 'structure of mutually oriented and dependent people' (Elias 1978:261), represents the key element of Elias's work. He suggested that figuration may be visualized as formations of dancers on a dance floor (or athletes on a playing field), which makes it easier to imagine states, cities, families, or entire social systems as figurations. Figurations are historically produced and reproduced networks of interdependence — another core concept in the figurational approach. Interdependence is a constraining as well as enabling influence on individuals' actions.

Furthermore, Elias (1978, 1982) elaborated the conception of the 'civilizing process', which constitutes a historical secular tendency in human societies to increasing external and internalized control over individual 'affects' (acts) and social behaviour, particularly violence, the gradual transformation of manners, and a general distancing from nature (Horne, Jary, and Tomlinson 1987). This civilizing process was accompanied by a tendency towards democratization, which also intensified class and individual competition in manners, and introduced courtly and aristocratic manners to society at large. Elias's (1971) suggestion that premodern sports (such as the original Olympic games or the folk games in preindustrial societies) involved much greater levels of violence than do modern sports will be of interest when we examine the history of leisure and sports.

Given the growing consensus on the need to formulate perspectives that transcend the dualisms that have hampered social analysis in general and leisure studies in particular, Mommaas and van der Poel (1988) consider the single most important thing in this respect to be the shift from studying either the individual or society to the examination of 'figurations' (Elias), 'habitus' (Bourdieu), and 'practices' (Giddens); in other words, the situated activities of interdependent actors *vis-à-vis* one another. Furthermore, the concept of hegemony has become for many sociologists a central notion in the historical study of leisure. They situate it within a broader framework of struggles over the freedoms social classes allow one another and how these freedoms should be used, thus drawing attention to processes of legitimation and control. Clarke and Critcher (1985) comment that hegemony identifies cultural conflict as a process that happens not just at the level of political ideologies but involves everyday thinking and habits of mind as well. Hegemony has become a significant concept especially in cultural studies as it embraces a number of major themes about the processes of cultural domination and conflict. We will apply it later when we comment on the development of leisure and sports in Canada.

Canadian sociologist Peter Heron (1991) argues that leisure is becoming increasingly institutionalized. Basic to his argument are several assumptions, among them the notion that leisure and culture are inseparable, and that institutions seek to influence cultures that are expressive and irrational rather than technical and rational. He points to the phenomenon of the interpenetration of institutional values into the values and belief systems of the environment, originally conceptualized by Jepperson and Meyer (1989). This phenomenon of institutional interpenetration can also be termed 'cultural hegemony'. Heron's propositions further stem from Goldman and Wilson's (1977) suggestion that rational institutionalism is a dominating feature of capitalist societies and that non-rational, expressive recreational activities and existential leisure are marginalized both within and outside of institutions. Related to these trends in the theory and paradigm development is a growing awareness that the way people spend their free time cannot be studied in isolation from their other daily activities nor from their past.

The new orientation in the sociology of leisure, especially its neo-Marxist branch, has focused on three contemporary trends in leisure (Wilson 1987): firstly, the commodification of leisure has turned leisure into an item to be bought and sold on the market instead of providing an experience that grows out of family and community life; secondly, the privatization of leisure makes leisure home-centred and, with the aid of technological advances like the telephone, television, radio, and vcrs, increasingly room-centred. Privatization also entails the individuation of leisure styles and is coupled with consumerism. Thirdly, the rationalization of leisure makes sports more bureaucratized and performance-oriented. The rational administration of leisure becomes treated as a technological imperative, a natural part of a computerized and automated world (Guttman 1978). Furthermore, sociologists are more aware that leisure, ostensibly the most free part of people's lives, is just as much contested terrain as the world of work (Clarke and Critcher 1985). People now include leisure among their life entitlements, they look increasingly to their governments to protect their leisure rights, to rectify leisure injustices, and to provide leisure opportunities where the market has not provided them.

▬ New criticism

As can be expected, not all leisure scholars embrace new radical propositions in the sociology of leisure. New radicals are criticized, among other things, for not having an agreed-upon alternative and for wresting the terms of political debate from the new right (Roberts 1990). Others, like Rosemary Deem (1986), are as critical of efforts to absorb the analysis of leisure into critiques of capitalism and orthodox leisure studies.

Another critic of earlier approaches to leisure, Chris Rojek (1985) who, as we have already seen, rejects the social formalism of orthodox approaches, proposes a reconstruction that would focus on the permissible rules of pleasure. He maintains that leisure relations should not be conceived of as relations of freedom. Instead, the structure and development of leisure relations should be studied as an effect of legitimating rules concerning pleasure and displeasure.

In his later analysis, Rojek (1989) argues that most postwar theories of leisure and recreation can be approached through the agency/structure dichotomy. Theories of *agency* focus on the thoughts, feelings, and conduct of the actor. They subscribe to a *voluntaristic* model of social action in which freedom, choice, and self-determination are attributed to the actor. Conversely, theories of *structure* focus on the social context in which the individual is situated. They endorse a *deterministic* model of personal conduct that emphasizes that individual behaviour is influenced by social structures arising from the interactions of individuals through time, but are beyond the capacity of any single individual or group of individuals to control. Rojek's reaction against the agency/structure schema leads him to the concept of *process* in which social life is seen as *movement*. This approach retains the concepts of action and structure, but situates them indissolubly *in time*. Action is no longer seen as autonomous and self-determining; it is seen as contingent and interdependent. Structure is no longer regarded as merely constraining; it is regarded as both enabling and constraining.

However promising the new perspectives on theorizing leisure may be, more questions are raised about the association of leisure with freedom and control. Recently, several theorists express their opinion that this issue often results in either ignoring the question of freedom in leisure altogether and puts the notion aside as a mere ideological one, or leads to moving away from freedom as the main characteristic of leisure to something else. Mommaas and van der Poel (1987:169) propose to

> look at freedom as something more than just a personal experience (as so many students of leisure would have it) and something more down to earth than transcendental of social reality (as so many critical students of leisure would have it). Freedom is a positive and indivisible part of social order, not opposed to it, but intrinsically involved in its reproduction.

In sum, there is no consensus as yet among leisure sociologists regarding theoretical approaches to leisure. Sociological approaches to leisure, which originated from traditional sociological theories, have subsequently undergone considerable scrutiny, self-examination, and development. The sociology of leisure has lately become a fertile and quite challenging field in which new theoretical and conceptual propositions not only expand our understanding and interpretation of leisure itself but contribute to further theory-building processes in sociological studies in general. Our readers will see them at work in later sections that address specific issues of leisure times, perceptions, and outcomes.

▮▮ Feminist orientation in leisure analysis

The theoretical conceptualization of women's oppression under patriarchy, both historically and in contemporary societies, has found its application in leisure studies as well. However, there is no one feminist approach and feminist theory is not a single body of work (Deem 1986; Mackie 1991; Stanley and Wise 1983). Feminist perspective primarily provides a theoretical framework for studying numerous facets of society, including leisure, by placing women at the forefront of its analysis, and by regarding them as an oppressed group with certain common experiences and interests. This emphasis does not deny that women also differ in their social background, interests, economic status, sexual orientation, and group membership.

Feminist approaches in general and in leisure studies in particular emphasize the importance of linking analysis and theory to political action and change. Feminists insist on avoiding an artificial break between theoretical and empirical analysis of other people and the politics of their own lives and practices (Deem 1986). Stanley and Wise (1983) have identified three propositions that are shared by all feminist theories: (a) women are oppressed and share a common set of oppressions; (b) the personal is political in that the personal experience is affected by the 'system' in everyday life; and (c) a feminist consciousness and the understanding of what it means to be a woman can be developed.

Several specific feminist approaches are typically applied in analysing women's position in society. Perreault (1984) identifies three feminist perspectives—liberal, leftist, and radical. She suggests that equality, liberation, and integrity are the key ideas related to each of these perspectives. Liberal feminism addresses the need for equality of opportunity for women in society. Leftist feminists exhort liberation and the transformation of social institutions. Radical feminists are concerned with women's integrity and the need for a complete countering of the patriarchal society through revolutionary rather than incremental social changes. Regardless of perspective or theoretical emphasis, virtually all have recognized that the family and the economy constitute the central arenas where gender stratification is produced and sustained (Chafetz 1988).

Henderson et al. (1989) posit that feminist interpretations of women's reality have particular implications for examining and understanding the leisure of women. Women's opportunities for leisure differ because of their oppression (Deem 1990, 1992; Henderson 1986). In general, feminist approaches provide a means for addressing social change that may result in greater opportunities for women to experience leisure. Carpenter (1985) addresses the elements of freedom and choice that are at the core of leisure and feminism. She argues that the goal of both feminism and leisure is to encourage choices, not to set limits. Today, both feminism and leisure focus on a revolt against male domination.

Feminist points of view suggest that leisure has been largely an androcentric concept, just as society has been largely patriarchal, with women and leisure devalued by those in power. Women's leisure experience in the past often did not fit with existing conceptualizations and theories, and research into leisure behaviour has tended to neglect the effect of gender roles on opportunities for leisure and needs satisfied in leisure (Colley 1984). Leisure literature often excluded women and assumed that the study of men represents women as well, thus serving to justify women's subordination and oppression. According to feminist theorists, an understanding of leisure behaviour will not be comprehensive until leisure research addresses the unique experiences of women and builds theory upon this information.

A particular critique by Rosemary Deem (1986) focuses on the traditional way of making connections between leisure and industrialization. In her opinion, that framework typically traces the gradual shift among working-class males from the interwoven work-leisure pattern of feudal Britain to the separate work-leisure routines of a society in which time spent in paid employment is distinct from time spent on leisure or at home. While such a traditional framework examines the relationship between industrialization, work, leisure, and time for the male working-class, it leaves out the parallel influences on women's experiences. Deem posits that this framework assumes that capitalism permanently altered the perception and notation of time. It shifted from time's irregularity, dependence on daylight, seasonality, and task orientation to a concept in which time is measured precisely and is controlled by owners of means of production, and clearly distinguishes between different parts of the day, week, and year according to work and non-work periods. Such a male-oriented framework assumes that contemporary leisure structures, including paid holidays and work-time regulations, apply to all, while in fact they represent only one of several relevant links in women's lives. For most women, their leisure time and activities are determined by the leisure, work, needs, and demands of others. Often women's leisure occurs simultaneously with work activities or is indistinguishable from work (for example, watching television and doing housework, or cooking as both work and leisure).

One of the crucial goals of feminism is systematically changing and rectifying the distortion of female experience. Lather (1982) identified five tenets of feminist research: (1) it must integrate consciousness; (2) women must benefit from the research; (3) it must deal with the issue of getting women to speak in their own voices; (4) it must not contribute to the ideology of sex differences; and (5) it must be collaborative and interdisciplinary. A necessary precondition is to avoid an 'add on' philosophy related to women and leisure. Unlike the previous approaches, feminist perspectives question all established ways of thinking and propose new conceptualizations of leisure that will include women (Green, Hebron, and Woodward 1990; Henderson et al. 1989; Stanley and Wise 1983).

In contrast to the androcentric approaches, all three feminist perspectives present a viable framework for viewing leisure as a universal right of women as well as men (Henderson et al. 1989). Liberal feminist views suggest that equality in leisure means that women have equal opportunity for participation in activities of their choice. They seek modifications towards leisure participation on an equal basis. Leftist feminists interpret women's lack of leisure as one example of a repressive society, and focus on the relationship between leisure and societal structures, especially economic ones. Leftists view the content and the process of leisure as reinforcing roles of dominance and submission. They call for the recognition of class and racial differences as influences on leisure. The radical feminist perspective goes further in its call for an end to the dichotomization of world views and gender roles. Radical feminists not only challenge leisure's androcentric orientation, they call for a radically altered perception of leisure for women and for new alternatives to the conceptualization and embodiment of leisure.

While some feminists dismiss leisure as an inappropriate concept (Coles 1980), most feminist writers propose to construct a concept of leisure that is appropriate and legitimate for women (O'Neill 1991; Wearing and Wearing 1988). Most feminists agree that women are exploited, devalued, and oppressed. There is, however, the growing recognition by feminist scholars of the very real differences among women (Henderson and Allen 1991) in terms of relative power and disadvantage associated with class, race, ethnicity, sexual preference, mothering, homosociality, occupation, education, as well as the differences in the possibilities and constraints for leisure in women's lives.

Feminist conceptualizations and research findings to date suggest that the culturally defined roles women have as homemakers and caregivers often conflict with the existing concept of leisure (Bella 1989; Bialeschki 1990; Henderson et al. 1989; Horna 1991; Kane 1990; O'Neill 1991; Scraton and Talbot 1989; Shaw 1989; Wimbush and Talbot 1988). Moreover, sex typing of both domestic and leisure activities is pervasive. Activities are or may be appropriate for both men and women, but are regarded as *not* being appropriate (Colley 1984).

Since the factors underlying the division of household labour may actually be more complex than existing explanatory models allow, Coleman (1988) proposes to view division of housework as an outcome variable within a larger model of gender stratification. Another feminist reappraisal of leisure points to the extent to which women's activities and values are structured in subordination by men's work and leisure patterns (D. Chambers 1986). In particular, the study of the double-day shift documents that women have less scope than men to transcend shift problems and exploit opportunities associated with unorthodox hours. Chambers argues that under the persistent division of labour by gender, the employment of women round-the-clock on rotating and continuous night work would accentuate their subordination rather than promote liberation.

The feminist approach to gender roles as applied in the work of Draper (1989) views leisure as a gendered construct. It recognizes that leisure is not only socially constructed within a set of gender relations but also plays a significant part in creating those gender relations. Wearing (1991), too, argues that adolescent leisure pursuits prepare males for the individual competitive aggressiveness necessary for success in the workplace and females for nurturing, caring, motherhood, and helpmate roles. However, she points out, leisure can be an area for the subordination of women and resistance to dominant ideologies and discourses. The servicing of men's leisure by women, which both excludes women from many leisure experiences and reinforces their nurturing/caring/selfless gender identity, is continued into old age. Such attitudes perpetuate conformity through leisure to identities that keep women in subordinate positions in the family and in the wider society. This 'ethic of care' (Gilligan 1982), defined as an activity of relationship, of seeing and responding to need, of taking care of the world by sustaining the web of connection so that no one is left alone, may serve to oppress women by keeping them in their place. The feminists attempt to understand how the ethic of care, even within leisure, continues to constrain women and empower men (Henderson and Allen 1991).

Similarly, feminists examine the process of socialization and its contribution to the gendered roles. We are already familiar with the argument by Dorothy E. Smith (1987), presented in the chapter on psychology and social psychology, regarding women's internalization of society's patriarchal view of them and the subsequent perpetuation of their powerlessness.

In sum, the androcentric concept of leisure and the near invisibility and distortion of women's leisure experience are being criticized by feminist leisure scholars. The three feminist perspectives offer alternative frameworks for examining and interpreting women's and men's leisure experiences. The feminists focus on the gendered construction of leisure and argue that the construction of gender identity influences women's leisure and, in turn, leisure experiences of women reinforce traditional gender identities. However, leisure can also provide an opportunity to challenge the tradition and create liberating identities and experiences for women. Our subsequent analysis of the data pertaining to men's and women's leisure behaviour and preferences will document how the feminist conceptualization of leisure contributes to the interpretation and understanding of the findings to date.

▐▌ Leisure in the sociology of the family

The sociology of the family has traditionally incorporated a variety of theoretical perspectives and paradigms. Talcott Parsons (Parsons and Bales 1955), with his model of the nuclear family and its functions, has influenced generations of sociologists. In their studies of the family, other sociologists primarily apply general sociological perspectives such as symbolic interactionism, conflict theory, systems theory, and exchange theory, as well as the developmental framework based on its central concept of the family life cycle. More recently the feminist perspectives exert growing influence in sociological studies of the family. Most of these sociologists recognize the role of leisure in various aspects of marital and familial relationships, interaction, satisfaction, and the socialization of children. Burgess and Locke (1945), the two influential sociologists of the family who traced historical transformation of the Western family, pointed to the change from the 'institutional phase' to the 'companionship phase' in the family. In their model, companionship in leisure is identified as a primary ingredient of the change in the family.

Most sociologists interpret contemporary leisure and the family as two thoroughly interwoven life spheres (Roberts 1981). Consequently, particular attention focuses on the interplay of the family and leisure domains. The family is viewed as the milieu in which most individuals first learn to play, and two-thirds of all leisure interests ever developed are initially practised with other family members. It is argued that even though industrialism separated work and leisure, it never fully segregated the family and leisure. The causal relationship between family and leisure, however, is difficult to establish since the direction of this relationship remains uncertain.

The studies that approach family leisure from the family perspective document that leisure may function either as a bonding factor in the family or as a divisive element in family life. The family can be an enabling or a constraining factor in leisure and, in turn, leisure may promote family togetherness or encourage family members to pursue their interests independently. The positive and negative potential of family leisure, which can become an arena for conflict, are widely recognized in the literature (ELRA 1983; Hantrais 1983, 1984; Hill 1988; Levy 1980; Marks 1989; Orthner and Mancini 1991). While leisure can bring out family conflicts, it can also help to eliminate them. Approaching family leisure from the leisure perspective leads to examining the family as a context of leisure activities in terms of time, space, material conditions, and as a group from which co-participants in an activity are recruited. Moreover, the family is viewed as either a facilitating or constraining factor in leisure in the way it socializes its members towards leisure attitudes and values, skills, provisions of free choice and personal development, or constrains family members' leisure.

The specific view of the family and leisure as two of the life domains (Dumazedier 1974; Horna 1989a, 1991; Kelly 1983; Rapoport and Rapoport

1978) emphasizes the relationship between the family and leisure and the overlap of these two domains. They change over the life cycle and across different families in a given society. Likewise, family leisure develops and dynamically changes over the family life cycle; it increases or decreases during certain stages; it can create bonds between the spouses or between parents and children; it can enhance or lower the quality of marital and familial relationships and affect the degree of marital satisfaction.

Among the most often applied theoretical perspectives in family studies is the developmental model influenced by several earlier sociologists of the family, such as Aldous (1978), Duvall (1957), and Hill and Rodgers (1964). This model of the family life cycle views family development as a series of stages. The passage from one stage to the next is associated with a change in family composition—for example, the birth of the first child or children growing up and leaving the parental home. These changes are accompanied by distinctive roles and developmental tasks.

Rhona Rapoport and Robert Rapoport use this developmental family life cycle approach to leisure activities in their frequently cited work, *Leisure and the Family Life Cycle* (1978). The Rapoports argue that individuals have specific preoccupations that can change with age. Preoccupations may be manifested in interests that may change or remain constant and, in turn, may be channelled into various activities. Individuals change their preoccupations, interests, and activities as they develop in the course of the life cycle. Within the sociology of the family, the roles and tasks associated with marriage, childbirth, and all subsequent critical transitions as children develop and eventually leave home are important foci of interest and activity including, of course, leisure.

The family life cycle overlaps with the establishment phase of people's lives. Since we will examine all life cycle stages in the next section, let us now concentrate on the family life cycle. In addition to analysing the establishment phase, Rapoport and Rapoport propose to examine the three subphases that are demarcated by children's development (1978:190). The first subphase relates roughly to families with young children of preschool age, the second to families with children still in school, and the third to families in which the children have left school. In each of these subphases, families experience shifts in their preoccupations and corresponding activities.

Whether conceptualized as consisting of eight stages (Duvall 1957) or three subphases of the establishment phase, each stage of the family life cycle significantly influences the meaning, motivations, satisfactions, and pursuits in the family leisure domain (Horna 1987d, 1989a; Kelly 1978b, 1987; Orthner and Axelson 1980; Rapoport, Rapoport, and Strelitz 1977). We will have ample opportunity to examine details of empirical evidence in support of leisure throughout the family life cycle later in this book.

Viewed from the perspective of the social role theory, the primary and most pervasive social roles for most adults are related to work and family: 'In general, despite vast differences in their relative salience for different persons or for the same person at different times in the life course, work and family roles tend to be dominant in their absorption of resources, especially time' (Kelly 1983:125). Work, family, leisure, and community, however, are not essentially separate, although their relative importance varies and their influences may be reciprocal as well as unidirectional. The overlap in time, resources, companions, and meanings is considerable.

Given the relative importance of different social contexts, social roles and immediate relationships (with family and close others) become crucial to leisure decisions. In fact, most findings indicate that adults seem to value the most leisure that is complementary and related to primary roles because of satisfactions attached to those relationships (Kelly 1983a). Although family leisure may be more constrained by expectations, it may also be more satisfying: 'It is not that we disvalue freedom, but that family interaction—even with somewhat less freedom—is valued highly' (Kelly 1983a:129).

These and other findings by Kelly show that marriage, family, and friendship associations appear to have a greater influence on the use of non-work time than the more traditional social factors (e.g., work, church, clubs, community), especially when informal and everyday kinds of leisure activity are included in the leisure spectrum. For example, of 1,203 activities reported in Kelly's survey, only fifty-seven were clearly job-related. Most leisure locales and companions were not related to work but to the family, thus indicating that leisure roles are intertwined with other non-work roles, especially familial (1978b).

The role theory perspective also points towards a growing tendency to delineate the recreational role in the family (Nye and Gecas 1976). This tendency is part of the current trend of wives sharing the provider role with their husbands, and husbands' willingness to share domestic and child care responsibilities.

Since both marriage and parenthood alter the role-expectation context and enactment of much leisure, Rees and Collins (1979) propose the concept of 'domestic age' encompassing age *and* gender *and* marital status *and* parenthood. It indicates that many leisure pursuits are markedly sensitive to change, associated in almost linear fashion with increasing age and domesticity. Children and the home are the major focus of people's interest during the early and middle years of parenting, so leisure styles at this time are usually distinctive.

An alternative analytical approach to family leisure during the parental stages of the life cycle interprets leisure as one of several means through which the parental role is enacted (Horna 1989a).

In this perspective, the starting analytical point is anchored in the unitary parental role that consists of work, semi-work, semi-leisure, and leisure participation both at home and outside the home, and is enacted because of intrinsic and/or extrinsic motivations. Thus, parental leisure is a component of the parental role. The empirical data that will be examined in more detail

Figure 5.1 A paradigm of the parental role

	Place		Motivation
Type	**Home**	**Outside home**	
Work	Unpaid labour: cooking, household chores, maintenance repairs, yard work, garage	Paid labour: employment, self-employment, overtime work, moonlighting	Extrinsic-obligatory
Semi-work	Child care, help with schoolwork, teaching skills, discipline	Volunteer work at school, taking child to activities, helping associations and organizations	
Semi-leisure	Role-determined leisure: games and play, children's TV, reading, telling stories, hobbies	Role-determined leisure: games and play, movies, shows and theatre, child's sports	
Leisure	Parallel and interactive leisure: TV, music, conversation, relaxation, entertainment	Parallel and interactive leisure, sports and spectator sports, movies, museums, visiting	Intrinsic-relational-pleasure

later in this book led me to conclude that the specific components of the parental role are enacted disproportionately and gender-asymmetrically. Furthermore, the asymmetrical pattern of the parental role enactment is reflected in the parents' perception of various activities.

It is often recognized in the literature that not all spouses or families follow the same lifestyles or patterns of marital and parental roles, authority and power structures, and division of labour in the household during different life stages. For example, Colin Bell and Patrick Healey (1973) find considerable differences between traditional and non-traditional marriage patterns and accompanying lifestyles. The patterns of leisure participation in the traditional marriage fundamentally differ between the spouses. The man's extradomestic world includes all his interests and pursuits, and his primary allegiance is oriented towards his peer group. Moreover, all his leisure activities are contained within this male world. On the other hand, the wife/homemaker's basic gender-role segregation results in leisure that is domestic and undifferentiated from the rest of her life.

Married couples are found to develop and prefer one of the four possible patterns of leisure styles that are based on the degree of their togetherness, similarity, closeness, and individuality:

a) The couples have the same leisure interests and like to do things together as much as possible;
b) These couples have many interests in common, but physical propinquity is not specifically searched for;
c) Physical closeness is highly valued, but doing different things while together is considered normal;
d) These couples value individuality: each individual has separate interests and pursues them according to his or her schedule (Carisse 1975:196).

These four patterns represent couples' preferred values that could be actualized differently. Carisse emphasizes that, although togetherness is usually indicative of family cohesion, a family can have a high cohesion while valuing autonomy expressed in individual pursuits. Furthermore, as Carisse assumes, any increase in free time and opportunity for new activities will be used according to rules already developed in the family system.

Likewise, Dennis Orthner (1975) argues that not all leisure activities are likely to influence a marriage equally. Even though leisure is primarily associated with pleasure and discretionary time, these conditions can be derived either alone or with others, with one's spouse, and with little or no interaction, despite the presence of others. Thus, Orthner identifies three leisure activity patterns: (1) *individual activities* that require no communication with others and may actually discourage interaction; (2) *joint activities* that require a high degree of interaction for successful completion of the activity, and tend to open communication and encourage role interchange; and (3) *parallel activities* that are little more than individual activities in group settings, allowing minimal interaction among the participants. Although people usually participate in each of these types of leisure activities to a greater or lesser degree, in a marital relationship, the interactional consequences may be quite different if one pattern dominates the others. In the course of a marital relationship, 'not all shared leisure activities are similar in their influence on marriage. Both parallel and joint activities are by definition participated in together by husbands and wives but, apparently, more than physical proximity is required to bring about a satisfactory relationship. A couple spending an evening watching T.V. or going to a play are communicating more with the source of their interest than with each other' (1975:99). However, if the couple is moving towards companionship as a source of marital solidarity, then the leisure factor is of critical importance. Orthner further argues (1976:102) that leisure activities are not the prime movers in marital interaction. Rather, the process of selecting activities appears to be somewhat circular, with people choosing activities that reinforce their relationships; the leisure activities, in turn, reinforce these orientations.

There is more similarity between joint and parallel participation during the middle life stage than during the first stage (Orthner 1976). In Orthner's view, this indicates that shared experiences per se, even if only parallel, may be as valuable to older couples as highly interactive experiences are to younger couples. Contrary to the popular belief that leisure patterns spill over into other life domains, Orthner's data suggest that increased leisure interaction is more likely to influence communication than role sharing. Orthner assumes that this is probably because 'the determination of household responsibilities is more culturally and subculturally defined and less subject to change than increased acceptance of the spouse and, therefore, accessible to communication' (1976:109).

Similarly, Roberts and his colleagues (1976) posit that the extent to which married people's leisure becomes home and television-centred depends on the style of marriage and conjugal roles. In a *companionate* style, the emphasis is on domestic togetherness and sharing, and home-centred leisure is related to this type of togetherness. In a *colleague* style of marriage, couples share leisure pursuits outside the home. Such styles of marriage and leisure increase the likelihood of spouses venturing jointly for leisure outside their homes. These authors also find that factors such as education and the wife's employment outside the home are associated with leisure styles. The more education people have, the less leisure time they spend in watching television and staying at home and the more time they spend in social pastimes with friends. Most women who work outside the home are beyond the child-rearing phase in the family cycle. However, if there are dependent children, the wife's work outside the home appears less relevant to leisure. According to Roberts et al., factors such as occupation and income are insignificant when set against the influence of the family. Regardless of occupation or income, women have more family responsibilities, and those responsibilities impinge on their leisure.

There are numerous findings that point towards somewhat different conclusions. The stream model of leisure (Horna 1987c), already briefly mentioned in connection with the familial context of early leisure socialization and learning, indicates salient similarity of leisure interests and activity sharing between spouses. The streams follow the influence of primary socialization for leisure preferences and behaviour. Later, similarity in leisure pursuits and preferences serves as a filtering factor during the courtship and mate selection process for most couples. This, then, results in the spouses' stream similarity in leisure (not necessarily specific pursuits). It occurs without the need to give up one's own pursuits in order to accommodate the other spouse's leisure preferences, nor does it mean that separate leisure lives is inevitable.

Family and leisure studies also address the relationship between leisure and marital satisfaction. Holman and Jacquard (1988) indicate that the direction and strength of the relationship between leisure and marital satisfaction are contingent upon the perceived communication during leisure activities. Joint spousal leisure is negatively related, or unrelated, to marital satisfaction when communication is low to moderate, and positively related when communication is high. Simply doing things together without a high level of perceived communication has at best no relationship to marital satisfaction; it may even have a negative relationship if the time together is accompanied by low communication. According to Holman and Jacquard, the greater the individual leisure, the less marital satisfaction. Low joint leisure is not significantly related to husbands' marital satisfaction, but is related to wives' marital satisfaction. Another view, however, indicates that children can contribute to marital dissolution in situations where the spouses have less shared leisure time (Hill 1988). Work issues have also been noted as barriers to shared leisure experiences.

To place the family and leisure, both individual and familial, into the context of one's life experience, Horna (1989c) proposes a multidimensional approach whereby the two life domains—the family and leisure—are visualized as two partially overlapping triangles that create a third triangle in the middle. The first triangle represents family roles and obligations, the second triangle represents leisure in general, including any potential leisure activities. The middle overlapping triangle represents family leisure.

Figure 5.2 Schematic representation of men's and women's family and leisure domains

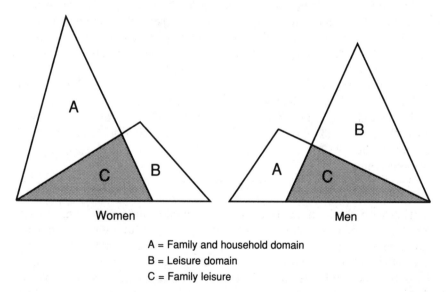

Women   Men

A = Family and household domain
B = Leisure domain
C = Family leisure

Source: J.L.A. Horna, 'Family and Leisure', in *Family and Marriage: Cross-Cultural Perspectives*, edited by G.K. Ishwaran (Toronto: Thompson Educational, 1992):302.

From this perspective, family leisure is conceptualized as those leisure activities that individuals participate in with their partner and/or children. This approach enables us to compare family leisure to couples' other life domains or to their individual leisure by analysing all three triangles, particularly the middle one. The nature and frequency of activities, the composition of participating groups who share activities, the perception of specific pursuits, and the reasons for participation or satisfaction derived from it are scrutinized. Thus, the male-female dual, asymmetrical experience becomes evident in marital and parental role enactments, the division of paid employment and domestic labour, the amount and distribution of discretionary time, access or barriers to leisure participation, as well as motivations for and perceptions of specific activities.

The earlier approaches to family leisure are presently under criticism, primarily by feminist and radical leisure scholars. A number of researchers question the advisability of using the family life cycle in general and specific stages in particular as empirical and explanatory variables in leisure research (Bella 1989; Green, Hebron, and Woodward 1990; Holman and Epperson 1984; Hudson and Murphy 1980; Witt and Goodale 1981). Life stages are becoming less distinct and the number of quality-of-life indicators is increasing. Also such phenomena as married couples who both work, 'blended' families, non-traditional careers, changing patterns in the division of domestic labour and the like make the course of a life cycle unpredictable and empirically less applicable.

The androcentric bias in many studies of leisure is expressed as familism—the tendency to treat women's leisure as an extension of the family. Critics of familism particularly criticize the assumption that the family is monolithic in its internal workings, approximates the nuclear two-parent family norm, and presumes that the family as a whole experiences leisure together (Bella 1989; Eichler 1988; O'Neill 1991). Familism disregards the fact that about 45 per cent of the population will likely be part of a one-parent family at some point, and most will also be part of a new two-parent family. Marxist feminists who apply the concept of reproductive labour and argue that homemaking is not leisure (Piché 1989:5) observe that 'family leisure is often experienced as work by women'.

Another type of familist bias appears in interpreting social interaction in favourite leisure activities. Much critique of familism refutes the notion that playing with children, family outings, and child-centred activity are leisure for all family members since it ignores the work spent in organizing to make this leisure and family recreation possible. For example, combining the work-like activity of cooking with the experience of a family meal may be leisurely for only some family members. Packing a picnic and making sure people are dressed appropriately is typically the woman/mother's unrecognized role. Thus, family leisure may not be interpreted as such by all members of the family if, for instance, camping holidays are more stressful than pleasurable for women

(Rosenblatt and Russell 1975), and the usual household chores move to a less convenient campground site (Cerullo and Ewen 1984). Therefore, the choices of recreation with family, friends, family and friends, or alone do not sufficiently differentiate between the different kinds of individual family members' experiences that are possible in family recreation.

Bella (1989) proposes to overcome the androcentric bias inherent in the work/leisure dichotomy by shifting to the idea of dialectic. According to her, the conception of leisure as entailing work would properly acknowledge women's contribution to that work. Furthermore, it would illuminate women's work in producing family leisure, as well as the work people do as employees to produce experiences for others, or individuals' work in producing leisure opportunities for themselves.

What about single-parent families? According to the Canadian government statistics, 13 per cent of all families in Canada are headed by a single parent, and women make up 94 per cent of all single parents (Statistics Canada 1984). It can be assumed that the interplay between parenting and leisure takes on a different pattern in single-parent families than in families with both parents present. Single parents must take on the parental roles that are typically shared by or divided between both spouses in two-parent families. In the absence of conjugal leisure, joint or parallel activities may be pursued with friends and children or abandoned altogether.

In contrast to the extensive literature that has focused on parents in two-parent families over several decades, there is only limited information about leisure patterns in one-parent families. We know somewhat more about their economic situation and specific challenges in parenting, especially experiences of emotional strain, constant demands of children, and the lack of adult company. One of the very few surveys of single parents shows that the leisure needs of one-parent families are not very different from those of other parents (Streather 1989). The findings indicate that single parents enjoy relaxing at home as well as meeting other adults. Furthermore, they would like to participate outside the home (either with or without their children) in activities that differ from their normal routines and responsibilities. But such leisure is severely limited for most of them, so their leisure pursuits reflect low expectations. Most of them are home-based and inexpensive, such as watching television or reading. As with other individuals or couples, television is a focus of single parents' leisure. Furthermore, in most single-parent families, especially those headed by women, low income is the main factor that prevents most single parents and their children from taking vacations.

We can conclude that analyses of leisure in combination with the sociology of the family went through several changes that reflected the rapid development of sociological paradigms and a more sophisticated understanding of families, as well as new perspectives on leisure. The seemingly contradictory propositions of scholars such as Carisse, Orthner, Roberts et al. on the one hand, and Horna's stream model on the other, or the feminist critique of most models should not be viewed with alarm. Rather, we need to incorporate these conceptualizations into an integrated explanatory model that expresses the continuum of leisure behaviour—from separate leisure styles to similar styles between spouses. Meanwhile, perhaps because of the recent criticism of the concept of family leisure itself, the focus of contemporary studies of family leisure is shifting towards individual family members, the inequality of leisure access and experience, and the family as a constraining factor in leisure.

▮▮ Leisure and the quality of life

A less frequently applied sociological framework, which incorporates multidisciplinary points of view, views leisure as one of the components that contribute to quality of life. In defining the quality of life, most theorists agree that the term 'quality' has the same meaning as 'grade', ranging from low to high, or from better to worse. 'Quality of life' and 'well-being' are often used interchangeably. Quality of life typically includes food and shelter, environment, work, freedom from poverty, attitudes, feelings, personal happiness, and opportunity for personal growth. Solomon and his collaborators (1980) posit that quality of life is an inclusive concept that covers all aspects of living as it is experienced by individuals. It therefore covers the material satisfaction of vital needs as well as personal development, self-realization, and a balanced ecosystem; it has objective conditions and subjective components.

Individuals' quality of life is closely related to the quality of life of social groups, communities, and nations. Some studies relate the components that make up the quality of life with ways or styles of life and with patterns of everyday life (Solomon et al. 1980). Groves and Lastovica (1977) propose a quality of life framework for family leisure activities. The seminal work by Campbell et al. (1976) views the quality of life as a general sense of well-being, and distinguishes between global satisfaction and domain-specific satisfactions. Blishen and Atkinson's (1980) conception of the quality of life is based on the individual's perception and assessment of satisfaction or dissatisfaction with life.

Because quality of life is difficult to measure directly, quality of life indicators are both objective and subjective. They are based on objectively observable facts and conditions of life in society, and on people's own subjective perception and assessment of their lives under given circumstances (Szalai 1980). For example, data about the number of people per room and people's expressed satisfaction with their housing have been used as indicators of housing quality (Andrews 1980). The monumental study of Canada and the United States by Michalos (1980) examined such quality of life indicators as population density and health, crime and political activity, science, education, environment, transportation, economics, housing, religion, and mortality, as well as leisure and recreation.

Studies of the quality of life show that subjective ratings of income, for example, are better predictors of feelings regarding the quality of life than are objective ratings, or a change in interpersonal relations appears to be more important in the quality of life than socio-economic status (Ackerman and Paolucci 1983; Scheussler and Fisher 1985; Wilkening and McGranahan 1978). Correspondingly, subjective experiences of leisure can be very import-ant components of the quality of life. The prominent sociologist of leisure, Dumazedier, argues that 'enhancing the quality of life by a new allocation of time and space ought to begin by reassessing the implications of leisure for all areas of social and personal life' (1974:213).

The available evidence suggests that, on the one hand, leisure has only limited power in predicting life quality (Andrews and Withey 1976). On the other hand, at least some forms of leisure seem to be correlated with overall quality of life (Flanagan 1978) or have no bearing on feelings about life and leisure except for individuals between forty-five and fifty-four years of age (Marans and Mohai 1991). Some researchers posit that out-of-home recrea-tion and the presence or absence of relevant leisure facilities are rarely consid-ered critical determinants of the quality of life (Roberts 1978). Similarly, Haavio-Mannila (1971) determines from her research in Helsinki that main life satisfaction is more often derived from work in the upper than in the lower class; in the lower class, family and leisure are more important. Furthermore, she shows that work (more so than leisure) is central to the life satisfaction of single women, while the opposite is true for single men. If, however, leisure were defined to include time with family, leisure may be the most important predictor of life satisfaction for married people.

A considerable amount of work by Neulinger (1974, 1981) also focuses specifically on leisure as a crucial prerequisite for an adequate quality of life. He argues that regardless of one's definition of leisure, the nature of that leisure will affect the person's quality of life, which will in turn affect one's leisure. Gunter and Stanley (1985) explain that the quality of any leisure experience is enhanced by the feeling that it is justified and deserved, or the knowledge that leisure is only a temporary interlude because there is an ac-tivity (e.g., work) to which one can return afterwards. It may also be that these feelings are affected by the duration of the interlude. Some argue that in considering any improvement in the quality of life in industrial societies, the conditions that bring about leisure must certainly be included (Govaerts 1985). For example, Shaw (1984) uses the experience and quality of leisure as one of the measurements of the quality of life.

As contextual and subjective factors in people's lives change continuously, so too do leisure experiences and the quality of life. To capture their dynamic nature, several studies of leisure and the quality of life utilize the developmen-tal theoretical perspective, which will be discussed later. In addition, many authors focus on variations and inequality in leisure experiences and in life quality, using the role theory perspective (Deem 1987; Govaerts 1985; Kelly

1983; Shaw 1984; Stebbins 1979) in which enactments of social roles and their impact on the experience and quality of leisure and life are analysed.

▥ Summary

The development of the sociology of leisure has never been a smooth, linear process. A number of schools of sociological thought, primarily the structuralist-functionalist, conflict, interpretive or symbolic interactionist, developmental, and later feminist perspectives, have been applied by different authors at different times in sociological approaches to leisure. Most of them, however, were to come under attack. The last few decades have seen some emerging consensus on a number of propositions about the character of leisure, as well as attempts to build holistic leisure paradigms that would expand the analysis of leisure.

The new orientation in the sociology of leisure has focused on the commodification of leisure, the privatization of leisure that makes it home-centred and room-centred and contributes to the individuation of leisure styles and consumerism. Many leisure theorists also became critical of the rationalization of leisure, which gives control to recreation professionals. Moreover, leisure ideas and practices are viewed as part of ideological reproduction that maintains capitalist social relations, and culture industries are interpreted as manufacturers and distributors of pleasure for profit.

This chapter has highlighted the traditional sociological theories and their later scrutiny and refinement. The feminist challenge to the androcentric concept of leisure, to the near invisibility and the distortion of women's leisure experience in particular is a critical development in the sociology of leisure. It influences the way leisure is interpreted as well as how contemporary leisure and the family are viewed by female and male sociologists. Leisure is either as a bonding factor or a divisive element in family life. In turn, the family is both an enabling and constraining factor in leisure. Leisure also contributes to the overall quality of life for individuals, social groups, or nations.

CHAPTER 6

Studies of life course variations in leisure

▮▮▮ Leisure over the life course

We have already learned about the developmental theoretical approach that views family experiences from the perspective of changes over the family life cycle. The concept of life cycle, however, does not apply only to families; it is one of the frequently applied psychological and sociological concepts. Most authors share the view that human life is an ongoing process of growth and development from birth to death, and that this process results from the interplay of biological, social, cultural, and environmental factors. Strictly defined, this concept addresses 'maturational and generational processes driven by mechanisms of reproduction in natural populations' (O'Rand and Krecker 1990). The socio-psychological and sociological literature includes many instances of applying the concept in a broader sense. The life cycle framework is useful for analysing the changing roles, obligations, and expectations throughout life.

Even though the stages may be conceptualized and temporally delineated by various scholars in different ways, most studies usually classify the life cycle stages into the preparation (childhood and adolescence), establishment (adulthood, 'second age'), and culmination ('later years', 'third age') periods (Kelly 1983, 1987; Neulinger 1981; Rapoport and Rapoport 1978). Neulinger also refers to milestones—important positive or negative events, highlights, or crises. The developmental and social role theories posit that the life course is characterized by a number of role transitions and adjustments to life events that leave their mark on the individual. As we have already seen in our discussion of the family life cycle and leisure, Rapoport and Rapoport introduced the key concepts that reflect the developmental nature of the changes during the life cycle:

1 *Preoccupations* are mental absorptions, less or more conscious, which arise from psychobiological development, maturation and ageing processes as they interact with social-environmental conditions.

2 *Interests* arise in people's awareness as ideas and feelings about what they want or would like to have or do, about which they are curious, to which they are drawn, through which they feel they might derive satisfaction.

3 *Activities* are spheres of action—such as driving, dancing, participating in or watching sports, attending clubs, etc. (1978:23–4).

Moreover, those who apply the developmental perspective recognize that contextual, cultural, economic, political, and other factors affect peoples' lives. As economic and political conditions change, the corresponding beliefs, values, and behaviour also change with each age group and generation.

More recently, several sociologists and psychologists have become critical of the life cycle conceptualization because of its explicit or implicit assumptions that the sequences are predetermined, rigid, and do not adequately reflect the broader contexts of people's lives. For example, Clausen (1986), Hagestad and Neugarten (1985), Hareven and Plakans (1987), Kelly (1989), and O'Rand and Krecker (1990) suggest the use of alternative conceptualizations, such as life course or life span that better express continuities and dynamic transitions as well as intersections of various roles and careers. To analyse leisure within such modified developmental frameworks means focusing on the dynamics and change of individuals' and groups' leisure socialization and behaviour as well as stability.

Most research findings document that a person's leisure needs and behaviour are both dynamic and static over a lifetime. The most popular activities that remain stable or show a marked increase in participation are often those that take place at home or nearby, are family-centred, and do not require a large amount of expensive equipment or planning.

Chronological age and gender combine to produce certain patterns. For example, Canadian males under thirty-five put ice hockey at the top of their favourite activities, older men prefer camping and golf, while women in all age groups cite walking as their number one favourite leisure activity (Alberta Recreation and Parks 1981, 1984, 1988). Creative activities lag considerably behind sports, ranking seventeenth among male and female respondents. Other age-related patterns indicate that as people age, their reasons for participation (such as improving skills or knowledge; learning new skills and abilities; spending time alone; a desire for competition, challenge, excitement) decline in importance. Other reasons increase in importance with age (helping the community, enjoying nature, relaxation). Moreover, some reasons are particularly important to young adults and older adults, but are less important in middle age (to show others they can do something, to keep busy, to be creative, to do things with friends, to meet new people, or because they are good at a particular activity). Other findings point to a high degree of continuity in behaviours, attitudes, and values in the second and third ages unless a major life event affected an individual's patterns. It follows, then, that analysis of leisure, especially in people's later years, should take into consideration major life events (Kleiber and Kelly 1980; McPherson 1990, 1991; Osgood and Howe 1984).

Additional variations are influenced by the historical time in which the individual lives. For example, Cribier (1979) argues that it is not so much one's chronological age but the cohort or generation factor, particularly among the postwar generations, that shapes one's leisure. Not surprisingly, scholars who focus on the preferences, needs, and benefits for future generations of seniors argue in favour of studying particular age groups when they are still in the early and middle years of the life cycle (McPherson 1991).

Turning now briefly to the work of psychologists and social psychologists, we are particularly interested in the learning theory of behavioural imitation and related studies of specific motivations, preoccupations, and interests. Psychologists' and social psychologists' models also typically follow the life cycle developmental perspective. It is interesting to note that these models often incorporate the process of leisure socialization (Bandura 1977; Bergier 1981; Brandenburg et al. 1982; Crandall 1980; DeFleur and Ball-Rokeach 1989; Featherman and Lerner 1985; Glass, Bengtson, and Dunham 1986; Iso-Ahola 1980a, 1989; Kelly 1983, 1989; Neulinger 1978, 1981; Osgood and Howe 1984; Rapoport and Rapoport 1978; and many others). Different physiological, psychological, and social changes and their interaction have different influences on leisure at various points in the life cycle (Osgood and Howe 1984). Leisure or recreation that contributes to full personality *development* during the younger age phase, may make its greatest contribution primarily to personality *adjustment* in middle age (Brightbill 1961). Only some elements of personality remain stable while others change as the individual ages.

According to the study by Crawford, Godbey, and Crouter (1986), who investigated the stability of leisure preferences across a two-year time span, preference for specific leisure activities generally declines over time, more so for men than women. Contrary to popular beliefs about spouses becoming more similar, the husbands and wives in this study did not become more similar in their leisure preferences over the first two years of marriage. Like Huston and Ashmore (1986), Crawford et al. propose that psychological *orientations* should not be conceptualized as psychological *traits* because of their potential for change over time. Expressed preference for a leisure activity appears to be but one component of individual psychological orientation, the extent to which the person *likes* the activity in question. The relative *skill* of the individual (or competence to participate in specific leisure activities) is another component of the individual's psychological orientation towards leisure activities, while what a person feels he or she *ought* to do for leisure is the third.

The study by Lounsbury and Hoopes (1988) further extends previous work on the stability of leisure variables. Lounsbury and Hoopes explore the stability of participation in leisure activities and related motivational factors by going beyond preferences for particular activities and by extending the surveyed time period to five years. Their research results indicate a 'most encouraging and even surprising' level of stability over a five-year period for leisure activity participation as well as (to a lesser extent) the leisure motivation variables studied. These authors find little systematic variation in leisure activity or motivation scores over the five-year period. Their other findings suggest that some subjects are more stable over time while others change more over time. A net effect at the group level, however, shows little or no change over time.

Some of these differences in stability and change are related to gender and age in a complex pattern. Kleiber (1980) and Kleiber and Kane (1984) suggest that women may draw different meanings from or benefit in different ways from various leisure activities. Thus, a tendency to participate *vigorously* in recreational activities, whether organizational, mechanical, physical, or artistic, is associated with a sense of control for women but not for men. Since physical activity is a stereotypically male pattern, women who are oriented towards it have a strong sense of control.

In sum, leisure behaviour viewed from the developmental perspective is dynamic and static, improvised and stable, and subject to personal interpretations. Participation in specific leisure activities may stem from individual factors and be gender and age specific; however, it is also influenced by contextual factors, stages of the life cycle, or events in people's lives, by historical events experienced by the same cohort, and may be affected by various constraints. Biologists, psychologists, and sociologists agree that transition points in people's lives cannot be defined in terms of precise chronological ages; however, the stages of childhood, adolescence, and adulthood are generally accepted. We will look at leisure during the three broad life phases: the preparation, the establishment, and the culmination. The role of leisure throughout those phases, while not necessarily paramount, is experienced at least to some degree most of the time.

These periods are covered unevenly in the literature. Most developmental psychology theorists who focus on early childhood and adolescence incorporate leisure as only secondary in their investigations. Leisure studies, on the other hand, seem to pay more attention to the middle period (with its corresponding issues of marital and parental leisure) at the expense of attention to the first period, while the third period is only recently being studied.

▮▮▮ Leisure and the preparation period

The preparation period of childhood and adolescence prepares one for adult roles, preoccupations, interests, and activities. As Kelly (1983) points out, it is a time of future-oriented meanings. Thus, the first years of one's life cannot be understood apart from the societal expectations that the child become something different in time as he or she grows up. We have already discussed the process of early socialization for leisure attitudes, values, and behaviour in the chapter on psychological and social-psychological perspectives. Now we can expand our discussion by showing that the emphasis during childhood and adolescence is on play or leisure in the family and with peer groups, and on the constantly expanding social world of children.

The work by Rapoport and Rapoport (1978), Kelly (1983), and several others stem from the seminal concepts first proposed by Erik Erikson (1950, 1968). Erikson, whose work concentrated mostly on young people's development, maintained that the developing individual is searching for his or her identity. In the search, various possible identities may be tried out, different roles may be adopted and relationships experimented with. Leisure scholars often emphasize the role of leisure in the process of identity formation, the search for autonomy and independence, and in experimentation with social interactions.

Childhood

Most leisure scholars pay no attention to infancy and some disregard childhood. A comprehensive review of the literature on children's peer cultures by Corsaro and Eder (1990) identifies two central themes that appear consistently—children's persistent attempts to *gain control* and to *share* that control with each other. These authors report consistent findings that solitary play is rare, and that gaining access to play groups, maintaining joint action, and making friends are complex processes for young children. Barnett (1991) discusses the propositions that play facilitates a child's transition from concrete to abstract thought processes. In play, children often use objects as symbols; the child's thoughts can be concrete and abstract. Similarly, play is likely to improve physical ability, strength, endurance, and skill. Kelly (1987) reminds us that one function of games in later childhood is to provide a comprehensible context for understanding that a child is not necessarily evaluated on what he or she is but according to agreed-upon criteria and formats. During early adolescence, leisure is partly associated with developing heterosexual attachments and self-definitions of acceptability and attractiveness. Leisure periods and settings are very important in this process.

Adolescence

One of the primary foci of studies on leisure in adolescence is on leisure's significance in searching for identity and testing one's abilities. Life in this period is both future-oriented and present-based. As Kelly (1983:62) points out, 'leisure roles may well be most central to working out intimacy, peer acceptance, cohort identification, self-definitional and independence tasks of adolescent development.' He suggests that with increased mobility and resources available to most teenagers, their leisure roles provide opportunities for experimentation, reinforcement, and affirmation. Leisure provides the fundamental arena for adolescents' development as well as the opportunities that are based on gender, age, social status, and culture. Adolescence, however, is not a generic phenomenon. For example, Glen Elder (1974, 1980) found that cohorts only a few years apart in age experienced different historical conditions. The effects of early hardships were very different for youngsters of various ages, and their later experiences and outcomes were also different.

Canadian authors Ouellet and Perron (1979) who examined leisure, particularly the relative importance of various elements in the leisure experience (i.e., status, achievement, atmosphere, risk, and freedom) found differences by age not only between adolescents and adults but also between high school and junior college students. High school students prize status, atmosphere, and risk more so than college students, who prefer freedom and achievement. Those interested in sports, especially team sports, seek status, atmosphere, and risk, while those favouring outdoor and socio-cultural activities are more oriented towards freedom. Groups showing preference for different leisure activities value achievement equally.

Several competing theories in sociology, psychology, and social psychology contribute to contradictory interpretations of youth cultures. Roberts (1983) in particular discusses the views of the bio-psychological, sociological, intergenerational conflict, and class theory approaches to adolescence. According to the bio-psychological approaches, adolescence expresses biological and psychological facts of life. The affluence and greater freedom of postwar years made adolescence more visible in society than during any previous era; that is, young people act out their problems in public, and have their own style of speech, music, dress, etc. The sociology of adolescence, born as a critique of the bio-psychological theory, does not accept adolescence as a universal life phase but views it as a social phenomenon. Since there is no single ritualized point of transition to adulthood in contemporary societies, individuals acquire different adult rights at different ages. Not surprisingly, young people occupy an ambiguous status of being neither children nor full adults. The sociology of adolescence suggests that through leisure activities in the company of peers, children and adolescents begin to assert their independence from teachers and parents.

The intergenerational conflict theory posits that contemporary societies fail to provide youth with secure and stable roles, but gives them access to freedom and money, which then lead to unstable and unruly youth cultures. Coleman (1961) originally viewed adolescence as an oppositional culture since adolescent peer groups and their culture seem to be separated from the world of adults and peers compete with parents in influencing adolescents. Some of these perspectives were later modified to emphasize the variety of peer cultures and to acknowledge that peer groups often reinforce the values of adult socializers. Also Youniss and Smollar (1985) find consistent evidence that suggests congruence of adolescent and parental values. Dornbusch (1989) suggests that the transition towards healthy independence in the peer group is facilitated by autonomy from parents in the emotional sense, not in the behavioural sense. Similarly, Willits and Willits (1987) posit that the effect of adolescent leisure on peer relations and independence from parental control should not obscure the importance of home and family to teenagers.

The class theory views societies as arenas for conflict, divided into dominant and subordinate groups. This seems to explain well, for example, the current youth unrest, particularly in the United Kingdom and in slum ghettos around the world. Roberts (1983) shows how the 'New Wave' (Brake 1980; Smith 1981) in youth theory made social class, not adolescence, its central concept. According to this conceptualization, young people who learn their culture in their homes and neighbourhoods attempt to resolve their contradictions primarily as class inequalities and conflicts, not as age divisions. Moreover, young people use popular culture as an additional resource to create solutions to their problems. It is argued within the class theory framework that the supposedly deviant social elements such as punks and skinheads are making important statements about their predicaments in a class society. The manifestations of these general class contradictions, however, further depend on age, gender, race, place of residence, and other circumstances.

The frequently disputed issue in class theory is whether the main division in youth cultures and leisure runs along age or class lines. According to class theory, youth subcultures are class divided. Its proponents note similarities between working-class youth styles and more general forms of working-class consciousness (Roberts 1983). The division between the rough and respectable youth cultures of early school-leavers and the middle-class youth styles of middle-class students is a persistent feature, at least in the United Kingdom. Although such divisions may have been blurred somewhat recently, they have never disappeared. In particular, there is a major difference in leisure between middle-class youth who continue full-time education until their early or mid-twenties and other young people. Middle-class youth have the resources— not just leisure equipment, but also access to a wide variety of cultures—that enable them to do many different things. This division is not absolute, however, since many students and working-class adolescents share many types of leisure activities and are served by the same leisure industries. Upon reviewing various approaches, Dornbusch (1989) concludes that the study of social processes linked to research on status groups holds the greatest promise for the development of knowledge within the sociology of adolescence.

Another persistent feature of youth cultures indicates that they are gender-segregated as well as class differentiated. Blyth et al. (1982), who examined the social world of adolescents, discovered noteworthy gender differences. For example, the nature of friendship is gender-differentiated. Males are more likely to spend time with groups of males, while females are more likely to interact with a single other female. This pattern is related to the degree of emotional intimacy among friends. Males are less likely to be emotionally close to their friends than are females. Also, as Ouellet and Perron (1979) found, boys give more importance to atmosphere and freedom in leisure than girls do. These gender differences in adolescents' interactions with peers of the same sex and age appear relatively stable cross-culturally as well.

Moreover, as Roberts (1983) posits, youth cultures have been mostly male-led. He cites findings that show that girls' participation seldom consists of equal sharing in leisure activities with their male counterparts; they are typically invited to participate by dressing, dancing, and otherwise acting to appeal to different types of male youth. There is empirical evidence that boys and girls make different uses of leisure, and that young middle-class and working-class males and females are involved in different youth cultures. Furthermore, most organized sports for girls continue to be led by men as coaches, officials, and administrators (Varpalotai 1992). Consequently, many girls seek leisure through all-female organizations such as Girl Guides where they feel free to experiment in a less competitive or non-competitive environment and where they can learn leadership roles.

These findings are not surprising given the 'ethic of care' concept, gender inequalities, and women's subordinate position in society in general and leisure in particular. Nevertheless, it does not necessarily mean that there is only uniformity in girls' leisure pursuits. Rather, there is a continuum that runs from an exclusively stereotypical feminine leisure through an androgynous (i.e., combined male/female style of leisure), to non-traditional leisure for women. Most adolescent females, however, do not prefer non-sexist leisure.

Several feminist theorists and researchers challenge the study of gender-differentiated adolescent leisure. Betsy Wearing, an Australian author, expresses the view of many feminist scholars by pointing out that women internalize a sense of inferiority to males through leisure in adolescence, and set an agenda for powerlessness and submission to male domination in all areas for the duration of their lives (1992). However, Wearing goes beyond descriptions of different leisure pursuits and agendas among young men and women in their late adolescence. She posits that there are ways in which leisure can provide the potential for developing individual identity that does not have to conform to the constraints of gendered categorization in contemporary society.

> In the period of late adolescence, before the impact of workforce segregation and segmentation of family responsibilities, there may be the opportunity for women with the material resources of middle-class position and expanded ideas from university education to challenge dominant gender stereotypes through their leisure. This is a moratorium time when there is a chance to explore or 'try on' different identities before integrating communal culture and individuality into a basic sense of the 'real me' which will underpin adult life (Wearing 1992:328).

We may add to this proposition that such non-gendered development of individual identity should prove beneficial to both female and male adolescents who will later form their own, hopefully non-gendered and symmetrical, families.

Most adolescents deviate from prevailing societal norms (Dornbusch 1989). Deviation and conformity, however, are relative terms. The definition of some behaviour as deviant, for example, sexual activity and drinking alcohol, is primarily based on a person's age. What may be considered appropriate at an older age is viewed as deviant and illegal when carried out by adolescents. Another factor affecting the view of deviant activities is history- or cohort-based. For example, young boys in nineteenth-century Canada were forbidden to play sports on the Sabbath. Recently, some supposedly deviant activities are so prevalent among most adolescents that they may indicate changing social trends. In other instances, an apparent type of deviant behaviour may be interpreted as a creative response to the ills of a class society. In most studies, attempts are made to distinguish between patterns of, for example, recreational use of drugs and alcohol and substance abuse (Kandel 1980). Stebbins (1988) defines deviance as nonconformity with social norms and focuses on tolerable forms of deviance. Certain forms of deviance are often seen as interesting leisure pastimes that offer freedom and pleasure.

These blurred definitions of deviant behaviour notwithstanding, some antisocial behaviour is clearly deviant regardless of age. Dornbusch (1989) finds that deviant behaviour increases dramatically and is disturbingly prevalent in adolescence. Interestingly, numerous studies cited by Kandel have usually failed to find a relationship between adolescent behaviours and social class. Rates of drug use (especially marijuana and alcohol) among young people in particular do not vary according to socio-economic status. Jessor and Jessor (1977) conceptualize marijuana and alcohol initiation as transitional behaviours in normal adolescent psychosocial development. Other researchers whose studies document peer similarities among delinquents and substance abusers seldom claim that such similarities result from the influence of peers during leisure. Rather, these similarities may result from selection of kindred-spirit peers or from socialization at home.

Our discussion of adolescents' leisure might have created an impression that adults have a *laissez-faire*, non-intrusive attitude regarding adolescents' leisure. It might appear that youngsters only respond to their physical and emotional maturation, and to indirect external factors in the process of creating their own leisure culture. In reality, parents, schools, civic authorities, and social reformers over the past few centuries have defined what they considered 'proper' leisure for children and adolescents. This has frequently resulted in a good deal of public investment in recreation facilities to provide 'proper' leisure. Social conceptions and interpretations of childhood and adolescence exert considerable influence on the quality, orientation, and provisions of leisure facilities and programs for children and adolescents.

▆▆ **Leisure during the establishment phase**

The establishment phase represents adulthood or the 'second age'. Most adults in their second age join the labour force, establish careers, find a spouse, and start a family. Rapoport and Rapoport (1978) suggest that the central preoccupation during this phase is with making commitments that constitute satisfying life investments. In particular, preoccupations during the early establishment phase are concerned with productivity (choices and plans). During mid-establishment, people are concerned with performance (effectiveness and competence at what is chosen), while people in the late establishment subphase are preoccupied with evaluation (the meaningfulness of commitments). We also remember that the subphases according to the Rapoports' classification by the age of children are closely associated with the family and parenthood.

Some theorists pay relatively more attention to the early period of transition to the establishment phase or to the pre-marital subphase. Thus Kelly (1987) identifies several themes of this period: the extraresidential leisure of student years moves to domestic entertainment and interaction; the sexual exploration of late preparation turns to commitment; some leisure becomes oriented towards establishing one's place in the community. Finally, Kelly posits that parenthood affects the resources and aims of leisure most significantly. Furthermore, the transition revolves around intimacy rather than work, which tends to be more instrumental and supportive of the consumer role for most young adults. Gordon (1976) divides the establishment phase into three parts as well, but labels them 'young adulthood', 'early maturity', and 'full maturity'. Although he suggests approximate chronological age categories for each stage, he and most other scholars posit that age as such is not an adequate predictor of preoccupations, interests, developmental dilemmas, or roles within the stages.

The contemporary changing sequence of transition points, roles, and preoccupations tends to differ from a typical sequence found in traditional societies. In particular, the current trend of postponing marriage and parenthood render the age-based classification inadequate. Nevertheless, however they are delineated, the establishment phase and its subphases are closely associated with leisure. Leisure is a means of expressing some basic life meanings such as self-worth, self-respect, autonomy, creativity, and social participation, and can be a source of status and prestige. It allows for expression of preoccupations and interests, and provides space and time for the socialization process. Leisure can be viewed as one of the progressive filters within the mate selection process, or interpreted from the perspective of systems theory as one of the means of boundary maintenance for the couple or the family.

Only a few studies have addressed leisure behaviour of single individuals, and those are concerned primarily with the general overview of the transition points, preoccupations, or social roles. We have at our disposal aggregate data by age, education, and other independent variables, and specific activities or preferences as dependent variables. However, most theorizing about leisure during the establishment phase concerns the interplay between the work, family, and leisure domains. Thus the study of leisure during the establishment phase overlaps to a great extent with the study of leisure and the family, which we have already examined. Additional conceptualizations to which we now turn originate with Osgood and Howe (1984) and Kelly (1983). In Kelly's view,

> One way of viewing life in the establishment period is as a set of nesting roles. The familial roles are the foundation of intimate acceptance, maintenance support, economic consumption, social position, community interaction and gender-role investment. From the family come the parenting roles, leisure roles that change significantly with the family life cycle progression, and the work roles that have their meaning for most primarily in their contribution to the family-home investment. The residence itself is more than shelter, especially in North America (1983:69).

Osgood and Howe (1984) delineate the broad age-based stages of the traditional American life cycle that relate changing activities, values, motivations, and meanings of leisure participation to various biological, psychological, and social developmental changes in particular life stages.

Middle adulthood is associated with two basic contradictions that characterize both leisure patterns during this phase and the studies that examine them. Some authors emphasize biological aging and a corresponding decline in physical strength and sexual power. According to this position, some middle-aged people are concerned with body image and physical health, while others focus on the middle-age peak of power, productivity, full engagement in work and community roles, and on the increased discretionary income and freedom when their children leave home. Rapoport and Rapoport (1978) posit that leisure in middle life is associated with new interests outside the home. Kelly (1982, 1987) views the age of full maturity and the postparental stage as the time when individuals start re-examining their lives and doing more activities for themselves. Leisure serves as a major vehicle for re-establishing previous personal and social identities or finding and trying out new ones.

Recent case-studies document that middle-aged individuals perceive themselves and the meaning of their lives as changed in comparison with young adulthood (Freysinger 1987). In particular, leisure becomes important for middle-aged people's well-being, effective functioning, adjustment, and adaptation to middle adulthood. Men indicate that their leisure is increasingly more important to them, and are involved in more leisure activities than before. Freysinger finds that, unlike in early adulthood when men's involvement in leisure leadership was motivated by the need for power and influence over others, middle-aged men are more oriented towards physical, mental, and emotional mastery over themselves.

Similarly, Osgood and Howe posit that leisure assumes a tremendous importance during middle age in reappraising one's life. Furthermore, Osgood and Howe assert that physical health concerns motivate leisure participation as 'more and more persons in midlife flock to diet and health spas and take up or reactivate participation in walking, biking, jogging, or some other form of physical recreation' (1984:186). Such assertions have empirical support from

Figure 6.1 Roles and changes over the adult life course: The traditional pattern

Key

- ☐ = Psychological tasks
- ◆ = Social roles / tasks (work, family, and community)
- ● = Leisure experiences
- ✳ = Biological milestones
- M = Males especially involved
- F = Females especially involved

Young adulthood (age 20–35 ◆◆)

- ☐ development of attitudes, beliefs, values
- ☐ establish autonomy
- ☐ establish intimacy or isolation
- ☐ 'Catch 30 Transition' occurs
- ☐ structure a dream
- ☐ culmination of self-determined goals
- ☐ make the 30s transition
- ◆ build life structure
- ☐ urge to merge
- ☐ seeker self emerges

Midlife (age 35–55)

- ☐ realization of mortality
- ☐ settling down
- ☐ creativity
- ☐ authenticity crisis
- ☐ self-reflection
- ☐ self-assessment of goals
- ☐ fulfilling the dream
- ☐ inward focus
- ☐ adjustment to aging parents
- ☐ mid-life transition (M)
- ☐ generation or stagnation
- ☐ restabilization of the sexes
- ☐ 'deadline decade'
- ◆ productivity, societal affirmation
- ✳ male mid-life crisis
- ✳ adjust to physiological changes
- ✳ menopause
- ✳ physical decline

Late life (age 55 ☐)

- ☐ integrity/integration vs despair
- ☐ time consciousness
- ☐ late adult transition
- ☐ flowering
- ☐ fulfil or fail at goals
- ☐ search for meaning of aging
- ☐ concern with unmet needs of self
- ✳ self-concept crisis
- ✳ physiological decline

- complete formal schooling
- first job, getting into the world
- first marriage
- buying a house
- managing a home
- first child born
- assume civic, social, and community responsibilities

- job promotion
- launch children from home
- civic/social responsibilities
- divorce
- mid-career change (M)
- return to work (F)
- care for aging parents
- 'empty nest'
- teach, train teenage children

- assume grandparent role
- retirement
- maintain independence—self-direction
- cope with loss—widowhood
- assume role of mentor
- maintain self-esteem and self-concept
- financial losses
- deal with issue of death
- life review, introspection

- culture bearers; support norms and values of culture
- socializing over sexualizing
- changing time sense
- develop mental flexibility

- peace, security, comfort
- personal autonomy
- meaningful integration
- shift concern from body to intellect
- decreased ego strength, change from active to passive mastery
- physical losses

- intimate other-related leisure
- work-related leisure (M)
- family-related leisure (F if care provided for children)
- instrumental activities (M)
- expressive activities (F)
- sensate-focused activities
- role-related
- social leisure
- sensual transcendance
- goal-directed

- new experiences
- flexible emotional investments
- intellectual pursuits
- sex-free social interaction
- reappraisal of self through leisure
- identity consolidation and/or exploration

- re-emergence of intimate other-related leisure
- social reintegration
- enrichment and extension of mental and spiritual activities
- more time for leisure
- relaxation and solitude

Source: N.J. Osgood and C.Z. Howe, 'Psychological Aspects of Leisure: A Life Cycle Developmental Perspective', in *Loisir et Société/Society and Leisure* 7 (1):175–96.

several studies; however, this support is not overwhelming and does not seem to pertain to the majority of middle-aged people or those in the postparental phase.

One of the typical changes when parents have older children, and even more so when they are in the postparental phase, is an increase in leisure time (Horna 1987d). The major reason for this change, however, varies between wives and their husbands. Women who experience an increase in their free time attribute that change to having fewer family obligations. Those few women who claim that they have even less free time blame it on new or extended occupational obligations. Men, however, whether they experience more or less free time, report the change as a result of their changing work situation. Having fewer family obligations does not noticeably affect men's leisure time. In general, some individuals describe their middle-age leisure experience as an opportunity to become more independent and to try new things, while others prefer to stay with their old comfortable routines and core activities.

Regularly pursued activities among postparental married couples aged forty to fifty-five are home-centred and require only minimal time, money, and physical exertion (Smith 1991). Consistent with reports from several other surveys, Smith reports that the leisure activity repertoire tends to expand during middle age. Like Freysinger's subjects, the majority in Smith's study indicate that leisure became more important to them in mid-life than it was during early adulthood. There are indications that leisure for middle-aged men and women becomes, in Kelly's terminology, less role-related as it becomes more unconditional in orientation — that is, more for its own sake. Furthermore, many of these people report that they experience more spontaneous leisure in their establishment phase. Leisure becomes less routine and structured, allowing for a greater freedom. More importantly, establishment phase leisure choices and preferences reflect the continuation of lifelong activities. Even with some variation among specific activities, men and women seem to engage in only those that they enjoyed in the past. This supports our earlier discussion about the continuity and change in leisure orientations throughout the life cycle.

Furthermore, middle-aged women (both single and married) use their increased freedom to pursue intrinsically satisfying activities that allow self-expression and self-fulfilment. This may suggest that decreased parental responsibilities and increased leisure time allow for self-actualization among women. For men, leisure's increased importance seems to be related to health concerns and is motivated by a sense of urgency to seek out various activities while they are still physically able to do so. Some men express a desire to develop a leisure repertoire that would fill in the free time anticipated after retirement. Despite these different reasons, the consequences are the same— both middle-aged men and women are becoming more aware of their leisure and are taking deliberate steps to participate in various leisure activities. Most researchers also document that many middle-aged people welcome opportunities to pursue leisure activities that they and their spouses can do together.

In sum, there is no uniformity in leisure patterns during the establishment phase. There is a shift towards leisure that can complement or support family roles and parental preoccupations. The gender inequity in the amount of leisure time and in the choice of pursuits appears to be more pronounced in the establishment phase than in the preparation phase.

▮▮ Leisure and the 'third age'

Diverse terms are used to describe the last part of the life cycle. While Erikson (1950) describes it as one of 'integrity', Kelly (1983, 1987) prefers the term 'culmination' to indicate the process of re-evaluating one's life and consolidating the 'strands of the life course'. Also Rapoport and Rapoport (1978) write about personal and social integration in the later-life phase. Rapoport and Rapoport divide the later life into preretirement, retirement, and old age subphases. Each of these subphases is associated with different preoccupations — anticipation of retirement, realignment of commitments, and death. Gordon (1976), too, points to integration during the retirement stage, which lasts from the beginning of retirement to the onset of severe illness, followed by the disability stage.

These positions clearly suggest that the focus in studying the later-life phase is on the culmination of the lifelong process. Aging does not begin at age sixty-five (McPherson 1991). As with the earlier life stages, aging is characterized by life events, transitions, and their associated effects, which differ considerably between individuals and groups. Not surprisingly, the elderly are no more homogeneous than the younger age groups. Individual differences in social characteristics, personality traits, and preferences continue for most people into their old age. The elderly themselves, as well as the society around them, impose their role expectations, enactments, and limitations. Moreover, because each cohort grows old under somewhat different circumstances, what existed for the elderly a generation ago may not be there for the subsequent cohort. Thus aging involves intertwined biological and social processes.

Retirement is often viewed as leisure earned through a lifetime of work, thus equating retirement with leisure. However, this popular conception is no longer valid. How do leisure theorists and researchers view leisure during the third age? Leisure scholars have applied various approaches found in the sociological, social-psychological, and gerontological literature and, in turn, enriched those perspectives.

One of the frequently cited gerontological approaches is the disengagement theory of aging. It was formulated in the early 1960s as a result of the research carried out by Elaine Cumming and William Henry (1961). It views aging as a progressive process of physical, psychological, and social withdrawal from the wider world. This approach suggests that the process of gradual withdrawal (disengagement) is mutually satisfying for both the individual and society. For seniors, disengagement provides increased opportunities for reflection, preoccupation with items of self-interest, and decreased emotional investment in people and events. This theory, however, has been challenged on several grounds. Firstly, it does not take into account the fact that people adjust throughout life. Secondly, it is not in agreement with substantial evidence that many older adults remain socially active and are happier than those who have withdrawn from their social system.

The other gerontological perspective, called the continuation or activity approach or the engagement model, originates with the work of Robert Havighurst, Bernice Neugarten, and Sheldon Tobin (1968). It proposes that seniors prefer to resist preoccupation with the self and do not want to distance themselves from society. This approach suggests that aside from the inevitable changes in biology and health, the elderly are the same as middle-aged people and have essentially the same psychological and social needs. Like the general developmental approach, the continuation perspective emphasizes that old age is not a period with distinct boundaries but is a part of the continuum of life. It includes changes that reflect the personality traits, attitudes, and preferences that occur over a lifetime. Gradual withdrawal from society tends to occur only in late old age. Gordon, Gaitz, and Scott (1976) and Kelly, Steinkamp, and Kelly (1986) report that the decline in participation is activity-specific. For example, lower rates of participation are most marked for travel, outdoor recreation, exercise, and sports. On the other hand, participation rates for social activities and family leisure remain relatively high, especially for men. Furthermore, various scholars argue that person-specific factors, such as health and economic status, represent key elements of life satisfaction among older adults (Larson 1978; Kelly, Steinkamp, and Kelly 1987; Mancini and Orthner 1980; Riddick and Daniel 1984). When older people's participation rates decline, their feelings of satisfaction, contentment, and happiness seem to decrease as well (Havighurst 1961; Maddox 1968; Neugarten 1964; Palmore 1975). One criticism of the activity approach is that this view does not adequately consider individuals who have been inactive throughout their lives and continue this pattern into old age, apparently quite satisfied to do so.

Since it became evident that personal perceptions and individual attitudes are very important in the aging process, MacNeil and Teague (1987), who drew upon the work of Iso-Ahola and his colleagues, proposed the attribution theory of aging. This theory assumes that people constantly search for meaning in human behaviour, look for explanations for their own behaviour and that of others, and assign meaning to behaviour by attempting to find causes for it. The types of assigned causality include dispositional attribution, which are behaviours caused by qualities inherent in the person (e.g., talent, skill), and environmental factors related to a situation, not the actor (e.g., opportunities).

Some propositions about the effect of retirement on the individual suggest that retirement may evolve into an identity crisis (Miller 1968), or it may become an opportunity for continuing leisure activities pursued in middle age (Atchley 1977). Others suggest that successful adjustment to retirement depends on the congruency between leisure wants and the person's ability to satisfy his or her perceived needs (Seleen 1982). Congruency theory posits that both life satisfaction and leisure satisfaction in retirement are results of the fit between perceived leisure needs and perceived fulfilment of those needs, and that they are not necessarily bound to a particular pattern among older adults (Mancini and Orthner 1980; Mobily 1989; Seleen 1982). Congruency theory recognizes that people can vary substantially in their need for leisure. Thus the absolute amount of leisure is not as important as leisure satisfaction. Further, congruency theory predicts that the 'leisure self' develops throughout life and would not do as well among incongruent types. Mobily (1987) comments that as recreation participation among seniors is quite low, the conflict between the congruency and involvement positions brings the question of leisure's worth back to the forefront. In particular, he asks which is more fundamental, more valuable—leisure satisfaction or leisure participation? This involvement approach is more than a hypothetical question since it has found some support in empirical research.

An application of two existing frameworks from mainstream sociology, the interactionist perspective and the exchange theory, is proposed by Stanley and Stanley (1985). These authors use the two frameworks to explain different patterns of leisure sports involvement by the elderly. They posit that in our society sports have traditionally been considered activities for the young and the skilled. People are encouraged to 'act their age' and are criticized for trying to hold on to youth; therefore, many adults do not consider physical activity appropriate for themselves because of their age. Furthermore, if someone was not skilled or successful when younger and was unable to define himself or herself as an athlete or winner, this person would not likely define sports activities as appropriate and would not attach a positive meaning to involvement in them. It is not likely that such meaning or interpretation will change with advancing age. The popular belief that this may no longer be the case for many elderly needs to be better documented.

From the perspective of exchange theory, which analyses social interaction as a series of transactions, a person would not engage in physical activities if he or she does not expect them to be rewarding. Stanley and Stanley go on to suggest that a person is not likely to continue to participate if not rewarded frequently (success proposition). Because of society's emphasis on extrinsic rewards that are difficult to achieve by most older persons who are unable to compete at a level that earns frequent rewards, some intrinsic satisfaction associated with participation is usually not enough. On the other hand, if a person was rewarded for performance in sports or physical activity in the past, he or she would be more likely to participate in leisure sports in later years (stimulus proposition). Since many are not rewarded frequently in early years, they are likely to withdraw and not participate when they are older. Thirdly, when extrinsic rewards are emphasized, and the likelihood of an older person obtaining them is not great, Stanley and Stanley propose to expect little (if any) involvement in that activity (rationality proposition). The subjective costs of participation in leisure sports—embarrassment, loss of self-esteem, and inconsistent self-image—may outweigh the benefits.

Canadian sociologist Alan Roadburg (1983) takes the perspective that leisure is a subjective experience that differs between working and retired people. While leisure may imply freedom to someone who is working, it does not necessarily have the same meaning for a retired person. Roadburg finds that the major difference is the retirees' emphasis on enjoyment and relaxation. Since only 17 per cent of his research subjects mentioned freedom, he concludes that most retired persons differentiate between activities that are relaxing or not relaxing, or between those that are enjoyable or not enjoyable. If a person is not part of the workforce with its inherent constraints on time and activity, freedom becomes less significant as a means of distinguishing between work and leisure. All of one's time is in a sense free time. Freedom is thus a necessary (but not sufficient) condition for leisure in retirement.

Roadburg detects yet another difference between working people's and retirees' definitions of leisure. While most working people do not have problems with defining leisure, many retirees are unable to define the term. Roadburg identifies the retirees' living arrangements, former occupation, and method of retirement as the factors associated with a particular definition. In particular, living arrangements appear to have the strongest influence on definitions of leisure. Older people who live in an institution are less likely to define leisure or to define it as enjoyment. People who live with a spouse tend to conceive of leisure as relaxation, and those who live alone generally define it as 'something to do'. Furthermore, Roadburg finds that if a person is forced to retire but would have preferred to remain at work, retirement may not be looked upon as freedom from the constraints of work. If poor health influenced the decision to retire, leisure implies the opportunity to rest or relax from the stress and strain that may accompany ill health.

Another Canadian study looks at how the elderly arrange all their free time and what factors determine how they spend it (Delisle 1982). It proposes that people's time is managed (by themselves or by society) and, therefore, one's activities are not chosen by chance. Thus some activities are more important than others and determine how time is divided among various activities. These are referred to as 'pivot activities', meaning those activities around which temporal order is determined and around which the other activities (contingent activities) are arranged. Individuals go through phases when they are very busy and other phases when they are less so. The busier these people are, the more activities they accomplish in a given space of time. They must synchronize or structure their activities and temporal order better, thus the density of the temporal order increases. The density of the temporal order is therefore both a measurement of how busy an individual is, and a measurement of the degree to which his or her temporal order is structured.

An application of this approach to the elderly implies that older persons do not live in the same sphere as people in the other groups, but in their own distinct sphere with specific alternations between dense periods. The seniors' week is divided into three relatively distinct periods: (1) weekdays, which are very busy, devoted to commitments and recreation; (2) the weekend, which is not very busy, devoted to recreation and fulfilling commitments; (3) the week in general, in which how weekdays are spent seems to be determined, at least in part, by the recreation activities of the weekend, which are primarily social or family-oriented (Delisle 1982). As with middle-aged persons, seniors' recreation appears to be their pivot activity of the weekend and for the week as a whole. Delisle's study finds no correlation between age or status of health and the parameters of time structuring. Men and women often participate in different activities; for example, women perform household tasks while men are involved in physical exercise. They also pursue a number of activities to about the same extent; for example, they frequent seniors' clubs and shows equally often. There is no significant difference in the frequency of visits to or from relatives and friends. In addition, those who learned to structure their time when they were younger continue to do so in their retirement. It also appears that economic status and personal characteristics determine how time is managed. Delisle suggests that leisure activities are probably the pivot of the temporal order of seniors, and the fulfilment of commitments is carried out as a function of the pivot.

Our discussion of leisure during the third age would be incomplete without a detailed look at senior women's leisure. As Szinovacz (1992) and numerous other authors point out, our knowledge concerning systematic differences in the retirement experiences of men and women remains limited. She argues that in order to reach a systematic analysis of gender differences in retirement, it is essential to go beyond mere demonstrations of male-female differences. Building on Lawton's (1983) conceptual model of the antecedents of activity, Szinovacz's model considers several domains, namely, the societal domain, the familial domain, and personality. Specifically, she argues that gender differences in retirement leisure are tied to gender stratification and gender differences in longevity at the societal level, the gender-segregated division of labour at the familial level, and gender-role socialization at the personality level. A special case are women who entered retirement because they were pressured by their husbands to retire when they did. They are likely to seek out retirement leisure activities that can provide the sense of achievement and accomplishment formerly gained in their occupational roles, for example, volunteering or community activities. Further restructuring of women's leisure from couple-oriented to other group or solitary activities is necessitated by the transition from wife to widow.

Women in their third age continue to perform the majority of household tasks, regardless of their employment status. They carry the major responsibility for the care of extended kin, and they function as the managers of social interactions, including relationships with relatives (Brody 1990; Di Leonardo 1987; Ferree 1991; Stone, Cafferata, and Sangl 1987; Szinovacz 1992). The gender-segregated division of responsibilities has several ramifications for retirement leisure. It influences the amount of leisure available to women, brings about changes in leisure time and activities after retirement, and contributes to the fact that women also enjoy less free time than men in their retirement years. Further reduction of women's leisure in retirement is often caused by their care for ill spouses or relatives (Szinovacz 1992). Moreover, since men's kin contacts and friendships are mediated by their wives, men's access to social networks and extended kin after retirement may be contingent on their wives' efforts and/or survival (Dorfman and Mertens 1990; Lee 1988). Single men become particularly vulnerable to social isolation.

Szinovacz (1989) and Szinovacz and Washo (1988) also note that work overload faced by many employed wives probably leads to a greater proportional increase in women's leisure after retirement than in men's. In anticipation of this increase in leisure, some women, and women more than men, make unrealistic leisure plans for retirement. According to Szinovacz (1989), women report significantly more leisure plans for retirement than men, and anticipate significantly more changes than men in time spent in leisure and obligatory activities after retirement. Nevertheless, as a consequence of the gender-based allocation of household duties before retirement, the establishment of spheres of influence after retirement may not be easy since the consolidation of existing spheres of influence after retirement may be used to bar the other spouse from participating in one's own domain.

As we have already addressed this issue, we know that gender role socialization predisposes most men and women to pursue different kinds of leisure activities, albeit within specific streams, or as a core and balance of activities. These differences tend to continue into the retirement years (Altergott 1988; Cutler and Hendricks 1990; Szinovacz 1992). Some women may never have developed the skills for 'male' activities. They may feel insecure about participating in male-dominated group activities, or they may be overly self-conscious about sports that would require exposure of their aging bodies to public scrutiny.

Studies of leisure during the consolidation phase of the life cycle are an unfinished endeavour. The complementary and contradictory propositions might at a first glance confuse the reader. However, these studies and their findings are inevitably diverse as they reflect the rapidly changing patterns of behaviour and leisure of contemporary aging cohorts as well as increase our theoretical understanding of them. In particular, the disengagement theory's interpretation of seniors' behaviour gets little theoretical and empirical support. Most theorists and researchers find that the third age does not begin at the age of sixty or sixty-five but represents an extension of the earlier life and leisure patterns and preferences. Seniors are no more homogeneous than the younger age groups, since gender differences, social characteristics, and personal traits continue to influence their lives. Some variations appear to stem from an individual's health and subjective differences between working and retired individuals.

▮▮▮ Summary

The developmental perspective perceives leisure behaviour as dynamic and static, improvised and stable, and subject to personal interpretations. Although specific leisure activities may be chosen on the basis of individual factors and may be gender and age specific, they are also influenced by contextual factors. The stages or events of the life cycle affect people's leisure behaviour. The transition points throughout people's lives, however, cannot be defined in terms of precise chronological ages. Most theorists agree on the three broad life course phases: the preparation, the establishment, and the culmination. Leisure is not necessarily predominant during those phases, but its contribution is felt at least to some degree most of the time.

Leisure during the preparation phase is primarily associated with the search for personal identity and testing one's abilities. Leisure pursuits provide one of the important means for this process. Among the most persistent features of this period is the peer-oriented youth culture and leisure activities that are class- and gender-differentiated and separated from the world of adults. They are congruent with the adult scene nevertheless.

During the establishment phase, including the parental, middle-age, and postparental stages, there is a shift towards leisure roles and pursuits that complement or support family and conjugal roles and preoccupations. The gender inequity in access to leisure time and the choice of pursuits appears to be more pronounced in the establishment phase than the preparation phase. The third age, which does not begin at the age of sixty or sixty-five, represents an extension of the earlier life and leisure patterns and preferences. Gender differences, social characteristics, and personal traits continue to influence the lives and leisure behaviour of older people.

CHAPTER 7

Leisure studies
and research

▉▉ **The institutionalization of leisure studies**

So far we have examined two broad disciplinary approaches to leisure—the psychology and the sociology—as well as their overlap in social psychology. The crucial characteristic of many leisure studies, however, is their multidisciplinary and/or interdisciplinary nature that goes beyond the boundaries of any one specific social science. Since leisure itself has many facets, it naturally calls for a much broader perspective than what a single discipline can offer.

Several leisure scholars make a distinction between leisure studies and leisure sciences. For example, Pronovost and D'Amours (1990:50) posit that leisure studies means a 'field of study with changing outlines, which has given rise to a certain institutionalization of teaching, research, and publication in universities.' Leisure sciences refers to 'fundamental modalities of scientific examination in the social and human sciences, examination into the definition of the object of research and the most appropriate methods, and constant examination of the foundations of a scientific discipline; in this sense, leisure sciences provide an interdisciplinary crossroads for the scientific examination of modern leisure.' Pronovost and D'Amours also point to the 'historicalness' of leisure sciences (as in all sciences). They posit that leisure sciences are constructed from the historical awareness of leisure and what it involves. The major themes change according to the historical contexts, while scientific examination and concerns become modified according to national situations. In addition, Pronovost and D'Amours point to the 'internal history of leisure sciences', made up of successive problematic issues, varied conceptualizations, pitfalls and monopolies, conflicts and debates.

The first, seminal analysis of leisure is Thorstein Veblen's *The Theory of the Leisure Class*, published at the turn of the century (Veblen 1899). Establishing the leisure field as a legitimate study and research discipline, in the United States in particular, coincided with the unprecedented economic growth, the implementation of social reforms, the reduction of the work week, and the growth of local public leisure institutions (Pronovost and D'Amours 1990). The emphasis in those early days was on parks and recreation. In Kraus's overview (1984), the founding of the American Association of Zoological Parks and Aquariums in 1924 was an indication that specialized recreational uses of parks were becoming increasingly widespread in American communities. This trend was further promoted by a national conference on outdoor recreation in 1924.

As the practice and theory of leisure influenced one another, the development of leisure studies and leisure sciences has become almost inextricably woven with the above events. The dominant ideologists of the decade were philosophers and philanthropists who influenced the great humanist and reformist movements and, at the same time, legitimized them. Expressing the theme of his times, an American, Arthur Newton Pack, believed in a significant and more than casual relationship between leisure and human happiness: 'It is only with leisure that we are able to taste happiness. It is only with leisure that we are able to measure in any human terms at all the value of living' (1934:23). In Pack's view, 'Education is the sine qua non of any adequate solution of the problem that has been brought about by an abundant leisure—this strange commodity that has such overwhelming potentialities for either discontent or happiness, for social or anti-social living' (1934:242).

The humanist and reformist orientations inspired American leisure (Pronovost and D'Amours 1990). Early leisure studies often dealt with mass education, 'rational leisure', play, idleness, and the underprivileged. Moreover, the field of leisure often dealt with élitist and militaristic concerns, and addressed the problems of hygiene and the moral and social conditions of the masses. Orientation on theoretical perspectives was much weaker.

Leisure studies primarily served pragmatic needs and political concerns regarding leisure and recreation, and therefore corresponded with the turning points and transitions in the leisure domain, particularly during the first half of the twentieth century (Neumeyer and Neumeyer 1958). For example, American publications between the two world wars followed the emphasis on recreation and parks prevalent at that time. In particular, these publications fulfilled the pragmatic need to cope with the new emphasis on recreation and parks and to train parks and recreation professionals. Sessoms, Meyer, and Brightbill (1975) posited that America has approached the provision of recreation opportunities and organized recreation in a manner similar to the way it organized its education and welfare programs.

After the Second World War, a strong drive to democratize leisure led to a marked increase in leisure participation. Charles Brightbill made a humanist plea to 'let recreation help us live a really democratic life and use it to attain sound emotional and physical health and make our daily lives more zestful' (1961:38). Articles on leisure began to appear in some of the leading sociology journals (Clarke 1956; Donald and Havighurst 1959; Havighurst and

Feigenbaum 1959; Michelon 1954; Reissman 1954; White 1955) beginning in the 1950s. Furthermore, several edited books on leisure were published (Donahue et al. 1958; Larrabee and Meyersohn 1958; Rosenberg and White 1957; Smigel 1963), and comprehensive texts for leisure courses or for work and leisure studies became available (Anderson 1961; de Grazia 1964; Kaplan 1960; Kleemeier 1961; Pieper 1963). Several of them responded to the trends and events that affected organized recreation service in the 1950s and 1960s (Kraus 1984). They included national concern with physical fitness, programs for the disabled, outdoor recreation and park development, increased federal assistance to recreation, involvement in the arts, growth of commercial recreation, unification of recreation and parks movement, concern with the poor and with minority groups. Moreover, new challenges created by the youth rebellion of the 1960s and special-interest groups (such as women, seniors, and homosexuals) who asserted their right to equal treatment, affected recreation services.

The above emphasis, as well as practices and policies, were supported by rapidly growing empirical research on linking the demographic and socioeconomic characteristics of the population with individual participation rates, preferences, and demands for recreation facilities. Such research trends, however, had their drawbacks. Research in recreation and parks remained largely mechanical—inventorying space, attempting to determine people's recreation interests, comparing one community with another, and so on (Sessoms, Meyer, and Brightbill 1975), while the theoretical development was confined mostly to the disciplines of sociology and psychology. Thus the postwar leisure field has been formed by (1) leisure ideologies that became the dominant professional models in American university textbooks; (2) the issue of mass culture, inspired by cultural anthropology; and (3) a clear reference to new methods of research and America's new concerns about growing bureaucracy, the influence of mass media, and problems of 'passivity' and conformism, as expounded by Mills and later by Vance Packard (Pronovost 1983; Pronovost and D'Amours 1990).

The controversy between the Veblen tradition's perspective and the mass society perspective affected leisure studies for decades. The former position views leisure as a function of socio-economic status and occupation, while the latter argues that with rising affluence, greater availability of discretionary time for all, and mass-produced leisure (such as TV, radio, printed materials, etc.), leisure functions as a prime unifier or equalizer of socio-economic inequities. Some researchers found support during the earlier stages of leisure studies development for class-differentiated leisure. For example, they documented significant differences in leisure activity involvement across and within different social subgroups (Wilensky 1961). Classes with higher educational, occupational, and income levels were found to be more involved in most forms of active leisure (Reissman 1954), or occupational prestige and educational level were directly related to active and passive leisure activity (Clarke 1956;

Robinson 1970; White 1955). Numerous researchers uncovered variable relationships between gender, age, and marital status and leisure involvement (Angrist 1967; de Grazia 1962; Graham 1959; Hoar 1961; Zuzanek 1976).

In contrast, other theorists and researchers claimed to have evidence for the democratization of leisure. Nels Anderson (1961) found support for his assertion that leisure involvement is evenly distributed across all social subgroups since 'all classes attend the same ball games, the same prize fights, the same night clubs, even the same opera. All listen to the radio and view the same TV programs.' Similarly, Joffre Dumazedier (1967) believed in the democratizing effects of contemporary and future leisure. The differences in theoretical premises and methodological approaches were only one part of the process of developing leisure studies and leisure sciences. The other part meant that leisure studies and leisure sciences were still more multidisciplinary than interdisciplinary in nature and therefore inseparable from their origins of psychology and sociology. Other disciplines, economics and geography in particular, have also contributed to the growth and refinement of the field of leisure studies. These are, however, outside the scope of our present examination of leisure.

Leisure studies have examined the relationship between work and leisure for decades. This area has been profoundly influenced by seminal works of Andersen (1961), Dubin (1956), Kornhauser (1965), Meissner (1971), Parker (1971, 1983), and Wilensky (1960).

As summarized by Zuzanek and Mannell (1983), seven major themes were applied in the study of the work-leisure relationship: (1) a statistical and time-budget perspective, (2) a socio-economic perspective, (3) a socio-organizational and planning perspective, (4) a sociological and socio-historical perspective, (5) the framework of socio-occupational status, (6) examination of the direct effects of work, and (7) socio-psychological studies. The conceptualization of the work-leisure relationship—whether as spillover/congruence, compensation/contrast, or neutrality/segmentation—received particularly wide attention.

The earlier orientation towards the typical work-leisure dichotomy and an uncritical reliance on some data sources were re-examined by several leisure theorists and researchers in the early 1960s. For example, de Grazia (1964) cautioned against an uncritical use of empirical data and pointed out that the figures gathered on consumer expenditures for recreation goods and services were not based on personal reports of expenditures but on sales of tickets or goods. Such expenditures can reflect an intention to spend free time but not necessarily its actual spending. Similarly, de Grazia argued that the government's expenditures for recreation must be considered from a separate angle: 'We cannot even say of taxes that they show an intention to spend the money. They show simply that Congress voted to spend tax receipts in this way' (1964:97).

When tracing the development of the leisure field in Canada, Burton (1979) proposed an analogy with the physical and mental growth and development of a human being, which proceeds through five stages: infancy, childhood, adolescence, young adulthood, and maturity. Burton posits that Canada experienced a relatively lengthy gestation period, followed by the birth and infancy of the field of leisure research in the 1950s. During that time,

> leisure was no longer solely of interest to historians, social commentators and the like as an expression or indicator of some greater concern, but became the immediate and primary concern of leisure and recreation professionals. Sport and physical fitness, for purposes of ensuring a healthy and morally sound population, were a special interest of the new municipal departments, and numerous research studies in this area emanate from the period (1979:14).

During the early 'childhood period', leisure and recreation came under scrutiny not simply as by-products of greater, more consuming interests; they advanced to being dependent variables in research directed towards an understanding of greater concerns, for example, the youth revolution of that time. Upon reaching adolescence in about 1967, Canada's leisure field experienced large and rapid growth in the number of organizations and individuals engaged in leisure research, in the volume of funds allocated for such research, and in the number of research studies being carried out at any one time. As in the United States, Canadian research of leisure was designed primarily to discover patterns of leisure behaviour and their associations with selected demographic and socio-economic variables of the population. Furthermore, it searched for particular indicators of the supply of leisure facilities, services, and programs. Some prominent examples of this research orientation include Canadian national surveys of the levels of attendance or participation in various events or activities, and perhaps as many as 100 local leisure surveys.

According to Burton's analogy, the leisure field in Canada entered the stage of young adulthood in about 1974–5. One of the elements of this stage was a restructuring of leisure researchers' attitudes towards acquiring and developing knowledge in the field, including the recognition that new knowledge is not necessarily or exclusively equated with the acquisition of new data. It would be safe to posit that by now, the Canadian leisure field has reached full maturity. The work of several prominent psychologists, social psychologists, and sociologists has contributed significantly to the development of the study and understanding of leisure. Several names deserve particular mention: Gruneau's ground-breaking theoretical work and discussion of cultural hegemony; Bella, Lenskyj, and Shaw's feminist theorizing and research of gender inequality; Mannell and Zuzanek's study of work-leisure relationships, leisure experience and social change, and innovative methodology; Jackson and Searle's study of leisure constraints and barriers; Roadburg's work on leisure, retirement, and aging; Burton's study of leisure administration and policies; Pronovost and D'Amours's examination of leisure from the francophone and cross-cultural perspectives.

In spite of the progress in the field of studying leisure, American sociology of leisure has been criticized for becoming a 'frozen' sociology. Pronovost and D'Amours view it as being torn between two models of analysis, represented on the one hand by American leisure institutions and dominated by the professionals, in which case the approaches are normative, do not stray far from common sense, and skim the surface theoretically. On the other hand, according to Pronovost and D'Amours, there is the model from the point of view of mass culture. In this other case, the sociology of leisure can easily slip into the pragmatic study of hobbies and trivial amusements. Although Pronovost and D'Amours speak specifically about sociology, their criticism is applicable to leisure studies beyond the boundaries of sociology.

The drive on the part of many theorists and researchers towards an inter-disciplinary integration is occasionally hampered by the uneasiness (even confrontation) between the two categories of 'leisurologists', the theorists and the leisure professionals. Such relationships have generated both occasional conflict and attempts at integration. The development of leisure studies, together with its specific priorities, responds to the scientific and technical culture peculiar to leisure departments, professional associations and institutions, the direction of research, and the choice of research methods. At the same time, leisure studies faces a series of epistemological obstacles, outlined by Pronovost (1983) and Pronovost and D'Amours as

- the 'first experience obstacle', which consists of an abundance of common sense notions, very little distancing between popular conceptions of leisure and sociological and psychological conceptions; makes the facts 'speak for themselves' too soon, and contrasts 'real life' with scientific activity
- the 'description obstacle', which consists of trying to define the fundamental properties of leisure by an accumulation of descriptive details, the utilization of diverse classifications and typologies to define the 'essence' or the foundations of modern leisure, and sometimes of the methodological excesses
- the 'pragmatism obstacle', which makes the character of a research, whether judged useful or not, a criterion of truth and pertinence, and all too often sustained by sort of latent anti-intellectualism on the part of leisure professionals; it becomes an obstacle to research when it starts to impose conditions, and when the expected practical application acts as a dominant criterion of evaluation
- the 'normative obstacle', by virtue of which many works on leisure too often still contain apologies for leisure
- and a tendency to copy methods and approaches from exact sciences in order to raise the status of human and social sciences (1990:53–4)

Likewise, Burton and Jackson (1990) find a significant discrepancy between the actual state of leisure studies and what scholars in the field believe that state ought to be. Their survey of leisure scholars confirms that, on the one hand, leisure studies has established a strong sense of legitimacy in academic scholarship. During the 1970s and 1980s, the field grew dramatically in the volume of research being conducted, in the numbers of specialist outlets for the findings of research studies, as well as in the number of organizations and forums that exchange research ideas, methods, and findings. Furthermore, a number of social science disciplines and interdisciplinary, multidisciplinary, and professional fields are contributing to the development of leisure studies. On the other hand, there is a widespread belief among leisure scholars that the quality of research and study has not kept pace with its growth in quantity. There is a prevailing sense of frustration with the lack of progress towards the development of a coherent and consistent body of theory about leisure.

In sum, the scholarly field of studying leisure has found its legitimate place within social sciences. During some ninety years of its existence, the analysis of leisure evolved within the context of humanist and reformist ideologies and movements, an increase in leisure participation, governments' intervention and involvement in leisure provisions, as well as the contribution from the humanities and social sciences. Leisure studies is not yet interdisciplinary. Its future development will likely be influenced by new orientations and integration that originate in both the leisure field itself and several 'parental' disciplines. Zuzanek (1991) already finds in the literature attempts to broaden and contextualize the methodological focus of leisure inquiry. In the substantive area, he points to attempts to revive interest in complex work-leisure, leisure-lifestyle relationships. In particular, there is a growing awareness that people's ways of spending their free time cannot be studied in isolation from their other activities and from their own history. Zuzanek maintains that leisure research could benefit from (1) building closer links between the analysis of leisure and other parts of everyday life, and interpreting leisure as a functional part of a daily lifestyle rather than as an entirely autonomous phenomenon; (2) examining leisure as free, yet socially patterned human behaviour, rather than simply as a state of mind; and (3) avoiding 'moralistic bias'.

▪▥ International comparisons

The pre-Second World War European focus on the masses and their education, similar to that in the United States, influenced leisure and leisure studies in France and several other European countries as well (Horna 1988a; Olszewska and Pronovost 1982; Pronovost 1983). North American and European leisure studies in the interval between the two world wars showed a growing awareness of and concern for the masses with their emphasis on the benefits of recreation and the democratization of leisure and education for leisure.

Following that 1930s' drive towards 'cultural leisure', French leisure sociology and leisure studies reached a major turning point in the 1960s. Three aspects of this reorientation stand out: (1) leisure is seen as an integral part of culture itself; (2) a multiplicity of cultures, for example, mass culture, high culture, regional cultures, and popular culture are recognized; and (3) in contrast to the earlier support for popular education, there is a growing movement called sociocultural animation, which supports the aspirations, cultural diversities, and self-sufficiency of common people. The typical topics of discussion in leisure studies revolve around questions of the mass culture industry, the integrating role of cultural politics, popular culture, and the professionalism among sociocultural leaders (Olszewska and Pronovost 1982; Pronovost 1983).

The dominant ideologists of leisure have originated from and belonged to different élite groups. While they were members of the clerical élite in the province of Quebec, in England they were reformists bent on improving the population's material and social conditions, and in France they came from among intellectuals concerned with educating the masses (Pronovost and D'Amours 1990). In each of these cases, just as in America, the dominant intellectual faction acted as spokespersons for that era's ideologies; the sociology of leisure was but the reflection of the era's leisure ideologies.

Czechoslovakia reflected the European trends between the world wars. As elsewhere in Europe, France and Britain in particular, Czechoslovak leisure studies focused on the impact of the shorter, eight-hour work day legislated in 1918; the lifestyle of the masses, family life, weekend activities, consumption patterns, and participation in the social affairs of small communities (Horna 1988a). The prevalent sociological thought in the 1930s' Czechoslovak republic was strongly politically oriented, and it lent an ideological form to the problems of leisure and free time, while the studies themselves were of less practical significance.

The changing trends in the perception of and approaches to leisure on both sides of the Atlantic prompted Parker to compare the American and British leisure scenes. He concluded that the American 'phenomenon of approaching leisure in a workmanlike, instrumental spirit is less common in Britain where there is perhaps more tolerance, and indeed celebration, of idleness' (1980:271). Parker's comparative study posits that leisure in other countries has low priority in terms of government expenditures; it is one of the first areas to be cut back in times of economic stringency. One of the most obvious differences between the United States and Britain is that the former has more developed training for professionals and a greater understanding of leisure behaviour and attitudes. Parker finds that unlike in Britain there is a significant relationship between academic recreation studies and public leisure provisions in the United States. Botterill and Brown (1985:270) also contend that leisure studies in the United States appear to be more functionalist as 'a philosophical difference, influenced by a range of political, social and economic factors, has led the US education system to be more pragmatic than its British counterpart.'

Similarly, Cherry (1979), in his survey of leisure studies in different countries, points out that in America economic analysis has made a prominent contribution to leisure research. Unlike in the United States, in Britain the scene has been dominated by a case-study data collection approach, while in France work towards sociological concepts has been more important. In quantitative terms, America has no rival to world leadership in leisure research and scholarship. The United States is distinguished in leisure scholarship not just for the sheer scale of its effort, but also in the extent to which leisure studies have gone independent (Parker 1980) of other disciplines. Throughout Europe, leisure is more likely to be researched and interpreted from within broader social science disciplines than studied as a separate subject.

Tropp (cited in Parry [1983]) and Parry (1983) suggest that in Britain, the proper understanding of leisure in people's lives has been hindered until recently because British sociology has been strongly reformist in orientation, and British sociologists have been mainly middle class by origin and intellectuals by education. Also, the various levels of British government have never possessed nor felt any need for comprehensive leisure or cultural policies nor has the country ever been aware of leisure problems that require political solutions. Of course, central and local government and their various agencies are major leisure providers in present-day Britain. They cater to the arts and sports, supervise broadcasting, run libraries, parks, and so on, but these provisions have never been seen as a means of promoting officially approved ways of life. Parry (1983) also notes that the sociology of leisure in Britain was and still is committed to the values of liberal and social democracy and reformism. Similarly, Horne, Jary, and Tomlinson (1987) identify three types of interest that evolved during the most formative period in leisure studies: a reformist strand in liberal sociology, elevation of providing-cum-caring professional expertise, and environmental concerns.

Unlike the above orientations, in Germany leisure is considered primarily a residual category (time left over after obligations), or viewed from the perspective of lifestyle or everyday life (Tokarski 1983). According to Tokarski, German studies of leisure are influenced by such approaches as the valve theory, which views leisure as a way of working off excess energy; recuperation theory, which interprets leisure as a major function towards recuperation; catharsis theory, which regards leisure as a release for suppressed emotions and psychological tensions; compensation theory, which purports that leisure compensates for deficiencies, failings, burdens, and constraints; consumer theory, which views leisure as an opportunity for the consumption of commodities; reduction theory, which shows impoverishment of leisure through restrictions at work; generalization theory, which maintains that leisure is an opportunity to reproduce the behaviour repertoire acquired at work; and identity theory, which regards work as that sphere in which an individual does what he or she would also do in leisure time.

To summarize our brief international comparison of leisure studies, Canada and the United States have shared a common emphasis and approaches for quite some time. In contrast, the Europeans differ from their overseas counterparts as well as among themselves. In addition, both Canadian and American leisure studies are becoming more informed about and influenced by the French and British.

▌▌▌ Leisure research

The development and institutionalization of leisure studies cannot be separated from leisure research and its advancements in refining and applying various research designs, procedures, and instruments. Of course, approaches may be selected to accomplish the goals depending on the researcher's theoretical orientation—his or her original discipline or multidisciplinary framework and conceptualizations within the discipline that correspond with the research task. This brief section on leisure research methodologies and techniques is not a substitute for the study of research methods in general. The goal here is to point to some selected, most frequently used research strategies, methodologies, and techniques that are typically applied in the investigation of leisure.

Students of social sciences are already familiar with the general divisions between the macro and micro perspectives, and between the quantitative and qualitative research approaches. Both quantitative and qualitative research seek to articulate dimensions of causality within social life (Scott and Godbey 1990). The two approaches differ in their respective paradigmatic assumptions and the tools needed for their methodological inquiry. Quantitative approaches, with their roots in logical positivism, are characterized by two principal features: human action is explained by social facts, and the methodological principles utilized in discovering facts are guided by the deductive logic of the natural sciences. Quantitative concepts that guide empirical investigation give depth to phenomena in terms of distinguishing characteristics, elemental properties, and empirical boundaries. Qualitative research is closely associated with interpretive paradigms that include symbolic interactionism, ethnomethodology, and phenomenology (Glaser and Strauss 1967; Scott and Godbey 1990). Unlike quantitative conceptualization, qualitative concepts are treated as sensitizing rather than definitive, and understanding human activity requires the researcher's sensitivity to the actor's point of view (Blumer 1954, 1966).

Numerous concrete methods available to the researcher can be placed on a continuum. For example, of the two observation and interviewing methods, neither one can be strictly categorized as a qualitative or a quantitative method. Observation can range from interpretive field research (qualitative) to sophisticated numeric check-lists (quantitative), and interviewing can range from structured close-ended telephone interviews with a random sample (quantitative) to an open-ended life history account using a theoretical sampling procedure (qualitative).

In addition to conducting primary research, secondary data have been used for research purposes by various leisure scholars and practitioners. Among the secondary data analyses, archival research is applied less frequently in leisure studies, with the exception of the history of leisure or, for example, the history of sports associations. The use of available documents, such as statistical data collected by the government or other agencies, is much more frequent. Official government statistics, such as population enumerations, employment and unemployment rates, data on spending by the government or citizens, travel destinations and frequencies of trips, and so on, are regularly collected and the publications are made available for research. In spite of the drawbacks of these sources, mainly because of different research goals pursued by the original agencies, leisure researchers have utilized them with success. Some government departments, for example, Canada Fitness or Alberta's Department of Recreation and Parks, collect information on the frequencies, preferences, and barriers in leisure, recreation, and sports.

Some secondary data originate from sources originally not intended for leisure investigations, such as marketing research or population expenditures surveys. An example of such data use will be presented when we later look at the study by Martin and Mason (1986). Similarly, content analysis of the mass media is popular among those researchers who are interested in, for example, perceptions of leisure or those who analyse the manipulation of leisure messages by the media and commercial interests. In another case, a series of magazine articles profiling local celebrities and their leisure styles was analysed over several years (Horna 1990). These profiles provided a wealth of information on the prominent individuals presented by the magazine as role models to the readers. The development of their leisure preferences and choices, and their current leisure behaviour helped to confirm further Horna's earlier stream model of leisure.

The study by George Lundberg and his colleagues, *Leisure: A Suburban Study*, carried out in the 1930s, is usually quoted as the first major comprehensive research of leisure in the United States. Similar goals were pursued by Robert Havighurst's series of reports, the Kansas City studies, published in the 1950s, and the Middletown studies by Robert S. Lynd and Helen Merrell Lynd, which was first published in 1929 and 1937 (reprinted in 1959 and 1965). The aforementioned Center for Leisure-Time Studies at the University of Chicago applied the interdisciplinary approach in its three major surveys on adaptation through leisure, work-leisure relationships, and the effects of the mass media in the 1950s.

An alternative investigative technique—the experimental method—is common in the natural sciences, but is used less often in the social sciences or leisure research in particular. In general, an experiment represents a test of the influence of one or more independent variables on dependent variables within artificial conditions created by the researcher. Of the few experiments used in leisure research, many were actually quasi-experiments (Havitz and Sell 1991). For example, experiments were designed to test the effectiveness of training programs or to measure the effects of recreational activities and leisure on skill development, changes in attitudes and behaviour, participant perception, and self-concept. Several studies examined the nature of the leisure experience itself, such as studying possible relationships between perceived freedom and pleasure. Havitz and Crompton (1990) examined the influence of attitudes towards the public and commercial sectors, and the effectiveness of persuasive messages on consumers' decisions about recreation. A field experiment to test the general effect of various types of information on consumer reaction to price increases was used by McCarvill and Crompton (1987). Their experiment consisted of providing information about municipal swimming-pools, and included various treatment groups and a control group. Those researchers who have applied experimental research methods do not suggest that this technique can ever replace other research approaches and methodologies. However, experimental studies can provide a valuable complementary function in studying specific aspects of leisure.

A variety of research methodologies, procedures, designs, and tools have been used to study leisure; they have been subsequently assessed and further defined (Gibson 1979; Henderson 1990; Howe 1985; Hunter 1983; Ng 1984, 1985; Ng and Smith 1982; Roadburg 1981; Scott and Godbey 1990; Singleton 1988; Wehman and Schleien 1981). Although none of them has received unqualified support, a brief overview of those applied most frequently is now in order.

▮▮ Quantitative and time-budget research

The typical quantitative approaches that are frequently used in leisure research include questionnaire surveys and structured interviews. The questionnaires used in leisure surveys usually employ both a standardized set of questions and open-ended questions to allow respondents to choose from among fixed-choice responses as well as to give answers in their own words. Most quantitative research projects fall within the traditional domain of sociology, employ univariate or multivariate data analysis techniques, and remain primarily descriptive in nature. The majority of these studies utilize leisure or recreation activities or free time designations as operational definitions of leisure, and demographic and/or socio-economic characteristics as independent variables.

Typical foci under quantitative investigation include a number of issues and leisure phenomena such as popular culture; high culture; the influences of social class relationships on leisure engagement; the 'problem' of leisure; leisure patterns within communities; demographic and socio-economic influences on leisure behaviour; influences of the family life cycle stage on leisure; work and leisure; gender and leisure; age and/or stage in the life course and leisure; life satisfaction/quality of life and involvement in leisure; the role of mass media in leisure; gender-role differences in leisure behaviour; leisure in rural and/or urban contexts; and leisure subcultures (Parry 1983). Howe (1985) maintains that much of the previous improvement in the quality of leisure research has been primarily in the positivist tradition and within the quantitative paradigm, like the works by Burdge (1983) or Tinsley (1984). Mannell (1983) concludes that most of the field research studies were applied and not basic research.

Since one of the most persistent orientations of leisure research has been to uncover and predict patterns of leisure participation and preferences among different social groups, varieties of large-scale quantitative survey research seemed to be the best way to accomplish the task. The 1960s and 1970s in particular were associated with a considerable number of such projects. Kelly's (1978a) study of leisure in three American communities examined life patterns of several hundreds of respondents. John P. Robinson's study (1977b) was based on a sample of over 2,000 American adults who kept complete diaries of their activities for a single day in 1965–6. Later he reported on the Leisure Activity Survey in the United States (Robinson 1983). The data for this study were collected in household surveys by the US Bureau of the Census, which conducted personal interviews with almost 18,000 respondents (approximately 1,500 respondents per month in 1982). British authors Young and Willmott (1975) analysed 2,644 interviews for their study, *The Symmetrical Family*, while Parker's study (1983) on the work-leisure extension, opposition, or neutrality relationship was similarly extensive. A Canadian leisure survey carried out in 1975 (Schliewen 1977) was based on 32,000 questionnaires attached to the regular labour force survey. More large-scale surveys carried out nationally and provincially followed in the 1980s. Horna and colleagues interviewed 562 married or cohabiting couples in 1980-1. The 1992 Alberta Recreation Survey, the fourth in a series of surveys conducted through the mail by the Alberta government, was based on a random sample of 10,299 households.

The surveys listed here still represent only a small portion of numerous surveys of this nature. Concerning the types of analysis, the study by Miriam Bernard (1984), utilizing cluster analysis, is an example. Her work based on lengthy questionnaire interviews dispels frequent misconceptions that young adults are a homogeneous group without problems where leisure is concerned. By applying cluster analysis, the author identifies types of young adults with similar patterns of leisure behaviour, rather than simply classifying activities. In particular, she identifies the characteristics of those who are 'leisure poor' and those who are 'leisure rich' (1984:350).

Other leisure research orientations can be illustrated by the work of researchers in the United Kingdom. We already know about the use of data collected originally for purposes other than leisure studies per se. Bill Martin and Sandra Mason (1986) demonstrate that it is possible to find out about the shifts in leisure interests, and to trace the trends in leisure from analysing the spending data. Their findings, for example, document that during the recession of the early 1980s, leisure spending increased by 2.5 per cent, primarily in home entertainment. Martin and Mason recorded a boom in purchases of video cassette recorders and television sets, and do-it-yourself products. The spending figures suggest to them that leisure during this period was very much home-centred.

Another extensively utilized quantitative approach to leisure research is the time-budget survey in which the distribution of daily life is studied by accounting for every minute and activity (Andorka 1987; Godbey 1981; Godbey and Parker 1976; Mills 1975; Robinson 1977a, 1977b; Szalai et al. 1972). Conventional time budgets concentrate on the distribution of time between various types of activities, time expenditures rather than on overall structures, ways of organizing time into the particular episodes and activity slots, but not on the factors behind them. The first time-budget surveys were carried out by Strumilin in the Soviet Union in 1924, and by Lundberg and colleagues in the Westchester County Survey in the United States in the 1930s, while Sorokin and Berger published their book on the methods and analysis of time budgets in 1939 (Andorka 1987). Further elaboration of time-budget survey methods and analysis was proposed by an international research team under the leadership of Alexander Szalai in one of the largest ever comparative time-budget surveys, *The Use of Time: Daily Activities of Urban and Suburban Populations in Twelve Countries* (1972).

One of the participants in that survey, Erwin K. Scheuch, described in considerable detail their time-budget interview that has subsequently been applied by several other researchers. Orthodox time budgets, however, share two weaknesses because they neither focus on *patterns* nor cover *total* ways of life (Gattas et al. 1986). Thus, although there is information on the amount of leisure activities pursued, the quality of experience or underlying attitudes and motivations are missing. Moreover, in Scheuch's experience (1972), it may be easy to collect answers that presumably show how people spend their time. However, it is very hard to collect answers that correspond with reality. Representing the expenditure of time is one of those subject matters where the reliability and validity of data are extremely sensitive to details in the manner of data collection. Scheuch also found that the perception of how one's time is spent is not only individual-related, but varies with the type of society. He was convinced that the difficulties their research team encountered in collecting and comparing information from twelve disparate countries were related to the structural properties of each society where the survey was carried out.

Similar concerns and questions regarding the accuracy of self-reporting participation rates in particular are raised by numerous other researchers (Chase and Godbey 1983; Sudman and Bradburn 1974). They are concerned not only about errors of omission but also about telescoping errors in which a person reports the occurrence of activities in a time period more recent than when they really happened, or he or she overestimates the number of occurrences. To document that such concerns are indeed warranted, we can examine Chase and Godbey's (1983) comparisons between self-reported frequencies of participation and club records of individuals' frequency of participation. These researchers show that more than 75 per cent of the respondents overestimated, and at least 43 per cent doubled their actual participation rate. Romsa and Blenman's (1985) test of the leisure activity data gathered by two different procedures also demonstrates the problems in this type of information-gathering. The test recorded a 230 per cent difference between the estimates obtained through the time budget (a week-long recording of the place and time of daily activities) and the information gathered by questionnaire. The next section will present a technique called the experiential sampling method (ESM) that can successfully minimize the troubling problem with respondents' self-reporting, inadequate recall of the time and frequency, and other types of under- or overreporting.

In spite of these problems with collecting data on the expenditure of time, the findings from Szalai's international study contributed to the accumulation of new knowledge about both leisure and leisure research techniques (Scheuch 1972). For example, the team observed that a 'yesterday interview' was the most effective procedure, combined with a self-reporting of a day in a diary. Another finding pointed out that the more a person is part of an industrial society with a high degree of communication, and the more educated he or she is, the more likely he or she is to do simultaneous activities. Using a term analogous to 'capital deepening', the Szalai team researchers coined the term 'time deepening' for this phenomenon. They also differentiated between primary and secondary activities. Although the team decided for practical reasons not to record more than two activities during any one time period, the tertiary activity might become crucial in a specific study of the time-deepening phenomenon. Another application of time deepening is the examination of women's leisure and comparisons of gender-differentiated leisure patterns. We have already addressed these concerns, particularly within the sociology of the family and leisure, and from the feminist perspectives. We will return to the empirical evidence in the forthcoming chapters.

Another concern regarding methodological inadequacies focuses on the incorrectly reported or interpreted frequency of participation in some specific activities. For example, people may check several leisure pursuits on a questionnaire, thereby making them seem like an important part of their lives. However, many of these pursuits—sports, games, and other active leisure—take up at most about 1 per cent of a typical adult's life. When participation in clubs, cultural activities, movies, and theatre is added, the frequency only goes up to about 2 per cent (Csikszentmihalyi and Graef 1980). This does not indicate that recreational leisure activities are unimportant in people's daily lives, but it suggests that at least quantitatively, such activities are less important than they are usually thought to be (Csikszentmihalyi and Kleiber 1991). Since passive leisure activities like watching television and reading take up slightly more than a third of discretionary time and socializing takes up another third, it still leaves quite a few hours each week for the kind of leisure that does not show up on most surveys. Csikszentmihalyi (1981) also argues that a single intense leisure experience may be more significant in determining the course of a person's life than thousands of more mundane obligatory experiences: 'a special fishing trip might be remembered forever, and its story told to one's grandchildren'. Thus, the frequency with which one does an activity and records it in a survey might not be its most important feature.

Over the years, various scholars of different theoretical orientations have criticized the excessive reliance on survey methodology (Godbey 1984; Henderson 1990; Mobily 1985). Also criticized have been situations in which method has dictated the problems to be studied by leisure researchers. Howe refers to such a narrow approach as 'the methodological cart driving the conceptual horse' (1985:221). Smith and Haley (1979) are critical of leisure research that depends predominantly on survey methods, is fascinated with statistics and number crunching, and substitutes statistics for theoretical understanding.

In Germany, Walter Tokarski has been disquieted by the state of leisure research in his country as recently as in 1983, but for another reason. Unlike in the United States where empirical, primarily quantitative approach has tended to rule for most of the time, German leisure research has been under a strong influence of theorists, many of them from educational studies. Tokarski charges that 'theoretical, even ideological treatments of leisure tend to predominate. Empirical data are often brought in only to support one's own point of view, while, as a rule, empirical material which might put the statements concerned into question is discarded. In the case of empirical studies it is often too limited in scope' (1983:502).

In sum, quantitative research methodologies and techniques have contributed to the knowledge about and interpretation of leisure patterns and relationships with other factors. Such positive contribution notwithstanding, several drawbacks still affect the quality of the findings as well as their theoretical importance and generalizability.

▥ Qualitative research

Corresponding to the trends among leisure scholars towards accepting or preferring psychological or subjective definitions of leisure as valid conceptualizations, qualitative approaches to leisure research became inevitable. The earlier prevalent focus on the positivist paradigm of studying leisure as time and activity has given way to an examination of leisure meaning associated with an interpretive paradigm. As a number of researchers and practitioners now realize, they are becoming more successful in solving some of the questions surrounding leisure behaviour by taking new ontological and epistemological approaches (Henderson 1990). The turn towards an interpretive, qualitative paradigm and its related methods enables researchers to better understand leisure behaviour. Cherry (1979) speaks for many leisure scholars when he advocates the trend of moving away from correlational models and towards looking at social processes, lifestyles, and leisure patterns from a social-psychological perspective. In Cherry's opinion, existing methods have been inadequate in handling the complexity and multidimensional nature of leisure. Leisure researchers all over the world agree that complex, multifaceted, and dynamic approaches are needed.

Iso-Ahola (1980a) also argues that the structured survey may supply basic quantitative data, but it does not provide information on the subject's own mental experience, for example, the quality of the individual experience and why people do certain things. Iso-Ahola posits that the preference should ideally be for in-depth studies, particularly among theoretically critical groups. Other scholars recommend that emphasis should be on understanding why a person spends leisure within personal 'boundaries', and how he or she is affected in leisure choices and behaviour by human social cognitions (Gattas et al. 1986). In in-depth interviews, subjects can recall earlier conditions and events, reconstruct personal leisure histories and thus assist investigators in understanding how past work, unemployment, family, and leisure experiences affect responses to current problems and opportunities. Respondents' introspection can be an invaluable source of information about the quality, meaning, and nuances of the leisure experience (Csikszentmihalyi 1975; Mannell 1980; Sági 1983).

Qualitative methods cover a wide range of interpretive techniques that 'describe, decode, translate, and otherwise come to terms with the meaning, not the frequency, of certain more or less naturally occurring phenomena in the social world' (Van Maanen 1983:9). Van Maanen further argues that the use of these methods does not exclude the use of the logic of scientific empiricism. Several researchers posit that the qualitative paradigm serves to analytically describe or reconstruct intact sociocultural scenes or groups (Goetz and Le Compte 1984), that qualitative data exist in the form of words, not numbers, and that words provide well-grounded, rich descriptions and explanations of processes occurring in the context of everyday life (Denzin 1978; Glaser and Strauss 1967; Miles and Huberman 1984). Since qualitative studies often occur in a single research setting or examine a single phenomenon, they are well suited for studies of a small group of people or the operation of social process. This is a naturalistic (Guba and Lincoln 1981) way as well as a holistic process of studying human life, systematically eliciting phenomenological information while avoiding purposive manipulation (Howe 1985). Scott and Godbey (1990) point to the unique understanding of leisure involvement that can be gleaned from utilizing a qualitative research process. Specifically, they emphasize those aspects of the qualitative research approach that examine (1) the experience of leisure within the context of day-to-day activities, (2) leisure behaviour as a formative process, and (3) leisure behaviour as a group phenomenon.

Among the frequently used techniques in the qualitative paradigm are the usual data collection techniques such as simple observation, participant observation, unstructured non-standardized interviews, key informant interviews, open-ended questionnaires, the review of documents or other artefacts and physical evidence, and/or some combination of these techniques in a case-study, ethnography, field study, life history, or other personal accounts (Van Maanen 1983). They aim to elicit direct and natural verbal or visual data in a variety of locales and focus on the respondents' views and interpretations. A popular way of illustrating the findings sometimes includes quotes or excerpts from transcribed material. The items are selected randomly or intentionally from the raw data. The interpretive paradigm focuses on the richness of meaning associated with the symbolic contexts of any culture (Rabinow and Sullivan 1987).

The qualitative interview technique, including the face-to-face individual interview, enables subjects to describe in their own words the role of leisure in their lives. Many of Susan Shaw's findings (1984, 1985b, 1988) were possible only thanks to her qualitative, in-depth interviews during which her respondents were encouraged to spontaneously mention specific subjective factors that related to their leisure experience. Like Shaw's findings, one of the most often-cited models of a specific leisure type—serious leisure—developed originally by Stebbins (1982), resulted from a series of in-depth interviews with amateur musicians, athletes, actors, comedians, and astronomers.

Another invaluable source of researchers' insight into the development of people's attitudes, motivations, and behaviour over the course of their lives can originate from life histories. Life histories consist of biographical material collected from individuals through written or tape-recorded recollections. They can provide rich information on the chronological sequence of events within their various personal and social contexts. Such reminiscences do not need to cover an individual's entire life but focus on important transition points, significant other persons and groups, or specific aspects of life experiences. For example, Horna's (1987c) stream model of leisure careers throughout the life cycle originated from taped in-depth interviews with respondents, who reminisced about their lives and the role of leisure.

Written diaries kept by the research subjects are also utilized in leisure research. Diaries record the day-to-day, hour-to-hour activities of individuals. The recorded entries can inform about actual activities at a given time, time expenditures, co-participants, as well as the context of an activity and the feelings about it. Neulinger (1981) applied his 'What Am I Doing' (WAID) diary not only for tracing people's leisure patterns but for helping them to better understand themselves and their leisure or lack of leisure. The WAID diary includes time entries every half hour for twenty-four hours daily and records activities, where they took place and with whom, how they rate the activity on a scale of 100, the reason they chose it, the need satisfied by that activity, and how they felt about it.

More recently, researchers turned their attention towards the experience sampling technique that is viewed as a viable alternative for studying human behaviour, including leisure experience (Larson and Csikszentmihalyi 1983; Mannell and Zuzanek 1991; Samdahl 1992). The experience sampling method (ESM) uses electronic pagers and questionnaire booklets that respondents carry with them everywhere for several days. At the sound of a randomly activated beeper, the respondent answers a series of questions in the questionnaire. The questions typically ask about the activity carried out at that moment, the social and environmental context of the activity as well as the accompanying feelings. One of the great advantages of this expensive and time-consuming technique is that it can minimize or eliminate the aforementioned problems of the respondent's recall. Graef, Csikszentmihalyi, and McManama Gianinno (1983) successfully used ESM in their study of intrinsic satisfactions, and Larson, Mannell, and Zuzanek (1986) applied it in the study of leisure activities as a context for social relationships.

Like quantitative approaches, qualitative methods have their drawbacks as well. In general, they tend to take longer and may be highly variable in content. Moreover, the presence of the interviewer may cause some reaction on the part of the respondent, which creates a potential for unintentional influence. In spite of these problems, qualitative research approaches allow leisure scholars to study those aspects of leisure experience that are inadequately explained by quantitative methods. At their best, the quantitative and qualitative methods complement and support each other in the effort to further our understanding of leisure.

▌▐▌ Research in leisure motivations

To discover people's motivation and participation in leisure activities, would it not be the easiest to ask them directly? A leisure researcher would provide subjects with a list of reasons and ask them to indicate which reasons are applicable for various activities. Although seemingly the most direct and simplest, such ways are considered inadequate by many leisure scholars. When people are asked why they participate in a leisure activity, they do not say 'because of optimal arousal' (Iso-Ahola 1980a:230). It may prove difficult to learn about leisure attitudes by approaching people with the question 'What's your leisure attitude?', since very few consider such general questions. Like so many other researchers, Nisbett and Wilson (1977) found that when people are asked to make judgements about causality or why they participate, they first resort to culturally supplied explanations; such responses are usually stereotypical, although they may accurately reflect a person's basic motivation. Furthermore, since psychological motives or attitudes are strongly shaped by the socialization process and decidedly affected by socio-economic, historical, and environmental factors, the methodology and survey instruments need to reflect these aspects of leisure behaviour as well.

The earlier scales and survey items measuring leisure behaviour, attitudes, or motivations often contrast work and leisure (Burdge 1969; Kelly 1972; Neulinger and Raps 1972; Yoesting and Burdge 1976). The seminal study of central life interests (Dubin 1956) applied a questionnaire that consisted of forty questions. A similar survey carried out by Parker (1983) contained questions such as 'What is your main interest in life?' and 'Do you find that your work encroaches on your free time?' French sociologist Dumazedier (1967) asked workers which activities gave them most satisfaction: leisure, family, or work.

Other primarily psychological and socio-psychological studies focused on leisure activities, but often investigated only one, usually the affective component of leisure attitudes (Fishbein 1967), or they focused on freedom in leisure. Neulinger's pioneering work (Neulinger 1974; Neulinger and Breit 1969, 1971) has stimulated considerable attention to leisure and leisure measurements. The sizeable literature published in the 1980s made a noteworthy contribution to both a better understanding of leisure and the systematic development of instruments and tests to measure leisure behaviour and its underlying factors, including leisure attitudes. Among these instruments are Witt and Ellis's leisure diagnostic battery (1984, 1985) designed to measure perceived freedom in leisure; instruments to measure leisure attitudes and motivations (Beard and Ragheb 1983; Crandall and Slivken 1980; Ragheb and Beard 1980, 1982); the self-as-entertainment construct by Mannell (1984); and Iso-Ahola and Wiessinger's (1987) scale that measures people's perception of leisure as boredom.

Of the two broad areas of attitude research, attitude measurements are becoming more and more relevant to leisure, mainly because of the increased emphasis on subjective aspects in leisure planning and policy decisions (Neulinger 1981). The motivation for leisure is typically studied from two basic aspects that include the motivation for a specific free time activity (similar to the marketing research conducted to identify a person's reason for buying a particular product), and the more general aspect that emphasizes the person and his or her whole repertoire of leisure behaviour, not just one or a few specific activities.

Among the most complex leisure attitude instruments, tested in several pilot studies before the final version was administered to 1,042 subjects, is Ragheb and Beard's leisure attitude scale (1982). This instrument stems from the component conceptualization of attitudes, thus including the cognitive, affective, and behavioural components. The cognitive component is conceptualized as (a) general knowledge and beliefs about leisure; (b) beliefs about leisure's relation to other concepts such as health, happiness, and work; and (c) beliefs about the qualities, virtues, characteristics, and benefits of leisure to individuals. The affective component is viewed as the individuals' (a) evaluation of their leisure experiences and activities, (b) liking of those experiences and activities, and (c) immediate and direct feelings towards leisure experiences and activities. Finally, the behavioural component includes the individuals' (a) verbalized behavioural intentions towards leisure choices and activities, and (b) reports of current and past participation. Each of these components is tested through twelve statements that can be easily administered together or separately.

Another instrument developed by Beard and Ragheb (1983) examines leisure motivation, particularly the psychological and sociological reasons for participation in leisure activities. After initially including more than 150 subscales or items for assessing a large number of reasons, these researchers later suggested a forty-eight-item instrument, divided into four subscales. The four subscales correspond to four motivation components: intellectual, social, competence-mastery, and stimulus-avoidance. Unlike Beard and Ragheb, Witt and Ellis (1984, 1985) focus specifically on perceived freedom in leisure. The revised version of their instrument has twenty-five items representing five key concepts: perceived leisure competence, leisure locus of control, leisure needs, playfulness, and depth of involvement in leisure.

A self-administered leisure inventory, developed by Leisure Lifestyle Consultants (1978), contains items that help individuals to assess their current level of leisure well-being in the areas of coping in leisure; awareness and understanding of the impact of leisure on their lifestyles; knowledge of interests, resourcefulness, and fitness in leisure; and the ability to make time for and adopt healthy attitudes towards leisure.

These qualitative research approaches are used in the psychological and social-psychological instruments of studying particular aspects and contributing factors of leisure behaviour.

▮▮▮▮ Triangulation in leisure research

As we have seen so far, research may require different approaches to tackle different levels of reality (Haworth 1978), and methods or specific techniques are determined by the approach selected for a given research project. The methods selected will depend not only on the paradigm, the general approach, and the questions asked, but also upon pragmatic issues such as the resources available, the time, limits to one's abilities, the focus and priority of the research, and whether breadth or depth is desired (Patton 1980). Recognizing that various approaches have their own limitations, researchers in general combine two or more methods to control or supplement the information obtained from single methods. This process is called triangulation and is associated with its first proponent, Norman Denzin (1978) and his followers.

Triangulation is combining methodologies to study the same phenomenon (Denzin 1978; Jick 1983). It can also mean the use of multiple techniques within a given method to collect and interpret data (Denzin 1978), for example, different scales or indices focused on the same problem. The most prevalent type of combining various research methods is complementing survey methods with fieldwork, social observation, life histories, or in-depth (semi-structured or unstructured) interviews. The use of complementary methods can lead to more valid results and uncover unanticipated aspects of the issue under study. It can capture a more complete, holistic, and contextual portrayal of the units under study, and thus enrich our understanding by allowing new or deeper dimensions to emerge (Jick 1983).

Reichardt and Cook (1979) argue that combining methods is useful, particularly in evaluation because a variety of needs requires a variety of methods, one method can build upon another, and methods have biases so multiple methods can give more valid and reliable information. Since the goal in the study of leisure behaviour is to understand the meaning of the whole, this understanding can be achieved by combining the study of the parts with the study of the whole. To understand the meaning of recreation and leisure, a diversity and triangulation of methods may be essential. Research into individual behaviour, its psychological antecedents, the examination of the broader social context and outcomes can benefit from joining disciplinary perspectives and combining quantitative and qualitative methods through triangulation.

Calls for and applications of 'new' data analysis techniques that are qualitative in nature and triangulated in practice are increasingly mentioned in leisure literature (Dickason 1983; Horna 1987c; Kelly 1982; Shaw 1984; Unger 1982). Several writers who contrasted the differences between quantitative and qualitative research approaches consider the dichotomy between them to be artificial and inexact. They assert that a multidimensional continuum is a more accurate rendering of the research approaches (Cook and Reichardt 1979; Goetz and Le Compte 1984; Patton 1978).

Henderson (1990) offers a novel model for considering the paradigmatic, theoretical, conceptual, and methodological options available for leisure research. In this model, the choice of research methods is based on assumptions about one's world view and epistemological approaches. In Henderson's proposition, differences between the qualitative and quantitative approaches are not viewed as dichotomous, and the qualitative is not presented as the opposite of the quantitative. Rather, the relationship between the two approaches are compared to the Chinese concept of *yin* and *yang*. Henderson further suggests that each approach may be defined in relation to the other, with the differences complementing each other.

In sum, triangulation is gradually being used in leisure research. It represents the most comprehensive tool for investigating the complexity and dynamics of leisure that cannot be adequately revealed by any one limited approach. However, as with any tool, it is only as good as the researcher's overall theoretical perspectives and conceptualizations. It remains to be seen whether or not triangulation will be successfully proposed and applied beyond the methodological considerations.

▮▮▮ Summary

After decades of numerous and often extensive research projects by scores of leisure researchers, Ng and Smith still observed that 'leisure studies, despite the fervent wishes of researchers, is an undisciplined omnium-gatherium of competing ideas, observations, questions, theories, and personalities' (1982:6). The fact that such criticism is at all possible should also indicate to us that the leisure field as an academic and research discipline is a dynamic and rapidly growing area. In the first part of this chapter we examined how, during some ninety years of leisure studies, the analysis of leisure evolved within the context of humanist and reformist ideologies and movements. Furthermore, the increase in free time and leisure participation combined with government intervention and involvement in leisure provisions created a more positive atmosphere for leisure studies. Since the time of the first university programs in leisure in the 1930s, the number of institutions and the scope of their programs has increased dramatically. Regrettably, leisure studies has not yet become truly interdisciplinary in spite of its impressive academic and practical progress.

Canada and the United States have shared, and still do in many respects, common emphases and approaches in leisure studies. These two countries also have much in common with the Europeans. However, there are also differences. Canadian and American leisure studies are becoming more informed about and influenced by the French and British.

The second half of this chapter focused on various methodological approaches that are typically applied in leisure studies. We examined large-scale quantitative surveys that focus on patterns of leisure participation as they relate to demographic and social-economic characteristics and time budgets, as well as several methods that may become alternatives to the standard methodologies. In qualitative approaches, various ways of collecting information include interviews, life histories, and diaries. We have also found that because of the drawbacks of both the quantitative and qualitative perspectives, the process of triangulation can be used successfully to minimize the limitations of any single approach.

The future development of leisure studies and leisure sciences, leisure institutions and associations will likely be influenced by new theoretical and methodological orientations as well as by integrating original perspectives in the leisure field and in several 'parental' disciplines. Researchers will respond to the consistent calls to improve the quality of leisure theorizing and research, and at the same time might attempt to interpret the findings in such a way that they could be used more directly in professional practice.

PART 3

Leisure styles

▥ Part Three addresses the broad patterns or styles of leisure throughout life. It will include data on who does what with whom, when, and why. The focus will be on the forms and interpretation of leisure, the distribution of leisure time, the types of participants and their preferences, participation rates and patterns in leisure, as well as constraints in the pursuit of leisure. We will find out whether most people stay at home or go out, whether they are involved in group or solitary pursuits, whether they are engaged in unconventional activities, and how much of their time they devote to leisure. We will look at men, women, and their families; the young, middle-aged, and elderly.

In the following section, we will ask whether one prefers to listen to Bryan Adams, Guns n' Roses, or a Beethoven symphony? Does one curl up on a couch with a Harlequin romance or a book by Margaret Atwood, or perhaps with a TV remote control in hand to turn on 'Hockey Night in Canada', 'Masterpiece Theatre', or 'Cheers'? Does a person seek information from the dailies, magazines, Oprah Winfrey's talk show, or the CBC news? Are we more interested in Fergie and Di biographies or in the books by Pierre Berton and Peter Newman? Do we prefer to read a book or see its adaptation on television? Is anyone attending performing arts events or visiting museums and art galleries? Are people interested in such cultural pursuits at all or do they prefer to go for a stroll, swim, hike, or a sports game? Maybe bingo? Or perhaps none of the above because all of their free time is devoted solely to serious leisure of one kind or another. Do parents of young children pursue the same leisure activities as their childless counterparts or are they affected by parental responsibilities?

135

In the next chapters, we will examine the amount and allocation of leisure time, discuss the main points pertinent to the high, middle, and low types of culture, taste cultures, or just the binary distinction between popular and high culture. Then we will look at various other forms of leisure and summarize the patterns of participation in them throughout the different stages of the life cycle.

CHAPTER 8

The amount and allocation
of leisure time

The old maxim used to divide one's life into three unequal phases: youth and education, work life and marriage, and retirement. Similarly, it used to be said that the healthy division of daily life should be eight hours for work, eight hours for sleep, and eight hours for leisure. We know from our previous overview that such neat divisions never really applied to the majority of the population—certainly not to the underprivileged groups of society, nor to most women. Rather, they were just unmet recommendations by various kinds of reformers. Do these recommended divisions apply today? What activities do people do? In particular, what pursuits represent leisure in the lives of most people now? What is the empirical evidence at our disposal to document these existing patterns?

We have seen earlier that, by most of the recent definitions, leisure cannot be equated with free time. The amount and distribution of daily time, particularly its discretionary component, represent crucial factors in leisure. The structuralist and conflict approaches to leisure have alerted us to the availability or non-availability of time, facilities, or partners, and the constraints imposed on specific groups or individuals. Other theorists have shown the overwhelming impact of cultural hegemony on leisure. Feminists have emphasized gender inequality in access to leisure and in the degree of freedom of choice and experience. These multiple aspects represent a complex milieu for leisure during everybody's life cycle. This chapter presents further empirical evidence that supports (or contradicts) our earlier discussion of leisure patterns and information from the time-budget studies mentioned in the section on methodologies of leisure studies. The data are drawn from numerous studies undertaken in several industrial countries around the world, primarily Canada and the United States.

▮▮▮ Leisure time: When and how much?

The section on the history of leisure has already challenged the belief that people in the distant past had no leisure. We know that they too had leisure, but their leisure followed rhythms and cycles different from ours. We mentioned that medieval peasants and artisans had to cope with many days of imposed idleness, and that the Industrial Revolution drastically disrupted the lives and annual cycles of the majority of the urban population. A century or so ago, the average work week was about seventy hours long; it began to decline before the end of the nineteenth century. During the past century the amount of time spent at work was reduced sharply in urban industrial societies, particularly among certain segments of the population.

In the 1970s, the urban labour force in many countries generally worked an average of forty hours or less per week (Gist and Fava 1974). According to the German Institute for Economics, the length of the work week further declined during the 1980s and early 1990s in countries such as Germany (37.6 hours), Britain (38.8 hours), and France (39 hours) (*The New York Times*, 26 May 1992). The chief beneficiaries of free time in an urban industrial society are salaried white-collar workers and wage-earners, especially organized blue-collar workers. These employees can close their minds as well as the door on the job at the day's end, and turn their attention to other things. The relatively short work week does not apply to all occupational groups; for example, farm operators, small-business proprietors, and independent professionals tend to work longer hours. As Wilensky observed more than thirty years ago,

> It seems likely that we are headed toward an organization of work in which a small group of executives, merchants, professional experts, and politicians labour hard and long to control and service the masses, who in turn are going to 'take it easy' on a progressively shorter work week, in jobs which de-emphasize brawn and native shrewdness and play up discipline, reliability, and trained intelligence (Wilensky 1960:558).

We have already learned that the earlier prophecies about the imminent arrival of the leisure society have not materialized as yet; perhaps they were premature if not inaccurate. Not surprisingly then, John Kelly raises the question of the 'myth of the declining work week' (1982:121) related to the earlier expectations that the long-term decline of the average work week would continue at the rate experienced in the United States and other industrial countries between the 1850s and 1930s, from some seventy hours to forty-five hours per week. Contrary to those expectations, comparisons with time-use data in 1930s and 1950s show that people now have even less free time than in earlier eras (Robinson 1977a, 1977b, 1983; Robinson and Converse 1972).

Moreover, as historical statistics suggest, greater amounts of leisure time, in the United States in particular, have often been a by-product of job shortages rather than of social design or individual desire (Zuzanek 1976). The amount of time spent by Americans at work has increased rather than declined since the 1930s, for which the first time-budget information is available. Some of the findings, those concerning hours of work among men in particular, contradict the widely shared belief that the Second World War brought shorter hours and more free time.

The presumed consequence of such shorter work hours and more free time was that the nature of work itself would change and, above all, people would use their free time mostly for leisure. The more recent trends show that what is technologically possible is not always economically and socially feasible or acceptable. Furthermore, when it comes to more free time, most workers seem to prefer its accumulation in longer blocks on weekends and vacations, not shorter work days. Since the traditional societies' integration of work with leisure disappeared, the coffee break or tea time customary in offices or shops of most urban industrial countries provide opportunities for workers to find brief respite from their daily tasks (Gist and Fava 1974).

Over a lifetime, Canadians devote approximately one-quarter of their time to work, paid and unpaid, and one-quarter to free time activities, with the other half going to personal care (Harvey 1983). The workload tends to peak in the twenty-five to forty-four year age group rather than spread itself more evenly over a lifetime. Averaged over a lifetime from fifteen years of age, males spend thirty-one hours a week in paid work, fourteen hours a week on home and family care, seventy-seven hours a week on personal care, and have forty-six hours a week left for other activities. The data support our earlier assertions about gender differences, since the time allocations of women show the following distribution: seventeen hours spent on paid work, twenty-seven hours on home and family care, seventy-nine hours on personal care, and forty-five hours for all other activities.

Several societal trends may have affected time allocations (Robinson 1977a, 1977b). These include demographic shifts, a better educated population, women's increased participation in the labour force, and the postponement of marriage and childbearing. Robinson shows that for each increase (or decrease) of an hour of work, only about 60 per cent went into free time activities, with the other 40 per cent going into family care and personal care activities. The Robinson-Converse (1972) comparison of the time-allocation data is just one of numerous studies that show no indication of increasing free time in the adult population. The time spent on the routine aspects of housework had indeed been reduced. More time, however, is spent on the managerial aspects of housework, including the rearing of children and shopping—the tasks that are, as we already know, primarily women's responsibility. The greater drop in work hours for single men is likely due to the lower financial pressure on them to work longer hours, while the greater drop in work hours for married women could be due to the need for them to be at home while working part-time.

Further differences in time use are related to age and education attainment. For example, persons in the eighteen to twenty-five age group report much less work and housework than their counterparts reported previously (Robinson 1977a, 1977b). In contrast, the middle-aged group (twenty-six to fifty-five years of age) show increased time at work, as well as increases in free time. The oldest (fifty-six to sixty-five) age group shows some similarities to the eighteen to twenty-five age group and some contrasts, particularly the largest decline in paid work by almost 50 per cent. However, this has much less impact on the older generation's free time than it does on the younger for two reasons: the older group reports increased time in family care (mainly housework), personal care, and sleep.

The most profound differences in time distribution and leisure participation come with parenthood, affecting women (particularly those employed outside the home) more profoundly than men. The differences are affected by the employment status and weekly distribution of paid work as well as by the asymmetrical gender division of domestic and parental duties (Horna 1989d; Horna and Lupri 1987; Lupri and Symons 1982; Meissner et al. 1975; Zuzanek and Smale 1992). The General Social Survey conducted by Statistics Canada provides ample evidence that if paid work, domestic work, and child care are aggregated, employed mothers with small children, compared to mothers at home, report on workdays two to two-and-a-half more work hours, half an hour less of sleep, and one to two hours less of leisure (Zuzanek and Smale 1992). This difference is less on Saturdays, but is greater on Sundays. When time budgets of employed mothers are compared with those of employed fathers, the pattern shows less asymmetry in the total workload. However, employed mothers have about half an hour less of leisure on workdays, and between two to two-and-a-half hours less per day on weekends.

Contrary to the popular belief that things are getting better and that today's fathers are becoming more involved in domestic and parental tasks, the data indicate that traditional roles persist. The findings of the 1990 Project Canada adult survey indicate that change at home is gradual (Bibby and Posterski 1992). The current patterns of division of labour remain similar to those recorded earlier. Among today's married couples without children, 74 per cent of employed men and 61 per cent of employed women claim that they share the tasks at least equally. However, when couples have children, only 54 per cent of men and 31 per cent of women claim equal shares of the tasks. Not even younger fathers seem to be more inclined to share workloads, since fathers younger than forty are no more helpful than older fathers.

Likewise, the General Social Survey documents that marital and employment statuses strongly affect the amounts and distribution of domestic work, food preparation, and child care among women, but not so much among men (Zuzanek and Smale 1992). For employed mothers, Saturdays and Sundays are not days of leisure but days to take care of tasks not done during the week. Employed fathers, on the other hand, report almost identical amounts of housework throughout the week—levels that are very similar to those performed by single men. This gives both single and married men enough free time for watching television.

Related to this persistent asymmetry is the asymmetrical pattern of men's and women's personal sacrifices for the family. The available data show that wives are still more likely than husbands to sacrifice their career plans and their time for personal interests with the advent of parenthood (Thiessen and Singleton 1993). Given the general gender wage disparity, women's career sacrifice might be a rational choice for many families; however, there is also the issue of equity: if a wife sacrifices her career, will her husband make the sacrifices in leisure time? Thiessen and Singleton show that the negotiations are uneven—the spouse who sacrifices in one area, usually the wife, also sacrifices in other domains. The authors also document that age is related to the pattern of equity to a statistically significant extent, but in a surprising direction that challenges the popular belief that there is more symmetry among young couples. It is the younger couples who report a greater inequity, since the equity position of spouses under thirty years of age is substantially less gender-balanced than among those who are over thirty!

Summarizing the above empirical evidence, when measured by time budgets rather than aggregate labour statistics, work time did not decline during the postwar period nearly as much as expected. In particular, if the family rather than the individual were used as a unit for measurement of work, the total work hours outside the home for an average family would likely exceed those of the 1930s considerably, primarily due to the greater female labour force participation. Furthermore, because of longer hours of travelling to and from work, increased labour force participation, moonlighting, and more household obligations, some time-budget studies actually indicate a decline in leisure time (Robinson and Converse 1972; Zuzanek 1976). Other studies show continued gender differences and leave no doubt about the veracity of feminist claims of gender inequality in time distribution.

ⅡⅠ The core and balance leisure activities

The empirical evidence about participation in leisure activities proves to be both complementary and contradictory. Some researchers find mostly similarities, even identical patterns among individuals, social groups, and countries, while others' findings emphasize the variability and specific relationships with demographic, socio-economic, and individual role characteristics.

Some authors argue that the seemingly constant innovation in new leisure activities does not significantly alter the general leisure pattern. In fact, most innovations occur within well established social patterns and divisions (Roberts 1978), or within the leisure activity streams (Horna 1987c, 1987d). Although particular activities may be changed, dropped, or added frequently (Alberta Recreation and Parks 1981–92), only a minority make radical changes, which are mostly short-lived. Momentous changes—major shifts in societies' ways of life—tend to occur over generations, not years. In Roberts's opinion, this applies to changes instigated at the grass roots, such as the long-term trend towards home-centred living. It would be misleading to assume that leisure is a peculiarly resilient sphere in which people are able to hang on to tastes and styles of living that are handed down virtually intact from generation to generation. On the contrary, we can observe both rapidly spreading new leisure trends as well as new leisure patterns that will spread only gradually and then endure for very long periods.

An interpretive model that can assist us in sorting out some of the contradictions is the model of leisure patterns that divides leisure into core and balance activities (Kelly 1987). The core activities are almost resource-free for those living with others in a residence and are mostly relatively low cost and accessible. Watching television, interacting informally with other household members, conversing in a variety of settings, and engaging in sexual activity are common to adults throughout life. Other such activities include walking, residential enhancement, reading, and some regular events undertaken with kin and friends. Core activities occupy the greatest amount of time, especially those periods between scheduled events. Further, core activities that express and develop primary relationships are highly valued by most adults. Core activities tend to cross social lines largely due to their relative availability.

The balance or peripheral activities tend to vary more throughout life (Horna 1987d) as well as among individuals with different access to resources and of different sociocultural backgrounds (Kelly 1987). The balance may include occasional entertainment and cultural events or family outings. According to Kelly's and others' research, the similarities in patterns among different social strata are greater than the differences among them (Kelly 1987). Rates of camping, for example, vary little except for the upper élites and those who are poverty-stricken; however, styles of camping can be readily distinguished by cultural background and social position. Furthermore, practically all surveys reveal a significant number of activities that are common to most adults and do not vary greatly throughout life (Kelly 1983). We are reminded that Bella (1989) and several other feminists view camping or holiday-making, even if equally frequent, as more work than leisure for most women, particularly mothers of young children.

Clearly at odds with Kelly, Joan Smith (1987) reports that occupational status remains a generally relevant factor in leisure behaviour, at least in the United Kingdom, although in the number of activities, gender overrides differences of occupation. Women in general, regardless of occupation, take part in fewer activities than do men; however, a manual/non-manual divide in leisure activities appears to exist for both men and women. A distinctive semi-skilled/unskilled male workers' culture is also apparent, based on pub culture (darts and snooker) and betting, and these men are least likely to go dancing, which is a favourite leisure activity for women. The female version of this male culture is bingo. Women in the highest occupational group are the most active in cultural and civic pursuits, but not in physical ones.

According to Smith's analysis, several points stand out: while most home-based activities stay the same (watching television, listening to the radio, and visiting friends), others such as listening to records and reading books decline markedly for both men and women in households with small children in comparison with households without any children. Although the proportion of men who play darts and snooker is only slightly reduced for men with young children compared to those without children or with older children, pub-based leisure is common only for women without children, even though bingo is a frequent activity for women with small children. Activity rates for going to the theatre, films, or shows and for going dancing also decline for women with young children. There is a significant break in activity for adults in households with children under five; this break is apparent for both men and women, but it is more dramatic for women. Community activity and family commitments appear to be in conflict for men, but are more complementary for women.

Recall also our earlier discussion on perceptions or interpretation of specific activities and motivations for particular types of leisure. It makes it possible to distinguish between primary and secondary activities and to posit that an activity that takes place during a particular time period, for example, watching television or reading, could easily be specified as 'being home in the evening with the family'. That is, when an individual is at 'home in the evening with the family' while watching television or reading the paper, 'being home in the evening with the family' may be the primary activity and watching television or reading the paper the secondary activity. It will be useful to find out in future research whether not only the balance activities but also the primary or secondary activities are more prone to shifts in interests and preferences.

▥▮ Leisure patterns in Canada and the United States

Drawing on data available from the 1981 Canadian time-use pilot study (Statistics Canada 1983), we discover that respondents spend on average two-thirds of the day at home, 12 per cent at the workplace, 6 per cent in transit, and 5 per cent in someone else's home. Approximately 35 per cent of the day is spent alone, 30 per cent with family members, 15 per cent with co-workers, 15 per cent with relatives and friends, and approximately 25 per cent of leisure time is spent alone. Reading and listening to the radio are two activities mostly done alone; on the other hand, 50 per cent of television viewing time is spent with family members. For over 50 per cent of the time spent attending entertainment events and visiting cultural facilities, respondents are accompanied by relatives and friends, and for 33 per cent of this time, by family members. Three-quarters of the time devoted to the media, mostly television viewing and reading, is spent in the respondent's home; however, almost half of all listening to the radio, records, or tapes occurs away from the home. About 25 per cent of listening to the radio is done in transit, while 20 per cent of the time spent listening to records and tapes takes place at a neighbour's or friend's home.

Other sources, however, provide a somewhat different picture of the leisure time availability and distribution. According to the findings on the weekly time distribution, collected by Decima Research and Les Consultants Cultur' Inc (1992), there is some divergence in the amount of time Canadians say they have available to spend on leisure activities. Six in ten say they have between ten and thirty hours a week, the mean number of hours being seventeen. Many of these leisure activities appear to take Canadians out of their homes for a number of evenings a week. In fact, over half (52 per cent) of the population report that they are out of their homes at night for non-work related reasons at least three nights of the week. Only 6 per cent report that they do not go out of the house at least one night a week.

Among the non-work activities, respondents spend on average 42 per cent of the day doing two or more activities simultaneously as the primary and secondary activities (Statistics Canada 1983). An average of 5.3 hours of primary activities are spent in leisure pursuits. In secondary activities, 9.3 hours are spent on leisure in conjunction with some other activity. The most common secondary leisure activities include talking, relaxing, and listening to the radio. Thus, of the reported 5.8 hours per day spent on talking and relaxing, only 15 per cent occur as a primary activity. A sharp contrast is found in the primary/secondary breakdown of media activities: 95 per cent of the 2.2 hours is spent on average in listening to the radio while doing another activity such as eating, travelling to work, or reading, while television viewing is a primary activity 65 per cent of the time. This study also documents, perhaps not surprisingly, that 20 per cent more time is given to leisure activities on weekends than on weekdays. Activities showing the greatest time increase on weekends are entertaining and visiting family and friends, exercising, and attending entertainment and cultural events. The major exception to this pattern of increased leisure time on weekends is reading newspapers, since more time is spent on reading newspapers on Wednesdays and Fridays (approximately half an hour each day) than on any other day of the week.

One of the special features of this Canadian study about time use was asking respondents to record all activities occurring in the evening at 7 p.m. The recorded events were then categorized according to four variables: the respondent's age, number of children living at home, who participated with the respondent in the activity, and where the activity took place. Fifty-four subgroups were formed using these four variables, and the five subgroups most frequently participating in leisure as a primary activity were identified.

The five groups, which accounted for 45 per cent of leisure participation at 7 p.m., included (1) respondents fifty-five years of age and over, with no children living at home, who participated in the activity at home alone (accounting for 12 per cent of all 7 p.m. leisure activity); (2) respondents fifty-five years of age and over, with no children living at home, who participated in the activity at home with family members (10.8 per cent); (3) respondents fifteen to thirty-four years of age, with children living at home, who participated in the activity at home with family members (10.2 per cent); (4) respondents fifteen to thirty-four years of age, with no children living at home, who participated in the activity at home alone (6.4 per cent); and (5) respondents fifteen to thirty-four years of age, with no children living at home, who participated in the activity with persons other than family members away from home, but not in transit (6 per cent). For all groups except Group 5, media activities predominated. Of the individuals classified under Group 5, about 33 per cent were visiting friends, 22 per cent were talking or relaxing, and 15 per cent were engaged in media activities, while the remaining 29 per cent were involved in a wide range of activities, including exercising, playing sports, pursuing hobbies, and playing games. All five groups reported television viewing as the most frequent media activity, but Group 3 respondents differed from the others in some ways. They were three times as likely to watch television at 7 p.m. on the weekend than on a weekday, and their weekday evenings at 7 p.m. were more likely to be devoted to child care and housework.

Horna (1988b) reports that, similar to findings made by numerous other researchers, watching television is one of the core leisure activities for the overwhelming majority of her respondents in Calgary, Alberta. Approximately 80 per cent of both men and women in her study watch television often or at least sometimes on all days of the week. The proportion of those who go without television viewing is lowest on workdays (17.8 per cent of men, 16.6 per cent of women), however, the average length of time periods devoted to television on these days tends to be shorter. On Saturdays, 26.2 per cent of men and 30 per cent of women report watching no television at all, but this is the day when most of them go to the movies or live performances. Fewer couples watch television on Sundays than on workdays; however, those who do usually spend longer periods in front of their TV sets, while others typically visit relatives and friends or entertain in their homes.

The most frequent co-participant when watching television is the spouse or both the spouse and children; only 6 per cent of men and 2.7 per cent of women watch television alone. Most respondents watch television for fun or relaxation (74.2 per cent of men, 72.9 per cent of women), some (13.8 per cent of men, 16.2 per cent of women) do it because they have nothing else to do, while a mere 2.1 per cent of men and 3.1 per cent of women use television as their source of learning, and some even feel guilty about their television addiction. For example, one respondent said, 'I wish I did not watch TV. I watch too much TV and I could be doing something better with my time than sitting in front of the television.' Another reported 'I seldom watch TV without doing something else—a hobby maybe or chores, or ironing, but it's not a steady thing.'

Horna's respondents' reading habits differ more noticeably between men and women, as women tend to be somewhat more avid readers (34.5 per cent of men and 45.7 per cent of women read often, 20.8 per cent of men and 13.8 per cent of women read only rarely in 1980–1). Reading also varies by the day of the week, with more people reading on workdays than weekends; however, weekend readers spend more time doing so. Unlike in many other leisure activities, the gender gap in mass media use is not significant, particularly for television. Reading patterns for printed media show greater gender differences than for television or other visual media. More women than men read primarily fiction books, while a greater proportion of men prefer reading how-to and educational materials.

The comparative data drawn from the time diaries collected in Jackson, Michigan and Halifax, Nova Scotia show numerous cross-border similarities as well as some differences. According to Harvey's report (1982) on this project, the category of discretionary or free time activities, television, leisure travel, social visiting, and entertaining guests account for over half of all discretionary events in both Jackson and Halifax. In comparison with other countries of the multinational project, North Americans have more discretionary time and spend it in ways that differ from those of Europeans. In both Jackson and Halifax, the major portion of discretionary activity is home-oriented, spent in the company of other people, in the evening, and on activities of over an hour's duration. More than half of all discretionary time accrues in the evening, with approximately another quarter accruing in the afternoon. Although over one-third of discretionary events are of a short duration, they account for less than 7 per cent of total discretionary time. A greater portion of discretionary time is spent with the family.

The increase or decline in leisure participation is recorded by Warnick (1987). His recreation market calculations show that the participation changes are quite complex, as they respond to the process of aging as well as to the market offers and social movements such as the fitness movement. The expanded choice of activities may affect individual activity rates over and above the impact of demographic variables. It is likely that when a person has more activities to choose from, he or she may not change the total amount of leisure time but still participate in each activity less often or not at all in some of them, which would affect the overall statistics. Furthermore, overall participation rates by all adults seem to decline in many recreational activities; however, they appear to be somewhat cyclical even within a relatively short five- to ten-year period. For example, golfing, which decreased from 1975 on, increased again in the 1980s. Participation in the sport of the decade, racquetball, peaked and declined during the same decade. The 1980s also introduced a new phenomenon—leisure participation rates were higher among older adults than young adults in a wide variety of activities, some of which were traditionally thought to be youth- and young adult-oriented, such as fitness activities, health club membership, and travel.

The evidence collected by Geoffrey Godbey (1981) documents that the dif-

ferences between the more or less affluent or between the more or less educated are not in how much free time they have but in what activities they
choose. The commonality of life patterns found in various groups makes it
impossible to establish consistent, systematic, or significant differences in time
usage between different regions of the country, between urban and rural locations, or even by weather and seasons. Referring to various time-budget
studies, Godbey posits that overall, Americans spend more time with the mass
media than people in any other country surveyed, primarily watching television, and spending the least time in reading books. Participation in sports and
outdoor recreation activities, while an important part of leisure, represents
relatively minor expenditures of free time. Outdoor recreation activities consume less than 1 per cent and active sports 3 per cent of the free time of
employed men, 2 per cent for employed women, and 1 per cent for homemakers. Yet, according to Godbey, Americans still spend more time in active sports
participation than any other surveyed nation, and less time in outdoor recreation in comparison with those surveyed.

The results of a province-wide study carried out in Quebec (Morin 1992),
which pays particular attention to participation in cultural leisure activities,
show that women's participation in cultural activities has not lessened over
the years, and that women participate at greater rates than their male counterparts. However, specific rates of participation and preferences for particular
types of reading, television programs, performing arts, and sports are not only
gender-based but depend on age and socio-professional status of women as well.

Most preferences for specific leisure activities change among individuals.
The average reported preference for specific leisure activities generally declines over time, significantly more so for men than for women. Even over the
first two years of marriage, husbands and wives show no pattern of increased
leisure preference (Crawford, Godbey, and Crouter 1986). According to the
Alberta Public Opinion Survey on Recreation (Alberta Recreation and Parks
1981, 1984, 1988), males under thirty-five years of age put ice hockey at the
top of their favourite activities, older men prefer camping and golf, while their
female counterparts in all age groups list walking as their number one favourite. Creative activities, however, lag behind sports considerably, ranking seventeenth.

Tokarski's (1984) findings on working men aged twenty-five to fifty show
that adults not only pursue different activities but imbue some of these activities or groups of activities with different meanings. Some activities appear to
be multifunctional to varying degrees, while others are basically unifunctional.
For example, do-it-yourself activities and gardening are associated with happiness, satisfaction, activity, efficiency, self-confidence, subordination, accommodation; sports with activity and efficiency; and spending time with the
family, which includes watching television together, is associated with happiness, satisfaction, individual interests, and self-confidence.

Similarly, findings from the Alberta Public Opinion Survey on Recreation

(Alberta Recreation and Parks 1981, 1984, 1988) indicate several different patterns in reasons for participation, some of them age-related. Specifically, respondents feel that reasons for participation such as improving skills or knowledge, learning new skills and abilities, spending time alone, being away from the family, competing, looking for challenge or excitement decline in importance with age; however, other reasons, such as helping the community, enjoying nature, or relaxing increase in importance with age. Moreover, some reasons are particularly important to young adults and older adults, but are of less importance in the middle-age years, in particular reasons such as proving one's ability, keeping busy, being creative, doing things with friends, meeting new people, or doing something because one excels in it.

In spite of several inconsistencies, if not contradictions, it is possible to conclude that present Canadian leisure activity rates and patterns (aside from core activities, which show little differentiation) are associated with demographic and socio-economic characteristics of the population. We will attempt to find out later whether or not the cold climate, which has so far received little attention from leisure researchers, affects leisure participation rates as well, and whether it has a greater impact on sports and exercise or on cultural pursuits. Knowing the recreational activities of pioneer life, discussed earlier, we may speculate that the overall influence of the climate is quite likely mediated through the present social differentiation; for example, those with flexible work schedules or high incomes might find it easier to avoid cold climates by travelling to warm places than the poor, whose leisure opportunities are limited. These aspects are reflected in the preference for sports at the expense of culture among most Canadians.

▮ⅠⅠ Leisure patterns overseas

Most of us are curious about people in other parts of the world. We already know about some historic and geographic differences, but what about more recent trends? Are we similar in our leisure patterns or do we differ? If we are different, how much do we differ and in what areas? Finding answers to these questions can shed more light on general social phenomena and our own patterns.

The most detailed comparative information about the allocation of time originates from one time-budget study that covered twelve nations (Belgium, Bulgaria, Czechoslovakia, France, West Germany, East Germany, Hungary, Peru, Poland, the United States, the Soviet Union, and Yugoslavia) and was carried out by an international team of researchers headed by Alexander Szalai in 1965–6 (Szalai et al. 1972). This survey examined (1) working time and related time, (2) domestic work, (3) child care, (4) purchasing goods and services, (5) private needs such as meals, sleep, etc., (6) adult education and professional training, (7) civic and collective participation activities, (8) spectacles, entertainment, social life, (9) sports and active leisure, and (10) passive leisure. The team's findings document general gender discrepancies in the allotment of time, with additional differences related to specific countries or cultures. For example, European women experience a loss of about an hour of their free time daily if they are married, while married American women retain about the same amount of free time as they had before marriage. In some European countries, the presence of children did not seem to change the individual time pattern, while respondents in the United States recorded a loss of about 1.5 hours per day.

The time data for Australia, not included in Szalai's project, show that households with children spend more time on both household production and paid work in comparison with households without children (Ironmonger and Richardson 1991). In both types of households in Australia, women spend more time on household work, while men spend more time on paid work. Australian men spend much less time on household work, compared with both wage-earning and non-wage-earning women. Similar data are reported from Canada (Horna and Lupri 1987).

A shorter work week presented significant changes for most employed people and their families in former Czechoslovakia. The gradual shortening of the weekly work time from forty-eight hours (which lasted until 1956) to forty-six hours until 1966 was followed by a decrease to 42.5 hours in 1968 and accompanied by the introduction of the two-day non-work weekend. It necessitated an increase of daily work time to eight and a half hours, affected the availability of free time on those days, and shifted most household chores (done primarily by women) to Saturdays (Horna 1989b).

Comparing several European countries, Scardigli (1989) focuses on leisure and lifestyle in France and other European countries in the 1980s. According to him, the European style closely mirrors that of the United States and falls within a lifestyle of technological consumption, whereby the consumer is growing accustomed to everything that has a price, even activities formerly provided by the family or locality (education, leisure). In spite of this trend, Europeans' daily life is centred around the home at the expense of community life. The home is where an increasingly large part of social relations and leisure activities take place. The proportion of cultural activities outside the home is no higher than 15 to 19 per cent for the cinema and theatre in both Great Britain and France. In Scandinavia, Belgium, and Italy, people devote two hours per day to television, three hours in France and Spain, and four hours in England. Spare time has increased considerably through the extension of annual holidays and the reduction of the work week. Maria Carmen Belloni, in her study of Italians' daily use of time (1985), shows a substantial homogeneity in the choice of interest in everyday life and a stable distribution of time spent in various interest areas. In her opinion, the influence of biological or physiological variables is stronger than that of cultural variables in the organization of everyday life. The use of cafés and similar places appears to be a matter of national custom, especially in Poland, Hungary, France, and Yugo-slavia. For instance, not only men but women in Poland and Yugoslavia meet their friends in cafés (Kaplan 1975). Scardigli (1989) also notes the growing preoccupations related to individual expression and personal creativity, health and the body, as well as declining social and political involvement, including the decline in union membership and community life.

Reports on lifestyles and leisure patterns in Nottingham in the United King-dom, based on a survey and time-space diaries kept over a three-day period, including a weekend, come from Susan Glyptis (1989b). This survey asked respondents to record where each activity took place (which room in the house, or which facility or location outside the home) and with whom. In addition, they were asked to describe each activity as work, leisure, duty, chore, personal care, etc. On average, individuals recorded forty-eight events in the three-day period. Women's activity patterns were more fragmented than men's and more home-centred. On average, men undertook forty-three events, thirty-five at home and eight elsewhere; women undertook fifty-one events, forty-five at home and six elsewhere. Overall, 119 different activities were recorded, but individual lifestyles were quite specialized. Apart from gen-der differences, there were few statistically significant variations in the activ-ities undertaken by different social groups.

As in so many other places, almost all of the Nottingham respondents spent most of their time at home. Eighty-six per cent of all their daily activities took place there, and 61 per cent of all leisure time was spent in the home. Leisure accounted for 36 per cent of time, duties 11 per cent, and work 9 per cent. Thirty-nine per cent of time was spent alone, though leisure activities were slightly less solitary. Approximately 20 per cent of all time was spent with people apart from the immediate household. People living alone tended to lead a largely solitary existence, but they were more likely than family house-holds to spend some time with friends, and more likely to spend leisure time out of the home. Glyptis mentions several single people who did not take advantage of the spontaneity available to them as some left the house only for work and shopping, led highly structured lives, and were self-sufficient in the use of time.

According to yet another examination of specific patterns in the United Kingdom, 45 per cent of adults could be described as participants if a broad definition of sports is adopted, encompassing virtually all forms of physical recreation as well as some non-strenuous activities such as darts (Roberts and Brodie 1989). Wide differences in levels of sports activity, however, are found even among the more active members of the public. Furthermore, opening a new facility does not necessarily result in greater numbers of active particip-ants. After the initial novelty visits, the regular users, who tend to be those who already play, move into the more convenient or better appointed space. Thereafter, new participants are most likely to be drawn from groups with the strongest predisposition, who are most easily attracted, which generally means younger people (Roberts et al. 1989). Roberts and Brodie (1989) report no narrowing of age inequalities in participation.

Further evidence by Roberts and Brodie confirms that sports careers are most vulnerable during certain life cycle stages. A sharp drop in sports participation after completing full-time education is particularly evident, more so among women than men. The postparental phase is another critical period when individuals often reshape their domestic and recreational habits, and sometimes their work involvement also. Lapsed and infrequent players are likely to increase their involvement, given sufficient incentive and opportunity, during the years preceding retirement. Otherwise, there is no decline in the frequency of active participation in sports. More men than women play sports at all ages and in all socio-economic groups, although the gender gap in sports participation has narrowed in recent decades (Kamphorst and Roberts 1989). In Britain this gap is narrowest within the higher socio-economic strata, and widest within the lowest. For example, working-class women in Britain have an exceptionally low sports participation rate, and when they do take part, their participation in a sport tends to be less frequent than other players', male or female (Dench 1988). While sports are a more central interest in boys' peer groups, teenage girls in particular resort to all manner of strategies to avoid school games (Scraton 1987). Dependent children usually interfere with their mothers' time and activities, but they can also be a reason why some women visit sports centres.

Unlike many North American authors, scholars in the United Kingdom document that social class differences, especially in sports participation, show no recent trend towards narrowing class inequalities. The proportions playing sports have risen in all socio-economic strata, but without narrowing the gap. Thus some games are highly exclusive, whereas others have down-market appeal, for example, bowls, martial arts, and soccer had the highest proportions of working-class players (Dench et al. 1987; Roberts and Brodie 1989). These sports, plus swimming, are also particularly attractive to the unemployed. Even when they play the same games, individuals from different social strata tend to belong to different teams and leagues, and to use different facilities. However, according to these authors, the main class difference is in whether individuals play any sports at all. The exceptional groups are an upper middle class with unusually high participation, and the non-skilled working class whose members are most vulnerable to unemployment and poverty, where participation lags well behind average levels. For men and women who remain in postsecondary education, sports participation is the norm (Furlong et al. 1989; Roberts et al. 1988).

An example of leisure patterns in France is based on the study carried out in Rambouillet by Linda Hantrais (1983). At least 90 per cent of her respondents reported reading, watching television, listening to the radio, and entertaining or being entertained by family and friends. All daily and frequently mentioned activities required little prior planning or specialized equipment.

Since the French, particularly commuters, return home much later in the evening than their counterparts in, for example, England, and then spend more time over the evening meal, their evening activities rarely begin before 8:30 p.m. Consequently, young parents in particular curtail their social life. However, Hantrais also finds that marriage affected leisure behaviour in only about 30 per cent of cases, while the arrival of children brought about shifts in leisure for nearly half of the respondents. Cultural, social, and sports activities, particularly among women, are abandoned most often.

In Finland, 63 per cent of the population spend their free time at home, 10 per cent in another household, and 27 per cent go somewhere else (Niemi, Kiiski, and Liikanen 1986). Watching television and socializing top the list of leisure activities at 23 and 25 per cent of the total free time respectively. Almost 70 per cent of Finnish respondents watch television on weekdays and 80 per cent on weekends, men for longer periods of time than women. Other activities include reading at 14 per cent of free time, and sports and outdoor recreation (13 per cent of men, 8 per cent of women). According to the diaries, every third Finn on weekdays, and more than every second on Sundays is engaged in sports and outdoor recreation. The rates of participation in cultural and entertainment events, socializing, and organized sports and outdoor recreation, however, decrease with age. Reading books also decreases, but reading newspapers and listening to the radio as primary activities increase with age. Moreover, the rates for outdoor recreation, walking, and watching television are the highest among the youngest and oldest age groups.

In sum, it appears that Europeans and Australians have more similarities than differences with North Americans.

▉▉ Summary

The available findings on the patterns of leisure participation can be best summarized in the most comprehensive overviews drawn by Jiri Zuzanek. Published in 1976 and 1978, they are as applicable today as they were when they were first formulated. Most of the subsequent studies may have added further details; however, their major thrust remained unchanged. For example, Desaulniers and Théberge (1992) argue that the traditional gendered division of labour has been remarkably resistant to changes. Likewise, Luxton's (1980) analysis of couples in Flin Flon, Manitoba, Hochschild's (1989) analysis of US couples, as well as other related research findings, document very little variation from the findings by Meissner and his colleagues published in 1975.

In Zuzanek's overview of a number of leisure participation studies and surveys about the relationship between leisure, demographic characteristics, work, income, social class, and social status, he presents a complex picture of leisure. In relation to gender, he concludes that (1) the overall participation rates in leisure activities do not differ much between men and women; (2) women take somewhat greater part in cultural activities while lagging behind men in outdoor recreation, active sports, sports spectatorship, and home gardening; (3) non-employed women show slightly higher participation rates than employed women in most leisure activities, except going out to dinner, active sports, and sports spectatorship; (4) the total number of leisure activities in which women engage is smaller than that of men; and (5) the similarities in leisure participation rates between men and women are more striking than the differences.

However, the gender differences in the allocation of leisure time are considerable, particularly for middle-age groups and families with a large number of children. Generally, women have less leisure time than men. This is particularly true of employed women who have to carry the dual burden of the job and the household. In some societies, homemakers also have less free time than men. The inequalities increase considerably for married women with small children. The overall smaller amount of leisure time for women results in lower amounts of time for almost all leisure activities, and much less in active sports and outdoor recreation.

With regard to age and time, Zuzanek's overview indicates that the largest amounts of leisure time appear to be concentrated in adolescence or after retirement. The amount of leisure time over the life span changes curvilinearly with the younger and older age groups as both have more leisure time than the middle-aged. Moreover, the amount of leisure time is inversely related to rates of leisure participation as is obvious in old age when the increase in leisure time occurs simultaneously with a reduction in participation rates in most leisure activities. Another look at participation rates indicates that (1) the rates of participation for the overwhelming majority of leisure activities decline with age; (2) of activities that are relatively unaffected by the change in age, going to the opera, reading, working around the house, and watching television are quoted most often; (3) the decline in participation rates has a different slope for different activities—it is steeper for active sports or participation in public entertainment than it is for such activities as golfing or driving for pleasure; and (4) it is likely that, at least with respect to some activities such as entertaining at home, playing cards, and volunteering, there is a curvilinear trend with a slight increase of participation rates in the late preretirement, early postretirement years.

Among the socio-economic factors, Zuzanek finds formal education to be the best predictor of participation in leisure. However, he emphasizes two qualifications in this respect. First, the clear-cut positive relationship between education and participation rates in leisure activities appears only if the so-called minimal participation is measured. Minimal participation in leisure activities means participating at least once during a given period of time, usually twelve months. If more frequent participation is measured, educated individuals are significantly involved in only about half of the activities, perhaps because they may occasionally sample a wide variety of leisure activities, but are intensively involved in only a few of them. Secondly, the linear relationship between education and rates of participation in leisure activities does not hold true at the level of a master's degree and above. These findings allow Zuzanek to conclude that (1) the rates of participation for most leisure and recreational activities increase almost linearly with growing levels of education, (2) there may be a saturation point within this relationship at the very highest levels of college education, and (3) the few leisure activities that do not correlate positively with education include watching television, listening to the radio, playing cards, woodworking, knitting, attending sports events, fishing, and hunting.

Other conclusions made by Zuzanek show that participation in leisure activities is closely and positively associated with the social status and prestige of one's occupation. Professionals seem to be participating in a wider spectrum of leisure activities and at a higher rate than other occupational groups, while labourers and resource workers report the lowest rates of participation. Although attempts to connect certain leisure and recreational activities with particular occupations are subject to considerable disagreement between researchers, it appears that at least some activities acquire status through association, and intrastrata differences in rates of participation caused by the type of work and age composition of particular strata may be more pronounced than interstrata differences.

Since income correlates strongly with both education and socio-occupational status, Zuzanek is not surprised that the high-income groups report higher rates of participation in most leisure and recreational activities. In general, (1) rates of leisure participation correlate positively with a group's social centrality and social and educational status; (2) participation in leisure is of a cumulative rather than exclusive nature; thus, participation in certain leisure activities does not preclude but usually encourages participation in other even seemingly unrelated ones; for example, cultural participation usually parallels higher rates of participation in sports; and (3) the educational level is the most important predictor.

CHAPTER 9

Popular culture

The introduction and development of contemporary leisure forms and patterns are intertwined with popular culture. The definitions of popular culture are rooted in general sociological theories and approaches to leisure. Many definitions of popular culture are simply based on its content, through the inclusion or exclusion of specific components. For example, the *Handbook of American Popular Culture*, edited by Inge (1989) includes, among others, chapters on the automobile, circus and outdoor entertainment, computers and video games, and gardening. Other authors define or classify popular culture according to its popular, mass consumer appeal and its wide, ready acceptance, while yet others emphasize the mass-communication means of disseminating popular culture. The literature usually distinguishes among high (or élite) culture, middle culture, and low culture, or highbrow, middlebrow, and lowbrow culture (Glazer 1964). Sometimes we read about taste cultures or just two opposites—popular and high culture (Gans 1974). Frequently, the terms 'low culture' and 'mass culture' are used interchangeably with the term 'popular culture'.

The concept of popular culture is often conceived quite broadly as it covers a wide range of contemporary phenomena, cultural forms, and products that are relatively widespread in a given society (Barbu 1976). Barbu is one of a few authors who draw a distinction between the notion of a popular culture and that of a popularized culture, indicating the popularity or the quality of being widespread.

Other authors who discuss popular culture typically refer to those preferences and objects that are widely distributed across all the social classes in a society (Teevan 1989), or to the typical ways in which a society, or type of society, spends its time when not working (Kando 1980). Stebbins (1990) defines popular culture as a cultural subsystem of products shared by a large number of people who are in the same social class or group. He also points to its wide appeal, although the attraction is largely confined to a particular social class or other social grouping. Nye's definition implies that popular culture denotes majority culture, or the culture of the middle class, which in industrial societies represents a majority of the population. He states that 'popular culture is the most visible level of culture, the one found between the extremes of élite and folk culture' (1972:19). *The Encyclopedic Dictionary of Sociology* posits that

> Popular culture is often used as a synonym for mass culture and is contrasted with élite or high culture. While mass culture refers to all aspects of life in modern mass society, popular culture is usually limited to the popular arts and entertainment. It includes television, radio, recording, advertising, sports, hobbies, fads, and fashions.
>
> Mass culture (also called pop or popular culture), the way of life produced in advanced industrial countries. Mass culture involves standardized material goods, art, life styles, ideas, tastes, fashions, and values. It is a homogenized product of the mass media (1986:173, 216).

Most authors who point to the wide distribution of popular culture also suggest that societies develop a popular culture in relation to the availability of mechanisms and technologies for reaching mass audiences. It follows that the use and development of popular culture become dependent on the development of mass media that are widely distributed and inexpensive. How much daily leisure depends on the mass media will be discussed in the next sections.

Thus, according to the theorists of popular culture, popular culture consists of materials and activities that are mass-produced, acquired through some form of commercial exchange by members of a large and heterogeneous audience/consumer group, and is characterized by formulaic, conventionalized form and content (Sanders 1990a). The mass media and popular culture have developed hand in hand thanks to the rise of new technologies for reaching large numbers of people and the growth of new audiences with greater disposable incomes. More specifically, as Hebdige (1982) points out, 'what we call popular culture—a set of generally available artefacts: films, records, clothes, TV programs, modes of transport, etc.—did not emerge in its recognizable contemporary form until the post-War period when new consumer products were designed and manufactured for new consumer markets.' McPhail and McPhail (1990) also refer to standardized cultural products created solely for the mass market at minimal cost and without attention to excellence, and they note that the role of the media in bringing mass culture to audiences is unquestioned.

DiMaggio (1977:448) posits that 'the extent of diversity and innovation available to the public—and, conversely, the degree of massification of culture—has more to do with the market structures and organizational environment of specific industries than with strongly felt demands of either the masses or their masters for certain kinds of homogeneous cultural materials.' Similarly, MacDonald (1964) argues that mass culture represents a 'homogenized culture' and is fabricated for passive consumers by technicians hired by businessmen. Such mass culture is a debased, trivial culture that contributes to the 'infantilization' of the adults and 'adultization' (overstimulation) of the youth. However, Kelly (1981) challenges such views and claims that popular culture is more than a market response to taste; it symbolizes and expresses developmental reality and authenticity in people's lives. Kelly believes that the meaning and appeal of popular culture cannot be explained simply as entrepreneurial manipulation even though it is a product of the economic market.

Most of the following discussion will cover a more narrow interpretation of popular culture as the cultural objects and leisure activities that consist primarily but not exclusively of the mass media and popular arts shared by a large number of people in a given society.

ⅢⅡ Popular culture and élite culture

Typically, popular culture is contrasted with high culture and, sometimes, with folk culture as well. Folk culture is culture that is shared and transmitted through direct oral communication, which is typical of traditional or preindustrial societies. It can be interpreted as a traditional cultural subsystem (Stebbins 1984, 1990) that is shared, transmitted, and experienced directly through the senses. Thus folk culture is simple in form when contrasted with popular culture and high culture. In contrast with the known and often highly publicized creators of nearly all popular culture and high culture, creators of folk culture are unknown.

Élite/high culture refers to those preferences, habits, tastes, values, and norms that are characteristic of or supported by high-status groups in society. They include the fine arts, classical music, ballet, and other 'highbrow' pursuits (Tepperman and Rosenberg 1991), activities for which John Meisel (1974) uses the term 'aesthetic culture'. In addition to the wealthy who pursue high culture, people with more formal education are most likely to patronize high-culture events and products. Furthermore, popular culture, widely available at moderate cost to the consumer, contrasts with high culture, which is comparatively scarce and expensive. Both the critics and the defenders of popular culture seem to share a respect for the values of high culture, which is perceived as superior to mass culture, although perhaps not readily accessible to the masses (Zuzanek 1988). Apparently, high culture excludes many more people than it includes.

As we will see at the end of this section, Gans (1974) proposes a pluralistic view of culture. Within that, he defines high culture as a collection of those products that are consumed by a special public or category of consumers, a public that is dominated by creators and critics. In fact, most authors point out that popular culture is consumer-oriented, while élite culture is creator-oriented. The standards of high culture are set for the users or consumers by the creators and critics of high culture. The polarization of high/élite culture and popular culture is often expressed as the dichotomy between their creators, products, or performers. From Gans's pluralistic perspective, however, high culture and popular culture differ from one another in degree, not in kind. Gans urges a recognition of the plurality of taste cultures instead of a hierarchy of high and low cultures. Also, he believes that high culture is not threatened by popular culture.

Popular culture also reflects the influence of high culture and can contribute to the wider availability and acceptance of high culture. Zuzanek (1988) mentions the arguments of the defenders of mass culture represented by the writing of D.M. White (1957), who proclaimed after NBC's television production of Richard III that the mass media held the greatest promise for 'average' people. The contemporary mass media could provide a cultural richness not previously accessible to the majority of the population. Do people care? Gans (1974:114) observes that `there seems to be less resentment about cultural inequality than about other kinds of inequality. While poorer people want the money and power available to upper-income groups, lower taste publics apparently do not feel deprived by their inability to participate in higher taste cultures.' Apparently, lower taste publics strive for more education to gain occupational and social mobility rather than cultural mobility, and when they become upwardly mobile, they often maintain their former taste culture. Instead, middle- and working-class people develop and make use of a popular culture of their own (Tepperman and Rosenberg 1991).

We can see that the unequal distribution of taste cultures and cultural items across classes is not disputed. What is important is the role of such inequality. French sociologist Pierre Bourdieu (1984), whose work we already introduced in the chapter on sociological theories, shows how the unequal distribution of cultural items across social classes represents and reproduces social and political inequality. Bourdieu coined the term 'cultural capital', which refers to a body of knowledge, educational attainment, and interpersonal skills that help people to enhance social relationships and advance socially. One form of cultural capital is represented by high culture made available to the children of upper- and middle-class parents. For Bourdieu, culture is an instrument of ideological domination.

Unlike so many theorists who view popular culture as the opposite of élite culture, Herbert Gans (1974) offers a pluralistic view of culture and its popular component. Gans presents an image of society as composed of interdependent 'taste publics' with preferences for specific cultural items and events— taste cultures. Taste publics enjoy their particular cultural forms and differentiate 'good' from 'bad'.

> In reality, there are a number of popular cultures, and they as well as high culture are all *taste cultures* which function to entertain, inform, and beautify life, among other things, and which express values and standards of taste and aesthetics. Taste cultures, as I define them, consist of values, the cultural forms

which express these values: music, art, design, literature, drama, comedy, poetry, criticism, news, and the media in which these are expressed — books, magazines, newspapers, records, films and television programs, paintings and sculpture, architecture, and, insofar as ordinary consumer goods also express aesthetic values or functions, furnishings, clothes, appliances, and automobiles as well (Gans 1974:10).

Gans further posits that taste cultures are not cohesive value systems, and taste publics are not organized groups. Nevertheless, in his opinion, the major source of differentiation between taste cultures and publics is socio-economic level or class. The five publics and cultures that Gans distinguished are called high culture, upper-middle culture, lower-middle culture, low culture, and quasi-folk low culture (1974:71).

The pluralistic position advocated by Gans and a few other theorists is considerably less frequently presented in the literature than the view that emphasizes the dichotomy between popular culture and élite or high culture. We will see later that popular culture, like all forms of culture, is fragmented along age, gender, and social class lines, and is typically expressed as people's preferences and tastes in reading materials, types of music and television programs, dress codes, eating habits, and even living-room decorations, to name a few examples.

▓▌ Concerns and criticism

Élitist critics of popular culture—whether of the leftist or conservative orientation—tend to view popular culture (and mass culture in particular) with dislike, even distaste. The leftists, for example, Horkheimer and Adorno (1972) and Marcuse (1955), argue that mass culture is primarily profit driven, trivialized, and produces naïve, uncritical, and passive consumers. Although based on different premises, conservative criticism takes a similar position that emphasizes the trivial, brutal, or otherwise unworthy nature of popular culture resulting in the decline of society's moral standards. An example of specific criticism aimed at the peculiar sentimentality and superficial allusions to morality found in most modern mass culture is represented by Ann Douglas's *The Feminization of American Culture* (1977). She argues that those characteristics first appeared in nineteenth-century popular literature written for (and often by) women.

More recently, the concept of hegemony, originally proposed by Antonio Gramsci, is being applied in the critique of popular culture by several of Gramsci's followers. Gramsci's (1971) idea of hegemony suggests that the ruling class gains the subordinate groups' active consent to social and political inequality in large part not by the use of brutal force but through the use of ideological apparatus, including mass culture and the cultural industry. Gruneau, Whitson, and Cantelon's (1988:265) theoretical standpoint grounded in the work of Gramsci posits that 'cultural and ideological practices are important sites in the production and reproduction of social order'. Using the example of televised sports, these authors argue that meanings and practices that are integral to a class society and masculine hegemony are reinforced through sports and television. Their data show 'that sport on television maintains an especially reverent attitude towards the image of the individual, and that the theme of individual (as opposed to team) performance is one of the main structuring characteristics of sport programming' (1988:277).

Similarly, Hebdige (1982) suggests that the issue of taste—of where to draw the line between the good and bad, low and high, the ugly and the beautiful, the ephemeral and the substantial—emerges at certain points as a quite explicitly political one. In Hebdige's opinion, profound social and economic transformations have been mediated through aesthetic concepts like 'quality' and 'taste'.

Yet another argument related to the issue of taste comes from Gerald Kenyon (1991) who suggests that economics is a key ingredient, both in the production and consequences of taste, in fostering the use of taste as a symbolic power in social worlds beyond the arts. On the production side, taste is determined largely through the forces of the market-place. As paid admissions are inadequate in covering cultural institutions' financial needs, the corporate world has supported the arts. Kenyon argues that the greater corporate involvement in the arts is associated with stronger intercorporate ties and the reinforcement of dominant ideology. He finds that arts industries have become multinational, with interests mostly in large-scale productions of blockbuster exhibitions mounted by the world's major galleries and museums or the megaproductions of *Cats*, *Les Misérables*, and *Phantom of the Opera*. Furthermore, the market forces have become significant and powerful in the distribution of cultural products, and the multinational control of cultural industries has become well established. For example, the capacity of the film industry to open new films simultaneously in cities around the world has powerful influences upon taste, including its homogenization.

In Canada, a conscious struggle over its cultural identity represents a unique feature of Canadian life, culture, and politics. We have already touched upon this phenomenon in our discussion of historical origins, influences, and development of leisure in Canada. In comparing different countries, Merelman (1991) suggests that, unlike in the United States or Britain, Canada explicitly promotes or suppresses culture as such, be it French, British, or a mosaic of ethnic cultures. Culture in general and its Canadian production and content in particular are a legitimate political issue.

Although Merelman finds that individualism is less common in Canada than in the United States, the combination of religion, language, and region provides a sharp dividing line in Canada. A markedly dualistic cultural structure is often expressed through the choice of American mass media. American television series, especially those of the American sitcom family, that are popular south of the border are also popular in English-Canadian homes. By contrast, French Canadians do not watch most American television sitcoms, but prefer French-language programs. (The only programs with comparable French- and English-Canadian audiences are 'Dynasty', 'Dallas', and 'Hockey Night in Canada'.) Merelman suggests that the greater popularity of American programs among English Canadians than among French Canadians is probably a matter of culture—the culture of the family itself.

Bibby and Posterski (1992) also document that American television is exerting a dramatic influence in Canada, especially in the ways Canadians construct and interpret the world, including the Canadian world. They posit that 'Our concerns, from the economy to drugs; our dreams, from success to travel; our heroes, from rock stars to politicians; our perceptions of Canadians versus Americans—all are largely made *in the U.S.A.*' (1992:64). According to the survey of youth, carried out by Bibby and Posterski, virtually every choice made by teenagers in a number of areas, such as television programs, singers, movie stars, professional sports, authors, television newspersons, politicians, and world leaders, was American over Canadian. For example, tops in their respective categories were the likes of 'Beverly Hills 90210', Guns n' Roses, Julia Roberts and Arnold Schwarzenegger, Michael Jordan, Stephen King, Dan Rather of CBS, and Connie Chung of NBC.

In sum, the criticism addresses multiple issues—from the dichotomy between popular culture and high culture, the negative influences of mass, trivialized culture on the public to the manipulation and commodification of popular culture, the cultural hegemony mediated through the production of taste and aesthetic conceptualizations, the multinational control of cultural industries and of their products, and the Americanization of Canadian mass media.

▓ The products and the consumers of popular culture

We recognize that broadly conceptualized popular culture may incorporate a variety of elements, such as dress codes, speech patterns, automobiles, collecting popular artefacts, road signs, and much more. In this section, we focus on popular culture as leisure consumption of the mass media in general. The contrast with the pursuit of high- and middle-culture activities, and the utilization of performing arts, museums, and exhibitions is mentioned only cursorily. We will examine more specific patterns of the use of popular, mass-produced cultural products as well as élite culture in a later chapter when we turn to an examination of the socio-economic and socio-demographic variables and life cycle stages.

Mass media habits
Virtually all contemporary industrial societies devote a considerable amount of time and frequency of participation to the mass media, television in particu-

lar. Numerous studies have shown that the overwhelming majority of both youth and adults 'consume' one or more of the mass media on a daily basis (Hedinsson 1981; Horna 1988b; Kando 1980; Kelly 1983; Lull 1982; McQuail 1985; Parker 1983; Robinson 1981; Shaw 1984; Szalai 1972; Wilensky 1964). Canada is no exception.

The averages that are typically reported about the numbers or rates of participation do not adequately express differences across the entire population. Keeping in mind this shortcoming, we still find considerable revealing information. We learn that nearly 23 per cent of Canadians aged fifteen years and over allocate a good part of their typical day to some leisure activity. Over 53.5 per cent of these leisure pursuits involve the consumption of the media, primarily television, while listening to the radio, watching rented films, and reading newspapers and magazines come second (Parliament 1989). It becomes obvious that the most commonly reported activities are those that take place at home.

Of course, easy accessibility to the mass media makes these patterns possible, since 97 per cent of Canadians live in a household with at least one television set (Vipond 1989). Virtually every Canadian has access to radio service and all but 1 or 2 per cent of the population can receive at least one television station (McPhail and McPhail 1990). The average amount of time devoted to television viewing was 3.2 hours per day in 1976 and not much different in 1987 at 3.4 hours per day. Young men eighteen to twenty-four years old comprise the group that watches television the least, while older women sixty years of age and over watch the most. Among the provinces, the largest proportion of television viewers live in Newfoundland, while the fewest viewers live in Alberta (Gregg and Posner 1990). The average weekly rate of television viewing in the 1980s was almost twenty-five hours, the most frequent watchers being women (an average of 27.4 hours per week), Newfoundlanders (twenty-seven hours), older people, and lower-income earners (Vipond 1989).

In fact, as many researchers and marketing experts have asserted, the lives of most people have been rearranged over the past forty years to accommodate their viewing habits. For many, television is the prime controller of leisure time, since the television schedule plays a major role in the arrangement of people's schedules (Bibby and Posterski 1992). Married men and women in particular not only watch television often, but more than 50 per cent of them do so for up to three hours on weekdays. The proportion of those who watch television for three hours or longer is about 15 per cent on weekdays and some 20 per cent on Saturdays and Sundays (Horna 1988b).

Furthermore, 88 per cent of Canadians listen to records/tapes/CDs and 85 per cent read books (Decima Research and Les Consultants Cultur'Inc 1992). The average Canadian spends 19.9 hours per week listening to the radio (McPhail and McPhail 1990). Interestingly, radio audiences appear to make very selective individual decisions about their chosen programming, more so than television audiences. When calculating the rate of listening to the radio as a primary activity only, the frequency is, however, considerably lower (Horna 1988b). Only 5.8 per cent of men and 8.5 per cent of women report that they listen often, while 43.5 per cent and 38.9 per cent of men and women respectively say that they listen only infrequently. Almost half of all listening to the radio and other audio recordings occurs away from home, with about 25 per cent of this done in transit (Statistics Canada 1983b).

Decima Research and Les Consultants Cultur'Inc (1992) report that a little over half of the respondents in their representative sample of the Canadian population read a daily newspaper, and almost all report reading a paper at least once during the week, with regular weekend readership equalling if not surpassing weekday readership. Large proportions of the population also spend a good part of their week tuned into radio and television. Close to half the population report devoting at least ten hours to either media, and few report no exposure during the course of a week. In particular, about half the population indicates viewing popular culture programs regularly. Rates of viewing situation comedies follow behind news programs, then come sports, variety and talk shows, and night-time drama. There is considerable interest in television plays. Likewise, interest in popular types of the performing arts on television is quite high, with close to 40 per cent reporting that they watch this type of programming regularly.

Of the television shows watched regularly, the most popular are movies— in all, 87 per cent of the Decima Research and Les Consultants Cultur'Inc's respondents view TV movies. The researchers are not sure, however, of the extent to which these are rental videos or actual programming; if they are rented videotapes, then in fact news, current affairs, and documentaries represent the most frequently watched types of television programming.

Some reported differences in program preferences stem from the basic cultural orientation of the audience (Decima Research and Les Consultants Cultur'Inc 1992). The traditional performing arts audiences (enthusiasts of ballet, contemporary dance, drama, comedy, avant-garde theatre, symphonic music, pop symphonic music, chamber music and soloists, choral music, opera) are more likely to prefer dance, classical music, and opera on television too. A similar dividing line is found between performing arts audiences and the public overall. Both agree on the importance of news and documentary programs, but disagree widely on other types of programming preferred. Among performing arts audiences, no one type of program receives a clear second preference since all night-time drama, situation comedy, sports, and traditional performing arts shows are viewed at approximately the same level, albeit well below the rate for news and documentaries. Popular culture audiences (who prefer musicals, pop/rock, stand-up comedy, folk, jazz and blues, country and western) watch more pop, rock, and country music shows. At the same time, popular performing arts audiences also report that they are more frequent viewers of situation comedies, variety, and talk shows.

Vipond (1989) too finds that television remains primarily an entertainment medium. On English-language television, almost 80 per cent of the viewing time is spent on dramatic programs, variety programs, popular music, quiz shows, and sports. For French-language viewing, the comparable figure is 69 per cent. Of the total viewing time in English Canada, 71 per cent is spent watching foreign (mainly American) programs; the percentage being even greater during prime time from 7 to 11 p.m. While only 4 per cent of the prime-time drama programs are Canadian, 81 per cent of the news and 62 per cent of public affairs programs are domestically produced. Sixty-five per cent of all French-language viewing during prime time is of Canadian programs; however, 68 per cent of French-language drama programs are still foreign, many of them dubbed American movies.

Using the data from the Task Force on Broadcasting Policy, McPhail and McPhail (1990) likewise posit that Canadians are not only voracious consumers of electronic media products but prefer popular culture programs. The authors report the following distribution of viewing patterns (Monday to Sunday, 6 a.m. to 2 a.m.) for English- and French-language television audiences:

Table 9.1 Percentage of total television viewing

Program type	English language	French language
News	12	13
Public affairs	6	12
Sports	12	12
Drama	48	36
Variety/music/quiz	19	21
Other	3	6
Total number of program hours available	51,900	20,700

Together with Bibby and Posterski, we emphasize that a primary source of information for an ever-increasing number of Canadians comes from American television. The rate is growing thanks to cable television, which now reaches some 75 per cent of Canadian homes and offers packages of about fifteen US channels. 'In the course of watching an average of some three hours of TV a day, Canadians are gazing Stateside for two hours and viewing so-called Canadian programming for one hour ... even existing Canadian networks and local channels are swamped with U.S. programming, limited only by CRTC guidelines. Seemingly "pure", Canadian news programs on CBC and CTV draw liberally from American networks' "feeds"' (1992:63).

Another typical factor in mass media consumption, with the exception of reading, is its collective aspect. Most people watch television and go to movies with their family members or friends. Three-quarters of the time devoted to the media is spent at home (Statistics Canada 1983b). Bibby and Posterski (1992), Friesen (1990), and Markson (1990) observe that young people in particular listen to music with their friends, use music as a means of socializing, and are often oblivious to the lyrics. Statistics Canada (July 1983) reports that 20 per cent of time spent listening to records and tapes takes place at a neighbour's or friend's home. Horna's (1988b) data document that even with multiple television sets in many Canadian households, television viewing is a solitary activity for only 6 per cent of men and 2.7 per cent of women. Similarly, only 3.4 per cent of both men and women go to the movies alone. When adults listen to music while doing nothing else, about one-quarter of them is joined by the spouse.

Movies
This section examines only the trends in watching feature films in movie theatres, not watching films on television or playing rented films and recorded video tapes on vcrs. This discussion is related to our earlier history section that showed how movie theatres in the cities started shortly after the turn of century. The growth of movie theatres and attendances was quite rapid. The average Canadian saw twelve movies per year by 1936, eighteen by 1950. As movie-going peaked in 1952, almost 263 million paid admissions were recorded, only to end abruptly with the arrival of television in 1952. By 1975, however, paid movie admissions dropped to 97 million. In a period when the population of Canada grew by 57 per cent, the number of visits to the movie theatre fell by 63 per cent. Whether the rates of attendance were high or low, American influence in film distribution was as strong as in other forms of popular culture. For example, in the early 1950s, about three-quarters of all feature films shown in Canada originated in the United States, while the remainder were almost exclusively European, as only 0.1 per cent of the films were from Canada (Vipond 1989). It was not much better thirty years later since the percentage of theatrical time in Canada devoted to Canadian films in the 1980s was still only 3 per cent (Gregg and Posner 1990).

According to Vipond's (1989) assessment, movies began to cater increasingly to teenagers and young adults and to audiences desiring more explicit sex and violence than television allowed. Another change that came after twenty years of relative stability in the early 1980s and caused an abrupt drop in audience numbers resulted primarily from the introduction of vcrs and pay-tv movie channels. The availability of movies for viewing at home has likely negatively affected the need to go to movie theatres. vcrs in particular can satisfy the desire for increased choice in and control over the program and time of watching. Although the data indicate that vcr owners and cable subscribers are younger, better educated, have higher incomes than average, and are more likely to be professionals (McPhail and McPhail 1990), we may speculate that some lower-income people, home-bound individuals, and single parents may prefer vcrs as a source of entertainment that is cheaper, after recovering the initial purchasing cost, than going to the movies. Thus, it is perhaps not at all surprising that by the late 1980s, the average Canadian went to the movies only three times a year.

At the beginning of the 1990s, 67 per cent of Canadians reported going to a movie at least once a year; however, just 3 per cent see a movie at a movie theatre at least once a week, 14 per cent at least once a month, and 29 per cent never or less than once a year (Decima Research and Les Consultants Cultur'Inc 1992). Those who report going out to a movie theatre on at least a monthly basis, are invariably younger, since 48 per cent of those aged sixteen to twenty-four do so, and 19 per cent of twenty-five to thirty-four year olds do, while only 8 per cent of those thirty-five years or older report monthly movie attendances. The proportion of people who attend movies increases steadily in relation to the community size from a low of 46 per cent in communities of under 10,000 people to 64 per cent in cities of 100,000 to 999,999 population, and to a high of 72 per cent among people living in the three Canadian communities of 1 million or more.

The main pattern of visits at a movie theatre—low frequency—is basically the same among married people as well. Married couples apparently do not go to the movies too often, since 13 per cent of married men and 10.1 per cent of married women report never going, and only 10.7 per cent of both men and women indicate that they go often (Horna 1988b). Married people go to the movies almost exclusively with the spouse and/or with their children, while fewer than 5 per cent ever go alone.

In sum, we can observe that the mass media, especially television, represent the chief means of distributing and consuming popular culture. The numbers of television viewers are overwhelming and the daily or weekly duration of their activity is considerable. The audio-visual mass media provide entertainment and preferred grounds for socializing in and out of the home. Whether the audiences are aware of it or not, Canadian mass media remain under a strong American influence in both the anglophone and francophone regions of the country.

▮▮▮ Summary

This chapter introduced the concept of popular culture and its élite counterpart. Our interpretation emphasized popular culture as the cultural objects and leisure activities that consist primarily but not exclusively of the mass media and popular arts shared by a large number of people in a given society. We also contrasted popular culture with folk culture typical for traditional or preindustrial societies, and with élite or high culture, which is usually viewed as culture characteristic of or supported by high-status groups in society and include the fine arts, classical music, ballet, and other highbrow, aesthetic cultural pursuits. Furthermore, we presented the pluralistic view of culture based on the notion of taste publics and corresponding taste cultures.

Moreover, this chapter could not avoid the controversy about different types of culture and the criticism of popular culture in particular. Thus, we discussed the dichotomy between popular culture and high culture, and the negative influences of mass, trivialized culture on the public. This chapter also addressed the manipulation and commodification of popular culture and cultural hegemony through the production of taste and aesthetic conceptualizations and the multinational control of cultural industries and their products, as well as the Americanization of Canadian mass media.

Finally, we focused on patterns of mass media habits and movie theatre attendances. We discovered that three-quarters of the time devoted to the media is spent at home. In addition to examining specific rates of participation, we emphasized the collective aspect of mass-media consumption, with the exception of reading. We found that most people share especially television viewing and movie attendances with their family members or friends. Young people in particular listen to music with their friends and use music as a means of socializing. Such findings will be further explored in the next chapter.

CHAPTER **10**

More forms of leisure

The mass media may be omnipresent in the lives of most people in industrial societies, but people pursue other leisure activities. There is a man who built himself a climbing wall in his garage and now practises mountain climbing in the comfort of his home; there are members of the Society for Creative Anachronism, who play at being knights and fair ladies; there are stamp- and coin-collectors, white-water rafters, ham-radio operators, volunteers, gardeners, doll makers, archers, body-builders, builders of miniature trains and bridges made of toothpicks, tennis players, mushroom and berry pickers, players of 'Dungeons and Dragons', horseback riders, barbershop singers, dog fanciers, marathon runners, amateur actors, painters, and sculptors.

In this chapter we will focus primarily on physical recreation and sports, on high culture, and a few other forms of leisure in Canada. This discussion complements the overview of the amount and allocation of leisure time and the discussion of popular culture.

▮▮▮▮ Sports and physical recreation in Canada

As mentioned earlier, sports and physical recreation have always played an important role in the lives of many Canadians. We have seen the movement towards organized amateur sports, the establishment of parks and facilities, and various attempts to control the types of sports played by Canadians.

Rates of participation
Organized and non-organized amateur sports, physical recreation, fitness, and exercise pursuits are a relatively significant component of leisure in the lives of many Canadians. However, they were usually not among the core activities, even in the 1970s and 1980s. Physical activity for leisure reached high rates in total time and consistency of participation in the 1980s (Canada Fitness and Amateur Sport 1983). According to the findings from the Canada Fitness Survey, more than half of Canadians aged ten years and older are

physically active in their leisure time, while 11 per cent lead sedentary life-styles. Men's and women's rates of participation are becoming almost equal (57 per cent and 55 per cent respectively), with somewhat more women being sedentary (13 per cent vs 9 per cent of men), and still almost one-third being only moderately active (32 per cent of men, 30 per cent of women).

The active population, however, is not a representative cross-section; participants tend to be younger, better educated, more often single, in managerial or professional occupations, and live in the west (Canada Fitness and Amateur Sport 1983). Single Canadians in particular are more active (63 per cent), while married people are less active (49 per cent) than the national average of 54 per cent among those fifteen years of age and over. Young people are more active than their parents and grandparents, as there is a decreased participation rate from 68 per cent among the fifteen- to nineteen-year-old group to 47 per cent among the forty to fifty-nine year olds, to 53 per cent in the sixty and older category.

Conversely, more sedentary people are among the older generations; in particular, 13 per cent of those forty to fifty-nine, and 21 per cent among people in their sixties or older. Women sixty years of age and older are more active than women in their forties and fifties—as active as women in their twenties and thirties. Moreover, while 11 per cent of teenagers ice skate regularly, none of those forty and older do so regularly. Overall figures show that older Canadians do not skate even occasionally. Some 30 per cent of them are involved in curling on a regular basis (Canada Fitness and Amateur Sport December 1984–February 1985). There are also over 5,000 male and female Master Swimmers from eighteen to seventy-seven years of age who swim and compete regularly; many are also involved in the Red Cross and other Learn-to-Swim programs (Butcher 1993). In the natural resource-based activities, such as caving, rock climbing, and hang-gliding, men vastly outnumber women in the United States (Johnston and Blahna 1993), and the same seems to be the case in Canada. What is perhaps more surprising is that young people are leaving organized sports at an alarming rate (Stephens and Craig 1990).

Among the respondents recently surveyed by Decima Research and Les Consultants Cultur'Inc (1992), the following rates of participation in activities undertaken in the last year are reported: 56 per cent of respondents gardened in season, 47 per cent hiked or camped, 43 per cent biked recreationally, 31 per cent fished or hunted, 28 per cent skied cross-country or downhill, 23 per cent played golf, 18 per cent played a racquet sport, and 14 per cent went bird- and/or whale-watching. Of those who played some sports or exercised at a club, 29 per cent do so once per week, 12 per cent once per month, 9 per cent five to ten times per year, 10 per cent one to four times per year, and 30 per cent less than once a year or never.

Activity levels in sports and physical recreation pursuits show positive relationships with social status, occupation, or education. As the educational attainment increases, so does the likelihood of participation in sports and physical recreation: 63 per cent of people with university degrees, 56 per cent with high school education, and 41 per cent with primary education are active. Similarly, managers and professionals tend to be more active (60 per cent in comparison with 53 per cent of other white-collar workers and 48 per cent of blue-collar workers). Among women in particular, participation in both sports and exercise activities is on the increase (Canada Fitness and Amateur Sport October 1984); however, they vary widely in both the type and degree of activity. The highest rates are among well-educated, young, single, white-collar women.

The amounts of time devoted to various leisure activities differ. Also, some activities may peak and decline within a very short period. More important, however, would be what we already know about the prevalent preference for core leisure activities as well as the profound impact of parental and occupational roles in the lives of most adults. Women's obligations in the domestic and parental domain in particular impinge on their discretionary time. Curiously, Johnston and Blahna (1993) find that in the case of cavers, rock climbers, and hang-gliders, the men regard family and household responsibilities as the most constraining, while women's low participation seem to be influenced by socialization to more 'appropriate' activities for women.

Regional and seasonal differences
Overall regional differences expressed in lower proportions of sedentary people and higher proportions of active adults can be observed as one moves from East to West. Also, more physically active adults are more likely to live in urban environments (55 per cent) than in rural areas (48 per cent), although fewer differences for those classified as sedentary are documented (Canada Fitness and Amateur Sport January 1986). The greatest difference between active urban and rural residents in favour of urbanites is in the prairie provinces (62 per cent vs 48 per cent).

A study that examines participation rates according to the cold season and warm season variables (Mobily et al. 1993) compares seniors living in the midwestern United States with those in Saskatchewan. The findings show that the physical activity of this age group is generally oriented towards gardening, housework, walking, and yard work; that is, activities that are affected by seasonal variations. Fewer individuals participate in activities that are minimally affected by less favourable climatic conditions such as aerobics, calisthenics, dancing, and fitness or exercise. Instead of moving indoors and adopting alternative activities for the winter, seniors in both regions become less active in the winter and more active in the summer. We can fairly assume that these findings would be in all likelihood applicable to most other age groups as well.

Most popular activities
Data show that the most popular activities among respondents ten years of age and older include walking (57 per cent), bicycling (38 per cent), swim-

ming (36 per cent), jogging/running (31 per cent), and home exercises (28 per cent) (Canada Fitness and Amateur Sport October 1984). Somewhat less popular activities, yet mentioned by numerous Canadians, are ice skating (21 per cent), cross-country skiing (18 per cent), tennis (15 per cent), golf (13 per cent), baseball (11 per cent), alpine skiing (11 per cent), ice hockey (9 per cent), bowling (8 per cent), exercise classes (8 per cent), racquetball (6 per cent), and curling (5 per cent).

The popularity of various sports and exercise is, however, not necessarily expressed through high frequencies of participation. As long as reported participation is defined as 'at least once in the month preceding the survey', one should not assume that many people are heading for walking and biking paths, swimming-pools, gymnasiums, and fitness rooms.

The role of the government

Participation in physical recreation and sports is assisted by all levels of Canadian government through the provision of various sports and recreation programs and facilities. Over several decades, the governments have promoted participation in both physical recreation and competitive sports. The main role of Canada Fitness and Amateur Sport is to promote, encourage, and develop fitness and amateur sports. The Canada Games move around the country, and are always awarded to mid-size cities with a demonstrated need for additional facilities, thus leaving behind a legacy of high-quality facilities for the use of the host community (Westland 1979). The games are preceded by local, regional, and provincial events that lead up to the selection of the representative teams; in the 1980s they became less of a sports festival and more of an emphasis on sports development.

In contrast to Sport Canada's involvement with high-performance athletes, Fitness Canada stresses participation by all. With the goal of increasing public awareness of the benefits of fitness and encouraging greater participation in physical activity by Canadians of all ages and skill levels, it promotes a more active lifestyle and the benefits of being fit. Do Canadians heed such advice? The data presented above indicate an uncertain answer: yes, many do, and perhaps even more do not pursue sports and exercise. Those who are active may have been influenced by the governments' efforts, or maybe many would have been active regardless of the programs. At this juncture, we have inadequate information to confirm the effectiveness of the programs. However, we can speculate that for many people, physical exercise and sports participation would be curtailed without them.

▥ Cultural pursuits

High-culture venues

The general impression about the vitality of cultural life and high-culture leisure pursuits in Canada can be very positive. For example, over 250 professional performing arts companies in theatre, music, dance, and opera played to audiences totalling 9.7 million in 1982, an increase of almost 50 per cent in comparison with 1976 (Statistics Canada 1984b, 1985a). The data for 1982 indicate increases in the number of organizations in all four disciplines, ranging from 4 per cent in dance and 6 per cent in music to 14 per cent in opera and 19 per cent in theatre. By August 1991, there were 348 facilities for performing arts across Canada (Decima Research and Les Consultants Cultur'Inc 1992). Of those, the numbers were relatively proportionate to the population, with the exception of Ontario, which had fewer active facilities (16 per cent of facilities vs 26 per cent of the nation's population), and Montreal with 17 per cent of all facilities yet only 7 per cent of the population.

In spite of such increasing numbers of facilities, the total number of performances increased only slightly, by 4.6 per cent in theatre and 9 per cent in music, while other performing arts suffered losses of 12.3 per cent in dance and 11.9 per cent in opera (Statistics Canada 1984b, 1985a). In contrast to most other countries where general trends usually follow a straightforward pattern of gradual increase, decrease, or stagnation, the availability of performing arts events in Canada has been prone to erratic leaps and drops from one year to the next. Moreover, while one artistic area may experience a spectacular increase in one year, another area can go down sharply during the same year, and then reverse the pattern in the following year. Thus, establishing a regular pattern of Canadian cultural leisure pursuits may prove to be elusive.

Rates of participation
Overall participation in visits to cultural centres, cinemas, and other arts and cultural events generally increased; there were no signs of any significant reversal, even by the mid-1980s (Statistics Canada 1979, 1985a). Theatre attendances increased by 3.7 per cent, but attendances at other performing arts events decreased (music by 0.4 per cent, dance by 19.9 per cent, and opera by 0.5 per cent). In general, live theatre accounted for the highest proportion of total attendances, followed by proportionately much smaller audiences at musical performances (Statistics Canada 1984b, 1985a).

The earlier data on individual rates of attendance at performing arts events document that age, education, and socio-economic status not only influence participation in leisure activities, they also correspond with specific types of activities (Kirsh et al. 1973; Milton 1975; Statistics Canada 1979; Zuzanek 1978). The rates of cultural participation increase steadily from the lowest to the highest educational attainment categories and decrease with increasing age (Statistics Canada 1979). The factors that most affect attendances were, in order of importance, educational attainment, age, and gender. With paid attendances at live theatre, opera, ballet, music performances, museums, and art galleries, age was the best predictor, followed by education and gender. Moreover, as Milton discovered, age has a strong effect on spectator activities, but little effect on other low-interaction activities that take place outside the home. He found marital status and relation to the head of household to be poor predictors, but suggested that a particular combination of individual factors produced a change in patterns.

Zuzanek (1978) also determined that, in spite of the rates of participation in the overwhelming majority of leisure activities that generally decline with age, going to the opera remained unaffected by change in age. Among the socio-economic factors examined by Zuzanek, educational attainment appeared to be the best predictor of participation. It held true, however, only when minimal participation was measured. Furthermore, professionals ranked considerably higher than other groups for attending theatre, opera, symphonies, and cinemas, while the lowest participation levels were among resource industry workers. The least popular arts events—specialized films, classical concerts, and live theatre—were least affected by age.

By the early 1990s, 67 per cent of Canadians attended performing arts events at least once per year (Decima Research and Les Consultants Cultur'Inc 1992). The greatest proportion of them, 40 per cent, attend performances one to four times per year, just 1 per cent go at least once a week, while 29 per cent attend less frequently than once a year or never. Among those who frequent performing arts events at least once per month are primarily young people aged sixteen to twenty-four (10 per cent) and older people sixty-five or over (13 per cent), although these two groups also include 24 per cent and 33 per cent respectively of those who attend less than once per year or never. Individuals with household incomes over $75,000 and with graduate or professional degrees are found more frequently among the once-a-month attenders (10 per cent and 13 per cent respectively), and the least often among the non-attenders (16 per cent and 18 per cent respectively).

These data conceal the fact that the majority of Canadians report that they have never attended most types of traditional performing arts; the major exception is theatre where larger numbers report having seen a theatre comedy (47 per cent) and a theatre drama (40 per cent) (Decima Research and Les Consultants Cultur'Inc 1992). Symphonic and choral music goers report attendances at the rates of 12 per cent and 10 per cent respectively.

These current patterns do not differ significantly from leisure participation in leisure surveys of cultural pursuits conducted in the 1970s. They show that some 50 per cent of the total population within the frame of one survey (Kirsh et al. 1973), or over 60 per cent of the population within the survey sample for the Department of National Health and Welfare in 1976 (Statistics Canada 1977) accounted for 100 per cent of the attendances at the traditional cultural activities (theatre, opera, and ballet), visits to cultural sites, and popular culture events. In general, 14 per cent of the population attended cultural events; live theatre attracted 10 per cent of the population, opera about 2 per cent, ballet 1 per cent, while 6 per cent of the population attended classical music performances. Non-classical music performances attracted about 13 per cent of the population, other live performances 11 per cent, while 35 per cent of the respondents attended at least one commercial film during the study period (Kirsh et al. 1973:223–4).

Other cultural pursuits such as visits to public art galleries, museums, or historic sites (whether paid, free of charge, or both), attracted 13 per cent of the population (Kirsh et al. 1973:45). More than 8 per cent of the population paid to visit cultural sites, while art galleries attracted less than 3 per cent, museums almost 4 per cent, and historic sites about 5 per cent of Canadians.

Popular culture and traditional performing arts
When comparing the rates of attendance at the traditional performing arts with those for popular culture, we find that those for the traditional performing arts appear to be less frequent (Decima Research and Les Consultants Cultur'Inc 1992). Of those activities that have a high- or middle-culture flavour, few appear to be undertaken with any great frequency, although, as mentioned earlier, a substantial proportion of the population report involvement at least once a year.

Comparisons between the attendance rates at traditional performing arts and popular culture performances indicate that gender variations are minimal, and income and education variations are greatly reduced among audiences at popular performing arts events. This may be the case largely because the lower-income and less educated groups report greater attendance at popular events, while the more affluent and educated report similar levels of attendance for the traditional events. Moreover, different rates of attendance by age are limited for popular events, with the exception of less frequent attendance among seniors and greater attendance among those under twenty-five.

Other clear variations between attenders and non-attenders of the traditional performing arts can be observed by selected demographic variables. Women, together with the more affluent and educated social groups, are somewhat more likely to report attendance. Attendances appear to be quite strongly linked to educational level, with those with the highest level of education reporting the most frequent attendance. Contrary to the researchers' expectation, young Canadians are far more likely to report attending a traditional arts performance. The researchers (Decima Research and Les Consultants Cultur'Inc 1992) speculate that this might possibly reflect the impact of performing arts attended through school. It may be, though, that contemporary young people prefer to sample a variety of events.

Another discrepancy in the participation rates takes the form of metropolis-hinterland inequality. The availability of traditional performing arts events is an obvious problem for residents of smaller communities whose attendance rates are comparatively much lower, while no such problem appears to exist (or at least not to the same degree) for residents of the largest urban centres or for popular events in smaller communities.

Briefly said, there are several discrepancies between popular culture and traditional performing arts events with regard to the general rates of availability and attendance, as well as specific discrepancies within each culture group. We have seen the details of such discrepancies throughout several chapters of this book.

Preferences

If the rates of participation in physical recreation and sports seem to be on the rise, especially among middle-aged and older Canadians, is there a comparable increase in interest in attending high-culture events more often? On the one hand, yes, since for every five recent attenders of theatre, classical music, and dance performances, only one is content with his or her actual level of attendance, and four would like to attend more (Decima Research and Les Consultants Cultur'Inc 1992). On the other hand, not so much, since only a few of the occasional attenders and non-attenders are interested in attending more frequently. This finding likely indicates that those who never or only occasionally go to high-culture performances may choose or prefer not to attend. Or perhaps it is the case of cognitive dissonance, which would suggest that since they cannot attend more frequently, they choose not to want to attend more.

Decima Research and Les Consultants Cultur'Inc's (1992) findings show that going out to a concert or performance is a special event for two-thirds of participants. Women in particular (41 per cent of women vs 33 per cent of men) strongly agree with the statement 'I like to make an evening of going to a concert or theatre.' Sixty-nine per cent of all Decima Research and Les Consultants Cultur'Inc's respondents also strongly agree with the statement 'When going out for the evening, I basically want to relax and be entertained.' Furthermore, 40 per cent of these respondents strongly agree and another 30 per cent agree with the statement 'I like to attend a performance in a place where I can feel at home and relaxed'; among them 59 per cent are francophones and 33 per cent are anglophones. Homey atmosphere or not, star performers are a great attraction since close to two-thirds of respondents like to see star performers in person, and 50 per cent like to attend big hits.

Finally, what can be said about compatibility among various leisure pursuits, and about the more-or-less mutually exclusive, culture-based vs physical activity streams in leisure? The abovementioned survey of selected leisure activities in Canada (Schliewen 1977) found similarities between the types of performing arts attended and home-based, media-related leisure activities. Likewise, we have already seen similar findings with regard to the preferences for different programs on television, presented by Decima Research and Les Consultants Cultur'Inc (1992).

Seasonal and regional variations

We have seen examples of seasonality in physical recreational and sports participation, and we also recall from the chapter on development of leisure in

Canada that some seasonal sports, such as swimming, ice hockey, tennis, and other racquet sports, are becoming year-round indoor pursuits. Schliewen's (1977) findings document that seasonal variations are more pronounced for attendance at performing arts events when compared with in-home pursuits. Specifically, many cultural visits occur during the summer months as part of a typical summer vacation rather than as a recurring year-round or winter leisure interest.

Attendances at performing arts events and the cinema consistently decrease between the summer and fall by 5 per cent in music and 11 per cent in movies, while there are smaller decreases in attendances at live theatre. Moreover, Schliewen not only showed the strong relationship between visits to cultural institutions and the educational background of the attenders, he also confirmed high degrees of seasonality in participation regardless of variations in education.

Visits to historic sites, one of the most popular activities in the cultural category, decrease from 29 per cent in the summer months to 10 per cent in the autumn. More surprisingly perhaps, museum visits also drop from over 16 per cent to about 5 per cent. Since museums, unlike zoos or historic sites, are generally open throughout the year, such decreasing rates document the seasonality of visits, primarily influenced by summer holidays. This pattern is so deeply imbedded in public opinion that about 60 per cent of respondents in one study, *The Museums and the Canadian Public* (Dixon et al. 1974), felt that it is more appropriate to visit museums when on holiday.

Regional differences in attendances seem to follow the pattern of the distribution of facilities and performances presented at the beginning of this section. Provincial rates of attendance at traditional performing arts events show the highest proportion of attenders within the last six months in Quebec (51 per cent), followed by Alberta and British Columbia (47 per cent and 46 per cent respectively) (Decima Research and Les Consultants Cultur'Inc 1992). Manitoba and Ontario have the same rate (41 per cent), New Brunswick, Saskatchewan, and the Atlantic provinces follow (35 per cent, 34 per cent, and 31 per cent respectively). Residents of large cities with more than 100,000 inhabitants attend performing arts events at the rate of 63 per cent, but only 48 per cent of people living in cities with populations under 10,000 do so. The highest rates are found in Montreal (57 per cent), Toronto (54 per cent), and Vancouver (50 per cent).

According to Schliewen (1977), however, regional disparities do not reflect so much the presence or absence of facilities but stem from the attitudes, education, and language skills of the population in a given region. Other differences may result from the ethnic background of the residents. For example, Canadians whose mother tongue is English appear to be the most active ethnic group overall, rivalled only by those whose mother tongue is Dutch (Statistics Canada 1979). This phenomenon might be associated with the higher socio-economic status of many English-speaking Canadians, while the lower participation rates among some other ethnic groups can be partly explained by the language barrier. Additional regional differences are explored below in the provincial distribution of segmented psychographic profiles of Canadians.

Psychographic summary

The various types of attenders and non-attenders discussed earlier can be subdivided into distinct groups according to Decima Research and Les Consultants Cultur'Inc (1992). The eight groups are Devoted, Believers, Practitioners, Conditionals, Uncommitted, Uninvolved, Carefree Pop/Rockers, and Tuned Out.

The Devoted represent 8 per cent of the population, love the arts, and attend arts performances frequently. They enjoy somewhat above-average incomes, are highly educated, live mostly in major urban centres, and are older. Sixty-one per cent of this group are women.

Believers, who are similar in many ways to the Devoted, represent 17 per cent of the population. They are younger than the population overall; have above-average education; consist of 54 per cent females, 46 per cent males; and like to see stars and hits.

Practitioners (14 per cent of the population) and Conditionals (18 per cent of the population) have reasonably positive attitudes, but these attitudes do not translate into the same level of reported behaviour; also, they prefer mainstream performances and hit shows. The Conditionals have less enthusiasm for live performances and prefer to see a televised rather than a live performance.

Uncommitted (17 per cent of the population) and Uninvolved (14 per cent of the population) are less positive about the traditional arts. The Uncommitted have some interest in the traditional performing arts, mostly theatre. The infrequently attended performances take place mostly in clubs and bars. The Uninvolved prefer to see a show or performance on television, and when they occasionally go out, they seek a casual environment.

The Carefree Pop/Rocker group represents 6 per cent of the population. These people are young; 70 per cent of them are under thirty-five. They enjoy attending concerts that present music of their choice, and prefer live rather than televised concerts.

Tuned Out are just that—they have no interest in the arts and little intention of becoming involved. This group represents 6 per cent of the population, is predominantly male (71 per cent) and anglophone (91 per cent).

These groups are unevenly distributed throughout the population and across the provinces as well. Most of the Devoted live in the cities of Montreal, Vancouver, and Toronto, and in the provinces of Alberta and Manitoba. Fewer live in Saskatchewan and Atlantic Canada. Twenty-three per cent of the Believers live in British Columbia, 18 per cent in Alberta, 16 per cent in Saskatchewan, 14 per cent in Manitoba, 18 per cent in Ontario, 10 per cent in

Quebec, 12 per cent in New Brunswick, 17 per cent in other Atlantic provinces; 19 per cent are residents in Vancouver, 22 per cent in Toronto, and 16 per cent in Montreal.

In sum, most Canadians' daily leisure activities are not high culture. The rates of participation are associated with demographic and socio-economic characteristics, and are further influenced by the region and the size of community.

▮▮▮ Regional features: An example from Alberta

This section highlights leisure pursuits of residents living in one province—Alberta. We have examined enough of interprovincial and intraprovincial differences to know that Albertans cannot be taken as fully representative of all Canadians. However, many specific patterns of their leisure styles might be found in other parts of the continent as well. The data presented in this section are from the longitudinal survey of leisure and recreation, carried out by Alberta Recreation and Parks between 1981 and 1992. It was published as the *Public Opinion Survey on Recreation* in 1981 and 1984, the *General Recreation Survey* in 1988, as the *Alberta Recreation Survey* in 1992, and published over the years as a set of brochures under the title *A Look at Leisure*. The samples and methodologies varied to some extent from one stage to another, but the findings can be compared over the time periods. They illustrate many of the points made so far in the previous sections and those that will be made in the subsequent sections.

Rates of participation
The findings from the Alberta Recreation and Parks survey in 1984 provide a list of seventy-one leisure activities identified by members of households as those in which 'at least one member participated in the activity during the previous year' (Alberta Recreation and Parks 13:3). Twenty-one of them are social, creative, and cultural, while fifty represent outdoor and sports pursuits. The highest rates of participation are in personal entertainment, such as watching television, interacting with family and friends, and walking for pleasure; they correspond with Kelly's concept (1983, 1987) of the core leisure activities identified in the section on allocations of leisure time. The top twenty outdoor pursuits and sports include walking, swimming, overnight camping, fishing, golf, bicycling, aerobics and fitness, softball and baseball, hunting, curling, downhill skiing, jogging and running, picnicking, cross-country skiing, ice hockey, body-building and weightlifting, bowling, racquetball, motor or trail biking, and ice skating (Alberta Recreation and Parks 13:5).

In spite of the markedly varied rates of participation in these activities, the overall level of household participation in many of them appears to be quite high. However, the rates of participation by individual participants are less impressive. Proportions of actively involved individuals (not specified by gender or age) decrease from 30.2 per cent in walking to 16.3 per cent in golf, 9.9 per cent in softball or baseball, and 4.3 per cent in both ice skating and hiking.

At least one member of 47 per cent of households visited a museum, an art gallery, or a live theatre performance in 1992 (62 per cent in 1984, 65 per cent in 1988), and members of 45 per cent of households engaged in drama, music, or drawing (Alberta Recreation and Parks 13:3, 25:4; Alberta Tourism, Parks, and Recreation 1992). In comparison with other Canadians, Albertans visit art galleries, museums, historical sites, zoos, and libraries at above-average rates ranging from 105 per cent to 145.4 per cent (Schliewen 1977:44–5). Comparisons with the recent data collected by Decima Research and Les Consultants Cultur'Inc (1992) are difficult to make because activities are classified differently in the two surveys.

The findings about adult-only participation rates, based on additional calculations of the raw data available from the 1988 provincial survey, reveal that married couples' highest regular participation (over 70 per cent) is in entertaining guests in their home (76.9 per cent of urban couples with children, 75.5 per cent of urban childless couples, 78 per cent of rural couples with children, and 73.9 per cent of rural childless couples); about 20 per cent of all types of couples entertain occasionally. Rates of participation in sports is decidedly lower: 12.9 per cent of urban couples with children, 29.1 per cent of urban childless couples, 14 per cent of rural couples with children, and 9.1 per cent of rural childless couples participate regularly; 35.8 per cent, 29 per cent, 34 per cent, and 23.3 per cent of couples in these categories participate only occasionally. Other socio-relational or familial leisure activities are reported by some 90 per cent of all couples; among them, couples with children and rural couples show higher regular rates of participation than others. Overall, couples with children, especially those in early parental stages, are involved in leisure pursuits at the highest rates both regularly and occasionally. Very few couples indicate that they pursue cultural interests on a regular basis.

The data from different time periods of the Alberta Recreation and Parks survey show fairly stable participation rates for some activities, even some increase, or a slight decline during the 1980s and early 1990s, for example, walking (88 per cent of households in 1981, 89 per cent in 1988, 87 per cent in 1992), bicycling (62 per cent in 1981, 64 per cent in 1988, 59 per cent in 1992), golf (35 per cent in 1981, 40 per cent in 1988), downhill skiing (36 per cent in 1981, 34 per cent in 1988), soccer (20 per cent in 1981, 17 per cent in 1988). Other activities declined moderately, between 1981 and 1988 for example, spectatorship at sports events (75 per cent in 1981 and 64 per cent in 1988), camping (65 per cent, 51 per cent), ice skating (58 per cent, 46 per cent), softball and baseball (42 per cent, 34 per cent), curling (26 per cent, 21 per cent), cross-country skiing (31 per cent, 21 per cent), tennis (31 per cent, 20 per cent), and badminton (22 per cent, 16 per cent). Activities that showed the most decline were jogging and running (54 per cent, 33 per cent), bowling (43 per cent, 26 per cent), racquetball (28 per cent, 16 per cent), rollerskating (33 per cent, 11 per cent), football (24 per cent, 11 per cent), and backpacking (20 per cent, 8 per cent) (Alberta Recreation and Parks 31:4).

Preliminary data for 1992 (Alberta Tourism, Parks, and Recreation 1992) also indicate decreased rates in downhill skiing (33 per cent), spectatorship at sports events (58 per cent), camping (46 per cent), ice skating (43 per cent), softball (31 per cent), jogging and running (28 per cent). A slight increase to 41 per cent is recorded for golfing.

Intraprovincial variations

There are intraprovincial regional differences based on physical environment, population density, size of communities, and access to the mountains, ski resorts, and lakes. Of the twenty-five most frequent activities, horseback riding, ice hockey, ice skating, motorcycling, trail biking, racquetball, body-building or weightlifting, and cross-country skiing (except in southern Alberta) show similar rates across the province, while different rates of participation are found in other activities. Participation rates above the provincial average in swimming and golf are found in Calgary and Edmonton. These two cities also have higher rates of participation in aerobics, fitness, jogging, running, bicycling, and tennis. The close proximity of the Rocky Mountains undoubtedly contributes to the above-average rates of downhill skiing and hiking in Calgary (Alberta Recreation and Parks 17:3).

Residents of northern Alberta participate more frequently in overnight camping, fishing, softball, baseball, hunting, curling, boating, and snowmobiling, while southern Albertans prefer walking, camping, golf, picnicking, and bowling or lawn-bowling at above-average rates. (Residents of larger urban centres have more developed facilities and programs at their disposal, and swimming in Alberta takes place primarily at indoor swimming-pools. Northern residents have an additional advantage of a large land base and many lakes that encourage outdoor pursuits.)

Most popular activities

In Alberta, in spite of its markedly declining participation rate in the 1980s, camping was ranked number one both in 1981 and 1988, while walking for pleasure moved from number six to number two in popularity, and bicycling from fifteen to six (Alberta Recreation and Parks 31:6; Alberta Tourism, Parks, and Recreation 1992). In general, favourite types of activities among Albertans include exercise-oriented pursuits (25 per cent in 1981, 30 per cent in 1988), decreasingly popular team sports (14 per cent in 1981, 9 per cent in 1988), and relatively stable rates for fishing, hunting, golf, and skiing. Preliminary data for 1992 (Alberta Recreation and Parks 1992) put walking as the number one activity (but mentioned only by 11.9 per cent of respondents), camping as the second (7.45 per cent of respondents), golf as the third (6.72 per cent of respondents), and bicycling as the fourth (4.38 per cent of respondents).

Leisure pursuits in which Alberta households participate most often do not always coincide with the most favoured or the most desired activities (Alberta Recreation and Parks 11:3, 26:5, 28:4). Although people are most likely to participate in passive and social activities, many claim that they favour active sports, exercise, or outdoor pursuits. The ten favourite activities mentioned most often in 1988 are swimming, golf, cross-country or downhill skiing, aerobics, tennis, water sports, racquetball, handball or squash, and all types of boating or rowing (Alberta Recreation and Parks 28:4). Thus, both the most favoured and most desired ones include sports, outdoor, or fitness pursuits while cultural and artistic pursuits do not figure prominently in any of these actual preferred or desired activity categories.

Albertans appear to be satisfied with their leisure (Horna 1985b; Alberta Recreation and Parks 28:7). Most respondents report that they are satisfied with their existing leisure. Even if they were given an unlimited and unconstrained opportunity to participate in any additional or alternative activity, most respondents would still participate in the same activity, preferably spending more time on it. The degree of interest in any new activity, albeit only within the physical activity and sports leisure stream, varies in part according to age, education, income, and length of residence in Alberta. The greatest interest in innovation is found among Albertans who are under thirty-four years of age, university educated, earning higher incomes, or who are relative newcomers to the province; seniors and individuals with lower education and income are least interested in leisure innovations (Alberta Recreation and Parks 5:4).

In sum, the data gathered in Alberta document that living in one of the coldest provinces of Canada does not compel Albertans to opt for leisure patterns that are particularly different from those in other regions. In comparison with other Canadians, Albertans prefer in-home, sedentary and sociable, summer-or-winter-neutral orientation in leisure throughout the year.

▥ More variations of leisure

Serious leisure

The concept of serious leisure has been proposed and elaborated by its originator, Robert Stebbins, through his studies of amateurs who take their leisure very seriously indeed (Stebbins 1979, 1982, 1992). According to Stebbins's concept, serious leisure consists of three types—amateurism, hobbyist pursuits, and volunteering. These three types of serious leisure do not constitute paid work for most people who are engaged in them, although amateurs and volunteers are sometimes reimbursed for their efforts and expenses. Moreover, whereas amateurs, hobbyists, and volunteers frequently have important obligations, they have more freedom than breadwinners to cease their activity altogether. Nonetheless, serious leisure enthusiasts are usually more obliged to engage in their pursuits than are their less serious counterparts. Amateurs and volunteers, and a small number of hobbyists, have pleasant experiences and positive views about their activities because they contribute to their own well-being and to the life of the community.

Stebbins (1992) identifies six qualities of serious leisure that, taken together, distinguish it from casual leisure. One such quality is the occasional need to persevere. A second quality is the tendency for amateurs, hobbyists, and volunteers to have careers in their endeavours. Such careers in serious leisure frequently depend on a third quality: significant personal effort based on specially acquired knowledge, training, or skill, sometimes all three. Fourth, Stebbins finds eight durable benefits recognized by amateurs in their various pursuits: self-actualization, self-enrichment, self-expression, recreation or self-renewal, a feeling of accomplishment, enhancement of self-image, social interaction and a sense of belonging, and lasting tangible products of the activity. Only the ninth benefit—self-gratification or pure fun—is associated with casual leisure as well.

A fifth quality of serious leisure is the unique ethos of the experience. Amateurs, hobbyists, and volunteers tend to develop broad subcultures with their interests carried out within their own social worlds. Much of casual leisure cannot be conceived of in these terms. The sixth quality means that participants in serious leisure tend to identify strongly with their chosen pursuits; for example, they present themselves in terms of these pursuits rather than in terms of their occupations.

Hobbyists fall into four categories: (1) collectors who develop a technical knowledge of the commercial, social, and physical circumstances in which the desired items are acquired; (2) makers and tinkerers, for example, inventors, seamstresses, furniture and toy makers, boat-builders, quilters, indoor gardeners; (3) activity participants who steadfastly pursue leisure that requires systematic physical movement, is conducted within a set of rules, and often poses a challenge, albeit a non-competitive one, such as fishing, birdwatching, mountaineering, hang-gliding, body-building, barbershop singing; and (4) folk artists. When their pursuits are competitive, hobbyists can be classified as players of sports or games. They relate to each other according to a set of rules that structure their actions during a contest.

The amateurs in Stebbins's interpretation are guided by professional standards and share the same spirit of satisfaction. They are neither dabblers who approach the activity with little commitment or seriousness, nor professionals for whom it is an occupation and who make a living from that activity. Amateurs are sometimes ambivalent about the pursuit of an avocation. Family, work, and leisure pull them in two or three directions at once, making time demands that often far exceed the total available hours. In addition, there is an absence of community-wide institutional support for their leisure, such as the support that helps sustain serious involvement in family and work activities.

Finally, Stebbins argues that in contrast to most mass or popular leisure, which provides only short-term benefits and represents a low-yield use of free time, the pursuit of serious leisure can help solve the social problem of meaningless or empty leisure.

Collectors

Unlike people who just own things, collectors may become obsessed with their pursuit and turn into collecting addicts (Travis 1987, 1988). Assembling a collection legitimizes acquisitiveness and can make certain objects 'sacred' (Belk et al. 1988). On the positive side, collections provide self-esteem, an opportunity to display skills and knowledge, compensate for worries about problems in other life domains, and (for retired individuals in particular), they provide activities to replace work.

Collectors create their own social world; the practice of collecting, their events and formal organizations form a meaningful unit of social organization for its participants. Collecting provides an all-consuming organizing system for the collector's life (Olmsted 1991; Unruh 1980). Looking for new items takes collectors to flea markets and garage sales, to auctions, shows, exchanges, and meetings with fellow collectors, which contribute to social interaction, companionship, or competition. Within the collectors' social world, the collectibles serve as a substitute for personal interaction instrumental to the social self, communicated through the stories collectors tell (Stenross 1987). Preoccupation with collectible objects and with the social world of collecting takes place primarily during leisure time and also often at the expense of the time to be spent with the family or in other activities.

Gender differences in collecting, as in other leisure activities, are prevalent. More adult men than women are involved in serious collecting, although among children, more girls than boys have collections (Danet and Katriel 1987). In Olmsted's (1987) sample of stamp-collectors, 94 per cent were males; 98 per cent of males are found among breweriana collectors, and 86 per cent among baseball cards collectors (all cited in Olmsted 1991).

Collecting could be more stigmatized for women than for men, and the atmosphere at some shows or gatherings might overtly or subtly contribute to it. Also, because of their socialization for gender-appropriate roles, women are expected to be more caring and family-oriented rather than indulging in private collecting. Women may be blocked from acquiring the knowledge and skills necessary for collecting or for successful negotiations at auctions. And they may lack sufficient discretionary time and larger blocks of uninterrupted leisure time, as we have seen on several occasions. Furthermore, collectibles tend to be gendered and collections make gendered statements (Belk and Wallendorf 1990). Also social functions associated with collecting follow gender-differentiated patterns. Men's collections are often related to the masculine world of engines, science, world, and geography, while women's collections tend to reflect their preoccupation with the home, fine details, art, or sentimentality.

We can also find numerous instances of parents and grandparents using collecting with their children and grandchildren as a means of socialization *in* and *for* leisure. Parents of small children who are forced into temporary 'retirement' from their collecting pursuit often return to the collection as their children grow up and become co-participants (Horna 1989a; Olmsted 1987, 1991).

Collecting mania or crazes often result from skilful manipulation by manufacturers and distributors who might commercialize and commodify any object of collectors' desire, or artificially create such desire — be it baseball and hockey cards, Teenage Mutant Ninja Turtles, or various commemorative coins, plates, cups, hats, and pins. These crazes may be short-lived or last for decades.

In Calgary during the 1988 Winter Olympic games, Olympic pin collecting and trading swept through the city among its residents, Olympic athletes, and visitors alike (Horna and Olmsted 1989). What was unique about this craze was its spontaneity and enthusiasm. There could be no doubt that the pin collecting was skilfully created, orchestrated, and manipulated by the Olympic sponsors, pin manufacturers, and distributors, with the willing help of the mass media's search for human interest stories and 'lighter moments' reportage. Although most collectors quit shortly after the 1988 Olympics, pin collecting and trading became a leisure activity that provided a context for interpersonal contact during a festive event. Pin trading augmented the spontaneity and intimacy generated by crowd festivities, especially during the medal presentations attended each night at the Olympic Plaza by some 40,000 to 60,000 celebrating fans. Pin collecting and trading symbolized active, public, nonathletic participation in the games, reduced social distance, and facilitated communication with strangers. It was over for most participants in Calgary in less than three weeks, but was renewed by other collectors, who collected other games' pins elsewhere.

A case-study of local celebrities
By now, we are quite aware of several different patterns in leisure choices and preferences based on the demographic, educational, and occupational characteristics of various population groups. The main theme of such differences indicates that more variations appear in those activities that fall beyond core leisure activities than in the core itself. The examples presented in this section originate from a unique examination of leisure participation among local celebrities. These portraits are based on a content analysis of brief articles called 'Here's Looking at You' that appeared in a weekly supplement in *The Calgary Herald* between June 1985 and December 1989 (Horna 1990). These weekly columns presented interviews with locally prominent individuals who had outstanding achievements or remarkable involvement in sports, culture, government and political life, high-profile professions, charitable and volunteer work, or the mass media.

The featured personalities are unevenly distributed along the gender line in the sports group, with about one-third of them men and only four women, one of them being the twelve-year-old girl who lit the cauldron at the opening ceremonies of the Winter Olympic Games. The men who are not in sports are drawn almost equally from culture, charitable and volunteer work, government, and the media (19.5 per cent, 17.2 per cent, 16.1 per cent, and 13.8 per cent respectively). The women's backgrounds are primarily from culture (37 per cent) and charitable or volunteer work (25.9 per cent), while one woman's distinction is based on her husband's position in the local government.

The group of local celebrities is remarkably similar to the general population in its leisure pursuits and preferences. Most of their activities differ very little from the core leisure activities described earlier. They prefer recuperative, relational, or role-determined activities. The majority engage in sports and physical activities, which are mostly individual or partnered (such as fishing, racquet sports, boating, and sailing) rather than team-oriented. Fifty-nine per cent of men and 19 per cent of women are active in sports and physical pursuits, while culture is pursued by only 6.8 per cent. Occasional activities include music, photography, theatre and films, writing, composing music, collecting folk art, modelling and fashion, visiting museums, following politics, and working with computers. These particular activities were mentioned by only a few persons.

When asked about their idea of a great evening, almost 60 per cent of these celebrities mentioned good food and a fine wine at home or when dining out; over 70 per cent mentioned spending time with family and friends, perhaps drinking beer or wine; and about 15 per cent favoured a quiet evening at home, preferably by a fireplace. Perhaps due to the cold climate of Calgary, about 80 per cent of the celebrities prefer to vacation on tropical islands, near the ocean or at least a swimming-pool, and trips to warm climes—with more sports at the destination.

Furthermore, the celebrities' current leisure pursuits and preferences are similar to those in their childhood, showing no real crossover and little bridging between the streams. Some combination of the sports and physical activities stream with the culture stream can be deduced from activities of about one-quarter of the men and over half of the women. The top four most frequently cited pursuits include golf (30.9 per cent), skiing (22.2 per cent), gardening (19.7 per cent), and travel (16.0 per cent). For about 42 per cent of women, their top activity is reading, while skiing, aerobics, swimming, and needlework are mentioned by 16.7 per cent for each activity.

In sum, the leisure styles of Calgary's local celebrities do not differ substantially from those of others. The celebrities may have various claims to fame, but being innovative trail-blazers and inspirational role models in leisure does not appear to be among them.

Immigrants

Selected findings excerpted from historical studies, surveys of leisure and recreation patterns, time-budget studies, migration and ethnic studies, and sports
sociology and psychology literature suggest that most immigrants experience
modifications of their former leisure patterns, both voluntarily and involun-
tarily. Immigrants' leisure in the new country facilitates their dual identity,
bridging the consecutive phases of their adjustment in the host country. For
many new immigrants, particularly for those not proficient in their hosts'
language, leisure often performs the dual function of maintaining a separation from the outside world and creating a bubble of familiarity within an
unfamiliar community.

Common ethnic symbols such as shared language, leisure pursuits, food,
and music in particular appear to become sources of comforting familiarity in
a new environment. Participating with their compatriots in 'their' sports and
in voluntary organizations accentuates their exclusiveness and maintains traditions for many immigrants. The group may continue enacting traditional
roles within its confines, for example, filial piety among the Chinese or gender-segregated roles among immigrants from Islamic countries. Evidence of
continued gender-separated leisure pursuits of Italian 'urban villagers' in the
United States has been found by Herbert Gans (1962), and soccer clubs in
Toronto's Italian community were described by McKay (1980). Numerous
senior citizens' clubs and retirement homes are organized around common
ethnic backgrounds and traditional leisure pursuits. Another factor is related
to the adulation of top athletes and sports heroes. Often the psychological
gratification in leisure comes from having an ethnic or racial background
similar to the great performer (Spinrad 1981).

Frequently, ethnic food becomes a vital focus of social interaction and leisure (Anderson and Alleyne 1979; Mindel and Habenstein 1976). Canadians
of Ukrainian descent have festive family reunions, Germans in Canada organize their traditional beer festivals, and Caribbean mini-carnivals or Chinese
New Year celebrations are held in numerous Canadian cities, complete with
traditional delicacies.

A survey of Czech and Slovak immigrants in Alberta (Horna 1980) documents that immigration of these nationals resulted in several significant
changes in leisure patterns during the first five years after their arrival. Firstly,
the amount of their discretionary time for leisure decreased in comparison
with their premigration free time, mostly because of the pressing need to master the English language and attain required skills. Secondly, the scope and
diversity of these immigrants' leisure pursuits narrowed considerably because
of fewer resources at their disposal and fewer amenities in the province. Finally, in the absence of their former friends and extended-family members,
while simultaneously experiencing difficulties in making friends with Canadians, most immigrants curtailed their social contacts in leisure. Married couples in particular withdrew into their nuclear families and homes. The delib-

erate compartmentalization of personal identities resulted in the maintenance of their Canadian identity within the public life domain and their ethnic identity within the private, family, and leisure domains.

This observation is corroborated by Stebbins (1993). Although not examining immigrants, his study of francophones living in anglophone communities provides evidence that the French-language activities of both adults and children can be classified almost entirely as leisure. Moreover, both children and adults find additional leisure carried out in French within the wider community in francophone organizations and clubs, and in leisure activities where French is spoken with others, for example, bridge, cross-country skiing, volunteer activities, and choral singing.

Notable differences in the socializing and visiting patterns among the elderly of various Asian origins are found in Canada by Ujimoto and Naidoo (1984). Furthermore, as Ujimoto (1988, 1991) documents, of the more recent arrivals in Canada, Korean seniors have the highest percentage of family-oriented activities (49.3 per cent); their rates are followed by the Chinese seniors (32.7 per cent). Seniors' weekend activities at home tend to be pursued in the company of their compatriots by 72.4 per cent of the Koreans, 67 per cent of the Chinese, and 54.9 per cent of the Japanese. Likewise, George Karlis (1993) posits that the more recent and smaller groups of immigrants to Canada find community recreational services inadequate for their needs and must rely on their narrow family and ethnic circle.

Ethnic and racial situations elsewhere may not be any different. As the case of Britain suggests, under conditions of discrimination, members of black and Asian minorities, youth in particular, are propelled to the periphery of mainstream leisure (Roberts 1983). Many try to retain their ethnic cultures and identities, primarily through leisure activities.

In general, most empirical evidence about leisure of immigrant and ethnic groups point in one direction. Rather than undergoing a process of leisure desocialization and resocialization during the postmigration phase, immigrants pursue those leisure activities and styles that are an extension of their former leisure and a new complement to their past experiences. The influence of the host society over its new members appears to be less than complete, at least in the leisure domain of first-generation immigrants. Perhaps leisure provides a degree of freedom after all — similar to women's leisure experiences that provide the opportunity to challenge traditional stereotypes and patriarchal control (Wearing 1992).

Leisure travel
We have seen on several occasions in different sections of the book that, unlike core leisure, peripheral leisure is quite diverse in the choice of activities as well as in its relationship with particular demographic and socio-economic characteristics of the participants. One peripheral leisure activity that takes place less frequently but typically involves a considerable amount of plan-

ning, enjoyment, and recollection is tourism. Tourism has become an identifiable form of leisure that is often viewed as a part of popular culture (Kelly and Godbey 1992). Although there is no one agreed-upon definition of tourism, sociologists of leisure prefer to emphasize the aspects of pleasure and recreation, sociability, and self-actualization in tourism.

It is beyond the scope of this book to examine all aspects of leisure travel and tourism, including the entire process of travel decision making before the trip. We will focus on who pursues leisure travel (and with whom), why, and where. Are there specific preferences, motivations, and expectations for domestic leisure travel in contrast to leisure travel overseas and to Europe in particular?

The literature on tourism and leisure travel proposes diverse conceptualizations of tourism as a form of play and stimulus-seeking behaviour, as exploration, and as the search for the authentic. Other views interpret tourism as a change, compensation for or avoidance of boredom and routine, recreation, adventure, and learning—'to experience something different from the normal pattern of existence' (Butler 1989:572). Philip Pearce (1982), who proposes to apply Maslow's hierarchy of needs, finds that the principal reasons for and satisfactions with travel given by the majority of tourists can be interpreted as relating to Maslow's concept of the need for self-actualization (35 per cent), as well as the need for love and belonging (33 per cent).

Another approach suggested by Horne (1984) views the contemporary tourist as a modern pilgrim, carrying guidebooks as devotional texts, when the fame of the object becomes its meaning. It is further discussed by Urry (1990), who points to the shift 'from aura to nostalgia', which reflects the antiélitism of postmodernism. Allcock (1988) challenges the work of MacCannell (1976) and Horne (1984) who suggested that tourism can be treated legitimately as a surrogate religion in the Durkheimian tradition. Similarly, Cohen (1979:181) refers to people's 'spiritual center, whether religious or cultural—the center which for the individual symbolizes ultimate meanings.' Such a spiritual centre may be purely hedonistic, or it may be a new type of pilgrimage, with travellers seeking answers through experiential, experimental, or existential forms of travel. Cohen (1986) also elaborates on the temporal structure of tourist sights, the temporal quality of tourists' experiences, and the temporal organization of tourists' movements.

Related to these conceptualizations are various typologies of tourists themselves, typically linked with each type's motivation for travel. Murphy (1985) groups such tourist typologies into two general categories: interactional types (which emphasize the manner of interaction between visitors and destination areas) and the cognitive-normative models (which stress the motivations behind travel). Both approaches, however, indicate the strong links between visitors' expectations/motivations and the structure of destination areas. Plog's (1972, 1979, 1991) conceptualization is based on a polar continuum consisting of those who differ from the normal (centric) values of society and follow their independent vacation desires (allocentrics), and those who conform to society's norms and values and thus become part of the mass market of tourism (psychocentrics). Plog further suggests that tourist destinations are attractive to different types of visitors. Some authors find it useful to talk in terms of the roles tourists play (Pearce 1982; Yiannakis and Gibson 1992).

Most authors posit that tourism motivation involves all the components of personality and cannot be satisfactorily accounted for by the simple stimulus-response model (Parrinello 1993). Mannell and Iso-Ahola (1987) emphasize the dialectical interrelationships of the individual and social motivations of escaping and seeking over- or understimulating life conditions. Dann's (1977) push and pull—anomie and ego-enhancement—factors and motivations are frequently cited and further elaborated on, for example by Mansfeld (1992). Crompton (1979) groups motivations for pleasure vacations into socio-psychological motives (escape from a perceived mundane environment, exploration and evaluation of self, relaxation, prestige, regression, enhancement of kinship relationships, facilitation of social interaction) and cultural motives (novelty, education).

Numerous specific conceptualizations of travel and tourism motivations include the work by Murphy (1983) who identifies four basic motivators of leisure travel: physical or physiological, cultural, social, and fantasy. While the motives for leisure travel are many, a common reason is curiosity—a desire to see other people, other places, other cultures and political systems. A major component of travel motivation has been the cultural novelty of various destinations (Murphy 1985). Smith's (1977) focus is on the ethnic, cultural, historical, environmental, and recreational nature of tourism, and on the corresponding seven different types of tourists: explorer, élite, offbeat, unusual, incipient mass, mass, and charter. Some trips may be influenced by a single motivation; however, most trips seem to be undertaken in response to multiple motivations and have multiple destinations (Lue, Crompton, and Fesenmaier 1993; Mansfeld 1992).

No definite answers as to motivations have been given as yet and still more questions are being raised. One question is whether individuals possess different and person-specific needs that are relatively stable and that are satisfied within their particular roles. For example, an ongoing discussion focuses on the stability of travel motivations and the behaviour of individuals over time (Hamilton-Smith 1987; Pearce 1982; Yiannakis and Gibson 1992). Thus, we may ask from an applied point of view whether individual A would always tend to seek destinations compatible with his or her A needs and motivations, while individual B would seek destinations compatible with his or her B needs and motivations. Or would most individuals possess both A and B needs and motivations along a continuum and, consequently, alternatively seek A and B destinations or visit multiple destinations that offer a combination of A and B characteristics? Furthermore, do potential leisure travellers select their destinations according to some general site characteristics or do they demand very specific A and B characteristics? For example, would any historical, architectural, or natural attributes do or must it be only one specific site? We will present some empirical data to illustrate these points.

Tourism is pursued by numerous individuals and families. Parrinello (1993) quotes that more than 50 per cent of the population in postindustrial societies practise tourism.

Patterns of Canadians' leisure travel can be documented by the travel intensity index (see Table 10.1) based on selected demographic characteristics (Statistics Canada 1986).

According to Holecek (1990), of some 41 million Americans who travelled out of the country in 1988, 34 per cent visited Mexico, 32 per cent visited Canada, 16 per cent visited Europe, and 18 per cent went to other destinations. In addition to the growing numbers of tourists in general, trips to central and eastern Europe, the former Soviet Union, and previously little-known Asian destinations are becoming increasingly popular (Cook 1989). Likewise, the number of overseas holidays taken by UK residents continues to rise and includes a wider variety of leisure travel (Urry 1990).

According to Statistics Canada (1991), when taking the growth of Canada's population into account, domestic travel has diminished from 1980 to 1990. In 1990, 60 per cent of Canadians took at least one overnight trip in Canada, compared to 62 per cent in 1984 and a high of 64 per cent in 1986. The decrease in domestic leisure travel is attributed, at least in part, to increasing travel to international destinations, especially to the United States. This is particularly true of the baby-boom generation. Seniors represent one of the fastest growing travel market segments over the last decade, expanding at a faster rate than their population share.

These data indicate that several differences in travel destinations and degrees of participation related to demographic, socio-economic, and regional variables can be distinguished. They seem to contradict Card and Kestel's (1988) assertions that there is little relationship between travellers' demographics and destinations, perhaps because they interviewed travellers on the same airplane between the points of origin and destination. Further investigation of the travellers' comments should be carried out regarding their destination choices.

Case-study of leisure travellers in western Canada
Further illustrations of leisure travel patterns and preferences originate from two non-systematic samples of tourists, about the same proportion of men and women, most of them thirty-one to forty years old, who were travelling for leisure at the time of the interviews (Horna 1993). Similar to other Canadian findings, the interviews indicate that these tourists take a major vacation once a year (54 per cent) or two to three times per year (15 per cent); 26 per cent do so less frequently. Only 2 per cent of them typically travel over distances less than 200 km; most choose longer distances and usually vacation

Table 10.1 Travel intensity index

Travelling to:	Canada	US	Other	None
Province of origin				
Newfoundland	81	16	(	155
Prince Edward Island	90	39	83	116
Nova Scotia	102	47	(	110
New Brunswick	96	61	(	189
Quebec	94	80	87	114
Ontario	99	126	133	97
Manitoba	106	112	(	88
Saskatchewan	122	73	82	69
Alberta	121	91	(	62
British Columbia	96	119	109	103
Age				
15–24	100	84	89	103
25–34	113	98	74	83
35–44	108	120	110	82
45–54	96	128	141	99
55–64	97	92	134	104
65+	75	83	123	148
Marital status				
Married	105	108	104	90
Single	97	94	97	107
Widowed	72	58	71	156
Separated	91	80	93	119
Education				
1–8 years	73	59	72	155
Some secondary	98	91	79	103
Some postsecondary	115	105	91	77
Postsecondary certificate	122	151	128	54
University degree	122	167	242	52
Income				
Less than 9,000	72	38	37	161
9,000–14,999	82	59	43	136
15,000–19,999	98	80	75	109
20,000–24,999	105	88	55	99
25,000–29,999	107	95	79	86
30,000–34,999	119	137	117	57
35,000–39,999	124	136	111	54
More than 40,000	128	176	227	42
Occupation				
Professional	127	154	163	50
Clerical	113	135	133	67
Sales	107	113	73	81
Service	92	71	88	116
Primary	96	55	31	115
Manufacturing	92	77	82	114

Table 10.2 Main reasons for leisure travel (in percentages)

Main reason	Canada/US	Europe
Visiting family and friends	25	17
Sightseeing architecture, historic sites	15	26
Sightseeing nature, mountains, lakes	41	19
Experiencing culture, food, folklore	9	20
Meeting people	7	8
Retracing ethnic roots	—	8
Other	3	2
Total	100	100

in Canada (63 per cent) and the United States (27 per cent), while 10 per cent head for other destinations. Very few tend to travel alone (7 per cent overall, 9 per cent to Europe); family and friends are the preferred travel companions in North America (70 per cent and 23 per cent respectively) as well as in Europe (56 per cent and 20 per cent respectively). None of the respondents joined organized tour groups for leisure travel in North America, but 16 per cent would do so in Europe.

When asked about the main reasons for and interests during their leisure travel, the reasons listed in Table 10.2 were given.

According to the respondents, about one-third (33 per cent in Canada and the US, 29 per cent in Europe) stay with relatives or friends; 18 per cent in Canada and the US and 10 per cent in Europe opt for camping; 33 per cent in Canada and the US and 39 per cent in Europe book into economy-class accommodations; only 11 per cent in Canada and the US and 10 per cent in Europe stay at first-class, luxury hotels; and the remaining 5 per cent and 12 per cent respectively find other accommodations such as hostels. These figures can be compared with the data in Table 10.3 collected by Statistics Canada (1991b) that show the distribution of domestic tourist accommodations in Canada.

In terms of selecting a destination country or a combination of several countries, the following were listed: England (most frequently, perhaps because 37 per cent of respondents were of British heritage); England and France; England, Scotland, and France; England, Holland, Ireland, and all neighbouring countries; all western European countries; all western European countries and Yugoslavia; Sweden; Sweden and Italy; Portugal; Austria; Germany and Austria; Denmark, Germany, and Sweden; Italy, France, Germany, and England; Switzerland, Germany, Liechtenstein, France, Yugoslavia, and Austria. Mexico and India were the non-European destinations.

In most instances, respondents in the survey prefer multiple destinations.

Table 10.3 Domestic tourist accommodations (in percentages)

	1980	1990
Friends and relatives	52	50
Cottage	17	19
Hotel	4	7
Campgrounds	14	12
Motels	6	6
Other	7	6
Total	100	100

Such visits are usually of short duration in each country: 31 per cent stay in each of the visited countries for two to five days, 17 per cent for six to seven days, and 28 per cent for one to two weeks. However, further elaboration by respondents who went to Canada and the US or Europe reveal that the preferences and reasons for travel are rather general in nature for most of the respondents. For example, most interviewees feel that if one can find 'history', 'ruins', 'different people', 'natural wonders', and 'great food' in more than one country (especially in Europe), they need not single out one particular country, unless they also wish to visit friends and relatives or search for their family roots. This may reflect the inadequate, ethnocentric 'mental map' of the world (Gould and White 1974) that so many North Americans seem to possess.

In sum, the findings illustrate that (1) family and friends are the preferred travel companions, (2) organized tours are selected only by travellers visiting Europe, and (3) clear differences in reasons for travelling are obvious when North American and European destinations are compared. There is also much 'interchangeability' among destination countries when travelling for reasons other than visiting family or friends in the 'old country'.

As in other leisure pursuits, people's motivations to travel and choice of destinations may be both situation- and destination-specific. Furthermore, the roles played by leisure travellers are not constant but respond to multiple stimuli and personal circumstances over the social time (for example, economic cycles and political upheavals) as well as the individual life cycle.

Unconventional and questionable leisure pursuits
In the past, some people engaged in leisure pursuits of questionable morality, borderline acceptability, or cruelty—whether by contemporary or earlier standards. Various reformers attempted to eradicate those activities, but some still continue today as 'marginal recreation' (Kraus 1984) or are 'on the dark side of leisure' (Gunter and Stanley 1985).

There is no agreement among leisure theorists as to what leisure activities represent the unconventional or questionable. Most often such activities include gambling, pornography, prostitution, illicit drugs, violent sports, and blood sports involving cruelty to animals such as cock-fighting, dogfighting, and bull-baiting; some activities are perceived as blatantly deviant. Most Canadians and Americans do not think highly of the popularity of bullfights in Mexico, Spain, and southern France. They may also be critical of government-sanctioned leisure, such as gambling, to which people might become addicted and lose their earnings and savings.

Theoretical explanations of people's involvement in marginalized, stigmatized, and/or deviant forms of leisure suggest that they are motivated by the basic human need for play (Caillois 1961). As mentioned earlier, leisure can also be a search for excitement as an escape from the mundane—and deviant leisure activities might provide this. Smith and Preston (1985) document that the main motive in gambling is to engage in play, leisure, and recreation (according to 91 per cent of their respondents), and to relieve boredom and generate excitement (45 per cent); among additional reasons are the desire for new experience (32 per cent), and to be sociable and gregarious (21 per cent). It must be pointed out that respondents may be giving socially acceptable, leisure-related explanations for their own gambling, however, when it comes to other people's gambling, people think that others' motives for play, leisure, and recreation decrease in importance (to 43 per cent) and the motive for monetary profit assumes second place (42 per cent).

Cock-fighting is another example of deviant leisure. It has continued into the twentieth century, but because of public outcry against it and laws prohibiting it, this bloody 'sport' went underground (Bryant 1991). McCaghy and Neal (1974) estimate that some half a million people may be involved in some way in cock-fighting, but not all of them are active on a regular basis. In the United States, cock-fighting interests support three monthly magazines with circulations of over 10,000. Bryant (1991) cites the data from the National Gamefowl Fanciers survey, indicating that the majority of people involved in cock-fighting come from rural or small towns and grew up with cock-fighting. Cock-fighting is their major leisure activity, their hobby. Contrary to the popular negative stereotype of cock-fighters, almost 80 per cent of them are married, have children, and more than two-thirds of their spouses approve of cock-fighting and participate in it too.

Other types of popular but questionable leisure activities are the recreational use of alcohol and drugs, hunting, target shooting, and gun collecting. These activities are criticized primarily for the harm they can cause. The recreational use of alcohol and drugs harms the health and financial stability of the users, and perhaps their loved ones, employers, and the general public. Alcohol and drugs can also change perception and mood (Husch 1991). Most people claim that they do it to relax, to forget, or to feel free and uninhibited. These substances are symbolic of non-work, non-productivity, and non-regulated action. Sharing alcohol and other drugs with others in recreational use may serve as an expression of social interaction and intimacy.

Those who oppose hunting and gun collecting associate guns with violence and crime. The hobbyists themselves are often perceived in unflattering terms and their motivations are questioned. Hunters kill for pleasure, which critics perceive as morally controversial (Olmsted 1988). To counter such prejudice, gun enthusiasts try to justify the very aspects of their activities that others devalue (Stenross 1990).

In sum—and aside from our own values and attitudes or moral outrage— we recognize that the human need for play, excitement, thrills, escape, bonding, socialization, and companionship may lead to various marginalized, unconventional, even deviant leisure activities.

IIII Expenditures for leisure and recreation

An indirect indication of participation patterns, preferences, and rates of participation can be based on information about spending related to leisure, recreation, and culture. Leisure or recreation expenditures typically reported in statistical publications are for such items as admission fees, sporting goods and recreation equipment, television sets, stereos, musical instruments, toys and games, material and equipment for hobbies and crafts, and equipment for gardening. Of course not all equipment or memberships are used regularly, if at all, but to purchase them still suggests a degree of interest and commitment. Admission fees for events cannot adequately indicate the number of actual attendances by an individual or family.

In spite of these shortcomings associated with using expenditures to measure participation, corroborative evidence is revealed nevertheless. Overall, both in absolute and relative per capita terms, more money is spent for leisure and recreational goods and services by the younger and middle-aged groups than by older groups. Families of professionals and executives seem to spend more money for leisure products and services than other occupational groups. In absolute terms, the highest income groups spend considerably more for recreation than those with the lowest incomes. Zuzanek (1976) argues that with favourable job and overtime opportunities, even when leisure time decreases, leisure consumption tends to increase. He finds the same paradoxical relationship between leisure time, income, and leisure expenditures crosssectionally. Thus, groups with the largest amount of leisure time, such as old-age pensioners, often cannot afford large expenditures on leisure goods and services because of their low purchasing power.

Ownership of specific items corresponds with the age of the head of the family, educational attainment, and income bracket. For example, adult-size bicycles are found in 62 per cent of households where the head is in the twenty-five to forty-four group, but only in 20 per cent of the oldest heads of households. Downhill skis are distributed more evenly, from 17 per cent among the youngest households, to 19 per cent in the twenty-five to forty-four group and 20 per cent in the forty-five to sixty-four group. Snowmobiles are owned by 27 per cent of rural households, but by only 5 per cent of households in metropolitan areas (Statistics Canada 1983a). The percentage of households owning selected items changed slightly during the 1980s and varied by province. For example, the ownership of downhill skis increased between 1980 and 1987 from 21 per cent to 28 per cent in Alberta, from 17 per cent to 23 per cent in Quebec, and from 14 per cent to 16 per cent in Ontario (Statistics Canada 1988). In 1987, cross-country skis were owned by 21 per cent of Manitoba's households (an increase from 18 per cent in 1980), 13 per cent in British Columbia (from 10 per cent), and 26 per cent in Prince Edward Island (from 18 per cent).

In Alberta, 24 per cent own cross-country skis, 28 per cent alpine skis, 6 per cent own snowmobiles, and 55 per cent own adult-size bicycles (Statistics Canada 1988). There is also some difference between urban and rural areas in the mix of recreational equipment owned (Statistics Canada 1983a). Snowmobiles are more than five times more likely to be found in a rural than in a metropolitan area; similarly, boat ownership is lower in urban areas than elsewhere, while alpine skis and vacation homes are more commonly owned by metropolitan households. The ownership of skis is more widespread in Calgary than in Edmonton (33.8 per cent vs 24.5 per cent), and is the highest among all large cities across Canada (Statistics Canada 1986).

The smallest amount of dollars is spent on admission to cultural events, more on reading material and other printed matter, and the largest sum is allocated to purchases of home entertainment equipment and services (Statistics Canada 1985a). Further variations in family expenditure are related to the province of residence. Expenditures on cultural events in Alberta, Ontario, and British Columbia exceed or match the Canadian average; other provinces lag behind the Canadian average (Newfoundland and Nova Scotia by some $100, and Prince Edward Island by more than $200). Direct consumer expenditure on culture (home entertainment and services, reading material, and admissions to cultural events) represented 2.3 per cent of total consumer expenditure in 1982 (Statistics Canada 1985a).

The average price of the ticket paid for the last attendance in 1991–2 was $23, with prices ranging from $31 in Toronto, $26 in Vancouver, and $24 in Montreal to $19 in Manitoba, $18 in Saskatchewan, and $15 in New Brunswick (Decima Research and Les Consultants Cultur'Inc 1992). The more frequent attenders are prepared to pay more per event, but potential participants are reluctant to pay more, especially for an unfamiliar experience. Not only ticket prices differ between popular culture and élite culture performances, but audiences are prepared to pay different prices too: $22 for a pop or rock concert, $19 for a classical concert, and $16 for a dance.

Personal expenditures on recreation and sporting and camping equipment has fluctuated around 4 per cent of total expenditures since the late 1960s or early 1970s (Statistics Canada 1985b; Statistics Canada 1986, 1988). Interestingly, the range between the lowest and highest income groups is rather small in terms of these percentages (3.7 per cent to 4.1 per cent). The proportion of expenditures spent on recreation equipment and services increased slightly in 1980 to 5.6 per cent and to 6.7 per cent in 1989 (*Canadian Global Almanac* 1992). Purchases of reading and entertainment supplies remained remarkably constant over the years; the proportions of total personal expenditures on consumer goods and services were 1.6 per cent in 1966, 1.7 per cent in 1975, 1.8 per cent in 1980, and 1.7 per cent in 1989. With regard to purchases of art, 24 per cent of Canadians purchased at least one item within the previous year and 20 per cent had done so in the previous five years; however, 44 per cent reported that they never purchased a piece of art and 57 per cent never purchased a craft item either (Decima Research and Les Consultants Cultur'Inc 1992). Purchasers of artwork tend to be older, better educated, and enjoy higher incomes than the average population.

In comparison with some other industrial countries, Canadians appear to be among the lowest spenders on recreation. For example, in Table 10.4, the list of sixteen countries compiled by Max Kaplan (1975:133) documents that

Table 10.4 Expenditures for leisure and recreation

Rank order	Percentage per capita	Country
1	7.9	Italy
2	7.5	Belgium
3	7.3	West Germany
4	7.2	Norway
5	7.0	Sweden
6	6.7	Austria
7	6.6	France
8	6.6	United Kingdom
9	6.4	Ireland
10	6.3	Finland
11	5.9	Iceland
12	5.8	Greece
13	5.4	Luxembourg
14	5.2	United States
15	5.1	Netherlands
16	4.4	Canada

Canada was the last and only country whose residents were spending less than 5 per cent of their total expenditures on recreation in the 1970s.

Scardigli (1989) shows that in Europe in the 1980s, the average per capita expenditures allotted to leisure and culture varied between 4 and 7.5 per cent in all Mediterranean countries and Belgium, regardless of whether the countries were rich or poor, and between 8 and 10 per cent in Scandinavia, the Netherlands, and other Anglo-Saxon countries. He argues that these differences reflect specific cultural traditions and values rather than the countries' economic standing.

In sum, the data indicate that those who spend the most on leisure are married, middle-aged, and have children and high socio-economic status. If measured by the amount spent for recreation, social inequalities in leisure behaviour appear to be rather marked. However, the differences in leisure expenditures as a proportion of disposable income or total expenditures appear to be less stratified, since this proportion increases up to a certain point, but fails to grow in the highest socio-economic groups. The age of the head of household and the family income, rather than education or occupation, seem to have the most direct effects on the amount of leisure expenditures.

▮Ⅲ Summary

We have seen that leisure assumes several additional forms other than the consumption of the mass media. Sports and physical recreation are found throughout Canada; however, there are different rates and patterns of participation in these pursuits. Unlike pursuits of most core leisure activities, participation in sports and physical recreation is related to demographics, is gender- and age-sensitive, and also shows regional variations. The high-culture forms of leisure show lower rates of overall participation and are sensitive to factors similar to those affecting sports and physical recreation. Moreover, such differences are also activity-specific.

We examined serious leisure, which includes amateurism, hobbyism, and volunteering. Serious leisure requires commitment and perseverance, and, unlike most mass leisure activities, provides profound rewards to its enthusiasts. The hobby of collecting and collectors create their own world, which is gender-differentiated.

Leisure activities of immigrants and some ethnic groups can provide the means for identity preservation and boundary maintenance in the compartmentalized world of such groups.

Another form of peripheral, occasional leisure is travel. Like so many other types of leisure, leisure travel incorporates the desire to escape, to relax, to search for new experiences, to explore, and to build significant personal relationships. Leisure travel is not immune to differentiation in its goals and intensity according to demographic, socio-economic, regional, and life cycle stage variables. In contrast to other forms of leisure, unconventional or deviant leisure is often criticized and condemned by some people, but still satisfies the personal and collective needs of others.

Finally, we looked briefly at the expenditures for leisure items, services, and recreation and discovered that, on average, Canadians allocate less than 10 per cent of their total personal expenditures to leisure and recreation. A good part of that amount is spent on various equipment and goods, and less on books, performing arts events, and works of art.

CHAPTER **11**

Leisure throughout
the life cycle

This chapter presents selected data that illustrate the theoretical perspectives about the life cycle and leisure. As mentioned earlier, the literature typically divides the life cycle into three phases, which are spanned by conscious preoccupations, interests, and activities that are both stable and changeable. Furthermore, specific pursuits within the phases correspond not only with the chronological age of an individual but with his or her personal and group characteristics. Different physiological, psychological, and social changes influence leisure at various points in the life cycle as well. A person's leisure needs remain the same or change over time and in different situations. Finally, participation in specific leisure activities is gender- and age-specific, is influenced by contextual factors, and may be constrained by various barriers.

Attias-Donfut (1992) posits that cultural practices and leisure patterns define generations and contribute to the establishment of their collective identity. Rooted in history, cultural practices and leisure patterns make up the distinctive elements of a generational group. Like symbols, they serve as references through which generations are formed, recognized, and defined.

The unequal distribution of most people's time throughout their lives and among different groups contributes to generational differences. Furthermore, differences between generations and groups are related to varying gravitation towards popular culture (particularly the mass media) and to varying interests in sports, culture, leisure travel and tourism, and unconventional types of leisure.

▮▮▮ Youth and leisure

The origins of the following data are quite varied. The findings are based on different samples of various subgroups of youth, and result from applications of different methodologies. It will be interesting to note whether and to what extent these different sources lead to similar observations and conclusions.

Time and activities

The typical Canadian adolescent attends school for about six hours a day, then goes to work for another two (Bibby and Posterski 1992). In between, most students do about two hours of homework and watch about three hours of television, usually when eating or glancing at the newspaper. They also need some time to commute and for other necessary incidentals, such as meals and sleep.

Young people's leisure activities, carried out usually with their friends, are mostly social and cultural activities that take place during weekends and summer holidays. The main reasons for taking part in them are to have fun and to be with their peers (Gagnon and Harbour 1992). These findings are corroborated by the data from Quebec, collected by Paré (1992) in a study investigating 1,068 events in the daily lives of adolescents, and by numerous other surveys and observations. Paré's findings show that young people participate in leisure with their families and peers, and perceive school as a place for both leisure activities and for meeting friends. The home appears to be the primary location for leisure and other activities for most young people. Friendship, followed by music, are two main sources of adolescents' personal enjoyment (Bibby and Posterski 1992; Friesen 1990).

Another similarity in leisure pursuits among most adolescents and young adults is their preference for television and videos, and, above all, listening to 'their' kind of music. Books used to be a popular form of entertainment before the introduction of television. Today, approximately 50 per cent of female adolescents and 30 per cent of male adolescents claim to be frequent readers. The number of teenagers who say they enjoy reading stands at about 40 per cent, and only 18 per cent of teenagers say they enjoy reading 'a great deal' (Bibby and Posterski 1992).

Television is an important daily activity for most young people. More than 80 per cent of fifteen-year-olds watch television at least two hours a day, 35 per cent report four hours or more, while only less than 3 per cent watch television rarely or never. Furthermore, some six in ten say they receive 'a great deal' or 'quite a bit' of enjoyment from television and videos—about double the figure for adults (Bibby and Posterski 1992). On the other hand, interviews with grade ten students reveal that adolescents often say television is boring or associate watching television with having nothing better to do (Shaw, Kleiber, and Caldwell 1993).

The enjoyment of cars is examined in the literature less often. However, it needs to be mentioned at least briefly since driving for pleasure is considered by many people to be one of their most enjoyable leisure activities (Alberta Recreation and Parks 1981–92). According to Bibby and Posterski (1992), just under 40 per cent of all Canadian teens (44 per cent of males and 30 per cent of females) say that they receive a high level of enjoyment from their vehicles. Among those who have their own automobile, the enjoyment level is even higher at 77 per cent (males and females at 80 per cent and 75 per cent respectively). Bibby and Posterski (1992:22) quote a seventeen-year-old male who said, 'What I enjoy most is cruising in my car.'

Music

Perhaps more than any other topic, youth and music receive a great deal of attention by parents and leisure researchers alike. As Kelly (1981) states, various aspects of popular culture—such as vocabulary, clothes, dances, movies, cars, and possessions—make up a set of activities, symbols, and rituals that indicate to others and assure the self that one is really a part of the chosen youth culture. However, more than any other of these elements of popular culture, music is the special mark of the adolescent, the student, and pre-establishment adult. It also fulfils the need for change, since popular music groups, performers, and even their styles change. Of all the forms of popular culture, rock speaks most pointedly to teens (Markson 1990). While television and movies are shared with the adult world, rock music is virtually the exclusive property of the young and expresses adolescent resistance to adult authority.

Markson (1990) points out that, not surprisingly, rock is criticized for being profit-driven, lacking in higher aesthetics, and being thematically simple, technically uncomplicated, repetitive, formulaic, and thus ultimately not beneficial to its audience. Using a dazzling range of rhythms and sounds, the music industry has captivated young people. 'The music industry imprisoned their audience with alluring high-powered videos. For more than 10 years MTV has virtually handcuffed young people to their television sets' (Bibby and Posterski 1992:278).

Concerned parents, school authorities, and others are often horrified by rock music's alleged messages in lyrics. But, as Rosenbaum and Prinsky (1987) and Markson (1990) report, no more than 25 per cent of adolescent respondents are able to interpret lyrics accurately, even those of their favourite songs. These songs are listened to for background noise and to set the mood for other activities in which beat and sound are much more relevant than words and imagery.

One of the most detailed examinations of music interests is presented by Pronovost and Papillon (1988), who studied a representative sample of 2,013 respondents across Canada. These authors document that listening to recorded music is a widespread pursuit in the population. The majority listen to music on the radio, except for youth aged fifteen to twenty-four who listen to cassettes or FM radio stations more frequently. The primary reason for listening—pleasure and entertainment—is shared by both young people ages fifteen to twenty-four and older generations. Unlike older people whose second reason for listening to music is rest and relaxation, young people's is sociability. Furthermore, the young generation distinguishes itself from other age groups by the omnipresence of music in all daily activities, the amount of money spent on music-related purchases, the number of attendances at musical events, the importance of sociability associated with music, and the amount of attention given to the newest musical styles. The young and the most educated are the greatest consumers of music (Pronovost and Papillon 1988).

Similar to the findings of other researchers who find generational differences in genre preference, Pronovost and Papillon document the following preferences:

Ages fifteen to twenty-four: new wave or rock; popular groups and singers; chansonniers, songwriters, authors

Ages twenty-five to thirty-four: popular groups and singers; chansonniers, songwriters, authors; new wave or rock

Ages thirty-five to forty-four: chansonniers, songwriters, authors; easy listening, semi-classical; popular groups and singers

Ages forty-five to fifty-four: easy listening, semi-classical; country and western; chansonniers, songwriters, authors

Ages fifty-five and over: easy listening, semi-classical; country and western; classical music, opera and operetta

Fathi (1990) examines the musical tastes of Canadian male university students. He identifies three types of listeners, depending upon the frequency with which they listen to different types of recorded music: a high-culture listener who listens to high-culture music frequently, even though he may also listen to mass-culture music; a mixed listener who listens to mass-culture music and occasionally to high-culture music; and a mass-culture listener who listens only to mass-culture music. High-culture listeners tend to listen to music alone, while mass-culture listeners prefer to listen with other people, and mixed listeners are in between. The current taste in music among the majority of mass-culture listeners was acquired directly from radio rather than from attending live performances. Unlike these mass-culture listeners, high-culture listeners are more likely to come from homes where two or more family members play a musical instrument.

A special subgroup of the young music listeners are heavy-metal enthusiasts. Like almost all other young people, they claim that music is a big part of their lives and identify their involvement in the subculture as a leisure activity (although some of the activity is carried out during school hours) (Friesen 1990). The heavy-metal listeners' music interest, however, is also associated with various types of existential pleasures, such as getting drunk, driving fast, taking drugs, having sex, and partying. Friesen suggests that these pursuits are in contrast to the long-term, deferred gratification goals of 'normal' society.

Dividing lines

We examined class- and gender-differentiated and segregated youth cultures earlier when we discussed theoretical conceptualizations of leisure during the preparation stage of the life cycle. After searching for further empirical illustrations of such conceptualizations, we are assured that practically all examined literature indicate what Gans (1974) has posited—that the cultural innovations that are often presented by the mass media as parts of a single youth culture are actually parts of several different youth cultures. Likewise, Gagnon and Harbour (1992) find that adolescents aged twelve to seventeen in Quebec do not form a homogeneous group according to gender and age. Adolescents differ in their preferences for individual sports, outdoor recreation, and indoor games and activities, especially by gender. For example, about 60 per cent of male teens and 30 per cent of females say they actively follow sports; the NHL is closely followed by 44 per cent of teenagers, major league baseball by 33 per cent (Bibby and Posterski 1992).

Bynner and Ashford (1992) also document differences in preferred activities and leisure orientation. Even though males' and females' interests coincide to a degree on some of the preferences, they vary widely on others. For example, more male leisure activity in the late teens takes place in public venues like pubs, where storytelling and bravado are dominant features. Girls' social lives are spent mostly at home, where they are immersed in a 'bedroom culture', in which ideas of romance are nurtured by the magazines they read. Among grade ten students, the most common female sports activities are basketball, soccer, and gymnastics; the males are more likely than the females to participate in spontaneous 'pick-up' sports activities such as street hockey (Shaw, Kleiber, and Caldwell 1993).

There are other differences among the sixteen- to seventeen-year-olds as compared with the eighteen- to nineteen-year-olds, at least in the United Kingdom (Bynner and Ashford 1992). There is an increase in some activities, particularly going to pubs, parties, dances, discos, and drinking between the younger and older cohorts, and a decline in others, such as playing sports and attending youth clubs. The empirical evidence shows that members of the older cohort are spending more time with a partner rather than a group, and that there is a slight decline in the number of those who spend time with a group of the same sex.

There are gender differences in different preoccupations and interests as well as in actual activities. Findings from the Canadian national survey of students in grades eight to ten, carried out by Holmes and Silverman (1992), show that concerns about relationships (including those with families, friends, and the opposite sex) are greater among females than males. These gender differences persist across Canada and among different races. Likewise, the relative importance given to various elements of the leisure experience (i.e., status, achievement, atmosphere, risk, and freedom) differs among the high school and junior college male and female students. Ouellet and Perron (1979) document that the boys give more importance to atmosphere and freedom than girls do. Furthermore, males tend more than females to engage in active sports and sports spectatorship, while females' interests tend to lie more in dances and the cinema. When it comes to companions, girls spend more time with their parents or brothers and sisters than boys do, and boys spend more time in a single-sex group (Bynner and Ashford 1992).

Instead of such separate gender-based categories, Wearing's (1992) data suggest a continuum from traditional to non-traditional male and female leisure experiences and subjectivities. She finds that some elements of traditional stereotypes are present in the late adolescent period, but in varying degrees of acceptance, challenge, or resistance. Wearing presents five profiles to illustrate the spectrum of these types: a traditional female, a transitional female, a resistant female, a person who resists both male and female stereotypes, and a non-traditional male.

Further variations specific to Canada are based on linguistic origins and preferences. For example, watching and enjoying television and video appear to be slightly higher in Quebec, as well as among young male and female members of visible minorities (Bibby and Posterski 1992). Similarly, Pronovost and Papillon (1988), who draw from the national survey, are able to distinguish not only the youth subculture and popular and bourgeois subcultures but also cultural differences among anglophones, francophones, and allophones (whose culture or first language is neither English nor French). Although most anglophone or francophone audiences are oriented primarily towards American music, there are differences nevertheless. As Pronovost and Papillon (1988:332) document, these groups differ in their choice of mass media programs and performers, and show the following relationships between the mother tongue and the origin of music or songs.

Table 11.1 Origin of music/songs and the listener's mother tongue (in percentages)

Mother tongue	Franco-Canadian origin	Anglo-Canadian origin	Foreign origin
French	38.7	13.7	47.6
English	0.4	43.6	56.0
Other	2.5	50.8	46.7
Total	11.1	36.1	52.8

British data presented by Bynner and Ashford (1992) document class and gender divisions through a combination of education paths and cultural manifestations of teenage styles and values. The researchers find differences in how leisure time is used, in tastes in clothes and music, in the pubs and clubs attended, in styles of peer relationship and partnership, and in sexual mores.

Bynner and Ashford argue that lifestyle is influenced by the career routes on which young people embark in their teens, routes aimed at professional, skilled, or unskilled occupations. At the ages of sixteen and seventeen, those in academic and vocational routes tend to participate more in sports than those who went into jobs directly from school or via youth training schemes. However, at nineteen and twenty years of age, levels of participation decline in all groups, with broadly the same patterns of difference prevailing. School drop-outs favour watching soap operas, while those who pursue further academic or vocational studies prefer news and documentary programs; the differences are greater for the older than the younger cohort, with no differences for sports programs. By the age of twenty, the distinctive youth culture leisure style no longer differentiates career groups. The drop-outs in particular experience an accelerated transition to adulthood, as they begin to participate in the leisure activities of young adults sooner than those staying in school.

Socialization in leisure

We are already familiar with the role of leisure in identity formation, particularly during the preparation phase. Leisure is one of the most crucial means in this process. Shaw, Kleiber, and Caldwell (1993) take into account gender differences in both the developmental maturation processes and leisure activities. Using data from a survey and interviews with grade ten students, these authors examine the role of leisure activities in adolescents' identity formation. Their findings suggest that social activities with friends have a positive but insignificant effect on identity development for males and a significant negative effect on females. For female students, time spent with friends seems to be associated with lack of involvement in other activities. Furthermore, television viewing tends to be negatively associated with identity development for males but not for females. The authors conclude that for young women, the level of identity development seems to be positively associated with sports participation and negatively associated with time spent socializing. It might be that sports participation may challenge traditional feminine characteristics, while social activities may reinforce these same characteristics. For young men, however, none of the leisure activity categories shows a clear beneficial developmental effect, although high levels of television viewing seem to have a detrimental effect. Shaw, Kleiber, and Caldwell speculate that this is so possibly because identity development for males is more closely associated with a sense of future career or work roles than with current leisure activities.

Still, specific types of leisure activities are associated with higher levels of perceived physical, mental, and social health among college undergraduates. Caldwell, Smith, and Weissinger (1992), who studied the relationship between general health and overall life satisfaction of 525 students and their general leisure participation, report that leisure participation is beneficial from a number of perspectives.

Patterns of leisure activities among young people are so varied that the term 'youth culture', implying uniformity, is not accurate. Also, as Pronovost (1992) posits, the culture of young people covers two aspects of time: the short-term, in which they try to live intensely in the present and the mid-term, which is dominated by the traditional ideal of a warm family life and a rewarding job. Similarly, Gans (1974) suggests that youth cultures exist at two levels: as total cultures that exist apart from mainstream society and in fact try to change or overthrow it, and as partial cultures, which are practised by people who still belong to mainstream society. The total and partial cultures share many values and are opposed to various aspects of mainstream society. For example, they prefer film, music, and art to print culture. Gans concludes that their rejection of mainstream society has less to do with the generation gap than with a fundamental difference in values that is neither limited to the young alone nor shared by all young people.

▮▮▮ Leisure of establishment-phase adults

We will now examine in detail specific activities pursued by married people. Not all individuals in the establishment stage are married, but many of them are for most of that period. We have already examined selected data on leisure participation by age groups and marital status in the chapter on the amount and allocation of leisure time. The following sections focus on married or co-habiting couples and parents during the establishment stage.

Adults and their leisure
The most popular activities that remain stable or show a marked increase in participation among postpreparation adults are those that reflect the main preoccupations of marital and parental life. Contrary to the popular belief about the dominant importance of work in most people's lives, most establishment-phase adults indicate that the family, not work, is the most important thing in their lives (Horna 1985a; Pronovost 1989; Reszohazy 1982).

Married individuals like activities within the leisure and family domains and dislike household chores. These activities are mostly home-based and family-centred. Conjugal and parental leisure pursuits do not usually require a large amount of expensive equipment or advance planning, which suit the pressures and demands of marital and parental roles. Married women and employed mothers have obligations that often do not allow for large blocks of leisure time—a situation highlighted by many feminist studies.

Most adults (regardless of their marital status, age, or gender) are frequent consumers of popular culture, particularly music, reading material, and television. Married couples seem to be no exception to this trend. When people go out, it is to visit relatives and friends, see a movie, or take the family to some outdoor or indoor leisure venue; outdoor activities are reportedly undertaken by close to half of the population (Alberta Recreation and Parks 1981–92; Decima Research and Les Consultants Cultur'Inc 1992; Hantrais 1986; Horna 1985a, 1988b; Kelly 1982, 1983b). Other activities are undertaken regularly by only a small proportion of Canadians. Most of the population (67 per cent) also report attending 'performances in halls' (Decima Research and Les Consultants Cultur'Inc 1992). Although 40 per cent attend between one and four performances a year, almost 30 per cent do not attend at all throughout the year.

Calculations based on data from the Alberta Public Opinion Survey on recreation show that practically all family households watch television and listen to the radio. Married couples twenty-five to fifty-four years of age who have children at home participate in relational activities, visiting, crafts, hobbies, gardening, and home improvement more often than childless couples. Visiting and relational activities (those that people pursue because of their relationships with others) are more frequent in rural households than in urban households, perhaps because of closer family and community ties in the countryside. The rates of participation in fitness, cultural, and sports activities occupy fifth, sixth, and seventh rankings respectively, behind relational activities and visiting, watching television, manual activities, and reading. While regular participation in both cultural and sports activities is at the bottom of the rate ranking, occasional participation in these activities is slightly higher for sports and fitness, and somewhat higher in urban households.

The impact of marriage and parenthood

Leisure participation and specific pursuits change radically upon marriage, especially among women and those under thirty (Henderson et al. 1989; Hochschild 1989; Horna 1987c; Horna and Lupri 1987; Kelly 1982, 1987; Osgood and Howe 1984; Rapoport and Rapoport 1978; Roberts et al. 1976; Zuzanek and Smale 1992). For instance, a part of daily activities that is greater than it used to be before marriage (for example, domestic responsibilities) could not be classified as leisure, and the remaining leisure events are readjusted following marriage (Roberts et al. 1976). Similar to the concept of role-determined leisure noted earlier, Roberts's data indicate that it is marriage rather than parenthood that brings about the main break with adolescent lifestyles. As leisure becomes home-centred, time spent with friends declines sharply. For example, the rate of leisure with friends changes from the premarriage rate of 64 per cent to 17 per cent. Socialization becomes focused on a spouse rather than on a wider circle of friends. For married people, simply being with the family can become a major and valued aspect of leisure.

The importance of conjugal leisure is further corroborated by Horna's findings. When asked to name their favourite activities, relaxing with the spouse was listed more often than any other activity by respondents who have been married for up to ten years. This activity was also among the five most liked activities among men and women who were married for more than twenty years (Horna 1985a). Orthner and Mancini (1991) posit that by the 1980s, desires for companionship reached almost universal proportions. For example, a national sample of adults in the United States indicated that spending time with the family and companionship were the two most common objectives. Orthner and Mancini (1991) also show that the Lynds' Middletown study carried out in the 1920s reported shared family experiences as relatively rare, but the follow-up study in the 1970s found that Middletown couples and families were spending much more time together.

Next to marriage, parenthood creates even more profound change in leisure time and participation. As mentioned earlier, this change affects women more significantly than men. Other influences include employment status, weekly distribution of paid work, and the asymmetrical gender division of domestic and parental duties. Thus, employed mothers have less leisure on workdays and even less on weekends. On the other hand, both single and married men watch television more than twice as often as their female counterparts, and considerably more than mothers not employed outside the home. In fact, employed women with small children watch less television on weekends than during weekdays (Zuzanek and Smale 1992).

The comparative American-Canadian study presented earlier (Harvey 1982) confirms that an individual's marital and parental status affects both the amount of discretionary activity and the distribution of activity among settings. In Jackson, home-centred discretionary time ranged from a low of 45.3 per cent for single employed males with no children to a high of 74.6 per cent for married employed males with no children. This shows a significant reorientation of discretionary time for males upon marriage. In contrast, for employed females with no children, marriage has no effect on where discretionary time is spent as single women are spending 62.6 per cent of their discretionary time at home and married women 62.7 per cent.

These findings are similar to the information obtained by Decima Research and Les Consultants Cultur'Inc (1992). They also posit that age is clearly related to patterns of attending cultural events, and that life cycle stages clarify these patterns. Individuals who are single, under forty-five years of age, and with no children are more likely to attend cultural events, while those least likely to attend are married, with children at home, and under forty-five years of age. Only 13 per cent of this latter group report attending at least five times a year. Overall, these results suggest that attendance for young singles is quite high, but that once married or settled into a live-in relationship, attendance declines and further declines when children arrive. When the early child-raising years are over, attendance tends to increase. Attendance is also higher for older people, especially singles with no children at home.

Married couples in Calgary, Alberta: A case-study
The data reported in this case-study originate from two surveys of married couples carried out in Calgary, Alberta, during 1980–1 and 1985–6. A systematic random sample in 1980 yielded 562 couples, of whom both spouses were interviewed separately. Two survey instruments in 1980 addressed various issues of their work and domestic lives, including the division of labour and power in the family, marital satisfaction and conflict, enactment of pa-

rental roles, and background information on each respondent. Respondents were given a third survey instrument (a questionnaire and a self-addressed, prestamped envelope), to be completed and returned at the respondent's earliest convenience. There were completed questionnaires from 367 female and 359 male respondents, or 346 matched couples. The self-administered questionnaire included questions on estimated typical daily time expenditures (separately on weekdays, Saturdays, and Sundays). The time budget part was followed by questions on annual frequencies of involvement in all activities, co-participants in those activities, reasons for performing them, and the most liked or disliked activities.

The 1985–6 survey had follow-up interviews with a 10 per cent subsample of the original set, yielding fifty-six couples who were married for longer than five years. The interview, recorded in writing, consisted of semi-structured and open-ended questions administered by an interviewer to each spouse separately. The crucial section of the interview, which focused on the life history of each respondent (particularly leisure history), was recorded on audio tapes. In this part of the interview, the interviewer followed a prestructured sequence of questions, but allowed for a free flow of respondents' reminiscences. About 15 per cent of the couples requested a joint taped session during which each spouse expressed his or her opinion and described his or her leisure history before marriage.

The findings from this two-stage case-study document that leisure activities with consistently high rates of participation and relatively long time expenditures include having guests, visiting, talking to friends and relatives on the telephone, playing games with the children, and relaxing with the spouse. Some of the visits, as mentioned by quite a few respondents, extend over several days or a longer vacation period, while others are grandchildren's overnight stays with their grandparents. There tends to be greater joint or parallel family participation in sports, hobbies, television viewing, and going to the cinema, particularly when children are under sixteen years of age. Otherwise, men spend time away from the family for spectator sports more often than their wives do. Table 11.2 illustrates these points.

Of these activities, television viewing is the most prevalent even when only non-sports programs are counted. For most respondents, reading ranks among the regular activities, more so on weekdays than on weekends. The time devoted to reading is rather short, somewhat longer on Saturdays and Sundays among women, but not so among men. Similarly, individual and team sports and physical exercise take place mostly on weekdays, and then mostly for short periods of time. There is a sizeable group of those who do not participate in sports and exercise either on weekdays or weekends. The rate of non-participation on weekdays is about 50 per cent of both men and women; it rises on Saturdays to 52.9 per cent of men and 58.6 per cent of women, and on Sundays to 53.8 per cent of men and 59.9 per cent of women.

Hobbies, crafts, and gardening are especially popular among women and

Table 11.2 Participation (in percentages)

| | With family | | With no one else | |
	Males	Females	Males	Females
Reading	31.8	30.1	57.2	63.0
Exercise, sports	31.5	41.6	27.2	23.1
Hobbies	59.2	50.0	23.4	35.8
Spectator sports	50.3	56.1	22.8	5.8
Television	84.1	87.9	6.1	2.9
Movies	76.9	75.7	3.5	3.5

occur on all days of the week. There are, however, many respondents who do not participate in these pursuits (for example, about 50 per cent of men on weekdays and Sundays, and 39 per cent of men on Saturdays; over 35 per cent of women on weekdays and Saturdays, and 43 per cent of women on Sundays). The degree of participation in spectator sports, including those on television, shows a considerable gender gap, since significantly fewer women than men watch sports. Married couples go to the cinema, theatre, concerts, or other live entertainment infrequently, and when they do, it is usually on Saturdays. The frequency of visiting museums, art galleries, and exhibitions is extremely low on any day of the week, as well as throughout the year.

Thus, married couples' leisure is rather limited and involves only a few activities. Activities with the spouse, family, and friends; reading, hobbies, and sports are the most popular and frequent activities. There is gender asymmetry in leisure in the overall frequencies of participation, time expenditures on different days of the week, and involvement with co-participants. The presence and ages of children not only affect both parents' participation patterns but make the gender asymmetry more unbalanced. The in-depth interviews also showed that most respondents are so satisfied with their existing leisure that they would still choose the same activities and do more of them.

Another conclusion based on this case-study eventually led to the formulation of the stream model presented earlier. The model suggests that most leisure pursuits outside the core activities typically come from either the physical or cultural stream, at least in Calgary, Alberta, given the leisure opportunities available there. Even after experimenting with pursuits from another leisure stream, Calgarians' favourite activities come almost exclusively from the physical stream.

Parental leisure involvement
As mentioned earlier, the major turning point in the lives of married people occurs with the arrival of their first child. They begin to search for activities in

which they can participate with their child, taking into account their child's age and the limits of their discretionary time and finances. As pointed out earlier, Bella (1989) found that many supposedly family leisure activities involved work for women.

During the interviews in Horna's case-study, the majority of parents stressed their preference for activities that encourage togetherness, contribute to family communication, and support child socialization. The parents do not seem to regret giving up some of their former pursuits. Even when children are already in school, leisure is still a family affair, although occasionally only one parent and child participate together, while the other parent may be involved in non-leisure activities or in individual leisure pursuits. In the semi-leisure/semi-work area, more than half of the mothers (but very few fathers) reported volunteer activities. Most of the volunteer work is with schools, clubs, and associations, primarily because of their own child's needs. Not surprisingly, most of these volunteer mothers stop volunteering as soon as the children reach senior high school age. A similar pattern of temporary volunteer work is noted by Henderson et al. (1989) and Varpalotai (1992).

In spite of their emphasis on leisure as a family affair, there are differences in the way fathers and mothers allocate the amount of leisure time spent with their children. The participation frequency also varies between mothers and fathers. Rather surprisingly, husbands of non-employed wives play more often with their children (44.2 per cent) than husbands of full-time working mothers (27.3 per cent); part-time working wives' husbands are similar to homemakers' spouses (44.6 per cent). Perhaps these rates are more likely a function of the child's age than the mother's employment status, since mothers of young children work outside the home least often. Regardless of their employment status or the child's age, mothers are more active than fathers nevertheless.

Fathers seldom compensate for their lower rate of participation in children's games by involving the child in some of their own leisure activities. The data show that fewer than 10 per cent of fathers take their children along to active sports and physical exercise, spectator sports, movies and other commercial entertainment, nor do they share hobbies with their children. However, as the case-study of married couples in Calgary, Alberta, has shown, approximately one-quarter to one-third of the fathers reported that they did not participate with anyone else in sports and physical exercise, spectator sports, or hobbies. In contrast to fathers, mothers' lone participation in sports and physical exercise is lower, and much less so in spectator sports.

The effects of social status and wife/mother employment on family leisure time are complex. Social position has the greatest effect on father-children leisure time, but no effect on husband-wife leisure time (Jorgenson 1977). In Jorgenson's study, the employment of the wife/mother outside the home resulted in less husband-wife leisure time, but also resulted in more shared family leisure time. Wife/mother employment outside the home had little effect on a father's leisure time with children. Jorgenson's study also showed that social class is an important variable when considering leisure patterns and behaviour. Social position was effective in predicting the amount of husband-wife leisure time.

Thus the evidence shows that parents follow traditional roles: women remain more involved in domestic and child-care tasks than fathers do. Men tend to take more time for their individual sports-related leisure pursuits, especially spectatorship, while women spend more time on hobbies, crafts, and gardening, and play more with their children than their husbands do.

One-parent families and leisure
The impact of parenting on leisure is quite different when there is only one parent in the family. According to the Canadian government statistics, over the last decade approximately 13 per cent of all families in Canada were headed by a single parent, and women make up more than 90 per cent of all single parents. We have already noted Streather's (1989) study of one-parent families, which indicated that the leisure needs of single parents are similar to those of other parents: they wish to relax in their own homes and meet other adults; single parents' leisure is home-based and inexpensive, and related to popular culture, primarily watching television or reading.

Contrary to the general perception about the lives of single parents, Decima Research and Les Consultants Cultur'Inc (1992) made a surprising finding that 63 per cent of single parents, who supposedly have less time and money, report going to one or more performances a year. This is a little less than married parents aged forty-five or older (68 per cent), and slightly more than married couples of the same age group without children (61 per cent). Possibly single parents, despite generally more limited finances, have a greater need to get out of the home than other parents and see concerts as a way to do this. However, going to one or a few performances a year does not seem to constitute a rich cultural life.

In her study of single mothers in Nova Scotia, Elizabeth McNaughton (1993) found that on school days, mothers are most likely to spend between four to six hours a day with their children, averaging 5.25 hours; the average hours are 10.2 on Saturdays and 10.5 on Sundays. The children of single mothers receive more help with homework and spend over two hours less per week playing with friends than do the children of married mothers, most likely further curtailing their mothers' leisure time. Kissman and Allen (1993) suggest that depressed economic resources in single-parent families tend to affect family rituals, such as vacations, dining out, and celebrations of important events, and create new ones, such as local mini-vacations and picnics.

Empty-nest leisure
Our earlier discussion of the life cycle stages pointed out that when adult children leave home, middle-aged parents enjoy increased discretionary income and leisure time. This may be the case for many couples; however, not

all can enjoy this new freedom. The discretionary time of many middle-aged women is limited because they are caught between their remaining tasks as parents while taking on new tasks of caring for their elderly parents and in-laws. As Nett notes about this generation in the middle, 'These are the people who look forward to experiencing freedom of the empty nest when children grow up and leave home, but who instead must continue to be involved with adult children and grandchildren at the same time as a parent or parent-in-law requires assistance' (1993:320).

Furthermore, most married women continue to perform and even increase their traditional female role of 'kinkeepers', first studied by family sociologists Sussman (1965) and Reuben Hill with his collaborators (1970). Kinkeepers—who are almost exclusively mothers and mothers-in-law, daughters and daughters-in-law—assume primary responsibility for intergenerational contacts. The contacts may be through correspondence and telephone calls, through various kinds of assistance and emotional support, frequently in the form of semi-leisure or leisure such as family visits, reunions, celebrations, and vacations.

Some theorists suggest that parents in the empty-nest stage tend to move their leisure activities out of the home and embrace new interests. Almost three-quarters of postparental couples in Calgary, Alberta (Horna 1987d), report having the same amount or more of free time than they had five years earlier. The major reason for this change, however, varies between the wives and their husbands. Women who have more free time attribute that change to having fewer family obligations (37.4 per cent); those with less free time blame it on new or extended employment obligations. Men, however, whether they experience more or less free time, attribute the change to their changing work situation rather than changed family obligations.

One respondent described his middle-age leisure experience as follows: 'Most of my activities have been the same over the years except for sports. As we get older and become more independent, one can do so many more things. I try things and realize that is not what I wanted, so I try something else' (male respondent, age group fifty to fifty-four). A woman recalls that her 'leisure hasn't changed . . . not drastically, but my appreciation of life has changed. I enjoy things for what they are worth' (female respondent, age group forty to forty-four).

Smith (1991) conducted a study of postparental married respondents who ranged in age from forty to fifty-five. The results based on his leisure inventory questionnaire suggest that regularly pursued activities remain home-centred and require only minimal resources, such as watching television, reading, hobbies and crafts, cooking, and home maintenance or home improvements. Most of these activities do not involve much time, money, or physical exertion.

Occasional leisure activities are often pursued outside the home, although many are still home-centred and based on socializing, such as entertaining friends at home or relaxing with the spouse. The activities that are only sel-dom pursued are culture-oriented pursuits and community-related activities. They are reported about equally by both men and women.

Major differences in the participation patterns of men and women involve hobbies and crafts, cooking, and sports. The regular activities most frequently mentioned by female respondents include cooking for fun, reading, exercise (aerobics, biking, walking, swimming), hobbies and crafts (knitting, sewing, gardening, collecting, painting, photography), and watching television. Women's activities pursued only on an occasional basis consist of outdoor activities (hiking, backpacking, cross-country skiing), dining out, going to movies, entertaining at home, socializing away from home, relaxing with the spouse, and travelling. The activities in which female respondents seldom or never participate include those related to community involvement (volunteer work and church activities), both team and individual sports activities, and cultural activities (participating in music and singing, visiting museums and art galleries, going to the opera).

Activities most frequently pursued on a regular basis by men include home maintenance (home improvements, puttering around the house), reading, individual sports (golfing, tennis, squash, racquetball, fishing), exercise, and watching sports on television. The activities occasionally pursued by the majority of male respondents consist of outdoor activities, dining out, going to movies, entertaining at home, socializing outside the home, and activities done at home such as watching television, relaxing with the spouse, and listening to music. Most male respondents report infrequent or no involvement in hobbies and crafts, community-related activities, team sports, and cultural activities.

Consistent with reports from other surveys mentioned earlier, 64.3 per cent of Smith's respondents report that they participate in more activities during their middle-age phase than before, while 30 per cent participate in fewer activities. The corresponding percentage of women reporting fewer activities was less than that of their male counterparts. When comparing their current leisure activities with those in the past, almost half of the middle-aged respondents report that their current 'repertoires' are more often than not made up of both old and new leisure activities. Most respondents (60 per cent) currently pursue activities that can be done with their spouses; in fact, many report dramatically increased numbers of such activities.

Furthermore, as mentioned earlier, leisure becomes more important for most postparental adults. Smith's data document that about 70 per cent of the middle-aged adults believe that leisure had become more important to them than it was during their early adulthood years, and only 20 per cent (more men than women) state that leisure had become less important. Men and women feel that in their middle years, when they have more time and money than ever before, they can pursue more activities and enjoy them more often. Many welcome the opportunities to pursue leisure activities that they can do as a couple.

Middle-aged men and women describe their leisure experiences as corresponding with their life cycle changes and continuing from one stage to the next. Current leisure choices and preferences reflect lifelong participation. Most respondents tend to expand their repertoire of leisure choices and preferences (but only those activities they enjoyed in the past), rather than adopt unfamiliar types. The respondents' comments reflect a sense of continuity or at least some common element in past and current leisure activities. More women than men seem to experience greater degrees of change in leisure involvement over the life span, particularly in the opportunities for leisure.

The dual pattern of change and continuity in leisure pursuits, of giving more or less importance to leisure in the establishment phase, may reflect the process of structure building or structure changing (Levinson et al. 1978). This conceptualization posits that the unique pattern or design of an individual's life — life structure — undergoes changes that either reinforce the existing pattern or modify it, thus bringing about structure building or structure changing. Perhaps leisure is associated with such broader processes, although Carpenter (1989) finds little support for such a hypothesis. Her study of middle-aged adults suggests that neither the number of life events nor the positive or negative perception of them are significantly related to valuing leisure. Furthermore, valuing leisure remained constant whether respondents perceived themselves to be changing or not. This may be yet another of the contradictions and controversies related to leisure in our society.

▟ Leisure patterns during the 'third age'

Recent population statistics for Canada show that three-quarters of men over the age of sixty-five are married, but half of the women in this group are widowed, and that almost 15 per cent of men but 37.7 per cent of women live alone (Nett 1993). Furthermore, it is calculated that women born between 1931 and 1940, and between 1951 and 1960 will spend over twelve years of their lives in widowhood. In the group of people eighty years of age and over, 57 per cent of men are married, but only 15 per cent of women have a husband (Dulude 1991). These disproportions inevitably influence the availability of marital partners as primary co-participants in leisure activities. It does not mean, however, that widows live in seclusion with no social contacts. Znaniecka-Lopata (1973, 1979) discovered that the majority of widows have extensive networks of relatives and acquaintances with whom they socialize frequently. Some widows even enjoy greater freedom and independence following the death of their spouse.

The conclusions reached by most theorists about the preoccupations, interests, and corresponding activities during the third stage of the life cycle point out that contrary to the disengagement hypothesis, this 'third age' represents an extension of earlier life patterns. Most individuals do not experience major upheavals as they enter the third age; rather, they come prepared with skills and knowledge developed over a lifetime. Since individuals of different gender, marital status, education, and occupation followed somewhat different paths during the establishment phase, it cannot be expected that people would suddenly become more homogeneous in their behaviour upon reaching a certain age or retirement. As we have seen earlier, even the temporal order (time distribution and allocation) of leisure and recreation among the elderly continues the previous middle-aged pattern (Delisle 1982). Leisure activities among older adults are associated with eight dimensions: self-expression, companionship, power, compensation, security, service, intellectual aestheticism, and solitude (Tinsley et al. 1987). Consequently, the leisure behaviour of individuals in the third age is as varied and unpredictable as that in any other stage (McGuire, O'Leary, and Dottavio 1986).

All of the previous personal traits, gender differences, educational, and socioeconomic characteristics continue to affect the leisure preferences and patterns of the elderly. In addition, this population group has become influenced by such factors as contemporary expectations of increased longevity and generally good health as well as the concerted drive towards healthy lifestyles and active participation in the community. Also the categories of 'young-old' and 'old-old' age ranges need to be recognized in any examination of third age leisure patterns. Not only chronological age but other factors associated with aging, such as adequate resources and health, are increasingly interrelated with leisure. Active retirement with adequate resources and viable health likely contribute to relatively high levels of participation in some activities. Frailty, on the other hand, creates dependency and restricts most activities (Kelly 1987, 1990).

Yet continuation of leisure styles does not mean identical rates of involvement in specific activities. In fact, rates of participation in non-work activities are lower for each age category (Kelly, Steinkamp, and Kelly 1986). The Campbell's survey on well-being in Canada (Canadian Fitness and Lifestyle Research Institute 1989) also reports an age-related decline in participation, especially in more strenuous pursuits. Likewise, Lawton and colleagues (1982) document that advanced age is accompanied by lower rates of active pursuits outside the home. Although the constriction process sets in during the second half of life, it becomes more pronounced in the final period (Kelly 1987). A unique longitudinal study of continuity and discontinuity among two cohorts of people who were sixty to sixty-five and seventy-five years of age respectively at the time of first contact corroborates such North American findings. Tokarski (1989) reports that over the period of fifteen years of following the subjects, the research panel members experienced a reduction in the differentiation of patterns, as well as continuity rather than discontinuity. In his opinion, this supports the theory that lifestyles converge with advancing age.

Most studies that examine the relationship between activity patterns and age show that the primary difference in participation is activity-specific and continues to follow the well-known dividing line between core and peripheral activities. It is quite apparent that the repertoire of leisure pursuits associated with the third age does not differ considerably from those associated with other stages of the life cycle. Continuity is evident especially in the core that consists of accessible and relatively informal leisure activities that make up the ongoing day-to-day centre of non-required activity. The rates of participation tend to remain relatively high in social activities and family leisure in particular. The age-related decrease in participation is much more gradual for activities such as reading, culture, conversation, entertaining, and home improvements than for events and physically demanding activity outside the home (Gordon et al. 1976). In-home cultural activity and formal and informal social engagements are not significantly lower for those sixty-five to seventy-four or seventy-five and over (Kelly et al. 1986). Family interaction and to a lesser extent social leisure are lower for widows in the oldest age group. All this seems to indicate that much of the reduction in participation that is not caused by health trauma or other loss of capacity is at least partly a matter of choice. Older people continue to engage in those activities that bring them into contact with valued others and in which they feel comfortable with their abilities.

Surveys that focus on specific pursuits during the third age indicate that the elderly primarily participate in home-centred activities such as watching TV, reading, writing, doing arts and crafts, visiting, working around the yard (Kelly 1983; Mannell and Zuzanek 1991; Roadburg 1981; Sandrey, Simmons, and Devlin 1986; Singleton 1985; Zuzanek and Box 1988). Participation in most kinds of activities outside the home decreases with age, especially in travel, outdoor recreation, exercise, and sports. Furthermore, the physical and fitness activities in which the elderly take part outside the home do not require coordination and organization in advance (Pageot 1985, 1986). Generally, men are more interested than women in sports activities, including competitive sports; women prefer dancing and aerobic exercises. Although men and women participate in different activities, they are engaged in a number of activities to about the same extent. Both male and female seniors frequent seniors' clubs and shows equally often, and report no significant difference in the frequency of visits to or from relatives and friends (Delisle 1982).

According to the findings of the Alberta Recreation and Parks survey (1991), the top ten most frequently reported activities among those sixty-five or older include walking for pleasure (78 per cent); driving for pleasure (67 per cent); gardening (65 per cent); visiting a museum, live theatre, gallery (55 per cent); doing crafts and hobbies (49 per cent); attending sports events as spectator (38 per cent); picnicking in the countryside (38 per cent); fishing (29 per cent); dancing (26 per cent); swimming in pools (24 per cent). Curiously, television viewing and socializing are not included in this list; this is more likely because of the survey methodology than an indication that elderly Albertans do not watch television and do not engage in socializing with relatives and friends.

Even seniors visiting national parks are not uniform in their choices, motivations, and travel styles. For example, the most important motives given by seniors visiting Banff, Jasper, Kootenay, Waterton, and Elk Island national parks are being in an outdoor setting, learning about nature, and having a change from daily routines (Rollins 1993). They vary considerably in their preferences for travel styles and degrees of independence and spontaneity. Rollins's data make it possible to distinguish five groups of senior travellers:

Affluent
- do not look for special deals
- do not worry about money
- prefer longer trips

Independent planners
- enjoy planning a trip
- make travel arrangements well in advance
- do not like to travel in groups
- like special deals

Peer-conscious
- want to be with people their own age
- have similar interests as younger people
- like to do things on the spur of the moment
- like special deals

Cautious
- want everything organized for them
- do things on the spur of the moment
- want to travel in groups
- prefer day trips
- do not have interests similar to younger people's

Spontaneous
- like to do things on the spur of the moment
- prefer exotic foods
- do not usually like planning a holiday
- do not like making travel arrangements in advance
- do not like having everything organized for them

Although travel and taking part in community organizations might decrease somewhat with age, the participation is markedly lower only for those who are frail. Some even join Elderhostel, an international educational travel program that offers relatively inexpensive, short-term academic programs hosted by educational institutions around the world.

Estimates of leisure in the future suggest that the recent higher rates in some activities among those now in their twenties, thirties, and forties, in comparison with what today's older cohorts did when they were the same age, may lead to higher but still declining frequencies in the future. As Levy (1992:7) argues, 'never before in the history of society has there been an aging society that is as vigilant about its health as the present 50 year-old group.' In relative terms, the fifty-plus age group is the fastest-growing physically active cohort.

In sum, it may be suggested, as Kelly and Ross (1989) do, that in spite of no clear agreement on details, there is a general consensus on activity participation and satisfaction. In general, older people participate less than younger people in many kinds of activities, especially those that require physical exertion. The rates of participation, however, fall most precipitously for those age categories that have the largest proportion of the physically frail. In contrast, participation in social and family activities is consistently high for all age groups. Activities that are most accessible and involve interaction with family and friends seem most likely to be maintained in later years.

▮▮▮ Summary

We have learned that leisure activities in which young people participate most often are primarily social and cultural, provide fun and relaxation, and are carried out in the company of friends. Television and listening to music are the two most important daily activities for most young people. Rock music expresses adolescent resistance to adult authority. There are important gender-based dividing lines in young males' and females' interests and preferences for specific leisure pursuits, and differences in social origin influence the choice in future careers.

During the establishment phase, the most popular and frequent activities reflect the primary preoccupations of marital and parental life. Leisure participation and specific activities change radically upon marriage. The desire for companionship is reflected in leisure activities that couples can do together. The next major turning point in the lives of married people, especially women, occurs with the arrival of their first child. Leisure for married couples becomes limited to only a few activities. In spite of their emphasis on leisure as a family affair, men's and women's leisure patterns grow further apart during the establishment period.

The third age is a continuation of earlier leisure patterns; however, seniors' rates of participation are reduced in each age category, although less so in the core daily activities than in more strenuous pursuits like travel, outdoor recreation, exercise, and sports. Most of the older individuals engage in those activities that are manageable for them and that bring them into contact with family and friends. Most of the gender-based and other differences from earlier life cycle stages continue.

Such findings underscore our overall observation that most people of all ages focus their leisure around friends, spouse, and children, and prefer companionship over solitude in leisure.

Throughout the 1980s, Decima surveyed attitudes towards money and leisure time (Gregg and Posner 1990). Between 1980 and 1986, a majority of their respondents said that they would rather save their money for retirement than spend it. Two out of three said they would rather spend money on a house than on travel. Furthermore, most people prefer to eat dinner at home than in a restaurant (although their number had declined by 9 per cent by 1986).

On two occasions, Decima's respondents were asked what they would like to do if they were stranded on a desert island. Some 70 per cent said they would prefer to spend time with their current partner or spouse or with an attractive person of the opposite sex. Only 14 per cent said they would want a library of all books one would ever want to read, and just 6 per cent chose a television set with all the channels and videos available, while 3 per cent opted for all the music one would ever want to listen to.

CHAPTER **12**

Leisure constraints and barriers

$\mathbf{T}$he initial problem with examining barriers to leisure is defining what constitutes a barrier. Ellis and Rademacher propose the definition that 'a barrier to recreation participation is any factor which precludes or limits an individual's frequency, intensity, duration, or quality of participation in recreation activities' (1986:2). Since the commonly used term 'barriers' fails to capture the entire range of reasons for not participating in leisure or ceasing participation, the more generic term 'constraints' is proposed (Jackson 1988). Constraints inhibit people's ability to participate in leisure activities, to spend more time doing so, to take advantage of leisure services, or to achieve a desired level of satisfaction.

In addition to lack of time or a task overload, perceived competence and perceived control (based on Iso-Ahola's 1980 attribution theory), and personal attributions that hinder 'optimal leisure functioning' (Ellis and Witt 1984) are associated with leisure constraints. Other constraints may include impediments to enjoyment (Witt and Goodale 1981), leisure satisfaction (Beard and Ragheb 1980), or perceived freedom in leisure (Ellis and Witt 1984; Witt and Ellis 1985). In connection with these constraints, Tinsley and Tinsley (1986) examine the attributes of leisure experience and the conditions necessary to experience leisure. Empirical findings lead to the conclusion that conceptualizing barriers as impediments to a desired leisure activity may be too narrow since there is usually a weak relationship between preferences and participation (Crawford and Godbey 1987). Instead, there may be different types of relationships between preferences, barriers, and participation. For example, lack of interest may result from idiosyncracies on the part of some individuals or from deference to their partner's wishes.

Leisure constraints or barriers may also be conceptualized as the reduction of alternatives (Goodale and Witt 1989; Jackson 1988, 1991; Jackson and Searle 1985; Romsa and Hoffman 1980). This conceptualization recognizes that people initially have a broad range of choices at their disposal, not all of them practical or possible. In each case, the range of available choices becomes reduced. Some of the reducing factors or barriers block participation and consequently preclude it, while others inhibit and limit but do not preclude participation (Jackson and Searle 1985). For example, lack of interest and lack of knowledge represent blocking barriers.

▮▮▮ Classification of leisure constraints

Leisure researchers suggest that constraints include those that are external (environmental, often physical, but sometimes also social, economic, political, etc.), those internal to the individual (psychological, intrapersonal), and those that are social and relational (sociopsychological, interpersonal) (Goodale and Witt 1989). Another classification of leisure constraints groups them into intrapersonal, interpersonal, and structural (Crawford and Godbey 1987). Intrapersonal barriers include stress, depression, anxiety, religiosity, kin and non-kin reference group attitudes, socialization influences, sense of competence, and personal evaluations of the appropriateness and availability of leisure activities (Crawford and Godbey 1987). These barriers interfere with leisure preferences and are unstable and changeable. Interpersonal barriers include aspects of a marriage that may be brought into the partnership by each spouse or created by their interaction or by the parent-child relationship.

The combination of external, social, and relational constraints—perhaps all three types of constraints together—may be manifested through the division of domestic work, enactment of parental roles, and personal sacrifices—of leisure in particular. Interestingly, most individuals tend to perceive constraints associated with the external environment more readily than those associated with their personal characteristics or lifestyle (Soubrier, Ouellet, and Deshaies 1993).

A further distinction is made between those constraints or barriers that are permanent and those that are temporary (Iso-Ahola and Mannell 1985). Thus, some of the constraints may only partially inhibit leisure participation on occasion, or participation may be blocked entirely by other barriers or at other times. For example, there are people who are already participating in a given activity but are unable to increase the frequency of participation despite their wish to do so (Wall 1981). Lack of interest is interpreted not as a barrier or as an antecedent but as a consequence of non-participation. Likewise, lack of time and perhaps money are not so much barriers but reasons or just excuses for non-participation and, as such, may impede increased participation or continued participation (Jackson 1988).

Correspondingly, sources of constraints are classified into the social-personal, social-cultural, and physical categories (Iso-Ahola and Mannell 1985). Iso-Ahola and Mannell distinguish additional constraints that are felt during or following an activity, and set apart the enjoyment during the participation from satisfaction afterwards as a result. According to Ellis and Witt (1984) personal traits such as an individual's perception of control and competence, need satisfaction, capacity to become deeply involved in an activity, and play-fulness may endure over time and predispose individuals to experience leisure states, while a leisure state or condition may be transitory. A lack of such traits constitutes a barrier to leisure, which is primarily intrapersonal in nature and related to self-concept.

Neulinger's (1981) paradigm of leisure and non-leisure distinguishes these two states on the basis of personal perceptions and motivations. When individuals lose their ability to be spontaneous, when their leisure becomes more a means to an end than an end in itself, when leisure is perceived as a necessity (Godbey 1981), such personal barriers, perhaps also affected by external forces, contribute to the state of 'antileisure'.

▮▮▮ Activity-specific and age-specific constraints

Most studies of leisure barriers and constraints address those that are related to leisure globally or they examine particular activities, for example, hiking (Bialeschki and Henderson 1988), stamp-collecting (Olmsted 1987), bridge (Scott 1991), outdoor recreation (West and Merriam 1970), time with children (Nock and Kingston 1988), pool (Chick, Roberts, and Romney 1991), tennis (Thompson 1992), and aerobics (Frederick and Shaw 1993). Only a few studies to date have examined constraints affecting multiple activities, groups of activities, or specific constraints in relation to groups of leisure activities.

Among the complex examinations of leisure constraints and specific factors associated with them are the studies carried out by Edgar L. Jackson himself or in collaboration with Mark Searle, Elaine Dunn, and Peter Witt. The latest study (Jackson 1993) groups more than sixty specific activities into non-mechanized outdoor recreational activities, physical health and exercise activities, team sports, mechanized outdoor activities, and hobbies and home-based activities. The groups of constraints faced by people who would like to start a new activity are time commitments, facilities, costs of participating, social and geographic isolation, and lack of skills. For example, the findings document that costs affect primarily individuals who would like to participate in mechanized activities, followed by outdoor recreation, hobbies and home-based activities, physical exercise, and lastly, team sports. Facilities affect potential participants in the following activity groups (in decreasing order of importance): physical exercise, outdoor recreation, mechanized activities, team sports, hobbies and home-based activities. Individuals who would like to get involved in a hobby or home-based activity complain primarily about limiting time commitments.

Ouellet and Soubrier (1989) and Soubrier, Ouellet, and Deshaies (1993) studied leisure constraints. The first survey lists twelve activities mentioned by at least 10 per cent of respondents as those in which they would like to participate or those in which they would like to increase their participation (Ouellet and Soubrier 1989). These leisure activities include (in decreasing order of importance) downhill skiing, swimming, travel, reading, tennis, hockey, badminton, soccer, bicycling, movies, sailboarding, and socializing with friends.

The total of 235 activities mentioned by Ouellet and Soubrier's respondents is grouped into three categories: physical and sports activities; outdoor activities; and artistic, cultural, and social activities. Constraints include distance, transportation; high costs; time, schedule; inadequate selection of activities; administration of programs; services; inadequate staff; place; lack of partners; characteristics of associates; risk, danger; difficulty, effort; lack of stimulation; prohibiting values; fear, tension; lack of knowledge; and lack of competence. The findings indicate that physical and sports activities are affected primarily by time constraints, lack of partners, and high costs. Outdoor activities can be constrained by high costs, distance or transportation, or a lack of partners. Artistic, cultural, and social activities appear to be less constrained than the two previous groups, and primarily involve problems with time or schedule, high costs, or a lack of partners. All constraints and their effects on the three activity groups (Ouellet and Soubrier 1989) are listed in Appendix 1.

Age-specific examination of leisure constraints suggests that overall, age exerts a considerable influence on leisure activity preferences (Jackson 1993). Thus, isolation has the highest mean scores among the youngest and oldest groups. The influence of costs declines steadily with age, but the lack of skills increases in importance, and time commitments negatively affect middle-aged people in particular.

These findings, however, are somewhat inconsistent when each activity is examined according to age group. For example, the desire to participate in health and exercise activities remains relatively stable across all groups; also stable are preferences for mechanized outdoor recreational activities. In contrast, the desire to participate in team sports declines from the youngest group to those ages thirty-seven to forty-three, after which it remains stable. The preference for hobbies and home-based activities increases after the age of fifty and even more after the age of sixty-five.

McPherson (1990) concludes that seniors face both individual and institutional barriers. At the individual level, barriers include lack of motivation, negative attitudes towards leisure, and lack of experience, as well as a decline in health and energy, an inability to drive, a reduction in discretionary income, and the loss of a spouse. Barriers resulting from societal factors are numerous and varied; they include lack of information about leisure opportunities; a lack of community leisure programs, counselling, or facilities for seniors; unavailability of public transportation; prevailing myths or negative stereotypes concerning the supposed interests (or lack of) and abilities of older adults; a fear of being victimized if they leave their home or familiar neighbourhood; and local or regional norms or cultural values that discourage the involvement of older adults in certain activities or facilities.

The notion of age-specific constraints notwithstanding, only a relatively small proportion of individuals sixty-five years of age are affected by leisure constraints (McGuire, O'Leary, and Dottavio 1986). An examination of specific limitors and prohibitors reveals a u-shaped pattern characteristic for the lack of leisure companions as a limitor—the youngest and oldest respondents appear to be limited by this lack more so than middle-aged individuals. McGuire, O'Leary, and Dottavio report that lack of money, lack of transportation, safety concerns, and lack of information affect people of all ages differently. For example, a lack of leisure companions becomes less important as age increases, while lack of time, lack of money, and lack of transportation become more important in middle age compared to the earlier or later years. There are life cycle differences in the relative importance of time as a constraint in dependence on the stage of life cycle and also differences as to whether the concern is for reduced participation or cessation of an activity.

In sum, the multitudinal examination of leisure constraints in combination with activity-specific and age-specific approaches offer the greatest promise for assisting us to better understand leisure constraints, impediments, or barriers. However, it is not so much the chronological age of a person but his or her work and marital status, and the stage of the family life cycle that affect leisure most profoundly. A couple with a child below the age of six faces more challenges than a couple without children in the home (Witt and Goodale 1981; Witt and Jackson 1993). In addition, constraints for a single-parent family with a child younger than six are different compared to those of husband-wife families with children of the same age.

▥ Non-leisure and leisure non-participants

Why do people not participate in the first place, and why do so many quit once they start (Boothby, Tungatt, and Townsend 1981; Jackson and Dunn 1988)? Jackson and Searle (1985) identify some commonalities and categorize the types of barriers as follows: non-participation because of lack of interest; non-participation because of internal or person-specific barriers such as lack of information about opportunities, lack of motivation or skills; and non-participation because of external or situation-specific barriers such as lack of facilities or programs. In fact, it is also argued that those who are not interested in a specific leisure activity should not be included among the non-participants. Other types of non-participants may include those who face constraints or barriers as participants and want (but are unable) to increase the frequency or intensity of their participation; former participants who have ceased participating (Boothby, Tungatt, and Townsend 1981; Jackson and Dunn 1988); and people who participate but are unable to achieve the desired level of satisfaction or enjoyment (Beard and Ragheb 1980; Francken and van Raaij 1981; Witt and Goodale 1981).

The fact that certain people have ceased participating in an activity, however, does not automatically imply that they are no longer interested in it. People may cease participating because their personal, economic, or social circumstances have changed, or because recreation facilities may no longer be available to them. While all former participants can be classified as nonparticipants after ceasing participation, the reverse is not true. Some former participants may continue to want to participate in the activity in the future, while others may switch to another activity that would not be recognized if only activity-specific participation or discontinuity are recorded. Empirical data indicate that the rate of ceasing activities by some individuals may be compensated for by a number of new participants in a given activity. For example, replacement rates in an Alberta sample (Jackson and Dunn 1988) were 400 per cent in creative activities and handicrafts, 376 per cent in body-building, and 342 per cent in bicycling, but only 79 per cent in racquetball and squash, and 30 per cent in curling.

◧ Feminist contribution to the study of leisure constraints

It is not hyperbole to say that studying women's leisure means studying leisure constraints faced by women. Beyond the factual accounts showing that women have (or do not have) much leisure time that can be divided into longer or shorter blocks, feminists point to other crucial factors common to women's leisure experience (Bella 1989; Deem 1982, 1986, 1992; Green, Hebron, and Woodward 1990; Henderson et al. 1989; Shaw 1985b, 1989; Wimbush and Talbot 1988). We mentioned one such factor earlier — the ethic of care, originally conceptualized by Gilligan (1982), that pertains primarily to the lives of women.

The concept of the ethic of care implies that women's caretaking role may deprive them of leisure time and also preclude them from doing activities for themselves because of the belief that to do so would be selfish (Henderson and Allen 1991). The ethic of care may be considered both an antecedent that connotes an attitude resulting from socialization, as well as an intervening constraint to leisure because it may directly affect a decision to do an activity on a daily basis. Women also tend to be more accommodating when it comes to finding and coordinating leisure time, and selecting leisure activities carried out with the spouse, children, and friends.

Other factors that constrain leisure for women are the patriarchal and androgynous expectations that family leisure constitutes women's leisure (Bella 1989); women's interpretation of particular activities (for example, playing with children, which differs from men's interpretation) as leisure or non-leisure (Horna 1989d; J. Smith 1987); and women's subjective experience with leisure, for example, when women and men share similar objective constraints, but women subjectively experience them in a different fashion (Harrington, Dawson, and Bolla 1992). Issues such as concerns for personal safety and security during leisure outings (Henderson, Stalnaker, and Taylor 1988) and body image (Frederick and Shaw 1993; Miller and Penz 1991; Shaw 1991) also represent constraining factors for many women.

In sum, feminist analysis of leisure constraints deserves full credit for bringing to the forefront of leisure studies specific, qualitative aspects of leisure and non-leisure experiences.

▉▉ Substitutability and negotiations in leisure

Do the constraints and barriers to leisure mean that most people are limited in their leisure experience or perhaps entirely excluded from it? Can those individuals whose leisure activities are impeded or blocked find another acceptable substitute for the one that is not available for whatever reason? Some authors suggest that for many people, some of their activities may be substituted with little loss in satisfaction (Hendee and Burdge 1974).

Iso-Ahola posits that 'for the leisure participant, substitution means that the originally intended or desired behaviour is no longer possible' (1986:369), that the participant faces a barrier to his or her continued participation. Perceived freedom of choice and perceived comparability of alternatives from which to choose are central to substitutability. The determinants of one's willingness to substitute may be divided into those coming from the individual's perception and analysis of the need and reason to substitute, and the individual's perception and qualities of the activity to be replaced and the available alternatives.

Typically, a person evaluates the reason for substitution and tries to determine what can be done with the available activities. The substitution process is quite distinct from the general human need for change, novelty, variety, or optimal arousal. However, the general human need for change and novelty is present in the substitute leisure behaviour as it is in the original leisure behaviour (Iso-Ahola 1986). Katteler (1985) emphasizes that whether or not a substitute activity will provide a similar level of satisfaction will depend largely on the participants' motivations in relation to their age, gender, and education. There is inadequate information about specific substitutable activities beyond mostly anecdotal evidence. If a person cannot find a partner for a game of squash, will he or she look for a tennis partner instead, go for a solitary hike, or stay at home and watch television?

Do the actual constraints or the anticipation of constraints result in the process of substitution or in a suppressed desire to pursue one's selected activity? We are finding evidence that participation in desired activities depends, among other factors, on the ability to negotiate successfully through the constraints to leisure. Crawford, Jackson, and Godbey (1991) argue that leisure participation is heavily dependent on negotiating through multiple factors that must be overcome to experience leisure. This may be even more so for women with disabilities (Henderson, Bedini, Hecht, and Schuler 1993), especially when leisure is viewed as therapy, not as an entitlement in their lives.

The evidence collected by Samdahl and Jekubovich (1993) documents that leisure constraints are commonly confronted in daily routine, but people are often creative and successful at finding ways to negotiate those constraints. In the case of time constraints, people alter their routines or establish rules that reconcile the demands in their lives with leisure of their own choosing. They coordinate their leisure time with the schedules of desired co-participants, and may accept the fact that only smaller, not larger, blocks of time are available to them. People manage financial constraints by reducing the frequency of participation or they modify their options (perhaps by substituting other activities). They find alternative activities when facing health constraints.

▮▮▮ Experience of constraints

This section presents examples of some leisure constraints, such as work and family commitments and related time constraints, financial difficulties, a lack of opportunities or facilities, inadequate transportation, and a lack of partners for joint activities (Alberta Recreation and Parks, 1981, 1990, 1992; Canada Fitness and Amateur Sport 1986; Harrington and Dawson 1993; Harrington, Dawson, and Bolla 1992; Jackson 1983, 1993; Jackson and Searle 1985; Romsa and Hoffman 1980; Wall 1981; Witt and Goodale 1981; Witt and Jackson 1993).

Objective constraints
Work commitments, family commitments, overcrowding or lack of facilities, and a lack of partners are cited most frequently in Alberta (Alberta Recreation and Parks 5:Table II). In 1988, the cost of equipment and supplies was the most widely perceived barrier to participation (47.2 per cent), followed by work commitments (43.9 per cent), facility overcrowding (39.9 per cent), and admission fees (37.2 per cent) (Alberta Recreation and Parks 28:8). Curiously, the climate or unfavourable weather conditions are not mentioned among the barriers to Albertans' leisure and recreation. It cannot be determined from the findings whether this absence of the climate factor results from the survey methodology, since climate was not included on the list of possible barriers. Or perhaps the residents of cold-climate Alberta take their environment as unavoidable and accept climate limitations to their activities without giving them a second thought. The cross-country Canada Fitness survey (Canada Fitness and Amateur Sport 1983) documents that lack of time because of work is the main reason cited by people for not increasing their activity levels, while lack of partners ranks third and family commitments are in the fifth place.

Gender asymmetry, as we have seen earlier, implies that women tend to have less free time and married women's leisure in particular is most frequently hindered by their familial and parental obligations, while men's lack of time is often due to their work commitments (Henderson et al. 1989; Horna 1987d; Horna and Lupri 1987; Meissner et al. 1975; Shaw 1984, 1985a). When women report interference with their leisure, it is primarily because of their children's needs (Horna 1989d). We may reiterate that men, if they report interference with their leisure at all, claim that it is usually because of work rather than their children's needs. Also, the frequency of interference from the family and household is greater for women than for men. On the other hand, single parents experience both men's and women's types of impediments, and their incomes (which are often low) further curtail access to paid leisure pursuits or purchases of leisure and recreation equipment. Furthermore, practically all single parents complain about a lack of adult company and being on call since many are never able to spend any time away from their children (Streather 1989).

The results of the 1981, 1984, 1988, and 1992 Alberta surveys mentioned earlier document that by the 1988 survey, physical barriers increased in importance over the life span, while cost factors tended to decrease in importance (Alberta Recreation and Parks 28). Work and family commitments were particularly important for adults between twenty-five and forty-four years of age. Young adults and older adults over sixty-five again mentioned barriers of not knowing where to participate or learn the activity, and of having difficulty in finding partners to participate with. The effects of admission, equipment, and transportation costs are most strongly felt by those in the lower income categories (Alberta Recreation and Parks 28). In 1992, the cost of equipment and supplies was important to varying degrees for 28.7 per cent of respondents. On the other hand, the effects of time commitments associated with family and work increase in importance as income increases. The overall impact of barriers is the greatest for those with annual incomes below $30,000 and for single-parent families. Further details can be examined in the above-mentioned publications by Jackson since his calculations are based on the Alberta Recreation and Parks' surveys.

Subjective interpretations

Research into leisure behaviour, enjoyment, and constraints takes into consideration the effects of gender roles on opportunities for leisure and the interpretation of specific activities. We have already noted earlier that leisure as a block of time or as an activity separated from work is not as accessible for women as it is for men; women's leisure is woven into their daily lives (Bialeschki and Henderson 1986; Deem 1986). Men and women with similar lifestyles may have different needs for leisure and derive different satisfactions from the same leisure activities (Colley 1984). Consequently, they may interpret leisure constraints differently. Women may engage in family leisure experiences that are not their ideal choice but that provide interaction with other family members. Will they perceive such activities as leisure or will they find them impediments to leisure?

Horna's data (1989d, 1991) document that women and men view their daily activities as leisure, semi-leisure/semi-work, or work disproportionately. Such differences, however, are not the same across all activities. Regular paid work is perceived solely as work by only some 65 per cent of women and 58 per cent of men, while about a quarter of men and women report semi-leisure/semi-work qualities in their labour force participation. Child care tasks and domestic obligations and chores are perceived differently by women and men. Child care is perceived as semi-leisure/semi-work by 72.3 per cent of mothers, but only by 40.2 per cent of fathers; as pure work by 4.1 per cent of mothers, but by 15.1 per cent of fathers; and simply as leisure for 15.5 per cent of mothers and 25.5 per cent of fathers. Games and play with the children are mostly considered as leisure by 68.7 per cent of mothers and 77.1 per cent of fathers; it is considered semi-leisure/semi-work by 27.1 per cent of mothers and 14.6 per cent of fathers. Interestingly, 4.2 per cent of mothers and 6.2 per cent of fathers consider games with the children neither leisure nor work.

Over half of the women view cooking as their semi-leisure/semi-work activity, 26.8 per cent assign a work quality to it, and only 14.3 per cent view cooking as their leisure. In contrast, cooking is leisure for 35.7 per cent of men, semi-leisure/semi-work for the same proportion, and work for only 17.9 per cent of men. Household chores are perceived as work (60.7 per cent of women, 46.4 per cent of men) or semi-leisure/semi-work (32.1 per cent of women, 33.9 per cent of men). While almost no women or men consider these chores as leisure (5.4 per cent and 3.6 per cent respectively), 16.1 per cent of men view household chores as neither work nor leisure. The traditional male contribution to the family and household needs, such as maintaining and repairing things around the house, yard, and garage, is work for 17.9 per cent of men (39.2 per cent of women), leisure for 16.1 per cent (6.0 per cent), and semi-leisure/semi-work for 60.4 per cent of men (33.5 per cent of women).

Volunteer work in various capacities, which is often portrayed as leisure involvement, is semi-leisure/semi-work for 60.4 per cent of women and 48.4 per cent of men, with a somewhat greater tendency among women than men to view it as leisure, while 21 per cent of men view volunteer work as work (only 11.2 per cent of women do so); the rest consider volunteer work neither work nor leisure.

Reading is leisure for 92.9 per cent of women and 85.7 per cent of men. It is viewed as semi-leisure/semi-work by 5.4 per cent of women, but by 12.5 per cent of men, which likely reflects men's tendency to read more non-fiction. Sports and physical exercise are leisure for approximately 65 per cent of both men and women and semi-leisure/semi-work for 25 per cent of men and women. Similarly, hobbies and crafts are leisure for 62.5 per cent of both women and men, and semi-leisure/semi-work for more than 30 per cent of men and women, most likely reflecting extrinsic values of their products.

Additional free-time pursuits that are viewed primarily as leisure by over 80 to 93 per cent of both men and women include television, commercial entertainment and movies; listening to the radio, records, or tapes while doing nothing else; visiting friends and relatives; relaxing with the spouse; or relaxing and daydreaming alone. There are, however, greater differences between women's and men's perceptions of such activities as having guests in one's home and spectator sports. Having guests is more work than leisure for many, since 50 per cent of women and 44.6 per cent of men view this as semi-leisure/semi-work, and just 46.4 per cent of women and 55.4 per cent of men consider it as leisure (which most likely reflects all the work that goes into shopping, cooking, serving, and cleaning when guests are expected). Spectator sports are not only more frequent and time consuming among men than women, as mentioned earlier, more men than women (92.9 per cent vs 77.1 per cent) consider them leisure activities; a further 12.8 per cent of women view spectator sports as neither work nor leisure, or as work (6.2 per cent).

▪◫ Summary

A refined conceptualization of leisure constraints makes it possible to express variations better, particularly when it comes to the nature and role of constraints on leisure participation, the distinction between barriers and reasons for non-participation, and the classification of constraints. Constraints inhibit people's ability to participate in leisure activities, to spend more time doing so, to take advantage of leisure services, or to achieve a desired level of satisfaction. In short, leisure constraints or barriers may also be interpreted as the reduction of alternatives in leisure pursuits or choices. Leisure constraints include several types: external (environmental, often physical but sometimes also social, economic, political, etc.), those internal to the individual (psychological, intrapersonal), and those that are social and relational (socio-psychological, interpersonal). Furthermore, they are activity-specific, age-specific, and sensitive to different stages of the life cycle.

Numerous leisure theorists and researchers have contributed to the development of the theory and empirical examination of leisure constraints and barriers. However, feminist studies of leisure deserve special recognition for contributing to the better understanding of subjective leisure constraints, which include the effects of the ethic of care, women's different subjective interpretations of activities, and women's specific subjective experiences with leisure.

Postscript

$\mathbf{W}$e have seen that leisure means different things to different people, and that individual and group experiences with leisure and with constraints or barriers to leisure are also differentiated.

Theorists and researchers point out in their subjective and objective definitions of leisure that leisure is indeed a multifaceted phenomenon. Leisure cannot be equated with free time, but it definitely thrives better when there is adequate discretionary time. The retired or the unemployed do not enjoy the luxury of a neverending, unconstrained leisure; in fact, the retirees' perception of leisure differs from that of working people, not so much in terms of free time but in their emphasis on enjoyment and relaxation.

The chasm between those theorists who view leisure from a liberal democratic perspective and emphasize its therapeutic value, and those who emphasize that leisure does not represent real freedom, that the alienation, consumerism, and manipulation in and through leisure is becoming wider and does not show signs of being surmounted. Some, like Rojek (1985), propose reconstructing our understanding of leisure to focus on the permissible rules of pleasure. Others, like radical feminists, not only challenge leisure's androcentric orientation but call for a complete countering of the patriarchal society through revolutionary changes and radically altered leisure perceptions and experience for women. In between are numerous other conceptualizations and theoretical perspectives that require our attention and study.

Dividing one's life into three phases representing the youth and education period, work life and marriage, and retirement, and one's day into eight hours for work, eight hours for sleep, and eight hours for leisure do not seem to apply in our contemporary world any more. Furthermore, many researchers find that marriage, family, and friends are central elements in most people's leisure. Most people choose daily core leisure activities such as watching television, interacting and conversing with family or friends, reading, and walking. The peripheral activities are less frequent compared to core activities; however, several of them (such as cultural pursuits, sports, outdoor recreation, and leisure travel) may be more popular. Other peripheral activities, such as those that are morally controversial or deviant, may be condemned by many but practised by a few nevertheless. Urbanites may watch as much television as their rural counterparts, but the two groups differ in their preferences for various sports and community participation.

The male-female gender asymmetry in the work and household domains is strongly reflected in the amount and distribution of discretionary time and in access or constraints to leisure participation, as well as in different motivations for and perceptions of specific pursuits. There is little evidence of any improvement in this gender inequity; most fathers and mothers still spend their time with children differently, and most men take more time for spectator sports than women do.

Given the continued gender, social, and economic inequalities in our society, Charles Brightbill's (1961) humanist plea to 'let recreation help us live a really democratic life and use it to attain sound emotional and physical health and make our daily lives more zestful' is still waiting for its day of fulfilment. We still hope the time will come when everyone everywhere will be able to live according to Article 1 in the *Charter for Leisure*, proclaimed by the World Leisure and Recreation Association:

> Leisure is a basic human right. This implies the obligation of governments to recognize and protect this right, and of citizens to respect the right of fellow citizens to leisure.
>
> This means that no one shall be deprived of this right for reasons of colour, creed, sex, religion, race, handicap or economic condition.

Appendices

Appendix 1

Figure 1 Levels of constraints attributed to groups of leisure activities

Levels

1 Distance

2 High costs

3 Schedule

4 Inadequate offer

5 Administration of programs

6 Services

7 Inadequate staff

8 Place

9 Lack of co-participants

10 Characteristics of associates

11 Risk

12 Difficulty and effort

13 Lack of stimulation

14 Prohibiting values

15 Fear, tension

16 Lack of knowledge

17 Lack of skills, competence

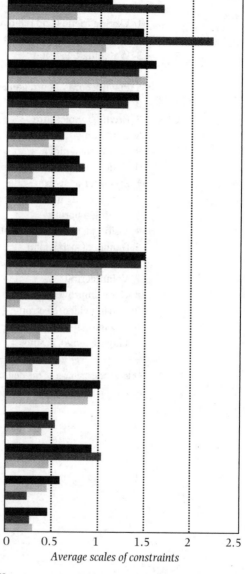

■ Physical and sports activities
▓ Outdoor activities
▒ Cultural, artistic, and social activities

Average scales of constraints

Source: G. Ouellet et R. Soubrier, 'Étude des contraintes perçues comme causes de la non-participation aux loisirs', *World Leisure and Recreation* 31(1):20, 1989.

Appendix 2

Table 1 Top activities by participating households,* Alberta, 1984 (in percentages)

Activity	Per cent
1 Visiting friends and relatives	90
2 Listening to radio, records	90
3 Watching television	90
4 Dining out	86
5 Playing cards, board games	82
6 Reading	81
7 Driving for pleasure	78
8 Gardening	75
9 Attending a movie	74
10 Crafts and hobbies	73
11 Spectator at sports events	71
12 Participating in groups or clubs	70
13 Visiting a library	70
14 Visiting a museum, art gallery, live theatre	62
15 Dancing (social, folk)	61
16 Attending educational courses	58
17 Volunteering	55
18 Home improvement	55
19 Playing video/electronic games	52
20 Engaging in drama, music, drawing	45
21 Playing bingo, casinos	27

*At least one member of the household participating

Source: Alberta Recreation and Parks 13:3.

Table 2 Top activities by participating households,* Alberta, 1988 (in percentages)

Activity	Per cent
1 Walking for pleasure	89
2 Driving for pleasure	79
3 Gardening	70
4 Doing a craft or hobby	68
5 Visiting a museum, art gallery, live theatre	65
6 Bicycling	64
7 Sports events as a spectator	64
8 Swimming (in pools)	60
9 Picnicking in the country	51
10 Overnight camping	51
11 Fishing	50
12 Dancing (social, folk, jazz, ballet)	47
13 Attending educational courses	46
14 Ice skating	46
15 Swimming (outdoors)	41
16 Golf	40
17 Playing video/electronic games	37
18 Aerobics/fitness	34
19 Downhill skiing	34
20 Softball, baseball	34

*At least one member of the household participating

Source: Alberta Recreation and Parks 25: Figure 1.

Table 3 Individuals pursuing outdoor and sports activities, Alberta, 1984 (in percentages)

Activity	Per cent
1 Walking for pleasure	30.2
2 Swimming	20.1
3 Overnight camping	16.7
4 Fishing	16.3
5 Golf	16.3
6 Bicycling	16.1
7 Aerobics, fitness	10.8
8 Softball, baseball	9.9
9 Hunting	7.8
10 Curling	7.6
11 Downhill skiing	7.5
12 Jogging, running	7.4
13 Picnicking	7.1
14 Cross-country skiing	6.1
15 Ice hockey	6.1
16 Body-building, weightlifting	5.4
17 Bowling, lawn bowling	5.3
18 Racquetball	4.9
19 Motor, trail biking	4.3
20. Ice skating	4.3
21. Day hiking	4.3

Source: E. Dunn, *1984 Public Opinion Survey on Recreation: Summary of Final Results* (Edmonton: Alberta Recreation and Parks, 1985).

Table 4 Top ten activities, Alberta, 1984

Most participated	Most favoured	Most desired
1 Visiting friends	Camping	Racquetball
2 Watching TV	Golf	Tennis
3 Radio listening	Downhill skiing	Swimming
4 Dining out	Fishing	Downhill skiing
5 Pleasure driving	Hockey	Cross-country
6 Board games	Pleasure walks	Golf
7 Pleasure walks	Reading	Curling
8 Reading	Swimming	Bowling
9 Picnicking	Racquetball	Calisthenics
10 Attending movies	Curling	Hockey

Source: Alberta Recreation and Parks 11:3.

Table 5 Trends in activities by participating households,* Alberta, 1981, 1984, 1988 (in percentages)

Activity	1981	1984	1988
Stable or slight decline			
1 Walking for pleasure	88	85	89
2 Gardening	74	75	70
3 Visiting museums, art galleries	74	62	65
4 Bicycling	62	63	64
5 Fishing	55	52	50
6 Golf	35	39	40
7 Downhill skiing	36	36	34
8 Soccer	20	21	17
9 Skateboarding	14	n/a	12
Moderate decline			
10 Crafts and hobbies	78	73	68
11 Spectator at sports events	75	71	64
12 Camping	65	57	51
13 Ice skating	58	53	46
14 Video, electronic games	44	52	37
15 Softball, baseball	42	44	34
16 Ice hockey	28	28	22
17 Hunting	28	22	22
18 Curling	26	23	21
19 Cross-country skiing	31	29	21
20 Tennis	31	25	20
21 Badminton	22	22	16
Marked decline			
22 Drama, music writing	47	45	33
23 Jogging, running	54	45	31
24 Bowling/lawn bowling	43	29	26
25 Racquetball	28	26	16
26 Rollerskating	33	24	11
27 Football	24	19	11
28 Backpacking	20	13	8

*At least one member of the household participating

Source: Alberta Recreation and Parks 31:Table 1.

Table 6 Top Ten activities for each age group, Alberta, 1988 (in percentages)

Activity	Per cent
Under twenty-five	
Walking for pleasure	89
Driving for pleasure	78
Attending sports events as spectator	69
Bicycling	67
Swimming (in pools)	64
Dancing	62
Crafts/hobbies	60
Visiting a museum, theatre, gallery	58
Overnight camping	58
Educational courses	54
Twenty-five to thirty-four	
Walking for pleasure	89
Driving for pleasure	80
Attending sports events as spectator	66
Crafts/hobbies	63
Bicycling	63
Swimming (in pools)	60
Visiting a museum, theatre, gallery	59
Overnight camping	57
Gardening	55
Picnicking in the countryside	52
Thirty-five to forty-nine	
Walking for pleasure	86
Driving for pleasure	77
Gardening	69
Visiting a museum, theatre, gallery	67
Attending sports events as spectator	64
Crafts/hobbies	59
Picnicking in the countryside	58
Bicycling	57
Swimming (in pools)	51
Overnight camping	51

Table 6 (continued)

Activity	Per cent
Fifty to sixty-four	
Walking for pleasure	83
Gardening	75
Driving for pleasure	74
Visiting a museum, theatre, gallery	60
Crafts/hobbies	57
Attending sports events as spectator	52
Picnicking in the countryside	50
Dancing	39
Bicycling	38
Fishing	36
Sixty-five or over	
Walking for pleasure	78
Driving for pleasure	67
Gardening	65
Visiting a museum, theatre, gallery	55
Crafts/hobbies	49
Attending sports events as spectator	38
Picnicking in the countryside	38
Fishing	29
Dancing	26
Swimming (in pools)	24

Source: Alberta Recreation and Parks 30: Table 2.

References

ACKERMAN, N., and B. PAOLUCCI. 1983. 'Objective and Subjective Income Adequacy: Their Relationship to Perceived Life Quality Measures'. *Social Indicators Research* 12:25–48.

ACOCK, A.C. 1984. 'Parents and Their Children: The Study of Inter-generation Influence'. *Sociology and Social Research* 68:151–71.

ACOCK, A.C., and V.L. BENGTSON. 1978. 'Socialization and Attribution Processes: Actual vs Perceived Similarity Among Parents and Youth'. *Journal of Marriage and the Family* 40:519–30.

ADORNO, T.W., E. FRENKEL-BRUNSWICK, D. LEVINSON, and R. SANFORD. 1950. *The Authoritarian Personality*. New York: Harper and Row.

AGGER, B. 1991. 'Critical Theory, Poststructuralism, Postmodernism: Their Sociological Relevance'. *Annual Review of Sociology* 17:105–31.

ALBERTA RECREATION AND PARKS. 1981–90. *Public Opinion Survey 1981, 1984, 1988, 1990, 1992. A Look at Leisure* series. Edmonton: Alberta Recreation and Parks.

ALBERTA TOURISM, PARKS, and RECREATION. 1992. *Alberta Recreation Survey 1992*. Edmonton: Alberta Tourism, Parks, and Recreation.

ALDOUS, J. 1978. *Family Careers: Developmental Change in Families*. Toronto: John Wiley.

ALLCOCK, J.B. 1988. 'Tourism as a Sacred Journey'. *Loisir et Société/Society and Leisure* 11 (1):33–48.

ALLEN, L.R., and M.A. DONNELLY. 1985. 'An Analysis of the Social Unit of Participation and the Perceived Psychological Outcomes Associated with Most Enjoyable Recreation Activities'. *Leisure Sciences* 7:421–46.

ALLPORT, G.W. 1968. 'The Historical Background of Modern Social Psychology'. In *The Handbook of Social Psychology*, Volume 1, edited by G. Lindzey and E. Aronson. Reading, MA: Addison-Wesley.

ALTERGOTT, K. 1988. *Daily Life in Later Life*. Newbury Park: Sage Publications.

AMABILE, M., W. DEJONG, and M.L. LEPPER. 1976. 'Effects of Externally Imposed Deadlines on Subsequent Intrinsic Motivation'. *Journal of Personality and Social Psychology* 34: 92–8.

ANDERSEN, N. 1961. *Work and Leisure*. London: Routledge and Kegan Paul.

ANDERSON, G.M., and J.M. ALLEYNE. 1979. 'Ethnicity, Food Preferences, and Habits of Consumption as Factors in Social Interaction'. *Canadian Ethnic Studies* 11 (1):83–7.

ANDERSON, R. 1975. *Leisure: An Inappropriate Concept for Women?* Canberra, Australia: Government Publishing Service.

ANDORKA, R. 1987. 'Time Budgets and Their Uses'. *Annual Review of Sociology* 13:149–64.

ANDREW, E. 1981. *Closing the Iron Cage: The Scientific Management of Work and Leisure.* Buffalo: Black Rose.

ANDREWS, F.M. 1980. 'Comparative Studies of Life Quality: Comments on the Current State of the Art and Some Issues for Future Reesearch'. In *The Quality of Life: Comparative Studies,* edited by A. Szalai and F.M. Andrews. London: Sage Publications, 273–85.

ANDREWS, F.M., and S.B. WITHEY. 1976. *Social Indicators of Well-Being: Americans' Perceptions of Life Quality.* New York: Plenum.

ANGRIST, S. 1967. 'Role Constellation as a Variable in Women's Leisure Activities'. *Social Forces* 45 (3):423–31.

ARIÈS, P. 1962. *Centuries of Childhood: A Social History of Family Life.* New York: Knopf.

ARMSTRONG, P., and H. ARMSTRONG. 1978. *The Double Ghetto: Canadian Women and Their Segregated Work.* Toronto: McClelland and Stewart.

ATCHLEY R.C. 1977. *The Social Forces in Later Life.* Belmont, CA: Wadsworth.

ATTIAS-DONFUT, C. 1992. 'Génération et repère culturels'. *Loisir et Société/Society and Leisure* 15 (2):419–35.

BAMMEL, G., and L.L. BURRUS-BAMMEL. 1982. *Leisure and Human Behavior.* Dubuque, Iowa: William C. Brown.

BANDURA, A. 1977. *Social Learning Theory.* Englewood Cliffs, NJ: Prentice-Hall.

———. 1986. *Social Foundations of Thought and Action: A Social Cognitive Theory.* Englewood Cliffs, NJ: Prentice-Hall.

BANNON, J.J. 1986. 'The United States: An Educational Overview'. In *International Directory of Academic Institutions in Leisure, Recreation and Related Fields,* edited by M. D'Amours. N.p.: World Leisure and Recreation Association, 259–66.

BARBU, Z. 1976. 'Popular Culture: A Sociological Approach'. In *Approaches to Popular Culture,* edited by C.W.E. Bigsby. London: Edward Arnold, 39–68.

BARNETT, L.A. 1991. 'Developmental Benefits of Play for Children'. In *Benefits of Leisure,* edited by B.L. Driver, P.J. Brown, and G.L. Peterson. State College, PA: Venture, 215–47.

———, and G.E. Chick. 1986. 'Chips Off the Ol' Block: Parents' Leisure and Their Children's Play'. *Journal of Leisure Research* 18 (4):266–83.

BAUMGARTNER, R., and T. HEBERLEIN. 1981. 'Process, Goal, and Social Interaction Differences in Recreation: What Makes an Activity Substitutable'. *Leisure Sciences* 4 (4):443–58.

BEARD, J.G., and M.G. RAGHEB. 1980. 'Measuring Leisure Satisfaction'. *Journal of Leisure Research* 12 (1):20–33.

———. 1983. 'Measuring Leisure Motivation'. *Journal of Leisure Research* 15 (3):219–28.

BECKER, B.W. 1976. 'Perceived Similarities Among Recreational Activities'. *Journal of Leisure Research* 8:112–22.

BELL, C., and P. HEALEY. 1973. 'The Family and Leisure'. In *Leisure and Society in Britain,* edited by M.A. Smith, S. Parker, and C.S. Smith. London: Allen Lane.

BELL, R., and L.V. HARPER. 1977. *Child Effects on Adults.* New York: Wiley.

BELLA, L. 1989. 'Women and Leisure: Beyond Androcentrism'. In *Understanding Leisure* and Recreation: Mapping the Past, Charting the Future, edited by E.L. Jackson and T.L. Burton. State College, PA: Venture, 151–79.

BELLEFLEUR, M. 1983. 'Loisir et pouvoir clérical au Québec, 1930–1960'. *Loisir et Société/ Society and Leisure* 6 (1):141–65.

BELLONI, M.C. 1985. 'Daily Use of Time and Social Behaviour: Reflections on an Italian Case'. *Loisir et Société/Society and Leisure* 8 (2):821–40.

BELK, R.W., and M. WALLENDORF. 1990. 'Of Mice and Men: Gender Identity in Collecting'. In *The Gender of Material Culture*, edited by K. Ames and K. Martinez. Ann Arbor: University of Michigan Press.

_____, et al. 1988. 'Collectors and Collecting'. *Advances in Consumer Research* 15:548–53.

BENGTSON, V.L. 1975. 'Generation and Family Effects in Value Socialization'. *American Sociological Review* 40:358–71.

_____, and L. TROLL. 1978. 'Youth and Their Parents: Feedback and Intergenerational Influence in Socialization'. In *Child Influence on Marital and Family Interaction*, edited by R.M. Lerner and G.B. Spanier. New York: Academic Press, 215–40.

BENNETT, T., and J. WOOLLACOTT. 1987. *Bond and Beyond: The Political Career of a Popular Hero*. New York: Methuen.

BERGIER, M.J. 1981. 'A Conceptual Model of Leisure-Time Choice Behaviour'. *Journal of Leisure Research* 13:139–58.

BERNARD, M. 1984. 'Leisure-Rich and Leisure-Poor: The Leisure Patterns of Young Adults'. *Leisure Studies* 3 (3):343–61.

BIALESCHKI, M.D. 1990. 'The Feminist Movement and Women's Participation in Physical Recreation'. *Journal of Physical Education, Recreation, and Dance* 61 (1):44–7.

_____, and K. HENDERSON. 1986. 'Leisure in the Common World of Women'. *Leisure Studies* 5:299–308.

_____. 1988. 'Constraints to Trail Use'. *Journal of Park and Recreation Administration* 6:20–8.

BIBBY, R.W., and D.C. POSTERSKI. 1985. *The Emerging Generation: An Inside Look at Canada's Teenagers*. Toronto: Irwin.

_____. 1992. *Teen Trends: A Nation in Motion*. Toronto: Stoddart.

BISHOP, D.W. 1970. 'Stability of the Factor Structure of Leisure Behavior: Analyses of Four Communities'. *Journal of Leisure Research* 2:160–71.

BLANCHARD, K., and A. CHESKA. 1985. *The Anthropology of Sport: An Introduction*. South Hadley, MA: Bergin and Garvey.

BLAU, J.R. 1988. 'Study of the Arts: A Reappraisal'. *Annual Review of Sociology* 14:269–92.

BLISHEN, B., and T. ATKINSON. 'Anglophone and Francophone Differences in Perceptions of the Quality of Life in Canada'. In *The Quality of Life*, edited by A. Szalai and F.M. Andrews. London: Sage Publications, 25–39.

BLUMER, H. 1954. 'What Is Wrong with Social Theory?' *American Sociological Review* 19:3–10.

_____. 1966. 'Sociological Implications of the Thought of George Herbert Mead'. *American Journal of Sociology* 71:535–44.

_____. 1969. *Symbolic Interaction*. Englewood Cliffs, NJ: Prentice-Hall.

BLYTH, D.A., et al. 1982. 'Mapping the Social World of Adolescents: Issues, Techniques, and Problems'. In *Social Cognitive Development in Context*, edited by F. Serafica. New York: Gilford.

BOLLA, P., D. DAWSON, and M. HARRINGTON. 1991. 'The Leisure Experience of Women in Ontario'. *Journal of Applied Recreation Research* 16 (4):322–48.

BOOTHBY, J., M.F. TUNGATT, and A.R. TOWNSEND. 1981. 'Ceasing Participation in Sports Activity: Reported Reasons and Their Implications'. *Journal of Leisure Research* 13 (1):1–14.

BOTTERILL, T.D., and G.P. BROWN. 1985. 'Leisure Studies in the United States: A British Perspective'. *Leisure Studies* 4:251–74.

BOURDIEU, P. 1984. *Distinction: A Social Critique of the Judgement of Taste.* London: Routledge and Kegan Paul.

BOYD, M. 1988. 'Changing Canadian Family Forms: Issues for Women'. In *Reconstructing the Canadian Family: Feminist Perspectives,* edited by N. Mandell and A. Duffy. Toronto: Butterworths, 85–109.

BRADLEY, I.M., and M. WARD. 1979. *The Nature of Exposure to the Performing Arts Among Audiences in 16 Canadian Communities.* Ottawa: Secretary of State, Arts and Culture Branch.

BRAKE, M. 1980. *The Sociology of Youth Culture and Youth Sub-Cultures.* London: Routledge and Kegan Paul.

BRANDENBURG, J., et al. 1982. 'A Conceptual Model of How People Adopt Recreation Activities'. *Leisure Studies* 1 (3):263–75.

BRANTLINGER, P. 1983. *Bread and Circuses: Theories of Mass Culture as Social Decay.* Ithaca: Cornell University Press.

BRAUN, C.M.J., and J. GIROUX. 1989. 'Arcade Video Games: Proxemic, Cognitive and Content Analyses'. *Journal of Leisure Research* 21:92–105.

BRIGHTBILL, C.K. 1960. *The Challenge of Leisure.* Englewood Cliffs, NJ: Prentice-Hall.

_____. 1961. *Man and Leisure: A Philosophy of Recreation.* Englewood Cliffs, NJ: Prentice-Hall.

BRODY, E.M. 1990. *Women in the Middle.* New York: Springer.

BROOKS, J., and D. ELLIOT. 1971. 'Prediction of Psychological Adjustment at Age Thirty from Leisure Time Activities and Satisfactions in Childhood'. *Human Development* 14:51–61.

BRYANT, C.D. 1991. 'Deviant Leisure and Clandestine Lifestyle: Cockfighting as a Socially Disvalued Sport'. *World Leisure and Recreation* 33 (2):17–21.

BULLOCK, C. 1983. 'Qualitative Research in Therapeutic Recreation'. *Therapeutic Recreation Journal* 17 (4): 36–43.

BURDGE, R.J. 1969. 'Levels of Occupational Prestige and Leisure Activity'. *Journal of Leisure Research* 1 (2):262–74.

_____. 1974. 'The State of Leisure Research as Reflected in the *Journal of Leisure Research*'. *Journal of Leisure Research* 6 (4):312–17.

_____. 1983. 'Making Leisure and Recreation Research a Scholarly Topic: Views of a Journal Editor, 1972–1982'. *Leisure Sciences* 6:99–126.

BURGESS, E.W., and H.J. LOCKE. 1945. *The Family: From Institution to Companionship.* New York: American Book Company.

BURT, R.S. 1987. 'Social Contagion and Innovation: Cohesion Versus Structural Equivalence'. *American Journal of Sociology* 92:1287–1335.

BURTON, T.L. 1971. *Experiments in Recreation Research.* London: Allen & Unwin.

_____. 1979. 'The Development of Leisure Research in Canada: An Analogical Tale'. *Loisir et Société/Society and Leisure* 2 (1):13–32.

_____, and E.L. Jackson. 1989. 'Leisure Research and the Social Sciences: An Exploratory Study of Active Researchers'. *Leisure Studies* 8:263–80.

_____. 1990. 'On the Road to Where We're Going: Leisure Studies in the Future'. *Loisir et Société/Society and Leisure* 13 (1):207–27.

Butcher, J. 1993. 'Physical Leisure Through the Lifespan: The Case of the Master Swimmer'. In *Proceeding of the 7th Canadian Congress on Leisure Research*, 155–8. Winnipeg: University of Manitoba.

Butler, R.W. 1989. 'Tourism and Tourism Research'. In *Understanding Leisure and Recreation: Mapping the Past, Charting the Future*, edited by E.L. Jackson and T.L. Burton. State College, PA: Venture, 567–95.

Bynner, J., and S. Ashford. 1992. 'Teenage Careers and Leisure Lives: An Analysis of Lifestyles'. *Loisir et Société/Society and Leisure* 15 (2):499–520.

Caillois, R. 1961. *Man, Play, and Games*. Glencoe, IL: Free Press.

Caldwell, L.L., E.A. Smith, and E. Weissinger. 1992. 'The Relationship of Leisure Activities and Perceived Health of College Students'. *Loisir et Société/Society and Leisure* 15 (2):545–56.

Campbell, A. 1981. *The Sense of Well-Being in America: Recent Patterns and Trends*. New York: Russell Sage Publications.

_____, P.E. Converse, and W.L. Rodgers. 1976. *The Quality of American Life: Perceptions, Evaluations, and Satisfactions*. New York: Russell Sage.

Campbell, E.Q. 1969. 'Adolescent Socialization'. In *Handbook of Socialization Theory and Research*, edited by D.A. Goslin. Chicago: Rand-McNally, 821–60.

Canada Fitness and Amateur Sport. 1979. *Partners in Pursuit of Excellence: A National Policy on Amateur Sports*. Ottawa: Government of Canada.

_____. 1983. *Canada Fitness Survey: Fitness and Lifestyle in Canada*. Ottawa: Government of Canada.

_____. 1984. *Canada Fitness Survey: Changing Times—Women and Physical Activity*. Ottawa: Government of Canada.

_____. December 1984-January 1986. *Canada Fitness Survey: Highlights, Numbers 42–6, 66, and 67*. Ottawa: Government of Canada.

_____. 1986. *Canada Fitness Survey: Regional and Community Type Differences in the Physical Activity Patterns of Canadian Adults*. Ottawa: Government of Canada.

Canadian Fitness and Lifestyle Research Institute. 1989. *Campbell's Survey on Well-Being in Canada: Highlights*. Ottawa: Canadian Fitness and Lifestyle Research Institute.

Canadian Global Almanac 1992: A Book of Facts. 1992. Toronto: Global Press.

Cantelon, H., and R.S. Gruneau. 1988. 'The Production of Sport for Television'. In *Not Just a Game*, edited by J. Harvey and H. Cantelon. Ottawa: University of Ottawa Press.

Card, J.A., and C. Kestel. 1988. 'Motivational Factors and Demographic Characteristics of Travel to and from Germany'. *Loisir et Société/Society and Leisure* 11 (1):49–58.

Carisse, C. 1975. 'Family and Leisure: A Set of Contradictions'. *Family Coordinator* (April):191–7.

Carpenter, G. 1985. 'The Leisure-Feminism Link'. *Leisure Information Quarterly* 11 (3):5–6.

_____. 1989. 'Life Change During Middle Adulthood and Valuing Leisure'. *World Leisure and Recreation* 31 (1):29–31.

CERULLO, M., and P. EWEN. 1984. 'The American Family Goes Camping: Gender, Family, and the Politics of Space'. *Antipode* 16:35–45.

CHACE, D.R., and N.H. CHEEK. 1979. 'Activity Preferences and Participation: Conclusions from a Factor Analytic Study'. *Journal of Leisure Research* 11:92–101.

CHAFETZ, J.S. 1988. 'The Gender Division of Labor and the Reproduction of Female Disadvantage'. *Journal of Family Issues* 9 (1):108–31.

CHAMBERS, D.A. 1986. 'The Constraints of Work and Domestic Schedules on Women's Leisure'. *Leisure Studies* 5:309–25.

CHAMBERS, I. 1986. *Popular Culture: The Metropolitan Experience*. New York: Methuen.

CHASE, D.R., and G.C. GODBEY. 1983. 'The Accuracy of Self-Reported Participation Rates'. *Leisure Studies* 2 (2):231–5.

CHEEK, N.H., and W. BURCH. 1976. *The Social Organization of Leisure in Human Society*. New York: Harper and Row.

_____, D.R. FIELD, and R.J. BURDGE. 1976. *Leisure and Recreation Places*. Ann Arbor, MI: Ann Arbor Science Publishers.

CHERRY, G.E. 1979. 'British Observations on Leisure Research in Canada'. *Loisir et Société/ Society and Leisure* 2 (1):239–54.

CHICK, G., J.M. ROBERTS, and A.K. Romney. 1991. 'Conflict and Quitting in the Monday Nite Pool League'. *Leisure Sciences* 13:295–308.

CHODOROW, N. 1978. *The Reproduction of Mothering: Psychoanalysis and the Sociology of Gender*. Berkeley: University of California Press.

CLARKE, A.C. 1956. 'The Use of Leisure and Its Relation to Levels of Occupational Prestige'. *American Sociological Review* 21:301–7.

CLARKE, J., and C. CRITCHER. 1985. *The Devil Makes Work: Leisure in Capitalist Britain*. Urbana, IL: University of Illinois Press.

_____, et al. 1976. 'Subcultures, Cultures, and Class'. In *Resistance Through Rituals*, edited by S. Hall and T. Jefferson. London: Hutchinson.

CLAUSEN, J. 1986. *The Life Course: A Sociological Perspective*. Englewood Cliffs, NJ: Prentice-Hall.

COAKLEY, J. 1990. *Sport in Society: Issues and Controversies*. St Louis: Mosby.

COHEN, E. 1979. 'Rethinking the Sociology of Tourism'. *Annals of Tourism Research* 6:18–38.

_____. 1986. 'Tourism and Time'. *World Leisure and Recreation* 28 (5):13–16.

COLEMAN, J.S. 1961. *The Adolescent Society*. New York: Free Press.

COLEMAN, M.T. 1988. 'The Division of Household Labor: Suggestions for Future Empirical Consideration and Theoretical Development'. *Journal of Family Issues* 9 (1):132–48.

COLES, L. 1980. 'Women and Leisure: A Critical Perspective'. In *Recreation Planning and Social Change in Urban Australia*, edited by D. Mercer and E. Hamilton-Smith. Malvern, Australia: Sorrett.

COLLEY, A. 1984. 'Sex Roles and Explanations of Leisure Behaviour'. *Leisure Studies* 3:335–41.

COLLEY, L. 1985. 'Work Occupation and Leisure Patterns of Selected Self-Supporting Women in Pre- and Post-Retirement'. *Loisir et Société/Society and Leisure* 8 (2):631–58.

COOK, S.D. 1989. 'U.S. Leisure Patterns and Outbound Travel'. *Travel and Tourism Analyst* 3:33–51.

Cook, T.D., and C.S. Reichardt, eds. 1979. *Qualitative and Quantitative Methods in Evaluation Research*. Beverly Hills: Sage Publications.

Corbet, E., and A. Rasporich, eds. 1990. *Winter Sports in the West*. Calgary: Historical Society of Alberta.

Corsaro, W.A., and D. Eder. 1990. 'Children's Peer Cultures'. *Annual Review of Sociology* 16:197–220.

Cox, A.E., et al. 1985. 'Sport in Canada, 1868–1900'. In *History of Sport in Canada*, edited by M.L. Howell and R.A. Howell. Champaign, IL: Stipes, 105–64.

Crandall, R. 1979. 'Social Interaction, Affect, and Leisure'. *Journal of Leisure Research* 11 (3):165–81.

———. 1980. 'Motivations for Leisure'. *Journal of Leisure Research* 12:45–54.

———, M. Nolan, and L. Morgan. 1980. 'Leisure and Social Interaction'. In *Social Psychological Perspectives on Leisure and Recreation*, edited by S. Iso-Ahola. Springfield, IL: Thomas.

———, and K. Slivken. 1980. 'Leisure Attitudes and Their Measurement'. In *Social Psychological Perspectives on Leisure and Recreation*, edited by S.E. Iso-Ahola. Springfield, IL: Charles C. Thomas.

Crawford, D.W., and G. Godbey. 1987. 'Reconceptualizing Barriers to Family Leisure'. *Leisure Sciences* 9:11–28.

———, G. Godbey, and A. Crouter. 1986. 'The Stability of Leisure Preferences'. *Journal of Leisure Research* 18 (2):96–115.

———, E.L. Jackson, and G. Godbey. 1991. 'A Hierarchical Model of Leisure Constraints'. *Leisure Sciences* 13 (4):309–20.

Cribier, F. 1979. 'Les vacances à l'heure de la retraite: Conduites d'âge, conduites de génération'. *Loisir et Société/Society and Leisure* 2 (2):399–426.

Crompton, J. 1979. 'Motivation for Pleasure Vacation'. *Annals of Tourism Research* 6:408–24.

Cross, G. 1990. *A Social History of Leisure Since 1600*. State College, PA: Venture.

Csikszentmihalyi, M. 1975. *Beyond Boredom and Anxiety*. San Francisco: Jossey-Bass.

———. 1976. 'What Play Says About Behavior'. *Ontario Psychologist* 8:5–11.

———. 1981. 'Leisure and Socialization'. *Social Forces* 60 (2):332–40.

———, and R. Graef. 1980. 'The Experience of Freedom in Daily Life'. *American Journal of Community Psychology* 8:401–14.

———, and D.A. Kleiber. 1991. 'Leisure and Self-Actualization'. In *Benefits of Leisure*, edited by B.L. Driver, P.J. Brown, and G.L. Peterson. State College, PA: Venture, 91–102.

———, R. Larson, and S. Prescott. 1977. 'The Ecology of Adolescent Activity and Experience'. *Journal of Youth and Adolescence* 6 (3):281–94.

Cumming, E., and W.E. Henry. 1961. *Growing Old: The Process of Disengagement*. New York: Basic Books.

Cutler, S.J., and J. Hendricks. 1985. 'Leisure and Time Use Across the Life Course'. In *Handbook of Aging and the Social Sciences* (2nd ed.), edited by R.H. Binstock and E. Shanas. New York: Van Nostrand Reinhold.

———. 1990. 'Leisure and Time Use Across the Life Course'. In *Handbook of Aging and the Social Sciences* (3rd ed.), edited by R.H. Binstock and E. Shanas. New York: Academic Press.

Dalton, R.J. 1980. 'Reassessing Parental Socialization: Indicator Unreliability versus Generational Transfer'. *American Political Science Review* 74:421–31.

D'Amours, Max, ed. 1986. *International Directory of Academic Institutions in Leisure, Recreation and Related Fields*. N.p.: World Leisure and Recreation Association.

Danet, B., and T. Katriel. 1987. 'Thing Magic: Closure and Paradox in Collecting'. Working Paper No. 2. Jerusalem: Hebrew University, Department of Communications and Sociology.

Dann. G.M.S. 1977. 'Anomie, Ego-Enhancement, and Tourism'. *Annals of Tourism Research* 4:184–94.

Dawson, D. 1984. 'Phenomenological Approaches to Leisure Research'. *Leisure Sciences* 11:18–23.

———. 1988. 'Social Class in Leisure: Reproduction and Resistance'. *Leisure Sciences* 10:193–202.

Deci, E.L. 1980. *The Psychology of Self-Determination*. Lexington, MA: Lexington Books.

———, and R.M. Ryan. 1985. *Intrinsic Motivation and Self-Determination in Human Behavior*. New York: Plenum.

Decima Research and Les Consultants Cultur'Inc. 1992. *Canadian Arts Consumer Profile 1990–1991*. N.p.: Decima Research and Les Consultants Cultur'Inc.

Deem, R. 1982. 'Women, Leisure and Inequality'. *Leisure Studies* 1 (1):29–46.

———. 1986. *All Work and No Play?* Milton Keynes: Open University Press.

———. 1987. 'The Politics of Women's Leisure'. In *Sport, Leisure and Social Relations*, edited by J. Horne, D. Jary, and A. Tomlinson. London: Routledge and Kegan Paul, 210–28.

———. 1990. 'Gender and Leisure: Past Progress, Future Prospects'. Paper presented at the XIIth World Congress of Sociology, Madrid, July.

———. 1992. 'The Sociology of Gender and Leisure in Britain—Past Progress and Future Prospects'. *Loisir et Société/Society and Leisure* 15 (1):21–38.

DeFleur, M.L., and S.J. Ball-Rokeach. 1989. *Theories of Mass Communication*. London: Longman.

de Grazia, S. 1964. *Of Time, Work, and Leisure*. Garden City, NY: Doubleday Anchor.

Delisle, M.-A. 1982. 'Loisir et structuration de temps chez les personnes âgées'. *Loisir et Société/Society and Leisure* 5 (2):387–413.

Dench, S. 1988. 'Women in Sport'. Paper presented at the Leisure Studies Association Conference, Brighton, UK.

———, C. York, and K. Roberts. 1987. 'Indoor Sport Provisions and Participants: Some Preliminary Findings'. Paper presented at the Conference on the Future of Adult Life, The Netherlands.

Denzin, N.K. 1978. *The Research Act: A Theoretical Introduction to Sociological Methods*. New York: McGraw-Hill.

Desaulniers, S., and N. Théberge. 1992. 'Gender Differences in the Likelihood That Work Reduction Will Lead to an Increase in Leisure'. *Loisir et Société/Society and Leisure* 15 (1):135–55.

Dickason, J.G., ed. 1983. 'Research Methodology'. *Therapeutic Recreation Journal* 17 (4).

Di Leonardo, M. 1987. 'The Female World of Cards and Holidays: Women, Families, and the Work of Kinship'. *Signs* 12:440–53.

DiMaggio, P. 1977. 'Market Structure, the Creative Process, and Popular Culture: Toward an Organizational Reinterpretation of Mass-Culture Theory'. *Journal of Popular Culture* 11:436–52.

Dixon, B., A. Courtney, and R. Bailey. 1974. *The Museum and the Canadian Public*. Ottawa: Secretary of State.

DONAHUE, W., et al., eds. 1958. *Free Time: Challenge to Later Maturity*. Ann Arbor: University of Michigan Press.

DONALD, M.N., and R.J. HAVIGHURST. 1959. 'The Meanings of Leisure'. *Social Forces* 37 (4):355–60.

DORFMAN, L.T., and C.E. MERTENS. 1990. 'Kinship Relations in Retired Rural Men and Women'. *Family Relations* 39:166–73.

DORNBUSCH, S.M. 1989. 'The Sociology of Adolescence'. *Annual Review of Sociology* 15:233–59.

DOUGLAS, A. 1977. *The Feminization of American Culture*. New York: Avon Books.

DOUGLASS, J.D. 1976. *Investigating Social Research: Individual and Team Field Research*. Beverly Hills: Sage Publications.

DRAPER, M. 1989. 'One Woman's Work Is Another Man's Leisure: Women and Leisure, Theoretical and Policy Issues'. Paper presented at the Australian Sociological Association Conference, La Trobe University, Bundoora, Victoria, Australia.

DRYDEN, K., and R. MACGREGOR. 1989. *Home Game: Hockey and Life in Canada*. Toronto: McClelland and Stewart.

DUBIN, R. 1956. 'Industrial Workers' Worlds: A Study of "Central Life Interests" of Industrial Workers'. *Social Problems* 3:131–42.

DULLES, F.R. 1963. *America Learns to Play: A History of Popular Recreation, 1607–1940*. Gloucester, MA: Peter Smith.

DULUDE, L. 1991. 'Getting Old: Men in Couples and Women Alone'. In *Continuity and Change in Marriage and Family*, edited by Jean E. Veevers. Toronto: Holt, Rinehart and Winston, 330–41.

DUMAZEDIER, J. 1960. 'Ambiguité du loisir et travail industriel'. *Cahiers Internationaux de Sociologie* 27:89–112.

_____. 1967. *Toward a Society of Leisure*. London: Collier.

_____. 1974. *Sociology of Leisure*. Amsterdam: Elsevier.

_____. 1990. 'Pour un renouveau de la recherche en sciences sociales du loisir'. *Loisir et Société/Society and Leisure* 13 (1):63–76.

DUNN, E. 1985. *1984 Public Opinion Survey on Recreation: Summary of Final Results*. Edmonton: Alberta Recreation and Parks.

DUVALL, E.M. 1957. *Family Development*. Philadelphia: Lippincott.

DYNES, W. 1977. 'Leisure Location and Family Centeredness'. *Journal of Leisure Research* 9 (4):281–91.

EICHLER, M. 1988. *Families in Canada Today: Recent Changes and Their Policy Consequences*. Agincourt, ON: Gage.

ELDER, G.H. 1974. *Children of the Great Depression*. Chicago: University of Chicago Press.

_____. 1980. 'Adolescence in Historical Perspective'. In *Handbook of Adolescent Psychology*, edited by J. Adelson. New York: Wiley, 3–46.

ELDERHOSTEL CANADA. 1993. *Fall Catalogue 1993*. Kingston, ON: Elderhostel Canada.

ELIAS, N. 1971. 'The Genesis of Sport as a Sociological Problem'. In *The Sociology of Sport*, edited by E. Dunning. London: Frank Cass, 88–115.

_____. 1978. *The Civilizing Process, Volume 1: The History of Manners*. Oxford: Blackwell.

_____. 1982. *The Civilizing Process, Volume 2: State and Civilization*. Oxford: Blackwell.

_____, and E.G. DUNNING. 1986. *Quest for Excitement: Sport and Leisure in the Civilizing Process*. Oxford: Blackwell.

ELLIOTT, P. 1974. 'Uses and Gratifications Research: A Critique and a Sociological Alternative'. In *The Uses of Mass Communications*, edited by J.G. Blumler and E. Katz. Beverly Hills: Sage Publications.

ELLIS, G., and C. RADEMACHER. 1989. 'Barriers to Recreation Participation'. Cited by Goodale and Witt in *Understanding Leisure and Recreation: Mapping the Past, Charting the Future*, edited by E.L. Jackson and T.L. Burton. State College, PA: Venture, 421–49.

_____, and P.A. WITT. 1984. 'The Measurement of Perceived Freedom in Leisure'. *Journal of Leisure Research* 16:110–23.

ELLIS, M.J. 1973. *Why People Play*. Englewood Cliffs, NJ: Prentice-Hall.

ELRA (EUROPEAN LEISURE AND RECREATION ASSOCIATION). 1983. 'ELRA Congress Examines Leisure Today and Tomorrow'. *World Leisure and Recreation* 25 (5):4–6.

ENCYCLOPEDIC DICTIONARY OF SOCIOLOGY. 1986. Guildford, CT: Dushkin.

ERIKSON, E.H. 1950. *Childhood and Society*. New York: Norton.

_____. 1968. 'Life Cycle'. In *International Encyclopedia of the Social Sciences*. New York: Macmillan and Free Press, 286–92.

EWERT, A. 1985. 'Why People Climb: The Relationship of Participant Motives and Experience Level to Mountaineering'. *Journal of Leisure Research* 17:241–50.

FATHI, A. 1990. *Canadian Studies in Mass Communication*. Toronto: Canadian Scholars' Press.

FEATHERMAN, D.L., and R.M. LERNER. 1985. 'Octogenesis and Sociogenesis: Problematics for Theory and Research About Development and Socialization Across the Lifespan'. *American Sociological Review* 50:659–76.

FEATHERSTONE, M. 1991. *Consumer Culture and Postmodernism*. London: Sage Publications.

FEREE, M.M. 1991. 'The Gender Division of Labor in Two-Earner Families'. *Journal of Family Issues* 12:158–80.

FERLAND, Y. 1979. 'A Comprehensive and Integrated System of Cultural Statistics and Indicators in Canada'. In *Social Research and Cultural Policy*, edited by J. Zuzanek. Waterloo, ON: Otium, 85–96.

FISHBEIN, M., ed. 1967. *Readings in Attitude Theory and Measurement*. New York: Wiley.

_____, and I. AJZEN. 1975. *Belief, Attitude, Intention, and Behavior: An Introduction to Theory and Research*. Reading: Addison-Wesley.

FISKE, J. 1989. *Understanding Popular Culture*. Boston: Unwin and Hyman.

FLANAGAN, J.C. 1978. 'A Research Approach to Improving Our Quality of Life'. *American Psychologist* 33:138–47.

FRANCKEN, D.A., and W.F. VAN RAAIJ. 1981. 'Satisfaction with Leisure Time Activities'. *Journal of Leisure Research* 13:337–52.

FREDERICK, C.J., and S.M. SHAW. 1993. 'An Exploration of Body Image as a Constraint to Participation in Aerobics'. In *Proceeding of the 7th Canadian Congress on Leisure Research*. Winnipeg: University of Manitoba, 224–7.

FREEDMAN, J.L., J.M. CARLSMITH, and D.O. SEARS. 1974. *Social Psychology*. Englewood Cliffs, NJ: Prentice-Hall.

FREY, J.H., and D.S. EITZEN. 1991. 'Sport and Society'. *Annual Review of Sociology* 17:503–22.

FREYSINGER, V.J. 1987. 'The Meaning of Leisure in Middle Adulthood'. *Journal of Physical Education, Recreation and Dance* 58 (8): 40–5.

FRIEDMANN, G. 1960. 'Leisure and Technological Civilization'. *International Social Science Journal* 12:509–21.

FRIESEN, B.K. 1990. 'Powerlessness in Adolescence: Exploiting Heavy Metal Listeners'. In *Marginal Conventions: Popular Culture, Mass Media and Social Deviance*, edited by C.R. Sanders. Bowling Green: Bowling Green State University Popular Press, 65–77.

FURLONG, A., R. CAMPBELL, and K. Roberts. 1989. *Class and Gender Divisions Among Young Adults at Leisure*. Edinburgh: University of Edinburgh.

GAGNON, P., and S. HARBOUR. 1992. 'Les loisirs des adolescents—le cas d'une municipalité de banlieue'. *Loisir et Société/Society and Leisure* 15 (2):521–44.

GANS, H.J. 1962. *The Urban Villagers*. New York: Free Press.

_____. 1974. *Popular Culture and High Culture: An Analysis and Evaluation of Taste*. New York: Basic Books.

GATTAS, J.T., et al. 1986. 'Leisure and Life-Styles: Towards a Research Agenda'. *Loisir et Société/Society and Leisure* 9 (2):529–39.

GERSON, E.M. 1976. 'On Quality of Life'. *American Sociological Review* 41:793–806.

GIBSON, P. 1979. 'Therapeutic Aspects of Wilderness Programs'. *Therapeutic Recreation Journal* 13 (2):21–37.

GIDDENS, A. 1964. 'Notes on the Concept of Play and Leisure'. *Sociological Review* 12 (March):73–89.

_____. 1984. *The Constitution of Society: Outline of the Theory of Structuration*. Oxford/ Cambridge: Polity Press.

GILLIGAN, C. 1982. *In a Different Voice: Psychological Theory and Women's Development*. Cambridge, MA: Harvard University Press.

GIST, N., and S.F. FAVA. 1974. *Urban Society*. New York: Crowell.

GLASER, B.G., and A.L. STRAUSS. 1967. *The Discovery of Grounded Theory: Strategies for Qualitative Research*. Chicago: Aldine.

GLASS, J., V.J. BENGTSON, and C.C. DUNHAM. 1986. 'Attitude Similarity in Three-Generation Families: Socialization, Status Inheritance, or Reciprocal Influence?' *American Sociological Review* 51:685–98.

GLASSFORD, R.G. 1976. *Application of a Theory of Games to the Transitional Eskimo Culture*. New York: Arno.

GLAZER, N. 1964. In discussion, in *Culture for the Millions? Mass Media in Modern Society*, edited by N. Jacobs. Boston: Beacon Press, 155–200.

GLYPTIS, S. 1989a. *Leisure and Unemployment*. Milton Keynes: Open University Press.

_____. 1989b. 'Lifestyles and Leisure Patterns: Methodological Approaches'. In *Life Styles: Theories, Concepts, Methods, and Results of Life Style Research in International Perspective*, edited by B. Filipcová, S. Glyptis, and W. Tokarski. Prague: Academy of Sciences and the ISA Research Committee on Leisure, 37–67.

GODBEY, G. 1981. *Leisure in Your Life: An Exploration*. Philadelphia: Saunders College Publishing.

_____. 1984. Letter to the editor. *Journal of Park and Recreation Administration* 2 (4): vii–ix.

_____. 1985. *Leisure in Your Life*. State College, PA: Venture.

_____ and S. PARKER. 1976. *Leisure Studies and Services: An Overview*. Philadelphia: Saunders College Publishing.

GOETZ, J.P., and M.D. LE COMPTE. 1984. *Ethnography and Qualitative Design in Educational Research*. Orlando, FL: Academic Press.

GOLDMAN, R., and J. WILSON. 1977. 'The Rationalization of Leisure'. *Politics and Society* 7 (2):157–87.

GOLDSMITH, E.B., ed. 1989. *Work and Family: Theory, Research, and Applications.* Newbury Park: Sage Publications.

GOODALE, T.L., and G.C. GODBEY. 1988. *The Evolution of Leisure.* State College, PA: Venture.

_____, and P.A. WITT. 1989. 'Recreation Non-Participation and Barriers to Leisure'. In *Understanding Leisure and Recreation: Mapping the Past, Charting the Future,* edited by E.L. Jackson and T.L. Burton. State College, PA: Venture, 421–49.

GORDON, C. 1976. 'Development of Evaluated Role Identities'. *Annual Review of Sociology* 2:405–33.

GORDON, D., C.M. GAITZ, and J. SCOTT. 1976. 'Leisure and Lives: Personal Expressivity Across the Life Span'. In *Handbook of Aging and the Social Sciences,* edited by R.H. Binstock and E. Shanas. New York: Van Nostrand Reinhold, 310–41.

GOSSELIN, L. 1985. 'Valeurs et loisir: Etude de validation de la théorie de Holland'. *Loisir et Société/Society and Leisure* 8 (2): 467–81.

GOULD, P., and R. WHITE. 1974. *Mental Maps.* Harmondsworth: Penguin.

GOVAERTS, F. 1985. 'Social Indicators of Leisure and the Quality of Life'. *World Leisure and Recreation* 27 (2):49–51.

GRAEF, R., M. CSIKSZENTMIHALYI, and S. MCMANAMA GIANINNO. 1983. 'Measuring Intrinsic Motivation in Everyday Life'. *Leisure Studies* 2 (2):155–68.

GRAEFE, A., and S. PARKER, eds. 1987. *Recreation and Leisure: An Introductory Handbook.* State College, PA: Venture.

GRAHAM, S. 1959. 'Social Correlates of Adult Leisure-Time Behavior'. In *Community Structure and Analysis,* edited by M.B. Sussman. New York: Crowell.

GRAMSCI, A. 1971. *Selections from the Prison Notebooks.* London: Lawrence and Wishart.

GREEN, E., S. HEBRON, and D. WOODWARD. 1990. *Women's Leisure, What Leisure?* London: Macmillan.

GREENDORFER, S.L., and J.H. LEWKO. 1978. 'Role of Family Members in Sport Socialization of Children'. *Research Quarterly* 49 (2):146–52.

GREGG, A., and M. POSNER. 1990. *The Big Picture: What Canadians Think About Almost Everything.* Toronto: Macfarlane Walter & Ross.

GREGORY, S. 1982. 'Women Among Others: Another View'. *Leisure Studies* 1 (1):47–52.

GRISWOLD, W. 1987. 'The Fabrication of Meaning: Literary Interpretation in the United States, Great Britain, and the West Indies'. *American Journal of Sociology* 92:1077–1117.

GROSS, E. 1961. 'A Functional Approach to Leisure Analysis'. *Social Problems* 9 (1): 2–8.

GROSSBERG, L., C. NELSON, and P.A. TREICHER, eds. 1991. *Cultural Studies.* New York: Routledge.

GROVES, D.L., and A.M. LASTOVICA. 1977. 'A Quality of Life Framework for Family Life Leisure Studies'. *International Journal of Family Counselling* 5 (2):59–65.

GRUNEAU, R. 1983. *Class, Sports and Social Development.* Amherst: University of Massachusetts Press.

_____. 1988. 'Modernization or Hegemony: Two Views of Sport and Social Development'. In *Not Just a Game,* edited by J. Harvey and H. Cantelon. Ottawa: University of Ottawa Press, 9–32.

_____, D. WHITSON, and H. CANTELON. 1988. 'Methods and Media: Studying the Sports/Television Discourse'. *Loisir et Société/Society and Leisure* 11 (2):265–81.

GUBA, E.G., and Y.S. LINCOLN. 1981. *Effective Evaluation*. San Francisco: Jossey-Bass.

GUNTER, B.G., and J. STANLEY. 1985. 'Theoretical Issues in Leisure Study' and 'The Dark Side of Leisure: Introduction'. In *Transitions to Leisure: Conceptual and Human Issues*, edited by B.G. Gunter, J. Stanley, and R. St Clair. Lanham: University Press of America, 35–51, 215–16.

GUTHRIE, R. 1986. 'Holland's Theory: An Extension into Leisure'. Unpublished Ph.D. dissertation, University of Calgary.

GUTTMAN, A. 1978. *From Ritual to Record: The Nature of Modern Sports*. New York: Columbia University Press.

HAAS, L. 1985. 'Love and Guilt: Normative Orientations and Their Implications for Accommodation and Resistance Among Women'. *Women's Studies International Forum* 8 (4):335–42.

HAAVIO-MANNILA, E. 1971. 'Satisfaction with Family, Work, Leisure, and Life Among Men and Women'. *Human Relations* 24 (6):585–601.

HAGESTAD, G.O. 1984. 'The Continuous Bond: A Dynamic Multigenerational Perspective on Parent-Child Relations Between Adults'. In *Minnesota Symposium on Child Psychology*, edited by M. Perlmutter. New York: Erlbaum, 129–58.

_____, and B.L. NEUGARTEN. 1985. 'Age and the Life Course'. In *Handbook of Aging and the Social Sciences*, edited by R.H. Binstock and E. Shanas. New York: Van Nostrand Reinhold.

HALL, A., et al. 1991. *Sport in Canadian Society*. Toronto: McClelland and Stewart.

HALL, S., and T. JEFFERSON. 1976. *Resistance Through Rituals: Youth Subcultures in Post-War Britain*. London: Hutchinson.

HAMILTON-SMITH, E. 1987. 'Four Kinds of Tourism'. *Annals of Tourism Research* 14:332–44.

HANTRAIS, L. 1983. *Leisure and the Family in Contemporary France*. Papers in Leisure Studies, No. 7. London: Polytechnic of North London.

_____. 1984. 'Leisure Policy in France'. *Leisure Studies* 3 (2):129–46.

_____. 1986. 'L'évolution des pratiques de loisir et le changement social'. *Loisir et Société/Society and Leisure* 9 (2):363–76.

_____, and T.J. KAMPHORST, eds. 1987. *Trends in the Arts: A Multinational Perspective*. Amersfoort: Giordano Bruno.

_____, P.A. CLARK, and N. SAMUEL. 1984. 'Time-Space Dimensions of Work, Family and Leisure in France and Great Britain'. *Leisure Studies* 3 (3):301–17.

HARACKIEWICZ, J.M., G. MANDERLINK, and C. SANSONE. 1984. 'Rewarding Pinball Wizardry: Effects of Evaluation and Cue Value on Intrinsic Interest'. *Journal of Personality and Social Psychology* 47:287–300.

HARE, J.E. 1983. 'Le théâtre comme loisir au Québec: Panorama historique avant 1920'. *Loisir et Société/Society and Leisure* 6 (1):43–70.

HAREVEN, T., ed. 1982. *Family Time and Industrial Time: The Relationship Between Family in a New England Industrial Community*. Cambridge: Cambridge University Press.

_____, and A. PLAKANS, eds. 1987. *Family History at the Crossroads*. Princeton, NJ: Princeton University Press.

HARGREAVES, J. 1986. *Sport, Power and Culture*. Oxford: Polity Press.

HARPER, W. 1981. 'The Experience of Leisure'. *Leisure Sciences* 4 (2):113–26.

HARRINGTON, M.A. 1991. 'Time After Work: Constraints on the Leisure of Working Women'. *Loisir et Société/Society and Leisure* 14 (1):115–32.

_____, and D. Dawson. 1993. 'No Rest for Mom: The Effects of Motherhood on Women's Leisure'. In *Proceeding of the 7th Canadian Congress on Leisure Research*. Winnipeg: University of Manitoba, 130–3.

_____, D. Dawson, and P. Bolla. 1992. 'Objective and Subjective Constraints on Women's Enjoyment of Leisure'. *Loisir et Société/Society and Leisure* 15 (1):203–21.

Harrison, A.A. 1976. *Individuals and Groups: Understanding Social Behavior*. Monterey: Brooks-Cole.

Harvey, A.S. 1982. 'Role and Context: Shapes of Behaviour'. *Studies of Broadcasting* 18:69–92.

_____. 1983. 'What in the World Do People Do?' *The Times Higher Education Supplement*, 7 January.

Harvey, J., and R. Proulx. 1988. 'Sport and the State in Canada'. In *Not Just a Game*, edited by J. Harvey and H. Cantelon. Ottawa: University of Ottawa Press.

Havighurst, R.J. 1961. 'The Nature and Values of Meaningful Free Time Activity'. In *Aging and Leisure: A Research Perspective into the Meaningful Use of Time*, edited by R.W. Kleemeier. New York: Oxford University Press, 309–41.

_____, and K. Feigenbaum. 1959. 'Leisure and Life Styles'. *American Journal of Sociology* 63:152–62.

_____, B.L. Neugarten, and S.S. Tobin. 1968. 'Disengagement and Patterns of Aging'. In *Middle Age and Aging*, edited by B.L. Neugarten. Chicago: University of Chicago Press.

Havitz, M.E., and J.L. Crompton. 1990. 'The Influence of Persuasive Messages on Propensity to Purchase Selected Recreational Services from Public or from Commercial Suppliers'. *Journal of Leisure Research* 22:71–88.

_____, and J.A. Sell. 1991. 'The Experimental Method and Leisure/Recreation Research: Promoting a More Active Role'. *Loisir et Société/Society and Leisure* 14 (1): 47–68.

Hawes, D.K. 1978. 'Satisfactions Derived from Leisure-Time Pursuits: An Exploratory Nationwide Survey'. *Journal of Leisure Research* 10:247–64.

Haworth, J.T. 1978. 'Leisure and the Individual'. *Loisir et Société/Society and Leisure* 1 (1):53–61.

Hebdige, D. 1979. *Subculture: The Meaning of Style*. London: Methuen.

_____. 1982. 'Towards a Cartography of Taste, 1935–1962'. In *Popular Culture: Past and Present*, edited by B. Waites, T. Bennett, and G. Martin. London: Croom Helm, 194–218.

_____. 1988. *Hiding in the Light: On Images and Things*. London: Routledge and Kegan Paul.

Hedinsson, E. 1981. *TV, Family and Society: The Social Origins and Effects of Adolescents' TV Use*. Stockholm: Almquist and Wiksell.

Heilbrun, A.B. 1965. 'An Empirical Test of the Modeling Theory of Sex-Role Learning'. *Child Development* 36:789–99.

Hendee, J.C., and R. Burdge. 1974. 'The Substitutability Concept: Implications for Recreation Research and Measurement'. *Journal of Leisure Research* 6:157–62.

_____, R.P. Gale, and W.R. Catton. 1971. 'A Typology of Outdoor Recreation Activity Preferences'. *Journal of Environmental Education* 3:28–34.

Henderson, K.A. 1986. 'Global Feminism and Leisure'. *World Leisure and Recreation* 28 (4):20–4.

_____. 1990. 'Reality Comes Through a Prism: Method Choices in Leisure Research'. *Loisir et Société/Society and Leisure* 13 (1):169–88.

_____. 1991. 'The Contribution of Feminism to an Understanding of Leisure Constraints'. *Journal of Leisure Research* 23 (4):363–77.

_____, and K.R. ALLEN. 1991. 'The Ethic of Care: Leisure Possibilities and Constraints for Women'. *Loisir et Société/Society and Leisure* 14 (1):97–113.

_____, L.A. BEDINI, L. HECHT, and R. SCHULER. 1993. 'The Negotiation of Leisure Constraints by Women with Disabilities'. In *Proceeding of the 7th Canadian Congress on Leisure Research*. Winnipeg: University of Manitoba, 235–41.

_____, and D. BIALESCHKI. 1992. 'Leisure Research and the Social Structure of Feminism'. *Loisir et Société/Society and Leisure* 15 (1):63–75.

_____, and J.S. RANNELLS. 1988. 'Farm Women and the Meaning of Work and Leisure: An Oral History Perspective'. *Leisure Sciences* 10 (1):41–50.

_____, D. STALNAKER, and G. TAYLOR. 1988. 'The Relationship between Barriers to Recreation and Gender-Role Personality Traits for Women'. *Journal of Leisure Research* 20 (1):69–80.

_____, et al. 1989. *A Leisure of One's Own: A Feminist Perspective on Women's Leisure*. State College, PA: Venture.

HERON, R.P. 1991. 'The Institutionalization of Leisure: Cultural Conflict and Hegemony'. *Loisir et Société/Society and Leisure* 14 (1): 171–90.

HILL, M.S. 1988. 'Marital Stability and Spouses' Shared Time'. *Journal of Family Issues* 9:427–51.

HILL, R., et al. 1970. *Family Development in Three Generations*. Cambridge: Shenkman.

_____, and R. RODGERS. 1964. 'The Development Approach'. In *Handbook of Marriage and the Family*, edited by H.T. Christensen. Chicago: Rand McNally, 171–211.

HOAR, J. 1961. 'A Study of Free Time Activities of 200 Aged Persons'. *Sociology and Social Research* 45:157–63.

HOCHSCHILD, A. 1989. *The Second Shift*. New York: Avon Books.

HOFF, A.E., and G.D. ELLIS. 1992. 'Influence of Agents of Leisure Socialization on Leisure Self-Efficacy of University Students'. *Journal of Leisure Research* 24 (2):114–26.

HOGAN, D.P., and N.M. ASTONE. 1986. 'The Transition to Adulthood'. *Annual Review of Sociology* 12:109–30.

HOGGART, R. 1958. *The Uses of Literacy*. New York: Oxford University Press.

HOLECEK, D. 1990. 'Tourism in the United States'. *World Leisure and Recreation* 32 (1): 32–9.

HOLLAND, J.L. 1973. *Making Vocational Choices: A Theory of Careers*. Englewood Cliffs, NJ: Prentice-Hall.

HOLLANDS, R.G. 1984. 'The Role of Cultural Studies and Social Criticism in the Sociology of Sport'. *Quest* 36:66–79.

_____. 1988. 'Leisure, Work and Working-Class Cultures: The Case of Leisure on the Shop Floor'. In *Leisure, Sport and Working-Class Cultures*, edited by H. Cantelon et al. Toronto: Garamond.

HOLMAN, T.B., and A. EPPERSON. 1984. 'Family and Leisure: A Review of the Literature with Research Recommendations'. *Journal of Leisure Research* 16 (4):277–94.

_____, and M. JACQUARD. 1988. 'Leisure Activity Patterns and Marital Satisfaction: A Further Test'. *Journal of Marriage and the Family* 50 (1):69–77.

HOLMES, J., and E.L. SILVERMAN. 1992. *We're Here, Listen to Us!* Ottawa: Canadian Advisory Council on the Status of Women.

HORKHEIMER, M., and T.W. ADORNO. 1972. *Dialectic of Enlightenment*. New York: Seabury.

HORNA, J.L.A., ed. 1979. *Alberta's Pioneers from Eastern Europe: Reminiscences No. 3.* Edmonton: University of Alberta.

_____. 1980. 'Leisure Re-socialization Among Immigrants in Canada'. *Loisir et Société/ Society and Leisure* (1):97–110.

_____. 1985a. 'The Social Dialectic of Life Career and Leisure: A Probe into the Pre-occupations Model'. *Loisir et Société/Society and Leisure* 8 (2):615–30.

_____. 1985b. 'Desires and Preferences for Leisure Activities: More of the Same?' *World Leisure and Recreation* 21 (1):28–32.

_____. 1987a. 'Leisure and Ethnic Minorities'. In *Recreation and Leisure: An Introductory Handbook*, edited by A. Graefe and S. Parker. State College, PA: Venture, 189–95.

_____. 1987b. 'The Arts in Canada'. In *Trends in the Arts: A Multinational Perspective*, edited by L. Hantrais and T. Kamphorst. Amersfoort: Giordano Bruno, 11–41.

_____. 1987c. 'The Process of Choosing Leisure Activities and Preferences: A Stream Model'. *Loisir et Société/Society and Leisure* 10 (2):219–34.

_____. 1987d. 'Leisure During the Postparental Stage of the Life Cycle'. *Journal of Physical Education, Recreation and Dance* 58 (8):46–8.

_____. 1988a. 'Leisure Studies in Czechoslovakia: Some East-West Parallels and Divergences'. *Leisure Sciences* 10 (1):79–94.

_____. 1988b. 'The Mass Media as Leisure: A Western-Canadian Case'. *Loisir et Société/ Society and Leisure* 11 (2):283–301.

_____. 1989a. 'The Leisure Component of the Parental Role'. *Journal of Leisure Research* 21 (3):228–41.

_____. 1989b. 'Work Time, Non-Work Time, and Leisure in Czechoslovakia During the 1970s and 1980s: A Survey of the Czech and Slovak Sources'. *East Central Europe* 16 (1-2):89–105.

_____. 1989c. 'Canada'. In *Trends in Sports: A Multinational Perspective*, edited by T. Kamphorst and K. Roberts. Culemborg: Giordano Bruno, 35–65.

_____. 1989d. 'The Dual Asymmetry in the Married Couple's Life: The Gender Differentiated Work, Family, and Leisure Domains'. *International Journal of Sociology of the Family* 19:113–30.

_____. 1990. 'Leisure Styles: A Case Study of Local Celebrities'. Paper presented at the XIIth World Congress of Sociology, Madrid, July.

_____. 1991. 'The Family and Leisure Domains: Women's Involvement and Perceptions'. *World Leisure and Recreation* 33:11–14.

_____. 1992. 'Family and Leisure'. In *Family and Marriage: Cross-Cultural Perspectives*, edited by K. Ishwaran. Toronto: Thompson, 293–304.

_____. 1993. '"Triple W" of Canadian Overseas Leisure Travel: Who, Why, and Where in Europe'. In *Proceeding of the 7th Canadian Congress on Leisure Research*. Winnipeg: University of Manitoba, 16–19.

_____, and E. LUPRI. 1987. 'Fathers' Participation in Work, Family Life and Leisure: A Canadian Experience'. In *Reassessing Fatherhood: New Observations on Fathers and the Modern Family*, edited by C. Lewis and M. O'Brien. London: Sage Publications, 54–73.

_____, and A.D. OLMSTED. 1989. 'Popular Festivities During the 1988 Winter Olympic Games: Olympic Pin Trading'. *World Leisure and Recreation* 31 (1):32–4.

HORNE, D. 1984. *The Great Museum: The Representation of History.* London: Pluto Press.

HORNE, J., D. JARY, and A. TOMLINSON, eds. 1987. *Sport, Leisure and Social Relations.* London: Routledge and Kegan Paul.

HOWARD, D.R., and J.L. CROMPTON. 1984. 'Who Are the Consumers of Public Park and Recreation Services?' *Journal of Park and Recreation Administration* 2:33–48.

HOWE, C.Z. 1985. 'Possibilities for Using a Qualitative Research Approach in the Sociological Study of Leisure'. *Journal of Leisure Research* 3–48.

———. 1988. 'Using Qualitative Structured Interviews in Leisure Research: Illustrations from One Case Study'. *Journal of Leisure Research* 20 (4):305–24.

HOWELL, M.L., and R.A. HOWELL, eds. 1985. *History of Sports in Canada*. Champaign, IL: Stipes.

HUDSON, W.W., and G.J. MURPHY. 1980. 'The Nonlinear Relationship between Marital Satisfaction and Stages of the Family Life Cycle: An Artifact of Type 1 Errors?' *Journal of Marriage and the Family* 42:263–7.

HUIZINGA, J. 1962. *Homo Ludens: A Story of the Play Element in Culture*. Boston: Beacon.

HUNNICUTT, B. 1980. 'Historical Attitudes Toward the Increase of Free Time in the Twentieth Century: Time for Work, for Leisure, or as Unemployment'. *Loisir et Société/Society and Leisure* 3 (2):195–215.

HUNTER, I.R. 1983. 'Methodological Issues in Therapeutic Recreation Research'. *Therapeutic Recreation Journal* 17:22–32.

HUSCH, J.A. 1991. 'Leisure, Work and Drugs: A Perspective of Use'. *Loisir et Société/ Society and Leisure* 14 (2):399–409.

HUSTON, T., and R. ASHMORE. 1986. 'Women and Men in Personal Relationships'. In *The Social Psychology of Female-Male Relations*, edited by R. Ashmore and F. Del Boca. New York: Academic Press, 167–210.

IBRAHIM, H. 1978. 'Gastronomy: The New American Pastime'. *Journal of Physical Education, Recreation and Dance/Leisure Today* October:21–2.

———. 1982a. 'Leisure and Islam'. *Leisure Studies* 1 (2):197–210.

———. 1982b. 'Leisure and Recreation in Egypt'. *Egypt* 1 (5):10–12.

———. 1991. *Leisure and Society: A Comparative Approach*. Dubuque, IA: William C. Brown.

INGE, M.T., ed. 1989. *Handbook of American Popular Culture*. New York: Greenwood Press.

INGHAM, R. 1986. 'Psychological Contributions to the Study of Leisure—Part One'. *Leisure Studies* 5 (3):255–79.

———. 1987. 'Psychological Contributions to the Study of Leisure—Part Two'. *Leisure Studies* 6 (1):1–14.

IRONMONGER, D., and E. RICHARDSON. 1991. *Leisure—An Input-Output Approach*. Melbourne: University of Melbourne Press.

ISO-AHOLA, S.E. 1980a. *The Social Psychology of Leisure and Recreation*. Dubuque: Brown.

———, ed. 1980b. *Social Psychological Perspectives on Leisure and Recreation*. Springfield, IL: Charles C. Thomas.

———. 1982. 'Towards a Social Psychology of Recreation Travel'. *Leisure Studies* 2 (1):35–47.

———. 1984. 'Social Psychological Foundations of Leisure and Resultant Implications for Leisure Counseling'. In *Leisure Counseling: Concepts and Applications*, edited by E.T. Dowd. Springfield, IL: Charles C. Thomas.

———. 1986. 'A Theory of Substitutability of Leisure Behavior'. *Leisure Sciences* 8 (4):367–89.

———. 1987. 'The Social Psychology of Leisure'. In *Recreation and Leisure: An Intro-*

ductory Handbook, edited by A. Graefe and S. Parker. State College, PA: Venture, 41–7.

_____. 1989. 'Motivation for Leisure'. In *Understanding Leisure and Recreation: Mapping the Past, Charting the Future*, edited by E.L. Jackson and T.L. Burton. State College, PA: Venture, 247–79.

_____, and J. ALLEN. 1982. 'The Dynamics of Leisure Motivation: The Effects of Outcome on Leisure Needs'. *Research Quarterly for Exercise and Sport* 53:141–9.

_____, and R.C. MANNELL. 1985. 'Social and Psychological Constraints on Leisure'. In *Constraints on Leisure*, edited by M.G. Wade. Springfield, IL: Charles C. Thomas, 11–154.

_____, and E. WIESSINGER. 1987. 'Leisure and Boredom'. *Journal of Social and Clinical Psychology* 5:356–64.

JACKSON, E.L. 1983. 'Activity-Specific Barriers to Recreation Participation'. *Leisure Sciences* 6:47–60.

_____. 1988. 'Leisure Constraints: A Survey of Past Research'. *Leisure Sciences* 10:203–15.

_____. 1991. 'Leisure Constraints/Constrained Leisure: Special Issue Introduction'. *Journal of Leisure Research* 23:279–85 and *Leisure Sciences* 13:273–8.

_____. 1993. 'Activity-Specific Constraints on Leisure Participation'. In *Proceeding of the 7th Canadian Congress on Leisure Research*. Winnipeg: University of Manitoba, 227–32.

_____, and T.L. BURTON, eds. 1989. *Understanding Leisure and Recreation: Mapping the Past, Charting the Future*. State College, PA: Venture.

_____, and E. DUNN. 1988. 'Integrating Ceasing Participation with Other Aspects of Leisure Behaviour'. *Journal of Leisure Research* 20 (1):31–45.

_____, and M.S. SEARLE. 1985. 'Recreation Non-Participation: Concepts and Models'. *Loisir et Société/Society and Leisure* 8 (2):693–707.

JENNINGS, M.K., and R. NIEMI. 1982. *Generations and Politics: A Panel Study of Young Adults and Their Parents*. Princeton: Princeton University Press.

JEPPERSON, R.L., and J.W. MEYER. 1989. 'The Public Order and the Construction of Formal Organizations'. In *The New Institutionalism in Organizational Analysis*, edited by W.W. Powell and P.J. DiMaggio. Chicago: University of Chicago Press.

JESSOR, R., and S.L. JESSOR. 1977. *Problem Behavior and Psychosocial Development—A Longitudinal Study of Youth*. New York: Academic Press.

JICK, T.D. 1983. 'Mixing Qualitative and Quantitative Methods: Triangulation in Action'. In *Qualitative Methodology*, edited by J. Van Maanen. Beverly Hills: Sage Publications, 135–48.

JOHNSTON, B.J., and D.J. BLAHNA. 1993. 'Gender Differences Among Intermountain West Cavers, Rock Climbers, and Hang Gliders in Relation to Psycho-Social Dimensions of Constraint to Participation'. In *Proceeding of the 7th Canadian Congress on Leisure Research*. Winnipeg: University of Manitoba, 213–16.

JORGENSON, D.E. 1977. 'The Effect of Social Position and Wife/Mother Employment on Family Leisure-Time: A Study of Fathers'. *International Journal of Sociology of the Family* 7:197–208.

JUSTER, F.T., et al. 1981. *Social Accounting Systems: Essays on the State of the Art*. New York: Academic Press.

KAMPHORST, T.J., and K. ROBERTS, eds. 1989. *Trends in Sports: A Multinational Perspective*. Culemborg: Giordano Bruno.

KANDEL, D.B. 1980. 'Drug and Drinking Behavior Among Youth'. *Annual Review of Sociology* 6:235–85.

KANDO, T.M. 1980. *Leisure and Popular Culture in Transition*. St Louis: Mosby.

KANE, M.J. 1990. 'Female Involvement in Physical Recreation—Gender Role as a Constraint'. *Journal of Physical Education, Recreation, and Dance* 61 (1):52–6.

KAPLAN, M. 1960. *Leisure in America: A Social Inquiry*. New York: Wiley.

_____. 1975. *Leisure: Theory and Policy*. New York: Wiley.

_____. 1979. *Leisure: Lifestyle and Lifespan*. Philadelphia: Saunders.

KARLIS, G. 1993. 'Ethnicity and Recreation in Canada: The Constraints of Canada's Ethnic Population'. In *Proceeding of the 7th Canadian Congress on Leisure Research*. Winnipeg: University of Manitoba, 284–5.

KATTELER, H.A. 1985. 'The Problem of Establishing Substitutability by Research'. In *Les temps libre et le loisir*, edited by Madeleine Romer. Paris: Association pour la Diffusion de la Recherche sur l'Action Culturelle, III–2–32 to III–2–38.

KATZ, E., and P.F. LAZARSFELD. 1955. *Personal Influence: The Part Played by People in the Flow of Mass Communication*. New York: Free Press.

KAY, T., and E.L. JACKSON. 1991. 'Leisure Despite Constraint: The Impact of Leisure Constraints on Leisure Participation'. *Journal of Leisure Research* 23 (4):301–13.

KELLY, J.R. 1972. 'Work and Leisure: A Simplified Paradigm'. *Journal of Leisure Research* 3 (4):50–62.

_____. 1976. 'Leisure as Compensation for Work Constraint'. *Society and Leisure* 8 (3):73–82.

_____. 1978a. 'Leisure Styles and Choices in Three Environments'. *Pacific Sociological Review* 21 (2):187–207.

_____. 1978b. 'Situational and Social Factors in Leisure Decisions'. *Pacific Sociological Review* 21 (3):313–30.

_____. 1981. 'Popular Culture: Why Is It Popular?' *Loisir et Société/Society and Leisure* 4 (1):83–94.

_____. 1982. *Leisure*. Englewood Cliffs, NJ: Prentice-Hall.

_____. 1983a. *Leisure Identities and Interactions*. Boston: Allen & Unwin.

_____. 1983b. 'Leisure Styles: A Hidden Core'. *Leisure Sciences* 5 (4):321–38.

_____. 1985. 'Sources of Leisure Styles'. In *Recreation and Leisure: Issues in an Era of Change*, edited by T. Goodale and P. Witt. State College, PA: Venture, 208–20.

_____. 1987. *Freedom to Be: A New Sociology of Leisure*. New York: Macmillan.

_____. 1989. 'Leisure Behaviors and Styles: Social, Economic, and Cultural Factors'. In *Understanding Leisure and Recreation: Mapping the Past, Charting the Future*, edited by E.L. Jackson and T.L. Burton. State College, PA: Venture, 89–111.

_____. 1990. 'Leisure and Aging: A Second Agenda'. *Loisir et Société/Society and Leisure* 13 (1):145–67.

_____, and G. GODBEY. 1992. *The Sociology of Leisure*. State College, PA: Venture.

_____, and J.-E. ROSS. 1989. 'Later-Life Leisure: Beginning a New Agenda'. *Leisure Sciences* 11:47–59.

_____, M. STEINKAMP, and J. KELLY. 1986. 'Later-Life Leisure: How They Play in Peoria'. *Gerontologist* 26 (5):531–7.

_____. 1987. 'Later-Life Satisfaction: Does Leisure Contribute?' *Leisure Sciences* 9:189–200.

KENYON, G.S. 1968. 'A Conceptual Model for Characterizing Physical Activity' and 'Six

Scales for Assessing Attitudes Toward Physical Activity'. *Research Quarterly* 39:96–106, 566–74.

_____. 1991. 'Beyond Entertainment: Economics and the Arts'. *World Leisure and Recreation* 33 (1):32–5.

KIDD, B. 1987. 'Sports and Masculinity'. In *Beyond Patriarchy: Essays by Men*, edited by M. Kaufman. Toronto: Oxford University.

KIRSCH, C., B. DIXON, and M. BOND. 1973. *A Leisure Study of Canada 1972*. Ottawa: Secretary of State.

KISSMAN, K., and J.A. ALLEN. 1993. *Single-Parent Families*. Newbury Park: Sage Publications.

KLEEMEIER, R.W., ed. 1961. *Aging and Leisure: A Research Perspective into the Meaningful Use of Time*. New York: Oxford University Press.

KLEIBER, D.A. 1979. 'Fate Control and Leisure Attitudes'. *Leisure Sciences* 3/4:239–48.

_____. 1980. 'Free Time Activity and Psycho-Social Adjustment in College Students: A Preliminary Analysis'. *Journal of Leisure Research* 12 (3):205–21.

_____, and M.J. KANE. 1984. 'Sex Differences and the Use of Leisure as Adaptive Potentiation'. *Loisir et Société/Society and Leisure* 7 (1):165–73.

_____, and J.R. KELLY. 1980. 'Leisure, Socialization, and the Life Cycle'. In *Social Psychological Perspectives on Leisure and Recreation*, edited by S.E. Iso-Ahola. Springfield, IL: Charles C. Thomas.

KOBASA, S. 1979. 'Stressful Life Events, Personality and Health: An Inquiry into Hardiness'. *Journal of Personality and Social Psychology* 37:1–11.

KOESTNER, R., M. ZUCKERMAN, and J. KOESTNER. 1987. 'Praise, Involvement, and Intrinsic Motivation'. *Journal of Personality and Social Psychology* 53:383–90.

KORNHAUSER, A. 1965. *Mental Health and the Industrial Worker*. New York: Wiley.

KRAUS, R. 1984. *Recreation and Leisure in Modern Society*. Glenview, IL: Scott Foresman and Company.

LAPPAGE, R. 1985. 'The Canadian Scene and Sport, 1921–1976'. In *History of Sport in Canada*, edited by M.L. Howell and R.A. Howell. Champaign, IL: Stipes, 224–302.

LARRABEE, E., and R. MEYERSOHN, eds. 1958. *Mass Leisure*. Glencoe, IL: Free Press.

LARSON, R. 1978. 'Thirty Years of Research on the Subjective Well-Being of Older Americans'. *Journal of Gerontology* 33:109–29.

_____, and M. CSIKSZENTMIHALYI. 1983. 'The Experience Sampling Method'. In *Naturalistic Approaches to Studying Social Interaction*, edited by H.T. Reis. San Francisco: Jossey-Bass, 41–56.

_____, R.C. MANNELL, and J. ZUZANEK. 1986. 'The Daily Experience of Older Adults with Friends Versus Family and Its Relation to Global Well-Being'. *Journal of Psychology and Aging* 1 (2):117–26.

LATHER, P. 1982. 'Notes Toward an Adequate Methodology in Doing Feminist Research'. Paper presented at the National Women's Studies Association Conference, Arcata, CA.

LAWTON, M.P. 1983. 'Time, Space, and Activity'. In *Aging and Milieu: Environmental Perspectives on Growing Old*, edited by G.D. Rowles and R.J. Onta. New York: Academic Press.

LAWTON, W.P., M. MOSS, and M. FULCOMER. 1982. *Determinants of the Activities of Older People*. Cited by Kelly in *Loisir et Société/Society and Leisure* 13 (1):145–67.

LEE, G.R. 1988. 'Marital Intimacy Among Older Persons: The Spouse as Confidant'. *Journal of Family Issues* 9:273–84.

LEISURE LIFESTYLE CONSULTANTS. 1978. *Leisure Wellbeing Inventory*. Eugene, OR: Leisure Lifestyle Consultants.

LENSKYJ, H. 1991. 'A New Ball Game? Historical and Contemporary Models of Women's Sport in Canada'. *World Leisure and Recreation* 33 (3):15–18.

LEPPER, M.R., and R.E. GREEN. 1975. 'Turning Play into Work: Effects of Adult Surveillance and Extrinsic Rewards on Children's Intrinsic Motivation'. *Journal of Personality and Social Psychology* 31:479–86.

LERNER, R.M., and G.B. SPANIER. 1978. *Child Influence on Marital and Family Interaction*. New York: Academic Press.

LEVINSON, D., et al. 1978. *The Seasons of a Man's Life*. New York: Knopf.

LEVY, J. 1980. 'Leisure and the Family: Towards Some Conceptual Clarity'. *Leisure Information Newsletter* 6 (3):6–7.

_____. 1992. 'Leisure and Retirement in the New Age Wave Society'. *World Leisure and Recreation* 34 (1):5–9.

LEWIS, G.H. 1978. 'The Sociology of Popular Culture'. *Current Sociology* 26 (3).

LINDEMAN, E.C. 1939. *Leisure: A National Issue*. New York: Association Press.

LINDER, S. 1970. *The Harried Leisure Class*. New York: Columbia University Press.

LINDSAY, P.L. 1969. *A History of Sport in Canada, 1807–1867*. Unpublished Ph.D. dissertation, University of Alberta, Edmonton.

LOFLAND, J. 1971. *Analyzing Social Settings: A Guide to Qualitative Observation and Analysis*. Belmond, CA: Wadsworth.

LONDON, M., R. CRANDALL, and D. FITZGIBBONS. 1977. 'The Psychological Structure of Leisure: Activities, Needs, People'. *Journal of Leisure Research* 9:252–63.

LOUNSBURY, J.W., and L.L. HOOPES. 1988. 'Five-Year Stability of Leisure Activity and Motivation Factors'. *Journal of Leisure Research* 20 (2):118–34.

LOWERY, S., and M.L. DeFLEUR. 1983. *Milestones in Mass Communication Research*. London: Longman.

LUE, C., J.L. CROMPTON, and D.R. FESENMAIER. 1993. 'Conceptualization of Multi-Destination Pleasure Trips'. *Annals of Tourism Research* 20:289–301.

LULL, J. 1982. 'The Social Uses of Television'. *Mass Communication Review Yearbook* 3:397–409.

LUNDBERG, G.A., M. KOMAROVSKY, and M.A. McINERNY. 1934. *Leisure: A Suburban Study*. New York: Columbia University Press.

LUPRI, E., and G. SYMONS. 1982. 'The Emerging Symmetrical Family: Fact or Fiction?' *International Journal of Comparative Sociology* 23 (3–4):166–89.

LUXTON, M. 1980. *More Than a Labour of Love*. Toronto: Women's Press.

LYND, R.S., and H.M. LYND. [1929] 1959. *Middletown: A Study in American Culture*. New York: Harcourt and Brace.

_____. [1937] 1965. *Middletown in Transition: A Study in Cultural Conflict*. New York: Harcourt and Brace.

McAVOY, L.L. 1979. 'The Leisure Preferences, Problems, and Needs of the Elderly'. *Journal of Leisure Research* 11:40–7.

McCAGHY, C.H., and A.G. NEAL. 1974. 'The Fraternity of Cockfighters: Ethical Embellishment of an Illegal Sport'. *Journal of Popular Culture* 8:557–69.

MacCANNELL, D. 1976. *The Tourist: A New Theory of Leisure Class*. New York: Schocken.

McCARVILLE, R.E., and J. CROMPTON. 1987. 'An Empirical Investigation of the Influence of Information on Reference Prices for Public Swimming Pools. *Journal of Leisure Research* 19:223–35.

McClelland, D.C. 1961. *The Achieving Society*. Princeton: Van Nostrand.

MacDonald, D. 1964. 'A Theory of Mass Culture'. In *Mass Culture: The Popular Arts in America*, edited by B. Rosenberg and D. Manning White. New York: Free Press.

McGuire, F.A., J.T. O'Leary, and F.D. Dottavio. 1986. 'Outdoor Recreation in the Third Age: Results from the United States Nationwide Recreation Survey'. *World Leisure and Recreation* 28 (2):18–21.

———. 1987. 'The Relationship of Early Life Experiences to Later Life Leisure Involvement'. *Leisure Sciences* 9 (4):251–7.

McKay, J. 1980. 'Soccer Clubs in Toronto's Italian Community'. *Canadian Ethnic Studies* 12 (3):56–80.

McKechnie, G.E. 1974. 'The Psychological Structure of Leisure: Past Behavior'. *Journal of Leisure Research* 6:27–45.

McKeever, E. 1992. '"What's Age Got to Do With It?": Leisure for the Over 50s—an Unfilled Market'. *World Leisure and Recreation* 34 (1):18–22.

Mackie, M.M. 1991. *Gender Relations in Canada*. Toronto: Butterworths.

McNaughton, E. 1993. 'The Relationship of Mother's Marital Status at the Time of Her First Child's Birth to Socialization and Development'. In *Single-Parent Families: Perspectives on Research and Policy*, edited by J. Hudson and B. Galaway. Toronto: Thompson.

MacNeil, R.D., and M.L. Teague. 1987. *Aging and Leisure: Vitality in Later Life*. Englewood Cliffs, NJ: Prentice-Hall.

McPhail, T.L., and B.M. McPhail. 1990. *Communication: The Canadian Experience*. Toronto: Copp Clark Pitman.

McPherson, B.D. 1976. 'Socialization into the Role of Sport Consumer: A Theory and Causal Model'. *Canadian Review of Sociology and Anthropology* 13:165–77.

———. 1990. *Aging as a Social Process*. Toronto: Butterworths.

———. 1991. 'Aging and Leisure Benefits: A Life Cycle Perspective'. In *Benefits of Leisure*, edited by B.L. Driver, P.J. Brown, and G.L. Peterson. State College, PA: Venture, 423–30.

McQuail, D. 1983. *Mass Communication Theory*. Beverly Hills: Sage Publications.

———. 1985. 'Sociology of Mass Communication'. *Annual Review of Sociology* 11:93–111.

McRobbie, A. 1981. 'Settling Accounts with Subcultures: A Feminist Critique'. In *Culture, Ideology and Social Process: A Reader*, edited by T. Bennett et al. London: Batsford, 113–23.

Maddi, S., and S. Kobasa. 1981. 'Intrinsic Motivation and Health'. In *Advances in Intrinsic Motivation and Aesthetics*, edited by H. Day. New York: Plenum, 299–321.

Maddox, G.L. 1968. 'Persistence of Life Style Among the Elderly: A Longitudinal Study of Patterns of Social Activity in Relation to Life Satisfaction'. In *Middle Age and Aging*, edited by B.L. Neugarten. Chicago: University of Chicago Press.

Malcomson, R. 1982. 'Popular Recreations under Attack'. In *Popular Culture: Past and Present*, edited by B. Waites, T. Bennett, and G. Martin. London: Croom Helm, 20–46.

Maltby, R. 1983. *Harmless Entertainment: Hollywood and the Ideology of Consensus*. Metuch, NJ: Scarecrow Press.

Mancini, J.A., and D.K. Orthner. 1980. 'Situational Influences in Leisure Satisfaction and Morale in Old Age'. *Journal of the American Geriatric Society* 28:466–71.

Mandell, N., and A. Duffy, eds. 1988. *Reconstructing the Canadian Family: Feminist Perspectives*. Toronto: Butterworths.

MANNELL, R.C. 1980. 'Social Psychological Techniques and Strategies for Studying Leisure Experiences'. In *Social Psychological Perspectives on Leisure and Recreation*, edited by S.E. Iso-Ahola. Springfield, IL: Charles C. Thomas, 62–88.

———. 1983. 'Research Methodology in Therapeutic Recreation'. *Therapeutic Recreation Journal* 17 (4):9–16.

———. 1984. 'A Psychology for Leisure Research'. *Loisir et Société/Society and Leisure* 7 (1):13–21.

———. 1989. 'Leisure Satisfaction'. In *Understanding Leisure and Recreation: Mapping the Past, Charting the Future*, edited by E.L. Jackson and T.L. Burton. State College, PA: Venture, 281–301.

———, and S.E. ISO-AHOLA. 1987. 'Psychological Nature of Leisure and Travel Experience'. *Annals of Tourism Research* 14:314–31.

———, and J. ZUZANEK. 1991. 'The Nature and Variability of Leisure Constraints in Daily Life: The Case of Physically Active Leisure of Older Adults'. *Leisure Sciences* 13:337–51.

———, J. ZUZANEK, and R. LARSON. 1988. 'Leisure States and "Flow" Experiences: Testing Freedom and Intrinsic Motivation Hypotheses'. *Journal of Leisure Research* 20:289–304.

MANSFELD, Y. 1992. 'From Motivation to Actual Travel'. *Annals of Tourism Research* 19:399–419.

MARANS, R.W., and P. MOHAI. 1991. 'Leisure Resources, Recreation Activity, and the Quality of Life'. In *Benefits of Leisure*, edited by B.L. Driver, P.J. Brown, and G.L. Peterson. State College, PA: Venture, 351–63.

MARCUSE, H. 1955. *Eros and Civilization*. New York: Vintage.

———. 1964. *One-Dimensional Man*. Boston: Beacon Press.

MARKHAM, S.E. 1991. 'The Impact of Prairie and Maritime Reformers and Boosters on the Development of Parks and Playgrounds, 1880 to 1930'. *Loisir et Société/Society and Leisure* 14 (1):219–33.

MARKS, S.R. 1989. 'Toward a Systems Theory of Marital Quality'. *Journal of Marriage and the Family* 51:15–26.

MARKSON, S.L. 'Claims-Making, Quasi-Theories, and the Social Construction of the Rock'n'Roll Menace'. In *Marginal Conventions: Popular Culture, Mass Media and Social Deviance*, edited by C.R. Sanders. Bowling Green: Bowling Green State University Popular Press, 29–40.

MARTIN, B., and S. MASON. 1986. 'Spending Patterns Show New Leisure Priorities'. *Leisure Studies* 5:233–6.

MASLOW, A. 1970. *Motivation and Personality*. New York: Harper and Row.

———. 1976. *The Further Reaches of Human Nature*. Harmondsworth: Penguin.

MEAD, M. 1928. *Coming of Age in Samoa*. New York: William Morrow.

MEISEL, J. 1974. 'Political Culture and the Politics of Culture'. *Canadian Journal of Political Science* 7 (4):602.

MEISSNER, M. 1971. 'The Long Arm of the Job: A Study of Work and Leisure'. *Industrial Relations* 10 (3):239–60.

———, et al. 1975. 'No Exit for Wives: Sexual Division of Labour and the Cumulation of Household Demands'. *Canadian Review of Sociology and Anthropology* 12 (4):424–39.

MERELMAN, R.M. 1991. *Partial Visions: Culture and Politics in Britain, Canada, and the United States*. Madison: University of Wisconsin Press.

MERTON, R.K. 1949. 'Patterns of Influence'. In *Communications Research*, edited by P. Lazarsfeld and F. Stanton. New York: Harper.

METCALFE, A. 1983. 'Le sport au Canada français au 19e siècle: Le cas de Montréal, 1800–1914. *Loisir et Société/Society and Leisure* 6 (1):105–20.

_____. 1987. *Canada Learns to Play: The Emergence of Organized Sport, 1807–1904*. Toronto: McClelland and Stewart.

MICHALOS, A.C. 1980. *North American Social Report*. Boston: Reidel.

MICHELON, L.C. 1954. 'The New Leisure Class'. *American Journal of Sociology* 59:371–8.

MILES, M.B., and A.M. HUBERMAN. 1984. *Qualitative Data Analysis: A Sourcebook of New Methods*. Beverly Hills: Sage Publications.

MILLER, L., and O. PENZ. 1991. 'Talking Bodies: Female Body-Builders Colonize a Male Preserve'. *Quest* 43:148–63.

MILLER, S.J. 1968. 'The Social Dilemma of the Aging Leisure Participant'. In *Middle Age and Aging*, edited by B.L. Neugarten. Chicago: University of Chicago Press.

MILLS, A.S. 1985. 'Participation Motivations for Outdoor Recreation: A Test of Maslow's Theory'. *Journal of Leisure Research* 17:184–99.

MILLS, C.W. 1963. *Power, Politics and People*. New York: Oxford University Press.

MILLS, R. 1975. 'The Time Budget Study'. In *The Symmetrical Family*, edited by M. Young and P. Willmott. London: Penguin, 336–60.

MILTON, B.G. 1975. *Social Status and Leisure Time Activities*. Montreal: Canadian Sociology and Anthropology Association.

MINDEL, C.H., and R.W. HABENSTEIN, eds. 1976. *Ethnic Families in America*. Amsterdam: Elsevier.

MOBILY, K.E. 1985. 'Thoughts on a Reconstruction of Leisure Research'. Paper presented at the National Recreation and Park Association/Leisure Research Symposium.

_____. 1987. 'Leisure, Lifestyle, and Life Span'. In *Ageing and Leisure: Vitality in Later Life*, edited by R.D. MacNeil and M.L. Teague. Englewood Cliffs: Prentice-Hall, 155–80.

_____. 1989. 'Meaning of Recreation and Leisure Among Adolescents'. In *Leisure Studies* 8 (1):11–23.

_____, et al. 1993. 'Seasonal Variation in Physical Activity in Elderly Adults'. In *Proceeding of the 7th Canadian Congress on Leisure Research*. Winnipeg: University of Manitoba, 175–80.

MOMMAAS, H., and H. VAN DER POEL. 1988. 'New Perspectives on Theorizing Leisure'. *Loisir et Société/Society and Leisure* 10 (2):161–76.

MONTPETIT, R. 1983. 'Culture et exotisme: Les panorams itinérants et le jardin Guilbault à Montréal au XIXe siècle'. *Loisir et Société/Society and Leisure* 6 (1):71–104.

MOORHOUSE, H.F. 1989. 'Models of Work, Models of Leisure'. In *Capitalism and Leisure Theory*, edited by C. Rojek. London: Tavistock, 15–35.

MORIN, F. 1992. 'Les loisirs culturels des femmes québécoises, une analyse de l'enquête de 1989'. *Loisir et Société/Society and Leisure* 15 (1):175–202.

MORROW, D., et al. 1989. *A Concise History of Sport in Canada*. Toronto: Oxford University Press.

MUKERJI, C., and M. SCHUDSON. 1986. 'Popular Culture'. *Annual Review of Sociology* 12:47–66.

MURPHY, J.F. 1974. *Concepts of Leisure: Philosophical Implications*. Englewood Cliffs, NJ: Prentice-Hall.

_____. 1981. *Concepts of Leisure.* Englewood Cliffs, NJ: Prentice-Hall.

_____. 1987. 'Concepts of Leisure'. In *Recreation and Leisure: An Introductory Handbook,* edited by A. Graefe and S. Parker. State College, PA: Venture, 11–17.

MURPHY, P.E. 1983. 'Perceptions and Attitudes of Decision-Making Groups in Tourism Centers'. *Journal of Travel Research* 21 (3):8–12.

_____. 1985. *Tourism: A Community Approach.* New York: Methuen.

NATIONAL COUNCIL ON WELFARE. 1988. *Poverty Profile 1988.* Ottawa: National Council on Welfare.

NETT, E.M. 1993. *Canadian Families: Past and Present.* Toronto: Butterworths.

NEUGARTEN, B.L. 1964. 'A Developmental View of Adult Personality'. In *Relations of Development and Aging,* edited by J.E. Birren. Springfield, IL: Charles C. Thomas, 7–32.

NEULINGER, J. 1981. *The Psychology of Leisure.* Springfield, IL: Charles C. Thomas.

_____. 1981. *To Leisure: An Introduction.* Boston: Allyn and Bacon.

_____. 1984. 'Key Questions Evoked by a State of Mind Conceptualizations of Leisure'. *Loisir et Société/Society and Leisure* 7 (1):25–36.

_____. 1987. 'The Psychology of Leisure'. In *Recreation and Leisure: An Introductory Handbook,* edited by A. Graefe and S. Parker. State College, PA: Venture, 37–40.

_____, and M. BREIT. 1969. 'Attitude Dimensions of Leisure'. *Journal of Leisure Research* 1:255–61.

_____. 1971. 'Attitude Dimensions of Leisure: A Replication Study'. *Journal of Leisure Research* 3:108–15.

NEULINGER, J., and C.S. RAPS. 1972. 'Leisure Attitudes of an Intellectual Elite'. *Journal of Leisure Research* 4:196–207.

NEUMEYER, M.H., and E.S. NEUMEYER. 1958. *Leisure and Society: A Study of Leisure and Recreation in Their Sociological Aspects.* New York: Ronald Press.

NG, D. 1984. 'On the Nature of Leisure Research Problem and Research Hypothesis'. Paper presented at the Fourth Canadian Congress on Leisure Research, Trois-Rivières, Quebec.

_____. 1985. 'La nature des problèmes et des hypothèses de recherche en loisir'. *Loisir et Société/Society and Leisure* 8 (2):351–8.

_____, and S. SMITH. 1982. *Perspectives on the Nature of Leisure Research.* Waterloo: University of Waterloo Press.

NIEMI, I., S. KIISKI, and M. LIIKKANEN. 1986. *Use of Time in Finland.* Helsinki: Central Statistical Office of Finland.

NISBETT, R.E., and T.D. WILSON. 1977. 'Telling More Than We Can Know: Verbal Reports on Mental Processes'. *Psychological Review* 84:231–59.

NOCK, S.L., and P.W. KINGSTON. 1988. 'Time with Children: The Impact of Couples' Work-Time Commitments'. *Social Forces* 67:59–85.

NYE, F.I. 1976. 'Family Roles in Comparative Perspective'. In *Role Structure and Analysis of the Family,* edited by I.F. Nye. Beverly Hills: Sage Publications, 149–74.

_____, and V. GECAS 1976. 'The Role Concept: Review and Delineation'. In *Role Structure and Analysis of the Family,* edited by F.I. Nye et al. London: Sage Publications, 3–14.

NYE, R.B. 1972. 'Notes on Popular Culture'. In *Side-Saddle on the Golden Calf: Social Structure and Popular Culture in America.* Pacific Palisades, CA: Goodyear, 13–19.

NYSTROM, E.P. 1974. 'Activity Patterns and Leisure Concepts Among the Elderly'. *American Journal of Occupational Therapy* 28:337–45.

OLMSTED, A.D. 1987. 'Stamp Collectors and Stamp Collecting'. Paper presented at the Popular Culture Association national meeting, Montreal.

———. 1988. 'Morally Controversial Leisure: The Social World of Gun Collectors'. *Symbolic Interaction* 11:277–87.

———. 1991. 'Collecting: Leisure, Investment or Obsession?' *Journal of Social Behaviour and Personality* 6 (6):287–306.

OLSZEWSKA, A., and G. PRONOVOST. 1982. 'Current Problems and Perspectives in the Sociology of Leisure'. In *Sociology: The State of the Art*, edited by T. Bottomore, S. Nowak, and M. Sokolowska. London: Sage Publications, 299–321.

O'NEILL, W. 1991. 'Women: The Unleisured Majority'. *World Leisure and Recreation* 33 (3):6–10.

O'RAND, A.M., and M.L. KRECKER. 1990. 'Concept of the Life Cycle: Their History, Meanings, and Uses in Social Sciences. *Annual Review of Sociology* 16:241–62.

ORTHNER, D.K. 1975. 'Leisure Activity Patterns and Marital Satisfaction over the Marital Career'. *Journal of Marriage and the Family* 37 (1):91–102.

———. 1976. 'Patterns of Leisure and Marital Interaction'. *Journal of Leisure Research* 8:98–111.

———, and L.J. AXELSON. 1980. 'The Effects of Wife Employment on Marital Sociability'. *Journal of Comparative Family Studies* 11:531–43.

———, and J.A. MANCINI. 1991. 'Benefits of Leisure for Family Bonding'. In *Benefits of Leisure*, edited by B.L. Driver, P.J. Brown, and G.L. Peterson. State College, PA: Venture, 290–301.

OSGOOD, N.J., and C.Z. HOWE. 1984. 'Psychological Aspects of Leisure: A Life Cycle Developmental Perspective'. *Loisir et Société/Society and Leisure* 7 (1):175–96.

OUELLET, G. 1985. 'Comportements de loisir et styles de personnalité'. *Loisir et Société/ Society and Leisure* 8 (2):425–52.

———, and J. PERRON. 1979. 'Etudes des liens entre les valeurs et les choix d'activités de loisir chez les étudiants'. *Loisir et Société/Society and Leisure* 2 (1):151–75.

———, and R. SOUBRIER. 1989. 'Etude des contraintes perçues comme causes de la non-participation aux loisirs'. *World Leisure and Recreation* 31 (1):16–21.

PACK, A.N. 1934. *The Challenge of Leisure*. Washington, DC: McGrath.

PACKARD, V. 1958. *The Hidden Persuaders*. New York: Pocket Books.

PAGEOT, J.C. 1985. *Inventory of Physical Fitness Programs and Services*. Ottawa: Secretariat for Fitness in the Third Age.

———. 1986. 'The Leisure Patterns of the Aged Canadians'. *World Leisure and Recreation* 28 (2):26–7.

PALMORE, E. 1975. *The Honorable Elders*. Durham, NC: Duke University Press.

PARÉ, J.-L. 1992. 'Connotations des lieux et du cadre social du loisir des adolescents'. *Loisir et Société/Society and Leisure* 15 (2):463–98.

PARKER, S.R. 1971. *The Future of Work and Leisure*. New York: Praeger.

———. 1980. 'Leisure and Leisure Studies in the United States and Britain—a Comparative Survey'. *Loisir et Société/Society and Leisure* 3 (2):269–80.

———. 1982. *Work and Retirement*. London: Allen & Unwin.

———. 1983. *Leisure and Work*. London: Allen & Unwin.

PARKIN, F. 1971. *Class Inequality and Political Order*. London: McGibbon and Kee.

PARLIAMENT, J.A.B. 1989. 'How Canadians Spend Their Day'. *Canadian Social Trends* 15 (Winter):23–7.

PARRINELLO, G.L. 1993. 'Motivation and Anticipation in Post-Industrial Tourism'. *Annals of Tourism Research* 20:233–49.

PARRY, N.C.A. 1983. 'Sociological Contributions to the Study of Leisure'. *Leisure Studies* 2:57–81.

_____, and J. PARRY. 1977. 'Theories of Culture and Leisure. In *Leisure and Urban Society*, edited by M.A. Smith. London: Leisure Studies Association.

PARSONS, T., and R.F. BALES. 1955. *Family, Socialization, and Interaction Process*. New York: Free Press.

PATTON, M.Q. 1978. *Utilization-Focused Evaluation*. Beverly Hills: Sage Publications.

_____. 1980. *Qualitative Evaluation Methods*. Beverly Hills: Sage Publications.

PEARCE, P.L. 1982. *The Social Psychology of Tourist Behaviour*. Oxford: Pergamon Press.

PERREAULT, G. 1984. 'Contemporary Feminist Perspectives on Women in Higher Education'. In *Beyond Domination*, edited by C. Gould. Totowa, NJ: Rowan and Allenhead, 283–309.

PICHÉ, D. 1989. 'Interacting with the Urban Environment: Two Case Studies of Women and Female Adolescents'. Cited by L. Bella in *Understanding Leisure and Recreation: Mapping the Past, Charting the Future*. State College, PA: Venture.

PIEPER, J. 1963. *Leisure: The Basis of Culture*. New York: New American Library.

PLOG, S.C. 1972. 'Why Destination Areas Rise and Fall in Popularity'. Paper for the Travel Research Association, Southern California Chapter.

_____. 1979. 'Where in the World Are People Going and Why Do They want to Go There?' Paper for the Tianguis Turistico, Mexico City.

_____. 1991. *Leisure Travel: Making It a Growth Market . . . Again!* New York: Wiley.

PRONOVOST, G. 1983. *Temps, Culture et Société*. Sillery: Presses de l'Université du Québec.

_____. 1989. 'The Sociology of Time'. *Current Sociology* 37 (3):1–129.

_____. 1992. 'Générations, cycles de vie et univers culturels'. *Loisir et Société/Society and Leisure* 15 (2):437–60.

_____, and M. D'AMOURS. 1990. 'Leisure Studies: A Re-examination of Society'. *Loisir et Société/Society and Leisure* 13 (1):39–62.

_____, and J. PAPILLON. 1988. 'Musique, culture de masse et culture de classes'. *Loisir et Société/Society and Leisure* 11 (2):325–49.

RABINOW, P., and W.M. SULLIVAN, eds. 1987. *Interpretive Social Science: A Second Look*. Berkeley: University of California Press.

RAGHEB, M.G., and J.G. BEARD. 1980. 'Leisure Satisfaction: Concept, Theory, and Measurement'. In *Social Psychological Perspectives on Leisure and Recreation*, edited by S.E. Iso-Ahola. Springfield, IL: Charles C. Thomas, 329–53.

_____. 1982. 'Measuring Leisure Attitudes'. *Journal of Leisure Research* 14 (2):155–67.

RAPOPORT, R., and R.N. RAPOPORT. 1978. *Leisure and the Family Life Cycle*. London: Routledge and Kegan Paul.

_____, R. RAPOPORT, and Z. STRELITZ. 1977. *Fathers, Mothers and Others*. London: Routledge and Kegan Paul.

READER, M., and S.J. DOLLINGER. 1982. 'Deadlines, Self-Perceptions, and Intrinsic Motivation'. *Personality and Social Psychology Bulletin* 8:742–7.

REDMOND, G. 1979. 'Some Aspects of Organized Sport and Leisure in Nineteenth-Century Canada'. *Loisir et Société/Society and Leisure* 2 (1):73–100.

REES, B.J., and M.F. COLLINS. 1979. 'The Family and Sport: A Review'. In *Leisure and*

Family Diversity, edited by Z. Strelitz. London: Leisure Studies Association, 16.1–16.15.

REICHARDT, C.S., and T.D. COOK. 1979. 'Beyond Qualitative Versus Quantitative Methods'. In *Qualitative and Quantitative Methods in Evaluation Research*, edited by T.D. Cook and C.S. Reichardt. Beverly Hills: Sage Publications, 7–32.

REISSMAN, L. 1954. 'Class, Leisure, and Social Participation'. *American Sociological Review* 19:76–84.

RESZOHAZY, R. 1982. *Le changement social en Belgique: Évolution des valeurs des Belges-Francophones*. Louvain, Belgium: Université Catholique de Louvain.

RIDDICK, C.C., and S.N. DANIEL. 1984. 'The Relative Contributions of Leisure Activities and Other Factors to the Mental Health of Older Women'. *Journal of Leisure Research* 16:136–48.

RITCHIE, J.R.B. 1975. 'On the Derivation of Leisure Activity Types: A Perceptual Mapping Approach'. *Journal of Leisure Research* 7:128–40.

ROADBURG, A. 1981. 'Perceptions of Work and Leisure Among the Elderly'. *The Gerontologist* 21 (2):142–5.

_____. 1983. 'Freedom and Enjoyment: Disentangling Perceived Leisure'. *Journal of Leisure Research* 15:15–26.

ROBERTS, K. 1978. 'The Society of Leisure: Myth and Reality'. *Loisir et Société/Society and Leisure* 1 (1):33–52.

_____. 1979. *Contemporary Society and the Growth of Leisure*. London: Longman.

_____. 1981. *Leisure*. London: Longman.

_____. 1983. *Youth and Leisure*. London: Allen & Unwin.

_____. 1990. 'Leisure and Sociological Theory in Britain'. *Loisir et Société/Society and Leisure* 13 (1):105–27.

_____, and D.A. BRODIE. 1989. 'The Rise of Sports Participation in the United Kingdom'. *Loisir et Société/Society and Leisure* 12 (2):307–24.

_____, et al. 1976. 'The Family Life-Cycle, Domestic Roles and the Meaning of Leisure'. *Society and Leisure* 3:7–20.

_____. 1989. *Community Response to Leisure Centre Provision in Belfast*. London: Sports Council.

ROBERTS, K., C.S. YORK, and D.A. BRODIE. 1988. 'Participant Sport in the Commercial Sector'. *Leisure Studies* 7:145–57.

ROBINSON, J.P. 1970. 'Daily Participation in Sport Across Twelve Countries'. In *Cross-Cultural Analysis of Sports and Games*, edited by G. Lüschen. Champaign, IL: Stipes.

_____. 1977a. *Changes in Americans' Use of Time: 1965–1975—A Progress Report*. Cleveland: Ohio State University, Communications Research Center.

_____. 1977b. *How Americans Use Time: A Social-Psychological Analysis of Everyday Behavior*. New York: Praeger.

_____. 1981. 'Television and Leisure Time: A New Scenario'. *Journal of Communication* 31 (1):120–30.

_____. 1983. 'Culture Indicators from the Leisure Activity Survey'. *American Behavioral Scientist* 26 (4):543–52.

_____, and P.E. CONVERSE. 1972. 'Social Change Reflected in the Use of Time'. In *The Human Meaning of Social Change*, edited by A. Campbell and P.E. Converse. New York: Russell Sage Foundation.

ROJEK, C. 1985. *Capitalism and Leisure*. London: Tavistock.

_____. 1987. 'Freedom, Power and Leisure'. *Loisir et Société/Society and Leisure* 10 (2):209–18.

_____, ed. 1989a. *Leisure for Leisure*. New York: Routledge.

_____. 1989b. 'Leisure and Recreation Theory'. In *Understanding Leisure and Recreation: Mapping the Past, Charting the Future*, edited by E.J. Jackson and T.L. Burton. State College, PA: Venture, 69–88.

ROLLINS, R. 1993. 'Senior Citizens Visiting National Parks'. In *Proceeding of the 7th Canadian Congress on Leisure Research*. Winnipeg: University of Manitoba, 117–18.

ROMSA, G., and M. BLENMAN. 1985. 'The Consistency of Two Data Gathering Procedures for Retirees' Leisure Activities'. *Loisir et Société/Society and Leisure* 8 (2):393–401.

_____, and W. HOFFMAN. 1980. 'An Application of Non-participation Data in Recreation Research: Testing the Opportunity Theory'. *Journal of Leisure Research* 12:321–8.

ROSENBAUM, J., and L. PRINSKY. 1987. 'Sex, Violence, and Rock'n'Roll: Youth's Perception of Popular Music'. *Popular Music and Society* 11 (2):79–89.

ROSENBERG, B., and D.M. WHITE, eds. 1957. *Mass Culture: The Popular Arts in America*. New York: Free Press.

ROSENBLATT, P.C., and M.G. RUSSELL. 1975. 'The Social Psychology of Potential Problems in Family Vacation Travel'. *Family Coordinator* 24:209–15.

ROSENGREN, K.E. 1983. 'Communication Research: One Paradigm, or Four?' *Journal of Communication* 33 (3):185–207.

ROSENZWEIG, R. 1983. *Eight Hours for What We Will: Workers and Leisure in an Industrial City, 1870–1920*. Cambridge: Cambridge University Press.

ROWNTREE, B. 1951. *English Life and Leisure*. London: Longman.

RUBIN, A.M. 1981. 'An Examination of Television Viewing Motivations'. *Communications Research* 8 (2):141–65.

RUSKIN, H., and B. SHAMIR. 1984. 'Motivation as a Factor Affecting Males' Participation in Physical Activity During Leisure Time'. *Loisir et Société/Society and Leisure* 7 (1):141–61.

RUSSELL, G. 1983. *The Changing Role of Fathers*. Milton Keynes: Open University Press.

RUSSELL, R.V. 1985. 'Simultaneous Structural Equations in Leisure Research'. *Loisir et Société/Society and Leisure* 8 (2):371–83.

SÁGI, M. 1983. 'The Motivation for Various Forms of Leisure Activity'. *Leisure Studies* 2 (1):111–14.

SAMDAHL, D.M. 1991. 'A Symbolic Interactionist Model of Leisure: Theory and Empirical Support'. *Leisure Sciences* 10:27–39.

_____. 1992. 'Leisure in Our Lives: Exploring the Common Leisure Occasion'. *Journal of Leisure Research* 24 (1):19–32.

_____, and N.J. JEKUBOVICH. 1993. 'Constraints and Constraint Negotiations in Common Daily Leisure'. In *Proceeding of the 7th Canadian Congress on Leisure Research*. Winnipeg: University of Manitoba, 244–8.

SANDERS, C.R. 1990a. '"A Lot of People Like It": The Relationship Between Deviance and Popular Culture'. In *Marginal Conventions, Popular Culture, Mass Media and Social Deviance*, edited by C.R. Sanders. Bowling Green: Bowling Green State University Popular Press, 3–13.

_____, ed. 1990b. *Marginal Conventions: Popular Culture, Mass Media and Social Deviance*. Bowling Green: Bowling Green State University Popular Press.

SANDREY, R.A., D.G. SIMMONS, and P.J. DEVLIN. 1986. 'Outdoor Recreation and the "Third Age" in New Zealand. *World Leisure and Recreation* 28 (2): 32–4.

SCARDIGLI, V. 1989. 'Consumption, Leisure and Lifestyle in Western Europe'. In *Life Styles: Theories, Concepts, Methods, and Results of Life Style Research in International Perspective*, edited by B. Filipcová, S. Glyptis, and W. Tokarski. Prague: Academy of Sciences and the ISA Research Committee on Leisure, 302–22.

SCHATZMAN, L., and A.L. STRAUSS. 1973. *Field Research*. Englewood Cliffs, NJ: Prentice-Hall.

SCHEUCH, E.K. 1960. 'Family Cohesion in Leisure Time'. *Sociological Review* 8 (1):37–61.

———. 1972. 'The Time-Budget Interview'. In *The Use of Time: Daily Activities of Urban and Suburban Populations in Twelve Countries*, edited by A. Szalai et al. The Hague: Mouton, 69–87.

SCHLIEWEN, R.E. 1977. *A Leisure Study of Canada 1975*. Ottawa: Secretary of State.

SCHMITZ-SCHERZER, R. 1979. 'Ageing and Leisure'. *Loisir et Société/Society and Leisure* 2 (2):377–96.

SCHUESSLER, K.F., and G.A. FISHER. 1985. 'Quality of Life Research and Sociology'. *Annual Review of Sociology* 11:129–49.

SCOTT, D. 1991. 'The Problematic Nature of Participation in Contract Bridge: A Qualitative Study of Group-Related Constraints'. *Leisure Sciences* 13:321–36.

———, and G.C. GODBEY. 1990. 'Reorienting Leisure Research: The Case for Qualitative Methods'. *Loisir et Société/Society and Leisure* 13 (1):189–205.

———, and F.K. WILLITS. 1989. 'Adolescent and Adult Leisure Patterns: A 37-Year Follow-Up Study'. *Leisure Sciences* 11 (4):323–35.

SCRATON, S. 1987. '"Boys Muscle in Where Angels Fear to Tread"— Girls' Subcultures and Physical Activities'. In *Sport, Leisure and Social Relations*, edited by J. Horne, D. Jary, and A. Tomlinson. London: Routledge and Kegan Paul, 160–86.

———, and M. TALBOT. 1989. 'A Response to "Leisure, Lifestyle and Status: A Pluralist Framework for Analysis"'. *Leisure Studies* 8:155–8.

SELEEN, P.R. 1982. 'The Congruence Between Actual and Desired Use of Time by Older Adults: A Predictor of Life Satisfaction'. *Gerontologist* 22:95–9.

SESSOMS, H.D., et al. 1975. *Leisure Services: The Organized Recreation and Park System*. Englewood Cliffs, NJ: Prentice-Hall.

SHAW, S.M. 1984. 'The Measurement of Leisure: A Quality of Life Issue'. *Loisir et Société/Society and Leisure* 7 (1):91–107.

———. 1985a 'Gender and Leisure: Inequality in the Distribution of Leisure Time'. *Journal of Leisure Research* 17 (4):266–82.

———. 1985b. 'The Meaning of Leisure in Everyday Life'. *Leisure Sciences* 7 (1):1–24.

———. 1986. 'Leisure, Recreation, or Free Time: Measuring Time Usage'. *Journal of Leisure Research* 18 (3):177–89.

———. 1988. 'Gender Differences in the Definitions and Perception of Household Labor'. *Family Relations* 37:333–7.

———. 1989. 'The Potential for Leisure in Women's Everyday Lives: Are Structural and Role Constraints Changing?' *World Leisure and Recreation* 31 (2):9–10.

———. 1991. 'Body Image Among Adolescent Women: The Role of Sports and Physically Active Leisure'. *Journal of Applied Recreation Research* 16 (4):349–67.

———, A. BONEN, and J.F. McCABE. 1991. 'Do More Constraints Mean Less Leisure? Examining the Relationship Between Constraints and Participation'. *Journal of Leisure Research* 23 (4):286–300.

_____, D.A. KLEIBER, and L.L. CALDWELL. 1993. 'The Role of Leisure Activities in the Identity Formation Process of Male and Female Adolescents'. In *Proceeding of the 7th Canadian Congress on Leisure Research*. Winnipeg: University of Manitoba, 166–8.

SINGLETON, J.F. 1985. 'Activity Patterns of the Elderly'. *Loisir et Société/Society and Leisure* 8 (2):805–19.

_____. 1988. 'Use of Secondary Data in Leisure Research'. *Journal of Leisure Research* 20 (3):233–6.

SMIGEL, E., ed. 1963. *Work and Leisure: A Contemporary Social Problem*. New Haven, CT: College and University Press.

SMITH, D.C. 1987. *The Everyday World as Problematic: A Feminist Sociology*. Toronto: University of Toronto Press.

SMITH, D.M. 1981. 'New Movements in the Sociology of Youth: A Critique'. *British Journal of Sociology* 32:239–51.

SMITH, J. 1987. 'Men and Women at Play: Gender, Life Cycle and Leisure'. In *Sport, Leisure and Social Relations*, edited by J. Horne, D. Jary, and A. Tomlinson. London: Routledge and Kegan Paul, 51–85.

SMITH, R.B. 1991. 'The Leisure Experience of Post-Parental Adults: A Time for Becoming'. Unpublished thesis, University of Calgary.

SMITH, R.W., and F.W. PRESTON. 1985. 'Expressed Gambling Motives: Accounts in Defense of Self'. In *Transitions to Leisure: Conceptual and Human Issues*, edited by B.G. Gunter, J. Stanley, and R. St Clair. Lanham: University Press of America, 217–42.

SMITH, S.L.J., and A.J. HALEY. 1979. 'Ratio Ex Machina: Notes on Leisure Research'. *Journal of Leisure Research* 11 (2):139–43.

SMITH, T.D. 1983. 'Parental Influence: A Review of the Evidence of Influence and Theoretical Model of the Parental Influence Process'. In *Research in Sociology of Educational Socialization*, edited by A. Kerkhoff. Greenwich, CT: JAI Press, 13–45.

SMITH, V.L., ed. 1977. *Hosts and Guests: The Anthropology of Tourism*. Philadelphia: University of Pennsylvania Press.

SOLOMON, E.S., et al. 1980. 'UNESCO's Policy-Relevant Quality of Life Research Program'. In *The Quality of Life: Comparative Studies*, edited by A. Szalai and F.M. Andrews. London: Sage Publications, 223–33.

SOUBRIER, R., G. OUELLET, and L. DESHAIES. 1993. 'Impact of Perceived Constraints on Latent or Actual Participation in Some Leisure Activities'. In *Proceeding of the 7th Canadian Congress on Leisure Research*. Winnipeg: University of Manitoba, 241–3.

SOULE, G.H. 1957. 'The Economics of Leisure'. *Annals of the American Academy of Political and Social Sciences* 313:16–24.

SPINRAD, W. 1981. 'The Function of Spectator Sports'. In *Handbook of Social Science of Sport*, edited by G.R.F. Lüschen and G.H. Sage. Champaign, IL: Stipes, 354–65.

STANKEY, G.H., and S.F. MCCOOL. 1989. 'Beyond Social Carrying Capacity'. In *Understanding Leisure and Recreation: Mapping the Past, Charting the Future*, edited by E.L. Jackson and T.L. Burton. State College, PA: Venture, 497–516.

STANLEY, L., and S. WISE. 1983. *Breaking Out*. London: Routledge and Kegan Paul.

STANLEY, S.C., and J. STANLEY. 1985. 'Sport Participation Among Older Adults: Myth or Reality?' In *Transitions to Leisure: Conceptual and Human Issues*, edited by B.G. Gunter, J. Stanley, and R. St Clair. Lanham: University Press of America, 179–91.

STATISTICS CANADA. 1977. *Recreational Activities, 1976*. Ottawa: Statistics Canada, Catalogue 87–501.

_____. 1979. *Selected Leisure Time Activities: February 1978*. Ottawa: Statistics Canada, Catalogue 87–001.

_____. 1980. *Cultural Facilities in Canada, 1977*. Ottawa: Statistics Canada, Catalogue 87–660.

_____. 1982. *1981 Census of Canada: Census Families in Private Households*. Ottawa: Statistics Canada, Catalogue 92–903.

_____. 1983a. *Ownership of Recreational Equipment*. Ottawa: Statistics Canada, Catalogue 87–003.

_____. 1983b. *Time Use in Canada*. Ottawa: Statistics Canada, Catalogue 87–001.

_____. 1984a. *Canada's Lone Parent Families*. Ottawa: Statistics Canada, Catalogue 99–933.

_____. 1984b. *1981 Census of Canada: Economic Families in Private Households, Income and Selected Characteristics*. Ottawa: Statistics Canada, Catalogue 92–937.

_____. 1985a. *Arts and Culture: A Statistical Profile*. Ottawa: Statistics Canada, Catalogue 87–527.

_____. 1985b. *Canada Year Book*. Ottawa: Statistics Canada.

_____. 1986. *Tourism in Canada: A Statistical Digest*. Ottawa: Statistics Canada.

_____. 1988. *Touriscope: 1988 Tourism in Canada, a Statistical Digest*. Ottawa: Statistics Canada.

_____. 1991a. *Canada's Elderly*. Ottawa: Statistics Canada.

_____. 1991b. *Travel-log, Vol. 10, No. 3*. Ottawa: Statistics Canada.

STEBBINS, R.A. 1979. *Amateurs: On the Margin Between Work and Leisure*. Beverly Hills: Sage Publications.

_____. 1982. 'Serious Leisure: A Conceptual Statement'. *Pacific Sociological Review* 25 (2):251–72.

_____. 1984. *Magician: Career, Culture, and Social Psychology in a Variety Art*. Toronto: Irwin.

_____. 1988. *Deviance: Tolerable Differences*. Beverly Hills: Sage Publications.

_____. 1990. *Sociology: The Study of Society*. New York: Harper & Row.

_____. 1992. *Amateurs, Professionals, and Serious Leisure*. Montreal: McGill–Queen's University Press.

_____. 1993. 'Leisure, Language, and Culture: The Francophones of Calgary'. In *Proceeding of the 7th Canadian Congress on Leisure Research*. Winnipeg: University of Manitoba, 281–4.

STENROSS, B. 1987. 'The Meaning of Guns'. Paper presented at the Popular Culture Association meeting, Montreal.

_____. 1990. 'Turning Vices into Virtues: The Dignifying Accounts of Gun Avocationists'. In *Marginal Conventions: Popular Culture, Mass Media and Social Deviance*, edited by C.R. Sanders. Bowling Green: Bowling Green State University Popular Press, 56–64.

STEPHENS, T., and C.L. CRAIG. 1990. *The Well-Being of Canadians*. Ottawa: Canadian Lifestyle and Fitness Research Institute.

STONE, R., G.L. CAFFERATA, and J. SANGL. 1987. 'Caregivers of the Frail Elderly: A National Profile'. *Gerontologist* 27:616–26.

STREATHER, J. 1989. 'One-Parent Families and Leisure (1979)'. In *Freedom and Constraint: The Paradoxes of Leisure*, edited by F. Coalter. London: Routledge and Kegan Paul, 175–86.

SUDMAN, B., and N.M. BRADBURN. 1974. *Response Effects in Surveys*. Chicago: Aldine.

SUSSMAN, M.B. 1965. 'Relationships of Adult Children with Their Parents in the United

States'. In *Social Structure and the Family*, edited by E. Shanas and G.F. Streib. Englewood Cliffs, NJ: Prentice-Hall.

SZALAI, A. 1980. 'The Meaning of Comparative Research on the Quality of Life'. In *The Quality of Life: Comparative Studies*, edited by A. Szalai and F.M. Andrews. London: Sage Publications, 7–21.

_____, et al. 1972. *The Use of Time: Daily Activities of Urban and Suburban Populations in Twelve Countries*. The Hague: Mouton.

SZINOVACZ, M. 1989. 'Decision-Making on Retirement Timing'. In *Dyadic Decision Making*, edited by D. Bringberg and J. Jaccard. New York: Springer.

_____. 1992. 'Leisure in Retirement: Gender Differences in Limitations and Opportunities'. *World Leisure and Recreation* 34 (1):14–17.

_____, and C. WASHO. 1988. 'Retirement Preparation and Planning: Gender Differences and Family Effects'. Paper presented at the Gerontological Society of America meeting, San Francisco.

TEEVAN, J.J., ed. 1989. *Introduction to Sociology: A Canadian Focus*. Scarborough, ON: Prentice-Hall.

TEPPERMAN, L., and M. ROSENBERG. 1991. *Macro/Micro: A Brief Introduction to Sociology*. Scarborough, ON: Prentice-Hall.

THIESSEN, V., and J.F. SINGLETON. 1993. 'Becoming a Family: Losing Leisure—Is There Subjective Equity?' In *Proceeding of the 7th Canadian Congress on Leisure Research*. Winnipeg: University of Manitoba, 136–9.

THOMAS, K. 1960. 'Work and Leisure in Pre-industrial Society'. *Past and Present* 29:50–62.

THOMPSON, E.P. 1963. *The Making of the English Working Class*. New York: Vintage.

THOMPSON, S. 1992. '"Mum's Tennis Day': The Gendered Definition of Older Women's Leisure'. *Loisir et Société/Society and Leisure* 15 (1):271–89.

TINSLEY, H.E.A. 1978. 'The Ubiquitous Question of Why'. In *New Thoughts on Leisure*, edited by D.J. Brademas. Champaign, IL: University of Illinois.

_____. 1984. 'The Psychological Benefits of Leisure Counseling'. *Loisir et Société/Society and Leisure* 7:125–40.

_____, and R.A. KASS. 1978. 'Leisure Activities and Need Satisfaction: A Replication and an Extension'. *Journal of Leisure Research* 10:191–202.

_____, and D. TINSLEY. 1982. *Psychological and Health Benefits of the Leisure Experience*. Carbondale, IL: Southern Illinois University Press.

_____. 1986. 'A Theory of Attributes, Benefits, and Causes of Leisure Experience'. *Leisure Sciences* 8:1–45.

_____, T.C. BARRETT, and R.A. KASS. 1977. 'Leisure Activities and Need Satisfaction'. *Journal of Leisure Research* 16:234–44.

_____, et al. 1987. 'The Relationship of Age, Gender, Health, and Economic Status to the Psychological Benefits Older Persons Report from Participation in Leisure Activities'. *Leisure Sciences* 9:53–65.

TOKARSKI, W. 1983. 'The Situation of Leisure Research in Western Germany with an Emphasis on the Methodological Aspects'. *Loisir et Société/Society and Leisure* 6 (2):493–506.

_____. 1984. 'Interrelationships Between Leisure and Life Styles'. *World Leisure and Recreation* 27 (1):9–13.

_____. 1989. 'Continuity and Discontinuity of Leisure Life Styles in Old Age: Results of a Reanalysis.' *World Leisure and Recreation* 31 (1):27–34.

TRAVIS, R. 1987. 'Collectors and Collecting; Self-Reported Obsessive Compulsive Behavior'. Paper presented at the Popular Culture Association national meeting, Montreal.

———. 1988. 'Why People Collect: Motivational Tendencies and the Addictive Factor'. Paper presented at the Popular Culture Association national meeting, New Orleans.

TRIANDIS, H.C. 1967. *Attitude and Attitude Change*. New York: Wiley.

TROPP, A. 1983. 'The Study of Leisure in Great Britain'. Cited by N.C.A. Parry in 'Sociological Contributions to the Study of Leisure'. *Leisure Studies* 2:57–81.

TURNER, V., ed. 1982. *Celebration: Study in Festivity and Ritual*. Washington, DC: Smithsonian Institute.

UJIMOTO, K.V. 1988. 'Sociodemographic Factors and Variations in the Allocation of Time in Later Life'. In *Daily Life in Later Life: Comparative Perspectives*, edited by K. Altergott. Beverly Hills: Sage Publications, 186–204.

———. 1991. 'Ethnic Variations in the Allocation of Time to Daily Activities'. *Loisir et Société/Society and Leisure* 14 (2):557–73.

———, and J. NAIDOO, eds. 1984. *Asian Canadians: Aspects of Social Change*. Guelph: University of Guelph.

UNGER, L.S. 1982. 'The Interaction of Situational and Personal Variables Affecting Subjective Leisure'. Paper presented at the National Recreation and Park Association/Leisure Research Symposium.

———. 1984. 'The Effect of Situational Variables on the Subjective Leisure Experience'. *Leisure Sciences* 6 (3):291–312.

UNRUH, D.R. 1980. 'The Nature of Social Worlds'. *Pacific Sociological Review* 23:271–96.

URRY, J. 1990. *The Tourist Gaze*. London: Sage Publications.

VAN MAANEN, J., ed. 1983. *Qualitative Methodology*. Beverly Hills: Sage Publications.

VARPALOTAI, A. 1992. 'A "Safe Place" for Leisure and Learning—the Girl Guides of Canada'. *Loisir et Société/Society and Leisure* 15 (1):115–33.

VASKE, J., et al. 1982. 'Differences in Reported Satisfaction Ratings by Consumptive and Non-consumptive Recreationists'. *Journal of Leisure Research* 14 (3):195–206.

VEBLEN, T. 1899. *The Theory of the Leisure Class*. New York: Macmillan.

VIPOND, M. 1989. *The Mass Media in Canada*. Toronto: Lorimer.

WADE, M.G., ed. 1985. *Constraints on Leisure*. Springfield, IL: Charles C. Thomas.

WALL, G. 1981. 'Research in Canadian Recreation Planning and Management'. In *Canadian Resource Policies: Problems and Prospects*, edited by B. Mitchell and W.R.D. Sewell. Toronto: Methuen, 233–61.

WANKEL, L.M., and C.E. THOMPSON. 1977. 'Motivating People to Be Physically Active: Self-Persuasion vs Balanced Decision Making'. *Journal of Applied Social Psychology* 7:332–40.

WARNICK, R.B. 1987. 'Recreation and Leisure Participation Patterns Among the Adult Middle-Aged Market from 1975 to 1984'. *Journal of Physical Education, Recreation and Dance* 58 (8):49–55.

WEARING, B. 1991. 'Leisure and Women's Identity: Conformity or Individuality?' *Loisir et Société/Society and Leisure* 14 (2):575–86.

———. 1992. 'Leisure and Women's Identity in Late Adolescence: Constraints and Opportunities'. *Loisir et Société/Society and Leisure* 15 (1):323–43.

_____, and S. WEARING. 1988. 'All in a Day's Leisure: Gender and the Concept of Leisure'. *Leisure Studies* 7:111–23.

WEBB, E.J., et al. 1981. *Nonreactive Measures in the Social Sciences*. Boston: Houghton Mifflin.

WEBER, M. 1958. *The Protestant Ethic and the Spirit of Capitalism*. New York: Scribner.

_____. 1964. *Basic Concepts in Sociology*. New York: Citadel.

WEHMAN, P., and S. SCHLEIEN. 1981. *Leisure Programs for Handicapped Persons*. Baltimore: University Park Press.

WEISSINGER, E., and S.E. ISO-AHOLA. 1984. 'Intrinsic Leisure Motivation, Personality and Physical Health'. *Loisir et Société/Society and Leisure* 7 (1):217–28.

WEST, P.C., and L.C. MERRIAM. 1970. 'Outdoor Recreation and Family Cohesiveness: Research Approach'. *Journal of Leisure Research* 2:251–9.

WESTLAND, C. 1979. *Fitness and Amateur Sport in Canada: An Historical Perspective*. Ottawa: Canadian Parks and Recreation Association.

WETHERELL, D.G. 1990. 'A Season of Mixed Blessings: Winter and Leisure in Alberta Before World War II'. In *Winter Sports in the West*, edited by E.A. Corbet and A.W. Rasporich. Calgary: Historical Society of Alberta, 38–51.

WHITE, D.M. 1957. 'Mass Culture in America: Another Point of View'. In *Mass Culture: The Popular Arts in America*, edited by B. Rosenberg and D.M. White. New York: Free Press, 13–21.

WHITE, R.C. 1955. 'Social Class Differences in the Use of Leisure'. *American Journal of Sociology* 61 (2):145–50.

WILENSKY, H.L. 1960. 'Work, Careers, and Social Integration'. *International Social Science Journal* 12:543–60.

_____. 1961. 'The Uneven Distribution of Leisure: The Impact of Economic Growth on "Free-Time"'. In *Work and Leisure: A Contemporary Social Problem*, edited by E. Smigel. New Haven, CT: College and University Press.

_____. 1964. 'Mass Society and Mass Culture: Interdependence or Independence?' *American Sociological Review* 29:173–97.

WILKENING, E.A., and D. McGRANAHAN. 1978. 'Correlates of Subjective Well-Being in Northern Wisconsin'. *Social Indicators Research* 1:301–27.

WILLIAMS, R. 1958. *Culture and Society 1780–1950*. London: Chatto and Windus.

_____. 1961. *The Long Revolution*. London: Penguin.

WILLITS, W.L., and F.K. WILLITS. 1987. 'Adolescent Leisure Patterns'. In *Recreation and Leisure: An Introductory Handbook*, edited by A. Graefe and S. Parker. State College, PA: Venture, 177–81.

WILMETH, D.B. 1989. 'Circus and Outdoor Entertainment'. In *Handbook of American Popular Culture* (2nd ed.), edited by M.T. Inge. New York: Greenwood Press, 173–203.

WILSON, J. 1987. 'The Sociology of Leisure'. In *Recreation and Leisure: An Introductory Handbook*, edited by A. Graefe and S. Parker. State College, PA: Venture, 49–58.

WIMBUSH, E., and M. TALBOT, eds. 1988. *Relative Freedoms*. Milton Keynes: Open University Press.

WINSHIP, J. 1987. *Inside Women's Magazines*. London: Pandora.

WITT, P.A. 1971. 'Factor Structure of Leisure Behavior for High School Age Youth in Three Communities'. *Journal of Leisure Research* 3:213–19.

_____, and G.D. ELLIS. 1984. 'The Leisure Diagnostic Battery: Measuring Perceived Freedom in Leisure'. *Loisir et Société/Society and Leisure* 7 (1):109–24.

_____. 1985. 'Development of a Short Form to Assess Perceived Freedom in Leisure'. *Journal of Leisure Research* 17 (3):225–33.

_____, and T.L. GOODALE. 1981. 'The Relationships Between Barriers to Leisure Enjoyment and Family Stages'. *Leisure Sciences* 4 (1):29–49.

_____, and E.L. JACKSON. 1993. 'Constraints to Leisure Across the Family Lifecycle: Re-examination and Extension'. In *Proceeding of the 7th Canadian Congress on Leisure Research*. Winnipeg: University of Manitoba, 162–5.

WUTHNOW, R., and M. WITTEN. 1988. 'New Directions in the Study of Culture'. *Annual Review of Sociology* 14:49–67.

YEO, E., and S. YEO, eds. 1981. *Popular Culture and Class Conflict 1590–1914: Explorations in the History of Labour and Leisure*. Sussex: Harvester.

YIANNAKIS, A., and H. GIBSON. 1992. 'Roles Tourists Play'. *Annals of Tourism Research* 19:287–303.

YOESTING, D.R., and R. BURDGE. 1976. 'Utility of a Leisure-Orientation Scale'. *Iowa State Journal of Research* 50 (5):345–56.

_____, and D. BURKHEAD. 1973. 'Significance of Childhood Recreation Experience on Adult Leisure Behavior'. *Journal of Leisure Research* 5 (1):25–36.

_____, and J. CHRISTENSEN. 1978. 'Reexamining the Significance of Childhood Recreation Patterns on Adult Leisure Behavior'. *Leisure Sciences* 1 (3):219–29.

YOUNG, M., and P. WILLMOTT. 1975. *The Symmetrical Family*. London: Penguin.

YOUNISS, J., and J. SMOLLAR. 1985. *Adolescent Relations with Mothers, Fathers, and Friends*. Chicago: University of Chicago Press.

ZNANIECKA-LOPATA, H.L. 1973. *Widowhood in an American City*. Cambridge, MA: Schenkman.

_____. 1979. *Women as Widows: Support Systems*. New York: Elsevier Holland.

ZUZANEK, J. 1976. *Leisure and Social Change*. Waterloo, ON: University of Waterloo, Faculty of Human Kinetics and Leisure Studies.

_____. 1978. 'Social Differences in Leisure Behavior: Measurement and Interpretation'. *Leisure Sciences* 1 (3):271–93.

_____. 1988. 'Semantic Images of High and Popular Culture: Opera vs Soap Opera?' *Loisir et Société/Society and Leisure* 11 (2):351–63.

_____. 1991. 'Leisure Research in North America: A Critical Perspective'. *Loisir et Société/Society and Leisure* 14 (2):587–96.

_____, and S. BOX. 1988. 'Life Course and the Daily Lives of Older Adults in Canada'. In *Daily Life in Later Life: Comparative Perspectives*, edited by K. Altergott. Newbury Park: Sage Publications, 147–85.

_____, and R.C. MANNELL. 1983. 'Work-Leisure Relationships from a Sociological and Social Psychological Perspective'. *Leisure Studies* 2 (3):327–44.

_____, and B.J.A. SMALE. 1992. 'Life-Cycle Variations in Across-the-Week Allocation of Time to Selected Daily Activities'. *Loisir et Société/Society and Leisure* 15 (2):559–86.

Index